THE WRITTEN GOSPEL

This book comprehensively surveys the origin, production and reception of the canonical gospels in the early church. The discussion unfolds in three steps. Part One traces the origin of the 'gospel' of Jesus, its significance in Jewish and Hellenistic contexts of the first century, and its development from eyewitness memory to oral tradition and written text. Part Two then more specifically examines the composition, design and intentions of each of the four canonical gospels. Widening the focus, Part Three first asks about gospel-writing as viewed from the perspective of ancient Jews and pagans before turning to the question of reception history in the proliferation of 'apocryphal' gospels, in the formation of the canon, and in the beginnings of a gospel commentary tradition.

MARKUS BOCKMUEHL is Professor of Biblical and Early Christian Studies at the University of Cambridge and Fellow of Fitzwilliam College. His publications include *Jewish Law in Gentile Churches* (2000) and (ed.) *The Cambridge Companion to Jesus* (2001).

DONALD A. HAGNER is George Eldon Ladd Professor of New Testament at Fuller Theological Seminary. He is author of commentaries on Matthew (1993, 1995) and Hebrews (1990); among his other books is *The Jewish Reclamation of Jesus* (1984).

THE WRITTEN GOSPEL

EDITED BY

MARKUS BOCKMUEHL

AND

DONALD A. HAGNER

CAMBRIDGE
UNIVERSITY PRESS

CAMBRIDGE UNIVERSITY PRESS
Cambridge, New York, Melbourne, Madrid, Cape Town, Singapore, São Paulo

Cambridge University Press
The Edinburgh Building, Cambridge CB2 8RU, UK

Published in the United States of America by Cambridge University Press, New York

www.cambridge.org
Information on this title: www.cambridge.org/9780521540407

First published 2005
Reprinted 2007

Printed in the United Kingdom at the University Press, Cambridge

A catalogue record for this book is available from the British Library

Library of Congress Cataloguing in Publication data

ISBN-13 978-0-521-83285-4 hardback
ISBN-13 978-0-521-54040-7 paperback

GRAHAM N. STANTON
SAPIENTI EVANGELII MAGISTRO ET ARDENTI
ANNO AETATIS LXV
AB AMICIS DISCIPVLISQVE GRATISSIME OBLATVM

Contents

vii

Contributors

LOVEDAY ALEXANDER is Professor of Biblical Studies in the University of Sheffield, and Canon Theologian at Chester Cathedral. Her publications include *The Preface to Luke's Gospel* (SNTSMS 78; Cambridge: Cambridge University Press, 1993) and *Images of Empire* (JSOTSup 122; Sheffield: Sheffield Academic Press, 1991).

RICHARD C. BEATON is Associate Professor of New Testament Studies at Fuller Theological Seminary, Pasadena, California. His publications include *Isaiah's Christ in Matthew's Gospel* (SNTSMS 123; Cambridge: Cambridge University Press, 2002).

MARKUS BOCKMUEHL is Professor of Biblical and Early Christian Studies in the University of Cambridge and Fellow of Fitzwilliam College. His publications include *Jewish Law in Gentile Churches* (Edinburgh: T. & T. Clark, 2000) and (ed.) *The Cambridge Companion to Jesus* (Cambridge: Cambridge University Press, 2001).

RICHARD A. BURRIDGE is Dean of King's College, London, where he also teaches New Testament Studies. He was originally a classicist; his books include his recently revised *What Are the Gospels?* (Grand Rapids: Eerdmans, 2004), *Four Gospels, One Jesus?* (London: SPCK/Grand Rapids: Eerdmans, 2005), and *Jesus Now and Then* (London: SPCK/Grand Rapids: Eerdmans, 2004).

JAMES CARLETON PAGET is Lecturer in New Testament Studies at the University of Cambridge and Fellow and Tutor of Peterhouse. His publications include *The Epistle of Barnabas: Outlook and Background* (Tübingen: Mohr (Siebeck), 1994) and a number of articles on subjects related to early Christianity and its origins.

JAMES D. G. DUNN is Emeritus Lightfoot Professor of Divinity in the University of Durham. His recent publications include *The Theology of Paul the Apostle* (Edinburgh: T. & T. Clark, 1998) and *Christianity in the Making*, volume 1: *Jesus Remembered* (Grand Rapids: Eerdmans, 2003).

CRAIG A. EVANS is The Payzant Distinguished Professor of New Testament in Acadia Divinity College, Acadia University. His publications include *Jesus and His Contemporaries* (AGJU 25; Leiden: E. J. Brill, 1995), *Mark* (WBC; Nashville: Thomas Nelson, 2001), and *Jesus and the Ossuaries* (Waco: Baylor University Press, 2003).

DONALD A. HAGNER is George Eldon Ladd Professor of New Testament at Fuller Theological Seminary, Pasadena, California. He is the author of commentaries on Matthew (WBC; Dallas: Word, 1993, 1995) and Hebrews (NIBC; Peabody: Hendrickson, 1990); among his other books is *The Jewish Reclamation of Jesus* (Grand Rapids: Academie, 1984).

MARTIN HENGEL is Professor Emeritus of New Testament Studies in the University of Tübingen and Director of its Philipp Melanchthon Institute. His most recent books include *The Four Gospels and the One Gospel of Jesus Christ* (London: SCM; Harrisburg: TPI, 2000), *Paulus and Jakobus* (WUNT 141; Tübingen: Mohr (Siebeck), 2002) and *The Septuagint as Christian Scripture* (Edinburgh: T. & T. Clark, 2002).

MORNA D. HOOKER is the Lady Margaret's Professor of Divinity Emerita in the University of Cambridge, and a Fellow of Robinson College. Her publications include *A Commentary on the Gospel according to St Mark* (BNTC; London: A. & C. Black, 1991; Peabody: Hendrickson, 1992) and *The Signs of a Prophet* (London: SCM; Harrisburg: TPI, 1997).

WILLIAM HORBURY is Professor of Jewish and Early Christian Studies in the University of Cambridge, a Fellow of Corpus Christi College, Cambridge, and a Fellow of the British Academy. His publications include *Jewish Messianism and the Cult of Christ* (London: SCM, 1998), *Jews and Christians in Contact and Controversy* (Edinburgh: T. & T. Clark, 1998), and *Messianism among Jews and Christians* (London/New York: T. & T. Clark International, 2003).

JUDITH LIEU is Professor of New Testament Studies and Head of the Department of Theology and Religious Studies, King's College London. Her publications include *Neither Jew nor Greek? Constructing Early Christianity* (Edinburgh: T. & T. Clark, 2002) and *Christian*

Identity in the Jewish and Graeco-Roman World (Oxford: Oxford University Press, 2004).

DAVID P. MOESSNER is Professor of Biblical Theology in the University of Dubuque Theological Seminary. His publications include *Lord of the Banquet* (Harrisburg: Trinity Press International, 1998) and (ed.) *Jesus and the Heritage of Israel*, Vol. 1 of Luke the Interpreter of Israel (Harrisburg: Trinity Press International, 1999).

RONALD A. PIPER is Professor of Christian Origins in the University of St Andrews, and University Vice-Principal for Learning and Teaching. His publications include *Wisdom in the Q-Tradition: The Aphoristic Teaching of Jesus* (SNTSMS 61; Cambridge: Cambridge University Press, 1989) and (ed.) *The Gospel Behind the Gospels: Current Studies on Q* (NovTSup 75; Leiden: Brill, 1995).

KLYNE SNODGRASS is Paul W. Brandel Professor of New Testament Studies, North Park Theological Seminary, Chicago. He is the editor of *Ex Auditu*, a journal for the theological interpretation of Scripture, and his publications include *Ephesians* in *The NIV Application Commentary* (Grand Rapids: Zondervan, 1996) and *Between Two Truths* (Grand Rapids: Zondervan, 1990).

CHRISTOPHER TUCKETT is Professor of New Testament Studies in the University of Oxford and a Fellow of Pembroke College. His publications include *Q and the History of Early Christianity* (Edinburgh: T. & T. Clark, 1996) and *Christology and the New Testament* (Edinburgh: Edinburgh University Press, 2001).

Abbreviations

AB   Anchor Bible
ABD   *The Anchor Bible Dictionary*, ed. David Noel Freedman.
              6 vols. New York: Doubleday, 1992
ABG   Arbeiten zur Bibel und ihrer Geschichte
ABRL   Anchor Bible Reference Library
ACCSNT   Ancient Christian Commentary on Scripture, New
              Testament
AF   The Apostolic Fathers
AGJU   Arbeiten zur Geschichte des antiken Judentums
              und des Urchristentums
AGSU   Arbeiten zur Geschichte des Spätjudentums
              und Urchristentums
ALUB   Annales Littéraires de l'Université de Besançon
AnBib   Analecta Biblica
ANQ   *Andover Newton Quarterly*
ANRW   *Aufstieg und Niedergang der römischen Welt: Geschichte
              und Kultur Roms im Spiegel der neueren Forschung*, ed.
              H. Temporini and W. Haase. Berlin: de Gruyter, 1972–
Apoc   *Apocrypha*
ASNU   Acta Seminarii Neotestamentici Upsaliensis
ATDan   Acta Theologica Danica
Aug   *Augustinianum*
AUSDDS   Andrews University Seminary Doctoral Dissertation Series
b.   born
BAlt   Beiträge zur Altertumskunde
BBCom   Blackwell Bible Commentaries
BBR   *Bulletin for Biblical Research*
BETL   Bibliotheca Ephemeridum Theologicarum Lovaniensium

BFCT	Beiträge zur Förderung christlicher Theologie
BG	Berlin Gnostic Codex
BGBE	Beiträge zur Geschichte der biblischen Exegese
BHP	Bibliothèque d'Histoire de la Philosophie
BHT	Beiträge zur historischen Theologie
BNTC	Black's New Testament Commentaries
BRBS	Brill's Readers in Biblical Studies
BRS	Biblical Resource Series
BSL	Biblical Studies Library
BZ	*Biblische Zeitschrift*
BZAW	Beihefte zur Zeitschrift für die alttestamentliche Wissenschaft
BZNW	Beihefte zur Zeitschrift für die neutestamentliche Wissenschaft und die Kunde der älteren Kirche
CC	Continental Commentaries
CCAMA	Clavis Commentariorum Antiquitatis et Medii Aevi
CCCM	Corpus Christianorum: Continuatio Mediaevalis
CCSL	Corpus Christianorum: Series Latina. Turnhout, 1953–
cent.	century
CEQ	*The Critical Edition of Q*, ed. J. M. Robinson et al. Leuven and Minneapolis: Peeters and Fortress, 2000
CJA	Christianity and Judaism in Antiquity
cod.	codex
col(s).	column(s)
CQ	*Classical Quarterly*
CQS	Companion to the Qumran Scrolls
CR	Colloquium Rauricum
CRINT	Compendia Rerum Iudaicarum ad Novum Testamentum
CrIS	The Critical Idiom Series
CSHJ	Chicago Studies in the History of Judaism
d.	died
DJD	Discoveries in the Judaean Desert
DJSS	Duke Judaic Studies Series
DL	*Deutsche Literaturzeitung*
DNP	*Der neue Pauly: Enzyklopädie der Antike.* Ed. H. Cancik and H. Schneider. Stuttgart: J. B. Metzler, 1996–
DNTB	*Dictionary of New Testament Background*, ed. C. A. Evans and S. E. Porter. Downers Grove and Leicester: InterVarsity Press, 2000
DSD	*Dead Sea Discoveries*

EBib	Etudes Bibliques
EdF	Erträge der Forschung
EKKNT	Evangelisch-katholischer Kommentar zum Neuen Testament
ET	English translation
Exp	*The Expositor*
FBBS	Facet Books, Biblical Series
FC	Fathers of the Church. Washington, D.C., 1947–
FF	Foundations and Facets
fl.	*floruit,* flourished
Forum	*Foundations and Facets Forum*
frag.	fragment
FRLANT	Forschungen zur Religion und Literatur des Alten und Neuen Testaments
GBS	Guides to Biblical Scholarship
GCS	Die griechischen christlichen Schriftsteller der ersten [drei] Jahrhunderte
GRBS	*Greek, Roman and Byzantine Studies*
HOC	Histoire des Origines du Christianisme
HTKNT	Herders theologischer Kommentar zum Neuen Testament
HTR	*Harvard Theological Review*
Hyp	*Hyperboreus*
HZ	*Historische Zeitschrift*
IBS	Irish Biblical Studies
ICC	International Critical Commentary
IG	*Inscriptiones Graecae.* Editio minor. Berlin, 1924–
Int	*Interpretation*
IThS	Innsbrucker Theologische Studien
JAAR	*Journal of the American Academy of Religion*
JBL	*Journal of Biblical Literature*
JCH	Jewish and Christian Heritage
JEH	*Journal of Ecclesiastical History*
JGRCJ	*Journal of Greco-Roman Christianity and Judaism*
JJS	*Journal of Jewish Studies*
JSJSup	Supplements to the Journal for the Study of Judaism
JSNT	*Journal for the Study of the New Testament*
JSNTSup	Journal for the Study of the New Testament: Supplement Series
JSOTSup	Journal for the Study of the Old Testament: Supplement Series

JSPSup	Journal for the Study of the Pseudepigrapha: Supplement Series
JSRC	Jerusalem Studies in Religion and Culture
JTS	*Journal of Theological Studies*
KAV	Kommentar zu den Apostolischen Vätern
KBANT	Kommentare und Beiträge zum Alten und Neuen Testament
KEK	Kritisch-exegetischer Kommentar über das Neue Testament (Meyer-Kommentar)
LACL	*Lexikon der antiken christlichen Literatur*, ed. S. Döpp and W. Geerlings, 2nd edn. Freiburg: Herder, 1999
LCL	Loeb Classical Library
LEC	Library of Early Christianity
LXX	Septuagint
MCS	Monographs in Classical Studies
MS(S)	manuscript(s)
MT	Masoretic Text (of the OT)
MThS	Marburger theologische Studien
Mus	*Muséon: Revue d'Etudes Orientales*
n.d.	no date
NGS	New Gospel Studies
NHC	Nag Hammadi Codex
NIBC	New International Biblical Commentary
NovT	*Novum Testamentum*
NovTSup	Supplements to Novum Testamentum
NTC	New Testament in Context
NTL	New Testament Library
NTOA	Novum Testamentum et Orbis Antiquus
NTS	*New Testament Studies*
NTTh	New Testament Theology
NTTS	New Testament Tools and Studies
OCD	*The Oxford Classical Dictionary*, ed. S. Hornblower and A. Spawforth, 3rd edn, Oxford: Oxford University Press, 1996
OGIS	*Orientis Graeci Inscriptiones Selectae*, ed. W. Dittenberger, Leipzig: Hirzel, 1903–5, 103–5
PapyCast	Papyrologica Castroctaviana, Studia et Textus. Barcelona, 1967–
par.	parallel(s)
PillNTC	The Pillar New Testament Commentary

PL	Patrologia Latina [= Patrologiae Cursus Completus: Series Latina], ed. J.-P. Migne. 217 vols. Paris, 1844–64
Ps.-	Pseudo-
PTMS	Princeton Theological Monograph Series
PTSDSSP	Princeton Theological Seminary Dead Sea Scrolls Project
Q	'Q', hypothetical source of Jesus sayings used by Matthew and Luke
RAC	*Reallexikon für Antike und Christentum,* ed. T. Kluser et al. Stuttgart: Hiersemann, 1950–
RevQ	*Revue de Qumrân*
RhetR	*Rhetoric Review*
RhetSQ	*Rhetoric Society Quarterly*
RHPR	*Revue d'Histoire et de Philosophie Religieuses*
RivBSup	Supplementi alla Rivista Biblica
SAQ	Sammlung ausgewählter kirchen- und dogmengeschichtlicher Quellenschriften als Grundlage für Seminar-übungen
SBAltW	Schweizerische Beiträge zur Altertumswissenschaft
SBEC	Studies in the Bible and Early Christianity
SBL	Society of Biblical Literature
SBLDS	Society of Biblical Literature Dissertation Series
SBLSemeiaSup	Society of Biblical Literature Semeia Supplements
SBLSP	Society of Biblical Literature Seminar Papers
SBLSymS	Society of Biblical Literature Symposium Series
SBT	Studies in Biblical Theology
SC	Sources Chrétiennes. Paris: Cerf, 1943–
SemeiaSt	Semeia Studies
SFSHJ	South Florida Studies in the History of Judaism
SHAW.PH	Sitzungsberichte der Heidelberger Akademie der Wissenschaften, Philosophisch-Historische Klasse
SHJ	Studying the Historical Jesus
SIJB	Schriften des Institutum Judaicum in Berlin
SJLA	Studies in Judaism in Late Antiquity
SJT	*Scottish Journal of Theology*
SNTA	Studiorum Novi Testamenti Auxilia
SNTI	Studies in New Testament Interpretation
SNTS	Studiorum Novi Testamenti Societas
SNTSMS	Society for New Testament Studies Monograph Series
SNTW	Studies of the New Testament and its World
SP	Sacra Pagina
SPap	*Studia Papyrologica*

SPNT	Studies on Personalities of the New Testament
SPS	Studies in Peace and Scripture
SSEJC	Studies in Scripture in Early Judaism and Christianity
STAC	Studien und Texte zu Antike und Christentum
STDJ	Studies on the Texts of the Desert of Judah
StPB	Studia Post-Biblica
SUNT	Studien zur Umwelt des Neuen Testaments
TANZ	Texte und Arbeiten zum neutestamentlichen Zeitalter
TB	Theologische Bücherei: Neudrucke und Berichte aus dem 20. Jahrhundert
TDNT	*Theological Dictionary of the New Testament.* Ed. G. Kittel and G. Friedrich. Trans. G. W. Bromiley. 10 vols. Grand Rapids: Eerdmans, 1964–76
TF	Theologische Forschung
Tg(s).	Targum(s); Targumic
ThI	Theological Inquiries
TLZ	*Theologische Literaturzeitung*
TPINTC	TPI New Testament Commentaries
TQ	*Theologische Quartalschrift*
TS	Texts and Studies: Contributions to Biblical and Patristic Literature
TU	Texte und Untersuchungen
TUGAL	Texte und Untersuchungen zur Geschichte der altchristlichen Literatur
TUMSR	Trinity University Monograph Series in Religion
TWNT	*Theologisches Wörterbuch zum Neuen Testament.* Ed. G. Kittel and G. Friedrich. Stuttgart: W. Kohlhammer, 1932–79
TZ	*Theologische Zeitschrift*
UCOP	University of Cambridge Oriental Publications
UTB	Uni-Taschenbücher
VC	*Vigiliae Christianae*
VCSup	Supplements to *Vigiliae Christianae*
VTSup	Supplements to Vetus Testamentum
WBC	Word Biblical Commentary
WMANT	Wissenschaftliche Monographien zum Alten und Neuen Testament
WUNT	Wissenschaftliche Untersuchungen zum Neuen Testament
ZNW	*Zeitschrift für die neutestamentliche Wissenschaft und die Kunde der älteren Kirche*
ZPE	*Zeitschrift für Papyrologie und Epigraphik*

PRIMARY SOURCES

Books of the Bible

Hebrew Old Testament

Gen	Genesis
Exod	Exodus
Lev	Leviticus
Num	Numbers
Deut	Deuteronomy
Josh	Joshua
Judg	Judges
Ruth	
1–2 Sam	1–2 Samuel
1–2 Kgs	1–2 Kings
1–2 Chr	1–2 Chronicles
Ezra	
Neh	Nehemiah
Esth	Esther
Job	
Ps/Pss	Psalm(s)
Prov	Proverbs
Eccl	Ecclesiastes
Song	Song of Songs
Isa	Isaiah
Jer	Jeremiah
Lam	Lamentations
Ezek	Ezekiel
Dan	Daniel
Hos	Hosea
Joel	
Amos	
Obad	Obadiah
Jon	Jonah
Mic	Micah
Nah	Nahum
Hab	Habakkuk
Zeph	Zephaniah
Hag	Haggai
Zech	Zechariah
Mal	Malachi

LXX/Deuterocanonical books cited

Bar	Baruch
1–2 Esd	1–2 Esdras
Jdt	Judith
1–4 Kgdms	1–4 Kingdoms
1–4 Macc	1–4 Maccabees
Sir	Sirach/Ecclesiasticus
Tob	Tobit
Wis	Wisdom of Solomon

Books of the New Testament

Matt	Matthew
Mark	
Luke	
John	
Acts	
Rom	Romans
1–2 Cor	1–2 Corinthians
Gal	Galatians
Eph	Ephesians
Phil	Philippians
Col	Colossians
1–2 Thess	1–2 Thessalonians
1–2 Tim	1–2 Timothy
Tit	Titus
Phlm	Philemon
Heb	Hebrews
Jas	James
1–2 Pet	1–2 Peter
1–3 John	
Jude	
Rev	Revelation

Old Testament Pseudepigrapha

As. Mos.	*Assumption of Moses*
1 En.	*1 Enoch (Ethiopic Apocalypse)*
2 En.	*2 Enoch (Slavonic Apocalypse)*
3 En.	*3 Enoch (Hebrew Apocalypse)*

Jos. Asen.	*Joseph and Aseneth*
Jub.	*Book of Jubilees*
Let. Aris.	*Letter of Aristeas*
Ps.-Phoc.	Pseudo-Phocylides
Ps(s). Sol.	*Psalm(s) of Solomon*
Sib. Or.	*Sibylline Oracles*
T. Benj.	*Testament of Benjamin*
T. Levi	*Testament of Levi*
T. Mos.	*Testament of Moses*
T. Zeb.	*Testament of Zebulon*

Other Jewish Writings

Dead Sea Scrolls

Abbreviations for the Dead Sea Scrolls are given in the standard format indicating the number of the cave at Qumran where the documents were found, followed by a number or alphabetic siglum for the title (e.g. 1QS, 4Q246). The most widely used edition of the text and translation at present is García Martínez and Tigchelaar 1997–8; for the standard critical edition see the Discoveries in the Judaean Desert (DJD) series, 39 vols. (Oxford: Clarendon, 1955–2002).

1QH	*Thanksgiving Hymns*
1QM	*War Scroll*
1QpHab	Pesher to Habakkuk
1QS	*Rule of the Community*
1QSa	*Rule of the Congregation*
4Q225	Pseudo-Jubilees[a]
4Q521	*Messianic Apocalypse*
4QFlor	*Florilegium*
4QMMT	*Miqṣat Maʿaśê ha-Torah*
4QpIsa	Isaiah Pesher
4QpNah	Nahum Pesher
4QShirShabb	Songs of the Sabbath Sacrifice
4QTest	*Testimonia*
11QT	*Temple Scroll*
11QMelch	*Melchizedek*
CD	*Damascus Document*

Josephus

Ant.	*Jewish Antiquities*

Ag. Ap.	*Against Apion*
J. W.	*On the Jewish War*
Life	*Life of Josephus*

Philo

Contempl.	*De Vita Contemplativa*
Legat.	*Legatio ad Gaium*
Mos.	*De Vita Mosis* or *On the Life of Moses*
Prob.	*Quod Omnis Probus Liber sit*

Rabbinic Literature

(1) Mishnah and Talmud

The Mishnah (*m.*) and Tosefta (*t.*) are quoted according to chapter and halakhah (e.g. *m. Sukkah* 2.3, *t. Sukkah* 2.3), the Babylonian Talmud (*b.*) according to folio, side a or b (e.g. *b. Sukkah* 17b). In quotations from the Palestinian Talmud (i.e. Yerushalmi, '*y.*'), the first two digits represent the chapter and halakhah as in the Mishnah, the third gives the folio and column, a–d (e.g. *y. Sukkah* 2.3, 17c). The tractates are abbreviated as follows:

ʿAbod. Zar.	*ʿAbodah Zarah*
ʾAbot	
B. Bat.	*Baba Batra*
B. Meṣiʿa	*Baba Meṣiʿa*
Ber.	*Berakhot*
Giṭṭ.	*Giṭṭin*
Ḥag.	*Ḥagigah*
Ḥull.	*Ḥullin*
Kelim	*Kelim*
Ketub.	*Ketubbot*
Meg.	*Megillah*
Men.	*Menaḥot*
Moʿed Qatan	
Ned.	*Nedarim*
Peʾah	
Pesaḥ.	*Pesaḥim*
Qidd.	*Qiddušin*
Šabb.	*Šabbat*
Sanh.	*Sanhedrin*
Sot.	*Sotah*

Sukkah
Taʿan.   *Taʿanit*
Yoma

(2)   Other Rabbinic writings
Abot R. Nat.   *Abot de-Rabbi Nathan*
Eccl. Rab.   *Ecclesiastes Rabbah*
Exod. Rab.   *Exodus Rabbah*
Gen. Rab.   *Genesis Rabbah*
Lam. Rab.   *Lamentations Rabbah*
Mek. deR. Ishmael   *Mekhilta de-Rabbi Ishmael*
Pirqe R. El.   *Pirqe de-Rabbi Eliezer*
Song Rab.   *Song of Songs Rabbah*
Soperim
Tg. Lam.   *Targum on Lamentations*
Yal.   *Yalqut*

Early Christian Writings

Apocryphal texts
Gos. Heb.   *Gospel of the Hebrews*
Gos. Pet.   *Gospel of Peter*
Gos. Thom.   *Gospel of Thomas*
Sec. Gos. Mk.   *Secret Gospel of Mark*

Apostolic Fathers
1–2 Clem.   *1–2 Clement*
Did.   *Didache*
Ign. *Smyrn.*   Ignatius, *To the Smyrnaeans*
Ign. *Rom.*   Ignatius, *To the Romans*

Augustine
De Cons.   *De Consensu Evangelistarum*

Clement of Alexandria
Hyp.   *Hypotyposeis*
Strom.   *Stromateis*

Didymus the Blind
Comm. Ps.   *Commentarii in Psalmos*

Epiphanius
Pan.   *Panarion* (or *Haereses*)

Eusebius
Hist. Eccl.   *Historia Ecclesiastica*

Hippolytus
Refut.   *Refutation of All Heresies*

Irenaeus
Haer.   *Adversus Haereses*

Jerome
Comm. Isa.   *Commentariorum in Isaiam*
Vir. Ill.   *De Viris Illustribus*

Justin Martyr
1, 2 Apol.   *First, Second Apology*
Dial.   *Dialogue with Trypho*

Lactantius
Div. Inst.   *Divinae Institutiones*

Melito of Sardis
Pasch.   *Peri Pascha*

Origen
C. Cels   *Contra Celsum*
Comm. Joh.   *In Johannem Commentarius*
Comm. Mt.   *In Matthaeum Commentarius*
Hom. Jer.   *Homilies on Jeremiah*

Photius
Bibl.   *Bibliotheca*

Tertullian
Apol.   *Apologeticus*
De Spect.   *De Spectaculis*
Test.   *De Testimonio Animae*

Classical and Hellenistic Writings

Aratus
Phaen.   *Phaenomena*

Aristotle
Poet.   *Poetica*
Rhet.   *Rhetorica*

Arrian
Anab.   *Anabasis*

Cicero
Att.   *Epistulae ad Atticum*

Diodorus Siculus
Bib. Hist.   *Bibliotheca Historica*

Dionysius of Halicarnassus
Ant. Rom.   *Antiquitates Romanae*
Dem.   *De Demosthene*
Gn. Pomp.   *Gnaeus Pompeius*
Thuc.   *De Thucydide*

Dioscorides
Mat. Med.   *De Materia Medica*

Epictetus
Disc.   *Discourses*

Euripides
Bacch.   *Bacchae*
El.   *Electra*
Med.   *Medea*

Horace
Od.   *Odes* or *Carmina*

Lucian of Samosata
Hist.   *Quomodo Historia Conscribenda Sit*
Conscr.
Peregr.   *De Morte Peregrini*

Marcus Aurelius
Med.   *Meditations*

Minucius Felix
Oct.   *Octavius*

Philostratus
Vit. Ap.   *Vita Apollonii*

Plato
Rep.   *Respublica* or *Republic*

Pliny the Younger
Ep.   *Epistolae*
Nat. Hist.   *Natural History*

Polybius
Hist.   *Histories*

Strabo
Geog.   *Geography*

Tacitus
Ann.   *Annales*
Hist.   *Historiae*

Other Ancient Sources

Nag Hammadi Codices
ApocJohn   *Apocryphon of John*
SJC   *Sophia of Jesus Christ*

Papyri

P. Cair.	*Papyrus Cairensis*
P. Eg.	Egerton Papyrus, British Museum, London
PGM	*Papyri Graecae Magicae: Die griechischen Zauberpapyri*, ed. K. Preisendanz et al. 2 vols. Stuttgart: Teubner, 1973–4
P. Köln	*Kölner Papyri*, ed. B. Kramer, R. Hübner, et al. Oplanden, 1976–
P. Oxy.	*The Oxyrhynchus Papyri*, ed. B. P. Grenfell, A. S. Hunt, et al. London, 1989–
P. Ryl.	*Catalogue of the Greek Papyri in the John Rylands Library at Manchester*

Introduction

Markus Bockmuehl and Donald A. Hagner

The gospels continue to captivate the world's attention. Christianity's burgeoning growth, especially in the southern hemisphere, means that they are being read by more people today than ever before. Even in the highly secularized West, millions flock to a blockbuster movie like Mel Gibson's *The Passion of the Christ*, and a renewed, broader interest in the gospels has been sparked by the recent flurry of popular Jesus books. The frequently exotic and far-fetched conclusions of these highly publicized books have driven Christians and interested non-Christians alike to go back to the gospels with questions concerning their origin, nature, and teachings. It goes without saying that these foundational documents continue to be critically important for the church and for the doctrine and practice of contemporary Christians.

At the beginning of the twenty-first century, scholarly research on the gospels is experiencing a renewal of textual, literary, and theological study. It is true that nothing ever stands still in biblical scholarship, but the study of the gospels in recent decades has made especially significant advances. New methods and approaches abound, with an emphasis on interdisciplinary work and new attention to such areas as sociology, literary or narrative criticism, and the history of influence of texts (*Wirkungsgeschichte*). The new emphases ought not to be thought of as superseding more traditional historical study of the gospels which necessarily retains its importance, but as supplementing and enriching it.

As our title indicates, the present volume of essays focuses on the written gospel. It intends to present an up-to-date treatment of major aspects of the production of the gospels, including the contexts in which they were composed, the process of writing, the character of the written gospels, and their publication and reception in the early church. Attention is furthermore given to the production of the individual canonical gospels, their position among and relation to non-canonical gospels, and the eventual writing of commentaries on the canonical texts.

Part I of the book, 'Before Writing', opens with an essay by William Horbury that explores the meaning of the word 'gospel' in the historical context of Herodian Judaea, showing it to be rooted in Scripture and applied in daily life and also in both Jewish and Graeco-Roman royal publicity and praise of God. The second chapter, by Klyne Snodgrass, looks specifically at the gospel of Jesus and its content. In chapter 3, James D. G. Dunn examines the oral tradition that underlies the written gospels and argues that the earliest stratum of the presumed sayings source 'Q' (so-called 'Q¹'), must have been oral rather than written. In the last chapter of Part I, Martin Hengel focuses on the historical character of the material in the gospels and the role of the gospel-writers in transmitting narrated history, criticizing much of form criticism in the process.

Part II, 'Writing the Four Gospels', focuses on the composition of the canonical gospels. Richard A. Burridge, in chapter 5, examines the four evangelists and the audiences for whom they wrote. This is followed by chapters devoted to each of the four evangelists. Richard C. Beaton provides insights into factors at play in the writing of Matthew, looking particularly at the sources of this gospel. Craig A. Evans examines the distinctive features of Mark, noting not only general aspects of Mark's style, but in particular the well-known device of Marcan sandwiching of one narrative within another. He suggests that the whole of the gospel in its bipartite structure can be conceived of as a Marcan sandwich. The composition of Luke is examined by David P. Moessner, particularly in view of its being part one of a two-part work, and the close interrelation between the gospel and Acts. Judith Lieu then provides a chapter on the distinctive aspects of the Gospel of John. She considers among other things the claim that this gospel is a 'spiritual' gospel, its symbolism, narrative and community-history readings of the gospel, and the composition of the gospel. In chapter 10, Morna D. Hooker looks in detail at the beginnings and endings of the gospels as providing clues to the meaning of the total compositions.

Part III deals with what transpired 'After Writing'. Here, in chapter 11, James Carleton Paget examines evidence of knowledge of the gospels among the (mainly non-Christian) Jews. In chapter 12, Loveday Alexander similarly looks at pagan views of the gospels, exemplified in the second-century writer Celsus. And in chapter 13, Christopher Tuckett writes concerning the many extant non-canonical gospels – narrative gospels, sayings gospels, infancy gospels, resurrection discourses – the light they throw upon the canonical gospels and their relation to them. The penultimate chapter, by Ronald A. Piper, documents the early church's acceptance of the four gospels as the canonical manifestation of the one gospel. In the final chapter of the book, Markus Bockmuehl explores the origins of gospel commentaries in the second century, looking at Jewish and Graeco-Roman antecedents, implications for the growing normative character of the gospels, and the balance of academic and pastoral interests in the early commentaries.

As editors we are particularly grateful to our fellow-authors for their contributions, and to Cambridge University Press for making this volume possible. Special thanks are also due to our Ph.D. students Wayne Coppins for translating chapter 4 and Stephen Young for invaluable assistance with the painful labour of formatting and indexing.

But why this book, and why this subject? Needless to say, we believe that there is clear merit and importance in making available a compendium of recent informed opinion – from the origins of the written gospel to its reception in canon and commentary. Above all, however, the contributors wish to honour Professor Graham N. Stanton, Lady Margaret's Professor of Divinity in the University of Cambridge, on the occasion of his sixty-fifth birthday (9 July 2005). Throughout the thirty-five years of his scholarly career at King's College London and at Cambridge, Graham has been a prolific scholar and a much-loved friend to colleagues and mentor to students. He has been an enabler and encourager of numerous doctoral students, all the while maintaining a close friendship with his own Cambridge *Doktorvater*, C. F. D. Moule. All of his major books thus far have focused either on Jesus or on the gospels or both. This interest was already evident with the publication of his doctoral thesis, *Jesus of Nazareth in New Testament Preaching* (1974). Graham is also the author of a popular textbook on the subject, *The Gospels and Jesus* (1989, 2nd edn, 2002). We may further mention his *Gospel Truth? New Light on Jesus and the Gospels* (1995), and his latest book on the subject, *Jesus and Gospel* (2004). Graham is renowned as a specialist in the Gospel of Matthew, on which he has written *A Gospel for a New People: Studies in Matthew* (1992) and numerous shorter studies. He has also edited or co-edited books on Matthew, on Resurrection, on Tolerance and Intolerance, and on Scripture and Theology, and published dozens of articles, too numerous to list here (see appendix). Noteworthy too is his tireless work as an editor, including the International Critical Commentary (since 1984) as well as the flagship journal *New Testament Studies* (1982–90) and the distinguished Monograph Series of Studiorum Novi Testamenti Societas (SNTS, 1982–91), the leading professional society in the field. He was elected a Fellow of King's College London in 1996 (the equivalent of an honorary doctorate) and served as President of the SNTS in 1996–7. A New Zealander who remains an inveterate All Blacks supporter even after forty years abroad, he was awarded an honorary DD in 2000 by his Alma Mater, the University of Otago. In 2002–3 he oversaw the 500th anniversary celebrations of the Lady Margaret's Professorship in Divinity, the oldest chair in the University of Cambridge.

It is our hope that Graham will be pleased with the subject of this book, so close to his heart, and with the quality of these essays written in his honour. Graham's scholarship is widely known and admired. Those who have met him personally cannot fail to be impressed by his unpretentious and self-giving gift of encouragement. We thank God for him and his wife, Esther, and for what they have meant over these many years not only to those involved in this book, but also to many other friends and acquaintances.

MARKUS BOCKMUEHL

DONALD A. HAGNER

PART I

Before writing

CHAPTER I

'Gospel' in Herodian Judaea

William Horbury

I

A link between the Jews of ancient Judaea and the Christian use of *euangelizein* or *euangelizesthai*, 'to announce', with the cognate noun *euangelion*, has regularly been postulated through comparison of the New Testament with the Old. These Greek words in their New Testament contexts have been perceived, through the LXX and the Vulgate, as sharing a good part of the semantic range of the Hebrew verb *l^ebasser*, 'to announce', and its cognate noun *b^esorah*, in the Old Testament. A signpost in the general direction of this view is formed by Heb 4.2 (cf. 4.6), 'we have been evangelized (*euēngelismenoi*) just as they' – the generation of the exodus – 'had been'.

The Epistle to the Hebrews here implicitly classifies as evangel the message of election, victory, and settlement to come which was conveyed through Moses, for example from the divine messenger (in Greek, *angelos*) at Exod 3.2–14, but was disregarded by the people and their princes other than Caleb, as shown above all in Num 13–14; cf. Ps 95.11. Of special note for scholarly assessment of the New Testament *euangelizesthai*, however, were a series of verses in the psalms and prophets which use the verb *l^ebasser* and its participle *m^ebasser*, rendered in the LXX by *euangelizesthai* and *euangelizomenos*, respectively, to speak expressly of the announcement and announcers of good tidings (Pss. 40.10; 68.12; Isa 40.9; 41.27; 52.7 (parallel with Nah 2.1 (1.15)); 61.1). The series is expanded in the LXX by Joel 2.32 (3.5), ending '*euangelizomenoi* whom the Lord shall call', where the Hebrew will have been read as *m^ebass^erim*. Note, however, that the noun *b^esorah* does not occur in this series; in the Hebrew biblical books it appears only in 2 Samuel and 2 Kings (six times in all).

These verses from the psalms and prophets are quoted or echoed in presentations of the teaching and work of Christ in the synoptic gospels, Acts, and Ephesians (Isa 61.1 in Matt 11.5, parallel with Luke 7.22, and in

Luke 4.18, with an echo in Acts 10.39; Isa 52.7 in Eph 2.17). They are also applied to the apostolic preaching in the Pauline corpus (Isa 52.7 quoted in Rom 10.15, and echoed in Eph 6.15), and probably in Acts (the end of Joel 2.32 (3.5) LXX not quoted but envisaged in Acts 2.21: see n. 28 below). These attestations of Old Testament passages which use the relevant vocabulary of course occur amid more widespread New Testament use of *euangelizesthai* and *euangelion.* The common share of the Old Testament in Greek and of the New Testament in this vocabulary is partially but strikingly recalled in the Vulgate Latin by the occurrence of *evangelizare* and *evangelista* in some of the passages on good tidings in the psalms and prophets (Ps 68 (67).12; Isa 40.9; 41.27; Nah 2.1 (1.15)).

This Old Testament-guided interpretation of Christian usage regularly also led to discussion of languages and vocabulary used by ancient Jews. The topic considered below is the place of the vocabulary associated with *lᵉbasser* and *euangelizesthai* in Herodian Judaea, that is the Roman province of Judaea (including Galilee, Samaria, Peraea, and Idumaea) in the period beginning when the Roman senate designated Herod the Great as king of the Jews in 40 BC, and ending at least in principle with the death of Herod's great-grandson Agrippa II, probably in AD 100.[1] Conditions which can be called Herodian will not have vanished overnight, and the full end of the Herodian period can be associated with the uprising of Bar-Kokhba in 132–5.

In this chapter some indications of the use of the relevant vocabulary in Judaea in this period will be reviewed in two main parts. To begin with, points which have emerged from biblically oriented study of *euangelion* against the background of the Old and New Testaments are gathered, and there is a fresh consideration of aspects of the Septuagint and its pseudepi-grapha, with kindred passages in Josephus and the New Testament, and of the Targum with some rabbinic texts (section 2 below). Then the discussion moves from this mainly biblical orientation to another viewpoint often taken in earlier study, the interpretation of this vocabulary in the setting of both gentile and Jewish religion (section 3 below). Herodian Judaea is still the focus of inquiry, and the use of the relevant words in ordinary life is not ignored; but attention is now paid to some primary texts of a more directly cultic character, notably honorific formulae, prophecy, and hymnody, including material from the Qumran finds and later Jewish literature. It is suggested overall (section 4 below) that, for Judaean Jews, the prominence of this vocabulary in scripture and its development in interpretative tradition were enhanced by contemporary more general

[1] Kokkinos 1998:396–9.

usage of the relevant Aramaic and Greek words, and their high profile in the honorific language of courts and temples.

2

The main lines of an approach to the New Testament vocabulary of 'gospel' guided especially by the Old Testament in Hebrew and Greek emerge in Matthew Poole's synopsis of seventeenth-century comment on *euangelion*.[2] He began by noting attestation in Greek authors of the meanings 'reward for good news' and 'sacrifice on account of good news' as well as 'good news' itself – the three meanings later distinguished in the Greek lexicon of Liddell, Scott, and Jones.[3] Christian understanding of the word as 'good news' thus emerged as continuous with Greek usage, even though it would increasingly be noted that the sense 'good news' was best attested in the relatively late Greek used by the bilingual Cicero, Plutarch, and (from Herodian Judaea) Josephus, and that the relevant Greek, Hebrew, and Aramaic vocabulary could sometimes be used for the announcement of bad news as well as good.[4] Poole gave most of his space, however, to Hugo Grotius' view (itself a development of earlier concern with the Semitic-language setting of the gospels)[5] that Hebrew or Aramaic here lay beneath New Testament Greek and was used by Christ, whose gospel (in Hebrew, *bᵉsorah*) consisted of the good tidings of peace and of the kingdom of God declared in Isa 52.7: 'the Christians received this term from their great teacher, and he from the prophets'. A motto for Grotius' approach could perhaps be taken from *1 Clem.* 42.1, 'the apostles had the gospel imparted to them (*euēngelisthēsan*) for us from the Lord Jesus Christ'.

The LXX and Hebrew and Aramaic continued to hold their place in comment on *euangelion* beside Greek usage, and were characteristically but not unjustly emphasized at the end of the nineteenth century in H. Cremer's biblical-theological New Testament lexicon (see n. 4 above).

---

[2] Poole (Pole) 1684–6 (corrected reprint of work issued first in 1669–76) IV, cols. 3–4, quoting among other authors Grotius 1641:4–5.

[3] Liddell et al. 1940:705a.

[4] On the relatively late attestation of *euangelion* in the sense 'good news', see Cremer 1893:30–1 (but Friedrich 1935, col. 719, ET 722, urged that some earlier instances of 'sacrifice on account of good news' presuppose the sense 'good news'); on use of relevant vocabulary for bad news as well as good, see Billerbeck in Strack and Billerbeck 1922–61:III (1926), 5 (the favourable sense predominates).

[5] Such concern was encouraged in the sixteenth century (Horbury 1999) by the patristic tradition that Matthew wrote in Hebrew, together with the printing of Jewish Hebrew versions of Matthew (1537, 1555) and of the gospels in Syriac (1555). The Aramaic words quoted by Grotius were the Syriac *sᵉbar*, 'to announce' and *sᵉbarta*, 'tidings'.

Yet it also remained clear both that Christian use of *euangelion* took up a sense attested in Greek authors, characteristically connected with the 'announcement' of births, victories, and new reigns, and that *euangelion* had quickly become a quintessentially Christian term. Thus it was already beginning to be used as a term for a written gospel-book by the time of Bar-Kokhba; it was adopted from Greek, without translation, by Christian speakers of Latin and Syriac; and the Greek word is also echoed in rabbinic literature with regard to Christianity.[6]

Within the New Testament, correspondingly, as many as sixty of its seventy-five or seventy-six occurrences are in the Pauline corpus; in the gospels and Acts, the noun is restricted to Matthew (four occurrences), Mark (seven or eight), and Acts (two), although the verb *euangelizesthai* is frequent in Luke and Acts. This distribution could in itself encourage the view that the noun was essentially a Pauline term derived from Greek-speaking circles, and was unlikely to reflect the (Aramaic or Hebrew) vocabulary of Jesus and his disciples.[7] Its rapid acquisition of a special Christian sense (a specialization which did not affect the verb to the same extent in Christian usage) perhaps contributed to the popularity in patristic authors of the related word *euangelismos* for the more general good announcement, above all for the 'annunciation' made to Mary by Gabriel, who had earlier been sent to 'announce' to Zacharias the future birth of John (*euangelisasthai*, Luke 1.19).[8]

These Greek and Christian aspects of *euangelion* were highlighted after the publication in 1899 of an inscription (ca. 9 BC) from Priene in Caria, using the plural *evangelia* for the good tidings which began with the birthday of the divine Caesar. Adolf Deissmann brought this epigraphic text together with papyri to present *euangelion* as a term of Augustan and

---

[6] Stanton 1997:334 (citing instances of *euangelion* as referring to a written text in *Did.* 8.2; 11.3; 15.3–4; Ign. *Smyrn.* 5.1; 7.2; *2 Clem.* 8.5); Mohrmann 1965 (reprint of articles issued in 1949 and 1950), 104, 113 (*evangelium* already found in the Latin version of *1 Clement*), 130–1 (*evangelium* one of a group of words adopted in Christian Latin together with the institutions which they designate); Brock 1967:399 (noting the currency of the translation *sᵉbarta* as well as the transliteration); Babylonian Talmud, *Šabb.* 116a, in Strack 1910:2, 19* (R. Meir (second century) said in condemnation *ᵃwen-gillayon*, 'trouble of *gillayon*', R. Yoḥanan b. Nappaḥa (third century)) *ᵃwon-gillayon*, 'iniquity of *gillayon*'), interpreted by Maier 1982:74–8 as originally referring not to the gospel but to blank parchment (Hebrew *gillayon*) considered unsuitable, but more probably, given the rarity of the use of *awen* attributed to Meir, alternative polemical malformations of Greek *euangelion*.

[7] Stanton 2004:18–25 argues in general on these lines. The unlikelihood of a link with the vocabulary of Jesus was stressed by Wellhausen 1911 (1st edn 1905), 99 (affirming the Paulinism of Mark) and Bousset 1921 (1st edn 1913), 42 n. 1; but it was allowed as possible by Harnack 1910:234, ET 324 (rejecting the Paulinism of Mark) and – now together with the opinion that Marcan usage reflected that of Paul – by Lagrange 1929:clvii, 17–18.

[8] Lampe 1961:559.

later Roman ruler-cult, attested in Asia Minor and Egypt with regard to the good news of an auspicious reign; he stressed that it was just one of a group of New Testament words which recall the idiom of ruler-cult, including *parousia, epiphaneia,* and *sotēr.*[9] Papyri and inscriptions published later on confirm the association with sovereigns, but also, like literary authors, attest more general announcement, notably in connection with birth, marriage, and victory.[10] The general and royal usages were of course intertwined; victory as well as birth well suits the ruler-cult context, especially given the dependence of many Hellenistic and Roman rulers, from the Seleucids to Herod the Great, Augustus, and Vespasian, on decisive battles and generalship for their sovereignty.[11]

J. Kögel, in his revision of Cremer, simply noted the fresh attestation of the sense 'good news' provided by the Priene inscription and related papyri.[12] This new contemporary context for New Testament usage, how-ever, also attested 'good news' in a sense strikingly comparable with Christian understandings of *euangelion* – as the gospel of a divine reign. Christian use of *euangelion* has often been derived ever since, as by the scholar honoured in this volume, not from Jewish Hebrew, Aramaic, or Greek usage related to the Old Testament, but from the language of Greek and Roman ruler-cult.[13] Mediating positions are exemplified by M. -J. Lagrange, who envisaged Jesus as having himself spoken of good news, but the evangelist Mark as setting the evangel of the messianic advent of Jesus Christ deliberately in contrast with the evangel of imperial advents.[14] In the discussion below I have taken it that influence from ruler-cult should indeed be recognized, but in convergence with rather than as an alternative to biblical and later Jewish influence.

At the time of the first consideration of the Priene inscription, however, the Hebrew and Aramaic setting of the gospels and their vocabulary of 'gospel' was being explored by G. Dalman and, from a more radically critical viewpoint, by J. Wellhausen; Wellhausen in turn was criticized in a

---

[9] Deissmann 1923 (4th rev. edn of work issued first in 1908), 312–24, ET (1910), 370–84; on the Augustus-cult at Priene see Mitchell 1993:1.102.

[10] Horsley 1983:10–15, no. 2.

[11] This is noted in connection with the autocratic rather than constitutional character of much Hellenistic kingship by Bi(c)kerman 1938:12–13.

[12] Cremer 1893, ed. Kögel (1911), 31.

[13] Sponsors of this view include Wellhausen 1911 (1st edn 1905), 98–9 (but he allowed that the term could have come from the ruler-cult to the church through Christian speakers of Aramaic); Bousset 1921 (1st edn 1913), 42 n. 1, 244; Lohmeyer 1919:54, n. 60; Strecker (1975 onwards), cited by Stuhlmacher 1991:151 n. 11; Koester 1990:3–4; Stanton 2004:20–35.

[14] Lagrange 1929:clvii, 2 (on Mark 1.1), 17–18 (on 1.15).

study of *euangelion* by A. Harnack, and Dalman's approach was taken further by P. Billerbeck. At the same time, in a contribution which gained less prominence in the biblical discussion overall, W. Bacher had shown the importance of the Hebrew verb *lᵉbasser* in rabbinic exegetical terminology. A revived and deepened Old Testament approach to *euangelion* began to emerge.

In this discussion, above all because of the importance of the verb as well as the noun in both Greek and Hebrew, the study of the vocabulary of 'gospel' was saved from some of the narrowness of concentration on a single word which has been viewed as a defect of this type of inquiry. The contexts of occurrences and the relationship of the words in Greek and Hebrew with other words of comparable signification received attention, and an attempt was made, in the footsteps of Grotius and others, to envisage the Semitic-language as well as the Greek-language idioms of the Judaean church. Hence, despite the prominence in debate of what were often questionably regarded as mutually exclusive alternatives – is this vocabulary essentially dominical or Pauline, Hebraic or Greek? – much was provided of value for inquiry directed towards the place of the 'gospel' vocabulary in Herodian Judaea.

Thus, to turn first to the LXX, with Judaean use of Greek in mind, it became a commonplace that Septuagintal attestation of *euangelion* in the sense 'good news' is slender or even non-existent; just one sure instance (2 Kingdoms = 2 Sam 18.25) was allowed by Billerbeck (as more recently by M. Hengel and G. N. Stanton), but the view in its most negative form was shared by scholars as different as Wellhausen, Harnack, Kögel, and G. Friedrich.[15] Since then, however, the interpretation and diffusion of the Greek scriptures at the time of Christian origins have been further discussed, and it seems likely that this mainly negative view should be modified, as noted below.

Secondly, now with Aramaic and Hebrew in Judaea in mind, the much more positive finding of this research with regard to Semitic-language texts is notable. Despite the assumed slenderness of clear Septuagintal attestation of *euangelion* in the required sense, G. Dalman, Harnack, and Billerbeck all took it, somewhat as Grotius had done, that the Hebrew noun *besorah* and the Aramaic *bᵉsorᵉta* were used in Judaea, by early Judaean Christians and possibly by Jesus (Dalman appears more cautious than Harnack on this point), in the sense of the good news of God's reign – a sense which would

---

[15] Wellhausen 1911 (1st edn 1905), 98; Harnack 1910:199–200, 235, ET 276, 325; Friedrich 1935, col. 723, ET 725; Hengel 2000:210–11 n. 9; Stanton 2004:13.

become central in the characteristic Christian understanding of *euangelion* as the preaching of the coming of the kingdom by Christ and his church. It was in Judaea, according to Harnack, that Greek-speaking Christians first adopted the Greek word in this sense, to gain an equivalent for the Hebrew or Aramaic used by fellow-members of the church.

From the New Testament side, this inference was encouraged especially by Mark, a gospel which attests the noun *euangelion* but not the cognate verb. Hence Aramaic, including Aramaic renderings of Hebrew scripture, would have formed the immediate background of the Christian use of the Greek noun. Yet this assumed new inner-Christian development in the use of the noun could readily have merged with the emphasis on the verb and its participle already received by Judaeans familiar with the Old Testament in Greek. Thus Judaean Christian Greek vocabulary, for Harnack, included the whole cluster *euangelizesthai, euangelion,* and *euangelistēs.*

Thirdly, this argument for the importance of the Aramaic *bᵉsorᵉta* in the awareness of Judaean hearers of scripture was supported by Dalman with evidence which is abidingly important in two respects. On the one hand he showed that the Aramaic vocabulary, like the corresponding Greek, was used for the significant announcements of family and national life, as when 28th Adar is remembered in an essentially pre-Mishnaic Aramaic text as the date when (probably after the death of Antiochus IV) 'good news (*bᵉsorᵉta tabᵉta*) came to the Jews, that they should not depart from the law' (*Megillat Taʿanit* as 36/17 12). On the other hand, the biblical attestation of *lᵉbasser* in the context of divine or prophetic announcement could itself be seen to heighten the prominence of *bᵉsorᵉtha.* Thus Dalman noted that the Syriac *Apocalypse of Baruch* (46.6; 77.12) spoke of the prophetic 'message', although he did not discuss the underlying Greek or Semitic-language term (considered further below). Attention was implicitly drawn by Dalman to the near-synonymous collocation in biblical and post biblical Hebrew of *lᵉbasser* with *lᵉhashmiaʿ,* 'to proclaim', and of *bᵉsorah* with *shᵉmuʿah,* 'report' or 'tidings', and by Billerbeck to the use of Aramaic *bᵉsorᵉta* to represent *shᵉemuʿah* as well as *bᵉsorah*; this collocation is well attested in Isa 52.7, parallel with Nah 2.1 (1.15).[16]

---

[16] Dalman 1898:85, ET 104, citing for a messianic announcer of good tidings *Az mi-liphne be-reshit,* in which the third stanza ends 'to make proclamation to us (*lᵉhashmiʿenu*) on mount Lebanon [the temple mount] a second time (Isa 11.11) by the hand of Yinnon [the messiah, 'Yinnon is his name' (Ps 72.17)]' (for a text with brief commentary see Goldschmidt 1970:II.410); Billerbeck (in Strack and Billerbeck 1922–61:III.5), citing parallel narratives of Yoḥanan b. Zakkai before Vespasian in Hebrew (*b.Giṭṭ.* 56b, with *shᵉmuʿah*) and Aramaic (*Lam. Rab.* 1.5, with *bᵉsorᵉta*); Clines et al. 1995:277a (collocation of synonyms in Isa 52.7).

The near-synonymity of the two Hebrew verbs and nouns, and the importance of Targumic rendering of *sh^{e}mu'ah* by *b^{e}sor^{e}ta*, was later explicitly underlined by P. Stuhlmacher, with acknowledgement of J. Buxtorf's registration of this rendering, from Obad 1, in his lexicon (first issued 1615).[17] Stuhlmacher's appeal to fresh evidence for the prominence of *b^{e}sor^{e}ta* was part of a broad review of Jewish and non-Jewish sources which marked a new stage in inquiry through scrutiny of newly published or neglected texts, especially but not only from the Targums and the Qumran writings; it included a study of *euangelizesthai* and *euangelion* in the LXX and Josephus which brought out contacts with Jewish tradition. Stuhlmacher's overall view was close to that of Harnack, and is followed in the main by M. Hengel and A. M. Schwemer when they argue against derivation of 'gospel' vocabulary from ruler-cult, and for a very early Christian development (already taken up by the Hellenists in the Jerusalem church) of a Greek vocabulary of *euangelion* on the basis of the Aramaic *b^{e}sor^{e}ta* and the Septuagintal renderings of Isaiah and the Psalter.[18]

Fourthly, to move from the question of the prominence of the relevant Hebrew and Aramaic vocabulary to its signification, particularly notable was the continuing connection between announcement and the vocabulary of divine kingship discerned by Dalman and Billerbeck; Dalman had drawn attention in this regard not only to biblical passages on the bearer of tidings such as Isa 40.9; 41.27; 52.7, but also to interpretations of this *m^{e}basser* in Isa 52.7 as the returning Elijah or the messianic king, in the midrash and synagogue poetry of later Roman and Byzantine Palestine.[19] Chronologically, their biblical and post-biblical Hebrew and Aramaic material ranges from the Second Temple period to the Byzantine age; but it suggests that Christian linkage of 'gospel' vocabulary with declaration of the kingdom of God and his Christ may belong to a series of Judaean Jewish developments of the biblical association of announcement with divine kingship.

Hence, lastly, it also emerged that the associations of *euangelion* in the context of Augustan ruler-cult were not far from those of the announcement vocabulary in its Old Testament contexts. Thus Joachim Jeremias stressed that the Hebrew verb *l^{e}basser* recalled ancient near eastern announcement

---

[17] Stuhlmacher 1968:122–53; Stuhlmacher 1991:151–2, 161–2.
[18] Hengel and Schwemer 1998:153–5.
[19] Dalman 1898:84–6, ET 102–4, citing among texts on the messiah *Tg. Lam.* 2.22, *Song. Rab.* on 2.13, and Kalir's piyyut *Az mi-liphne be-reshit*; Billerbeck (in Strack and Billerbeck 1922–61:III (1926)), 4–11 (8), on Rom 1.1.

of the new age of a new king.[20] Jeremias urged that associations with kingship – very like, it may be added, the associations highlighted by Deissmann from the ruler-cult of the eastern Roman provinces – did indeed already belong to the prophecy including the phrase 'to announce to the afflicted' (*l^ebasser* *^anawim*, LXX *euangelísasthai ptōchois*) in Isa 61.1; and that this prophecy was quoted by Jesus at the beginning of his ministry to declare the opening of a new age (Luke 4.18–19). It is implied in Jeremias's presentation that these associations of a 'gospel' with the publicity of a new reign would have reached Galilean Jews under Antipas not through the Greek idiom of the Augustan cult or its predecessors, but through the Hebrew biblical books and their own reflections of Israelite, Syrian, Mesopotamian, and Persian monarchy, transmitted in a mainly Semitic-language Jewish context. It could then seem, however, that the interpretation of 'gospel' from the Greek praises of Augustan ruler-cult and its interpretation against the background of Hebrew scripture fully converge in associating this vocabulary with the good tidings of a new reign. Both backgrounds loomed large in Herodian Judaea.

These considerations offered by earlier biblical study outline a good case for the familiarity of relevant Hebrew, Aramaic, and Greek vocabulary, especially the verbs, among Judaean Jews at the time of Christian origins. There are perhaps still more indications pointing in this direction. That is suggested by further aspects of some primary texts now to be considered, first from the LXX and its pseudepigrapha, with one or two passages of kindred content from Josephus and the New Testament, and then from the Targum, with a note of the rabbinic exegetical usage registered by Bacher.

First, then, with reference to the opinion that Septuagintal attestation of the noun *euangelion* is slender or non-existent, debate turns on those verses in 2 Samuel and 2 Kings (2 and 4 Kingdoms in the Greek) which in Hebrew attest the six biblical occurrences of the noun *b^esorah* noted above. In the Greek text of the great uncial codices the feminine noun *euangelía* is clearly attested in the sense of 'good news' at 2 Kingdoms = 2 Sam 18.20; 27; 4 Kingdoms = 2 Kgs 7.9, but the neuter noun *euangelion* appears with certainty only once, with the sense 'reward for good news' and in the accusative plural (2 Kingdoms = 2 Sam 4.10). Possible instances of its nominative plural *euangélia* in the sense 'good news' do indeed occur in the account of the bringing of the double news of victory over the rebels and the death of Absalom in 2 Kingdoms = 2 Sam 18.22, 25. In both verses the word is accentuated as the plural of *euangelion* by a corrector of Codex

---

[20] Jeremias 1930:17–18.

Vaticanus.[21] Verse 25 presents the single sure instance of *euangelion* in the sense of 'good news' allowed by Billerbeck and Hengel, as noted above. In both verses, however, the word could be accentuated as the nominative singular of the feminine noun *euangelia*, which is attested more clearly, as already noted, just before and after these two verses.[22] In all the verses cited MT gives the singular *b^esorah*.

Yet, as the corrections in Codex Vaticanus might already suggest, some cursive Greek witnesses to the account of the bearing of tidings to David attest the plural *euangélia*, 'good news', in the genitive in verses 20 (one manuscript) and 27, and in the nominative in verse 31.[23] In verses 27 and 31 the five manuscripts in question have long been taken to attest the Lucianic recension.[24] This is in general close to some Old Latin witnesses and to the biblical text of Josephus, and perhaps ultimately reflects revision in the Antiochene Jewish community of the first century AD.[25] In verses 27 and 31, accordingly, the plural *euangélia* is admitted into the 'Antiochene text' as reconstructed by N. Fernández Marcos and J. R. Busto Saiz, and these editors also accentuate *euangélia* in verse 22.[26] In verses 20 and 25, following the five Lucianic manuscripts, they print forms of *euangelismos*; this noun is not attested in the uncials of the New Testament but is common in patristic Greek, as noted above. Yet, despite its non-registration by Liddell and Scott and their revisers, it was not necessarily restricted to Christians in antiquity.

The Hebrew and the Greek texts of the books of Samuel were marked by variation and revision from long before the time of Christian origins. It seems very possible that, as Wellhausen, Harnack, and Friedrich held, the redactor responsible for 2 Kingdoms = 2 Sam 18.20–7 as transmitted in the great uncials envisaged the feminine noun *euangelia* throughout. On the other hand, given the attestation of the neuter *euangelion* in the sense of 'good news' in non-Jewish Greek texts from the first century BC onwards, it seems not unlikely that some Jews in this period may have understood 2 Kgdms 18.22, 25 as presenting *euangelion* in this sense in the plural (as in Cicero, e.g. *Att.* 2.3.1, the Priene inscription, and Josephus, *J. W.* 4.618, cited below); and that they may have also read this plural in verses 20, 27,

---

[21] Brooke et al. 1927:170–1.

[22] This accentuation is followed by Brooke et al. 1927 and by H. B. Swete and A. Rahlfs in their hand-editions. On the gradual introduction in Greek biblical manuscripts of diacritical signs (second century onwards) and then of fuller accentuation (fourth century onwards) see Biondi 1983:67.

[23] Brooke et al. 1927:170–1.

[24] Stuhlmacher 1968:155–6; Fernández Marcos and Busto Saiz 1989:xiv, lxxxvii.

[25] This is the view of Fernández Marcos 1998:238, ET (2000), 235–6; at ET 235, in the last line of the text, 'Antioch' should be read for 'Alexandria'.

[26] Fernández Marcos and Busto Saiz 1989:143–5.

and 31, in the fashion attested in the Vaticanus corrections and in some cursive manuscripts, most notably by witnesses to the Lucianic recension in verses 22, 27, and 31. Diffusion of Greek biblical versions for Jewish use in Judaea is confirmed for the time of Christian origins by Greek biblical fragments from Qumran Cave 7 and above all by the Nahal Hever (Wadi Habra) Greek text of the Minor Prophets.

At this period, therefore, Jews could have discerned in their Greek scriptures a number of instances of *euangelion* in the plural in the sense of 'good news', as well as widespread use of *euangelizesthai*. This point is supported, now with one or two indications of the singular, by pseudepigrapha from the later Second Temple period. Thus *euangelizesthai* is used for divine or prophetic announcement in the Greek texts of the *Psalms of Solomon*, on 'the voice of one announcing in Jerusalem' (11.1, considered below) and the *Paralipomena of Jeremiah*, on preaching by Jeremiah (3.11, 5.21). Again in connection with the prophetic message, the Syriac *Apocalypse of Baruch* as cited above refers to (plural) 'announcements' which he had given beforehand (46.6), and a 'scroll of tidings' (in the singular, 77.12) which he writes to the exiles in Babylon; both passages use Syriac *s'barta*, which often renders the Greek noun *euangelion* (n. 6 above), and there is therefore a fair possibility that *euangelion* stood in the lost Greek text translated here.

The association of *euangelizesthai* with the divine or prophetic message reappears in Josephus, when Joshua as prophet (compare his high profile as prophet in the Qumran texts) 'announced' beforehand to the people the fall of Jericho (*euēngelizeto*, *Ant.* 5.24, expanding Josh 6.16), and the apparition of an angel was 'announcing' beforehand the birth of Samson (*euangelizomenon*, *Ant.* 5.277, expanding Judg 13.3); and likewise in Luke, when angels 'announce' births to Zacharias and the shepherds (Luke 1.19, quoted above; 2.10; both with parts of *euangelizesthai*), and the Baptist 'announced' his prophetic exhortation to the people (*euēngelizeto*, Luke 3.18). In Revelation, close in expression to the Syriac Apocalypse of Baruch, God 'announced' the completion of his mystery to the prophets (Rev 10.7, with the verb *euēngelisen*), and an angel has an eternal *euangelion* (singular) to announce (Rev 14.6, with both verb and noun). These New Testament passages primarily attest not a specialized Christian usage, but Jewish usage of the Herodian age.[27]

This evidence from the Lucianic Greek text of the historical books, from pseudepigrapha transmitted in Greek and Syriac, from Josephus' biblical paraphrase, and from passages of Luke and the Revelation which lack

---

[27] They were assessed on these lines by Stuhlmacher 1968:216–17.

a specialized Christian stamp, should be set in turn beside the slight but significant Septuagintal heightening of the notion of a number of bearers of tidings (Joel 3.5 (2.32) end, implicitly recalled in Acts 2.21, as well as Ps 68 (67).12; Isa 52.7 is comparably quoted with a plural in Rom 10.15).[28] In all, then, the Greek noun (sometimes in the singular) as well as the verb, especially in the context of divine or prophetic announcement, and the group of biblical texts on announcing and announcers, were probably familiar to Greek-speaking Jews and Christians in Herodian Judaea.

Secondly, the Targumic renderings of the Isaianic prophecies of good tidings gave *b^esor^eta* a higher profile, as Stuhlmacher showed, by the use of *b^esor^eta* to render *shemu'ah*. This extended use of *b^esor^eta* is probably also relevant for Herodian Judaea, especially given the biblical collocation of Hebrew *b^esorah* and *shemu'ah* noted above; for *Targum Jonathan on the Prophets* is regarded as relatively early (before AD 200), and despite its exclusively Babylonian transmission is thought to reflect language either of Judaea itself or of Syria.[29] Neither Aramaic *b^esor^eta* nor Greek *euangelion* is therefore likely to have been unfamiliar in Herodian Judaea.

The view that *b^esor^eta* and cognate words became prominent in Aramaic biblical paraphrase receives some confirmation from their appearances in the Pentateuchal Targums of the Palestinian tradition. One or two of these appearances introduce into Pentateuchal contexts in Aramaic the phrases concerning a herald of good tidings which are prominent in Hebrew in the psalms and prophets. Thus Sarah exclaims 'how faithful was the bearer of tidings who announced (*m^ebass^era d^e-bassar*) to Abraham, saying Sarah will suckle children' (Gen 21.7, *Neofiti* and *Pseudo-Jonathan*). Again, Naphthali like 'a hind sent out, putting forth words of beauty' in Jacob's blessing (Gen 49.21) becomes a 'herald of good tidings', *m^ebassar b^esoran tabhan*, in *Neofiti* and *Pseudo-Jonathan*, in recognition of his position in the haggadah as the swift messenger among the patriarchs.[30] These Targums are closely linked with the haggadah as expounded in Galilee and elsewhere in Palestine well after the Herodian age, in the third, fourth, and fifth centuries; but they indicate the persistence of the relevant Aramaic vocabulary and of the image of the herald of good tidings, and thus confirm the suggestion of a high profile for this vocabulary which emerges from *Targum Jonathan on the Prophets*.

---

[28] For the implied reference to this part of Joel 3.5 (2.32) in Acts 2.21 see Dodd 1952:46–7; on Rom 10.15 against this background Stuhlmacher 1991:163.

[29] The setting of the Targum is discussed by Cook 1994.

[30] These passages were cited from *Pseudo-Jonathan* by Stuhlmacher 1968:128, 139 n. 2.

In the Galilean and Palestininan settings which shaped these Targums, the Hebrew verb *l^ebasser* came to the fore not dissimilarly in biblical interpretation transmitted in Hebrew. This point was made by Bacher with reference to literature from the Mishnah onwards.[31] The scripture or the holy spirit was viewed as a messenger bringing tidings, often with use of the feminine participle *m^ebasseret*, prominent in the biblical text at Isa 40.9, Ps 68.12 (pl.). Thus, to pick out two of Bacher's instances, in Mishnaic exposition of the Deuteronomic rite for expiation of an uncertain murder, 'the holy spirit announces to them (*m^ebassartan*) that when the rite is performed *the blood shall be forgiven them*'(Deut 21.9, interpreted in *m. Sot.* 9.6). Similarly, an exegesis attributed to Resh Laqish, who taught in third-century Tiberias, takes the suggestion of a future reference constituted by the unexpected use of imperfect tenses in Exod 1.12 *the more they afflicted them, the more they multiplied* as 'the holy spirit announcing to them (*m^ebassartan*)' that affliction will only make the Israelites multiply (*b. Sot.* 11a, foot; *Exod. Rab.* 1.11, on Exod 1.12). Thus the scripture or the spirit 'announces', in this Hebrew terminology, somewhat as a divine messenger or prophet 'announces' in the earlier Jewish Greek terminology noted above from the *Psalms of Solomon*, the *Paralipomena of Jeremiah*, Luke, and Revelation.

The Old Testament approach to 'gospel' vocabulary which has been followed thus far has highlighted biblical translation and interpretation in the Jewish community, from the LXX in the Hellenistic age to the Hebrew and Aramaic midrash and synagogue poetry of the later Roman empire. Some Greek biblical renderings have been freshly reviewed together with Greek pseudepigrapha, Josephus' biblical paraphrase, and some New Testament texts; and passages from the Targums have been reconsidered together with rabbinic comment. The biblically derived vocabulary of 'gospel', including the noun, has emerged as alive in Herodian Judaea in the transmission and development of biblical tradition not only in Aramaic, but also in Greek.

Its continuing life is accompanied by continuing interest in messenger-figures, evident in the concept of a number of *euangelizomenoi* in the LXX, in the added references to a bearer of good tidings in the Targum, and in the rabbinic concept of scripture or the holy spirit as giving tidings. This development can be linked with the persistence into Hellenistic and Roman times of that interest in messengers of God – prophetic, priestly, or angelic – which had became prominent in Hebrew biblical texts during

---

[31] Bacher 1899, 1905 (repr. in one vol. 1965), I:11; II:23, 203.

the Persian period (Isa 42.19; 44.26; Hag 1.13; Mal 2.7; 3.1; 2 Chr 36.15–16; cf. Exod 3.2; 23.12; 33.2, on the messenger or angel of the exodus). In Greek these passages use the word *angelos*, cognate with *euangelizesthai*. Against the background of this interest, together with widespread use of *euangelizesthai*, sometimes with *euangelion*, for the divine and prophetic message, it is not hard to see how the exodus generation could be viewed in Hebrews as *euēngelismenoi* (Heb 4.2, quoted above). At the same time this interpretation can be envisaged as current in Judaea, not simply in the diaspora.

The Greek and Aramaic vocabulary of 'gospel' has now been considered in the context of the scriptures and their Jewish interpretation and translation. The review confirmed that Jews in Herodian Judaea are likely to have been familiar with this vocabulary in both languages. At the same time, however, it became clear that the relevant words were used by gentiles as well as Jews in family life, and gained prominence in connection with temples and royal courts. A move can now appropriately be made from a focus on the Old and New Testaments to an overlapping but distinct focus on religion in Judaea. The place of 'gospel' vocabulary in ordinary life is not forgotten, but Jewish and gentile religion are primarily in view, with special reference to honorific formulae, hymnody, and prophecy.

3

Syrian, Idumaean, Greek, and Roman cults flourished in Herodian Judaea together with the Jewish cult of the one God. This old-established coexistence came to the fore under Herod the Great through the reincorporation into his kingdom of Greek cities which had once been subject to the Hasmonaeans, and his own zeal as a founder and benefactor of cities, now with Roman as well as Greek characteristics in cult and ethos.[32] Syrian and Greek mythology was correspondingly current in Judaea side by side with what may be called Jewish biblical mythology.

Recognition of a mythological aspect of biblical literature by such students of ancient Judaism as H. Gunkel and W. Bousset has been vividly restated for the later Second Temple period by S. Schwartz, with emphasis on the impact of successive empires.[33] He pictures Judaism as a covenantal religion focused on two institutions supported by Persian and Greek rulers, the sanctuary and the law of the one God; but he also stresses that it was permeated by and sometimes in tension with a mythology, most strikingly

---

[32] Millar 1993:353–9.   [33] Schwartz 2001:14–15, 49–87.

attested in the apocalypses. A similar permeation can be discerned, it may be added, through the prophets and psalms, Job and Proverbs, and the biblical versions in Greek and Aramaic. In this biblical mythology lesser divine beings – 'gods', 'holy ones', or 'messengers' (in English translation often 'angels') – are envisaged together with the sovereign deity in a kind of pantheon, comparable with the historically related pantheons of Syria and Greece.

Settings for the vocabulary of announcement which are brought into view in this context of religion then include not only ruler-cults but also the cults of deities envisaged as kings. Among these the most important for the present purpose is the Jewish cult of the most high God, 'a great king above all gods' (Ps 95.3), the 'king of heaven' (Dan 4.34 (37), in Aramaic; 1 Esdras 4.46, 58, in Greek). From the Persian period onwards a renewed Jewish emphasis on the deity as king and on his kingdom (for phrases which can be rendered 'kingdom of God' first become prominent in Chronicles) was concurrent with a Greek heightening of emphasis on the supreme deity as king, found in philosophical as well as poetic discourse.[34] The setting of these developments, for both Jews and Greeks, was the Persian monarchy and then the Greek monarchies which followed Alexander the Great.

The importance of heavenly heralds and messengers for Jews in this period has emerged already. Their equal importance for gentiles appears clearly in the broader context of the religions of Judaea. From the Olympians Hermes stands out. He was invoked as *euangelos,* and his attribute as the swift announcer of good news is emphasized by Philo. He was connected with the praise of Augustus, and he was one of the deities whose dress was adopted by Gaius Caligula: his likeness had been known in Syria, Phoenicia, and Samaria through gems and seals, and later he was known in Judaea under the Roman name Mercury, echoed in the Mishnah.[35] Herald-figures also include, however, kings (like Augustus and Gaius) in some aspects of ruler-cult.

Somewhat comparably in the *Assumption of Moses,* to return to a document of Herodian Judaism, Moses becomes a Hermes-like 'master of the word' and 'great messenger' (*dominus verbi, magnus nuntius*; 11.16–17), and at the appearing of God's kingdom (10.1–2) a 'messenger' (*nuntius*) is commissioned to

---

[34] Horbury 1998c:37–46, on biblical texts; Markschies 1991:408–18, on Hellenistic philosophy.

[35] Glare et al. 1996:135b, citing *IG* 12 (5).235 (Paros, first century AD); Horace, *Od.* 1.2, 41–4, addressed to Augustus, with the comments by Nisbet and Hubbard 1970; Philo, *Legat.* 99–102, on the attributes of Hermes and Gaius' claim to them; Leith 1997:39–48, and Plate i, on bullae originally attached to Aramaic papyri connected with Samaria found in the Wadi Daliyeh, north of Jericho; Elmslie 1911:62–3, on *m. 'Abod. Zar.* 4.1–2, 'by the side of the Merqolis ... on top of the Merqolis'.

avenge Israel (cf. Isa 61.1–2). Against this broader Judaean background of both gentile and Jewish concern with heavenly messengers, the *m^ebasser* or *euangelizomenos* of Isa 52.7 commanded attention.

The cults of Judaea and their mythology of course form the general setting of the biblical texts and versions considered above. Now, however, I should like to concentrate on some texts which are cultic in a more immediate sense. Honorific formulae, hymnody, and prophecy are mainly in view.

To begin with ruler-cult, it is likely, as noted already, that the associations of *euangelion* in this context will have been known to many Jews in Herodian Judaea. Ruler-cult had been familiar to Jews throughout the Greek period, and the cult of Augustus in particular was fostered by Herod in Judaea with magnificent temples at Paneas and at his new foundations of Sebaste and Caesarea; elements of ruler-cult surrounded the Herodian kings themselves.[36] Publicity correspondingly accompanied Herod the Great's accession day, chosen as the dedication day of the rebuilt Jerusalem sanctuary, and Antipas' birthday in his territories (Josephus, *Ant.* 15.421–3; Mark 6.20). Although the vocabulary of *euangelion* and *b^esor^eta* is unattested in the general notices of the 'good reports and praises' with which Herodian kings were hailed (*euphēmiai kai epainoi*, Josephus, *Ant.* 17.200, on the acclamation of Archelaus in Jerusalem), these recurrent Judaean occasions can be expected to have attracted it.

This vocabulary is attested, however, in connection with Vespasian's accession in Josephus (*euangélia* were celebrated with feasting in every city, *J.W.* 4.618, cf. 656); and rabbinic legend as later transmitted in Aramaic correspondingly imagines Yoḥanan b. Zakkai telling Vespasian *b^esor^eta tab^eta itbassart*, 'you have received good news' (*Lam. Rab.* 1.5).

Christian use of *euangelizesthai* and cognate words has often appeared principally, as noted above, as part of a more extensive overlap between New Testament and ruler-cult vocabulary, with a suggestion of gentile rather than Jewish derivation. This suggestion has probably been strengthened not only by recognition of the impact of ruler-cult on Judaea and its Jewish population, such as is advocated here, but also by the assumed yet questionable lack of attestation of the noun *euangelion* in an appropriate sense in Greek current among Jews. At any rate, it also became clear in earlier study that the theme of an auspicious reign belonged both to the

---

[36] On the interaction between Greek, Roman, and Herodian ruler-cult and Judaism and early Christianity, with an argument for its influence on messianism and the cult of Christ, see Horbury 1998c:68–77, 134–6; the prominence of the Augustan cult in Herodian Judaea is stressed by Collins 1999:242, 255–7, in her argument that the imperial cult was a decisive factor in the emergence of the worship of Christ.

newly discovered texts of ruler-cult and to the Old Testament passages on announcement and announcers of divine kingship which had influenced the New Testament. Moreover, both Jewish scriptural attestations and those linked with gentile ruler-cult were seen to be taking up usages familiar in family and national life, notably the announcement of births and victories.

Hence the overlap in this instance between Old and New Testament vocabulary and that associated with ruler-cult can be compared with the similar overlap between ruler-cult and the piety of Israel and the church in the vocabulary concerned with gift and benefaction. In this case too the overlap covers the Hebrew biblical texts themselves (as in Exod 28.28 on the 'holy gifts' of the people) as well as the LXX and the New Testament. The vocabulary of gift was current, like that of 'gospel', in everyday life from the Persian to the Hellenistic and Roman periods.[37]

In these cases there is probably less difficulty or paradox than has sometimes been thought when vocabulary which is prominent in gentile courts and temples is also employed in Jewish or Christian piety. The words in question are in more general currency, and receive a heightened profile and an attractive association with power from their honorific use by gentiles with regard to deities and to rulers. In biblical as in later times, the language of liturgical praise has characteristically been influenced by court usage.

To move now from ruler-cult to the Jewish cult of the 'king of heaven', the main texts still to be considered belong to Jewish praise and prophecy. The good news of the divine reign had been classically declared, from the beginning of the Persian period, in prophecies often cited already on the voice or the herald announcing that 'your God has become king' (Isa 40.3, 9; 52.7, etc.), and in commemorations of the 'kingdom' of God (Dan 3.33 (4.3); Ps 145.13) and its Davidic manifestation (1 Chr 28.5; 29.23; 2 Chr 13.8). The unabated vigour of prophetic formulae of announcement in Judaea, shortly before Herod the Great became king, is seen in respect of *lᵉbasser* and *euangelizesthai* in the Qumran Hodayoth and the *Psalms of Solomon*.

A fragmentarily preserved passage of the Hodayoth envisages the 'servant' of God who speaks as empowered 'to proclaim (*lᵉhashmiʿa*) from his understanding to a creature, and to interpret these things to dust like myself', 'to be a herald (*mᵉbasser*) of ... thy generosity, to preach good news (*lᵉbasser*) to the afflicted' (1QHᵃ 23.11–14, formerly 18.11–14).[38] In line 11

---

[37] On the impact of gift-culture on both ruler-cult and the piety attested in Philo, Josephus, rabbinic literature, and St Paul see Horbury 2003:70–8.

[38] García Martínez and Tigchelaar 1997–8:1.194–7.

lᵉhashmiᶜa ultimately evokes *mᵉbasser* and *lᵉbasser* in line 14, on the pattern of the Deutero-Isaianic collocation of the two verbs noted above. In the absence of context it can be surmised that here as in other similar compositions the speaker is the 'servant', despite his rueful reference to 'dust like myself'.[39] He stresses his abasement, but also the grace which has highly exalted him – to the status of the herald in Isa 52.7 (*mᵉbasser*), and of the one anointed with the spirit in Isa 61.1 to preach (*lᵉbasser*) to the afflicted.

Even through the oracular and allusive style of the Hodayoth, the 'herald' begins to emerge as a distinct figure. That is also the case in the eleventh Psalm of Solomon, already quoted above, from a collection now current in Greek and to be dated between 63 and 40 BC. This hymn on the ingathering of Jerusalem's children (cf. Isa 60.4) can be classified as a 'Zion psalm' outside the Davidic psalter, broadly comparable with the Jerusalem-centred psalm of Tobit or the Apostrophe to Zion from the psalms scroll of Qumran Cave 11, but particularly close to the poem addressed to Jerusalem in Bar 4.36–5.9. It begins 'Blow the trumpet of jubilee (Lev 25.9–10) for the saints, proclaim (*kēruxate*) in Jerusalem the voice of one who bears tidings (*euangelizomenou*), for God has had mercy on Israel in his visitation' (*Pss. Sol.* 11.1).[40] Here the voice is the particular 'voice' of the 'bringer of tidings' to Zion (Isa 40.6,9; 52.7) in the day of 'visitation' or divine deliverance (cf. 1QS 4.6, 19, 26; Wis 3.7), viewed as the supreme liberating jubilee (Lev 25.9–10, echoed in Isa 61.1, 'to proclaim release', LXX *kēruxai . . . aphesin*).

These two hymns therefore link the announcer of Isa 52.7 (*mᵉbasser*, LXX *euangelizomenos*) either with the anointed announcer of Isa 61.1 (in the passage from the Hodayoth) or with the unspecified announcer of the jubilee in Lev 25.9–10, the law which is echoed in Isa 61.1 (in the *Psalms of Solomon*); in *Pss. Sol.* 11.1 the announcer is also identified with the Deutero-Isaianic 'voice'. The figure of the announcer has thus become nodal in a nexus of Isaianic texts, with which the Pentateuchal jubilee law is linked, and which is used in differing ways in hymnody by the beginning of the Herodian age. Particularly notable is the extent of the nexus in *Pss. Sol.* 11.1, for which the existence of a Greek text suggests a wide currency.

---

[39] Following Delcor 1962:288, rather than Holm-Nielsen 1960:255 (arguing that the speaker differentiates himself from the 'servant' with this phrase).

[40] *Kēruxate* was conjecturally retroverted into Hebrew as *hashmiᶜu* by Frankenberg 1896:77; although *lᵉhashmia* is not rendered by this Greek verb in LXX, a Hebrew or Aramaic text of *Pss. Sol.* 11.1 could well have echoed Isa 42.2, 'proclaim (*yashmia*ᶜ) his voice', as happens in the later Hebrew and Aramaic synagogue poems quoted below (see nn. 45–6), and the collocation of *lᵉhashmiaᶜ* and *lᵉbasser* noted above would then have appeared not only in the Hodayoth but also in *Pss. Sol.* 11.1.

This impression is confirmed by two further fragmentary Qumran Hebrew texts. They probably represent prophetic compositions rather than hymns, although they use expressions which could also suit hymnody. First, the announcement of Isa 61.1 is linked with the future resurrection in an exhortation classified by E. Puech as a messianic apocalypse, perhaps of the later second century BC. 'Glorious things which were not before shall the Lord do, as he said; for he shall heal the stricken and revive the dead, he shall bring good tidings to the meek' (4Q521, fragment 2 ii, lines 11–12).[41] Puech emphasizes the resemblance in theme and language between these lines and the passage from the Hodayoth considered above, envisaging the possibility that they are by the same author. This resemblance should not, however, obscure the links between 4Q521 and texts not found at Qumran. Thus the Isaianic tidings to the meek are comparably linked with healing and resurrection in the Q passage Matt 11.5, parallel with Luke 7.22, noted above among the New Testament quotations of Old Testament texts using *euangelizesthai*. The association of Isa 61.1 with resurrection also broadly coheres with *Pss. Sol.* 11.1. Here Isa 52.7, *euangelizomenos*, and Lev 25.9–10 (echoed in Isa 61.1) are connected with divine 'visitation', which in the Qumran Community Rule can include the gift of everlasting life (1QS 4.6–7).

Then yet another Qumran find, the fragmentary Hebrew text 11Q13 (11Q Melchizedek), again perhaps from a prophetic composition, associates themes of Isa 61.1–2 (the jubilee-like proclamation of liberty, with its echo of Lev 25.9–10; the year of grace; the day of vengeance) with a definite figure, the priest-king Melchizedek coming again at the end of days, at the tenth jubilee (11Q13, col. ii, lines 4–7, 9, 13).[42] He is envisaged as returning from heaven, as is suggested later by tradition probably current in Tiberias at the end of the third century (*Pesikta de-Rab Kahana* 5.9, in the name of R. Isaac, and elsewhere); here Melchizedek is one of the four smiths seen in Zechariah's vision of four who would subdue the gentiles (Zech 2.3 (1.20)), the others being Elijah, the messiah, and the priest anointed for war, and the four together are the 'flowers' which 'appear' when the voice of the beloved is heard in Song 2.8–13, a passage read together with Isa 52.7, as noted below. In the Qumran text Melchizedek is indeed the 'god' who 'shall give judgment in the midst of gods', as David said in Ps 82.1–2 (11Q13 ii, lines 9–12).

Most importantly for the present purpose, the sequel in the Qumran Hebrew (col. ii, line 15 onwards) presents an extended interpretation of Isa

---

[41] Text, translation, and comment in Puech 1998:10–38.
[42] Text, translation, and comment in García Martínez et al. 1998:221–41.

52.7, in which the bearer of tidings (*m^ebasser*) is identified as 'the anointed of the spirit' (ii 18) – a title which alludes again to Isa 61.1. He announces 'your god reigns', and the 'god' is Melchizedek, according to a probable restoration (ii 23–5). The *m^ebasser* who makes this announcement is distinguished from Melchizedek by a number of interpreters;[43] but his title 'anointed of the spirit' (Isa 61.1, 'the spirit of the Lord God is upon me, for the Lord has anointed me to give good tidings (*l^ebasser*)') identifies him with Melchizedek, whose activity has just been presented in the terms of Isa 61.1–2 and the jubilee of Lev 25.9–10 (ii 4–7, 9, 13, cited above).

This identification in turn coheres once more with *Pss. Sol.* 11.1, in which, as in 11Q13 on this interpretation, the bearer of tidings in Isa 52.7 also announces the jubilee of Lev 25.9–10. The identification of this coming announcer with Melchizedek as anointed of the spirit and the 'god' who 'judges in the midst of gods' also coheres with later views of Melchizedek as a great spiritual being linked with Christ. These are met, for instance, in the Epistle to the Hebrews (7.3) and, at the end of the second century in Rome, in the monarchianism of Theodotus the banker, for whom Melchizedek was a great power, and Christ his image (Hippolytus, *Haer.* 7.36, 10.24).[44] Finally, 11Q13, in combination with *Pss. Sol.* 11.1, suggests a background for the later *Assumption of Moses*, cited above, on the commissioning of an avenging *nuntius* (10.1–2) at the appearing of the kingdom – perhaps once more an interpretation of Isa 61.1–2, where the anointed of the spirit announces the day of vengeance, in connection with Isa 52.7.

These further Hebrew fragments from the Qumran finds therefore fill out, through their contacts with texts not attested in the finds, the associations which had gathered round the Isaianic announcing and announcer at the beginning of the Herodian age. The announcer of Isa 52.7 had been identified with the anointed announcer of Isa 61.1 (the Hodayoth, 11Q13, and probably by implication *Pss. Sol.* 11.1), with the announcer of the jubilee of Lev 25.9–10 (11Q13, *Pss. Sol.* 11.1), and with the Deutero-Isaianic voice (*Pss. Sol.* 11.1). The announcing in Isa 61.1 (and Lev 25.9–10) had been connected with future life (4Q521, cf. *Pss. Sol.* 11.1), a link taken up in the later Herodian age in Matt 11.5, Luke 7.22, and with the great coming liberation (11Q13, *Pss. Sol.* 11.1). The verbs *l^ebasser* and *euangelizesthai* with their participles are therefore linked, through prophecy, with national hope and the figure of an expected announcer and

---

[43] For example, García Martínez et al. 1998:232.
[44] The line connecting 11Q13 with Hebrews, Theodotus the banker, and other Christian views of Melchizedek as an angelic spirit is traced by Gianotto 1984:264–6.

deliverer, and with the law as well as the prophets and psalms; they play a part in this connection in hymnody.

These associations of the verbs in their scriptural contexts reappear in the New Testament in Greek in connection with John the Baptist and Jesus; but they are also attested once more, as Dalman noted, in connection with Elijah and the messiah, in the synagogue poetry of later Roman and Byzantine Palestine. Through Hebrew and Aramaic texts from the Cairo Genizah this is now more extensively represented in print than in Dalman's time. One group of such attestations concerns the high priest, viewed as the angel or messenger of the Lord of hosts (Mal 2.7) when he brings the tidings of divine forgiveness on the Day of Atonement, in a liturgical embodiment of national hope. In Hebrew poems of about the fifth century and later he is the 'herald (*m^e basser*) of salvation' (Isa 52.7, quoted by Yose ben Yose), and 'as one crying in the wilderness to make straight the highways' (Isa 40.3, in an anonymous poem), so that even the angels tremble (compare the power over the 'gods' exercised by Melchizedek the *m^e basser*).[45]

In a second group these texts are applied to the messianic king. Some allusions play upon the resemblance noted already between Isa 52.7 (Nah 2.1 (1.15)) 'How beautiful upon the mountains are the feet of the *m^e basser*', together with Isa 40.3, 6; 42.2 on the 'voice', and the Song of Solomon on 'the voice of my beloved' who 'comes leaping upon the mountains', telling me that 'the voice of the turtle-dove is heard in our land' (Song 2.8, 12). Thus in an exegesis probably known in third-century Tiberias 'the voice of the turtle-dove' is 'the voice of king-messiah' (*Pesikta de-Rab Kahana* 5.9, in the name of Yoḥanan b. Nappaḥa (n. 6, above); this section was cited above for an exegesis of earlier words from Song 2.12). In poetry Yose ben Yose then asks correspondingly 'when will the turtle-dove cause his voice to be heard' (*yashmi^c a*, cf. Isa 42.2; 52.7)? Comparably, in a later poet, Yehudah, 'he shall make us hear the voice (Isa 42.2) crying in the wilderness (Isa 40.3)' – the messiah – and 'I will surely bring near the one crying in the wilderness'.[46] Lastly, in an Aramaic poem for 9th Ab the messiah is both voice and *m^e basser*:

> A great redeemer shall come to Zion (Isa 59.20),
> a branch shall sprout in Jerusalem (Jer 23.5);

---

[45] Yose ben Yose, *Azkir geburoth*, 269, in Mirsky 1977:171; anonymous *Az be-eyn kol*, 570–1, in Yahalom 1996:126.

[46] Yose ben Yose, *Anusah le-ezrah*, 25 in Mirsky 1977:108; Yehudah, poems 25.3, line 6; 30.6, line 41, in van Bekkum 1998:79, 196.

the voice of thy might shalt thou make heard in Zion
(Isa 40.3; 42.2; Song 2.12),
the feet of a bearer of tidings (Isa 52.7) in
Jerusalem.[47]

These poetic interpretations of the *m^e basser* are rooted in third- and fourth-century midrash. With their midrashic sources they form the culmination of a series of similar developments of the Old Testament texts using *l^e basser* and *euangelizesthai* into connected hints at the message of divine kingship and communal redemption. The series begins with the consistent and expanded use of the rendering *euangelizesthai* in the LXX prophets and psalms, perhaps from the early second century BC onwards, and the resultant echoes in Greek pseudepigrapha. Then another partly concurrent development, with clearer elements of a myth of a herald of the divine kingdom and deliverance, is evinced just before the Herodian age in the Qumran texts and the *Psalms of Solomon*, and probably also after the death of Herod the Great in the *Assumption of Moses*. Both these developments are reflected during the Herodian age in the New Testament, and they are taken further in specifically Christian applications to Christ and the apostolic preaching. In the non-Christian Jewish community they were later on continued in the midrashic and poetic development noted already. In Hasmonaean and Herodian times, and again in Byzantine Palestine, these interpretations were prominent enough to appear in hymnody.

The midrashic and poetic development could be understood as an implicit response to Christianity, but the signs of some continuity with pre-Christian sources, for instance in connection with Melchizedek and with the more general identification of the *m^e basser* as a coming deliverer, viewed together with the strength of messianic tradition in the Targums, make it unlikely that this development was wholly evoked by the rise of the church. This point is of some significance for the familiarity of the Old Testament texts using *l^e basser* and *euangelizesthai* in the Herodian age. They were heard with a tradition of interpretation which had flourished before Herod the Great's reign, and was still continuing among non-Christian Jews, irrespective of its interest for the church.

The religions of Herodian Judaea have formed the setting of this part of the inquiry. To summarize, the Aramaic and Greek vocabulary in question was in everyday use, but gained a high profile in cultic contexts. Thus the relevant verbs and nouns were prominent in ruler-cult, and this will have contributed indirectly to their vogue in Jewish piety, as suggested above.

---

[47] Poem 23, lines 17–20 in Sokoloff and Yahalom 1999:164.

The verbs with their participles came to the fore also in Jewish hymnody from the Qumran Hodayoth and the Greek *Psalms of Solomon,* and recur in later synagogue poetry. All these poetic compositions highlight scriptural texts which use *l^ebasser* and *euangelizesthai,* and together they indicate an old tradition of interpreting these prophecies which continued throughout and beyond the Herodian age. Ruler-cult and Jewish hymnody thus conferred still further éclat on a vocabulary which was already important for Jews in their scriptures and in ordinary life. This observation can be added to the argument for Herodian Jewish familiarity with the relevant words which was drawn from other primary sources in section 2, above.

4

The vocabulary under review has now been encountered in a number of distinct but related settings. In both Jewish and gentile environments it was used in daily life, as noted in the biblically oriented section 2 above, and it was emphasized by ruler-cult, as shown in the religion-oriented section 3. Among Jews the vocabulary derived special dignity from its scriptural employment, discussed in section 2, and especially from the use of *l^ebasser* and *euangelizesthai* in a group of prophecies which were themselves already influenced by court language, and from varied usage in biblical translation and interpretation. Its profile was further heightened for Jews, as shown in section 3, by hymnody which incorporated many of these biblical texts in a myth-like outline of the announcement of the divine kingdom and deliverance.

For Jews in Herodian Judaea this vocabulary then had a scriptural prestige which was accentuated in interpretative tradition, both Aramaic and Greek; but this prominence was further enhanced by the concomitant familiarity of the relevant Aramaic and Greek words in daily life, and by their high profile in the honorific language of court publicity and divine praise. Judaean Christians, whether Aramaic- or Greek-speaking, are likely to have felt the impact of this vocabulary above all through the Jewish community, its scriptural reading and interpretation, and the associated hymnody. Influences from ruler-cult and everyday life had already affected, and continued to affect, both non-Christian Jewish and Christian reception of the words.

A limited fresh study of primary sources, especially Aramaic and Greek biblical paraphrase and interpretation and Jewish hymnody, suggested some more particular observations which can now be summarized.

(1) From Grotius to Dalman, Wellhausen, Harnack, and Stuhlmacher the
     case for continuity between the Greek New Testament and the literature
     and languages of Herodian Judaea was clear in the case of *euangelizesthai*,
     which was strikingly attested in biblical prophecy. In the case of *euange-
     lion*, however, special argument was needed, in order to identify an
     immediate background for the Greek noun in an expanded use of
     Aramaic *bᵉsorᵉtha* – use which was in fact increasingly well documented.
(2) Nevertheless, Greek *euangelion* in the sense of 'tidings' was probably
     known in Herodian Judaea, as is suggested by the Lucianic text of the
     books of Kingdoms together with Josephus on Vespasian. In these
     sources the word is in the plural, but Judaean Jewish use of the singular
     also can be inferred from the Syriac *Apocalypse of Baruch* in conjunc-
     tion with Rev 14.6.
(3) The view that Aramaic *bᵉsorᵉta* was known as an equivalent term, partly
     through its expanded use as a rendering for *shᵉmuʿah* as well as *bᵉsorah*,
     was supported by Stuhlmacher from *Targum Jonathan to the Prophets*
     and from Palestinian Pentateuchal Targums (to which *Neofiti* can now
     be added); this combination of sources attests continuous currency
     from the second century AD onwards, probably with antecedents in
     Herodian Judaea.
(4) Both *euangelizesthai* and *lᵉbasser*, with its Aramaic cognate, came to be
     used in scriptural interpretation for the giving of a divine or prophetic
     message, sometimes with the relevant nouns. This emerges from the
     pseudepigrapha and the New Testament in Greek, and from Targumic
     and rabbinic terminology in Aramaic and Hebrew. Judaean Christian
     use can best be derived from this Jewish use.
(5) The interest in messengers of God evinced in biblical tradition cor-
     responded to non-Jewish concern with divine messengers, and encouraged
     attention to the herald(s) mentioned in prophecy and psalmody as *mᵉbas-
     ser* or *euangelizomenos*. By the late Hasmonaean period this had led to a
     nexus between Isa 40.3; 52.7; 61.1 and other passages including Lev 25.10,
     and in one instance to an identification of the herald with the returning
     Melchizedek. In later midrash and poetry from the third century onwards
     the herald was comparably identified also with Elijah, the high priest or
     the messianic king. The New Testament association of the herald with the
     Baptist and Jesus should be set within this series of interpretations.

Now it is a pleasure to offer Graham Stanton, with grateful recollection
of many years' friendship, this essay on vocabulary which comes to the fore
in his own scholarship, but is also very suitable for a birthday.

CHAPTER 2

The gospel of Jesus

Klyne Snodgrass

The gospel of Jesus, i.e., the gospel Jesus preached, is quite different from the gospel about Jesus which the early church preached.[1] The church's gospel is rightly summarized as the proclamation of the death and resurrection of Jesus; but as crucial as that focus is, it makes little sense apart from the gospel Jesus proclaimed. The preaching *of* Jesus is not inferior to the preaching *about* Jesus and is not merely an antecedent necessity or presupposition for the church's message.[2] The message of Jesus was and had to be the foundation of both the thought and the life of early Christians, a reality attested by the existence of the canonical and apocryphal Gospels, even though outside the Gospels reference to the sayings of Jesus is not as direct as we would expect.[3] It is a privilege to address this topic in honour of someone whose career has contributed so much to the discussion.

The concern must be for the message, the good news, of Jesus and not for his possible use of the Aramaic word *b^esora'* or some other equivalent to our word 'gospel'. Whether he used such an equivalent to refer to his message cannot be determined, given the freedom with which the evangelists framed their material.[4]

The choices of the evangelists with regard to the Greek noun *euangelion* and the verb *euangelizesthai* merit attention. Matthew uses *euangelion* only four times, twice in his summary statements and twice reporting sayings of Jesus, and *euangelizesthai* only once (in a statement from Jesus). Mark uses *euangelion* seven times (excluding 16.15), five in sayings of Jesus, and does

---

[1] The difference is between the subjective and objective genitive.

[2] Bultmann (Bultmann 1951–5:1.3) is famous for saying that the message of Jesus is a presupposition for the theology of the NT rather than a part of that theology.

[3] On the other hand, allusions are more frequent than often noticed. Allusions in James are most obvious, but for a treatment of allusions to Jesus' teaching, esp. in Romans, see Thompson 1991.

[4] I do not exclude the possibility that Jesus used such language, just that it cannot be demonstrated. As Horbury shows in chapter 1 above, both the noun and the verb were in use in Herodian Judaea because of the convergence of the influence of OT Scriptures like Isa 52.7 and the influence of the ruler cult.

not use the verb at all. Luke does not use the noun at all (although he uses it twice in Acts) but uses *euangelizesthai* ten times, four of which are in sayings of Jesus. John uses neither the noun nor the verb. No doubt exists that Jesus believed he was announcing good news to his contemporaries.[5] As we will see, the verb stems from the influence of Isaianic promises; the noun seems to be a convenient and natural summary word.[6] The secular use of these words to designate the good news of the new reign of an emperor (among other things) made the words, at least for some, singularly appropriate for understanding Jesus' proclamation of the kingdom, and this framed his message at least partly as a political confrontation.

The task of summarizing Jesus' message in brief scope is daunting. The reported sayings of Jesus are numerous, diverse, and at times perplexing, and it is surprisingly difficult to find brief, coherent summaries of his message.[7] Multi-volume attempts are more the order of the day. Some would say that the attempt to isolate and summarize Jesus' message is foolhardy, and they doubt our ability to get back to the message of Jesus. But the old methods attempting to strip off layers of ecclesial accretions to get back to the message of Jesus have proved a dead end too burdened by methodological uncertainties and the subjectivity of the particular scholar.[8] Recent attempts have rightly pointed to a much more sane approach, one less content with stratifying the Jesus tradition to attempt to authenticate individual sayings but, instead, one that offers a broader and more coherent picture of Jesus and does justice to the way oral tradition was passed down.[9] Necessary too is James Dunn's reminder that what is available to us is the 'remembered Jesus', not Jesus himself.[10]

We know too well of attempts to make Jesus conform to the spirit of the time. Jesus' message has often been summarized as the highest ethic known to humanity, but this will not work. Jesus did not come to preach a universal ethic, and much of his ethic is often deemed unattractive and irrational, even if people like the sound of his words.[11] If Jesus came to

---

[5] Although especially later the terms can be used of bad news.   [6] Cf. Stanton 2004:9–62.

[7] Although the contribution of the Gospel of John is significant, this attempt to describe Jesus' message will focus almost exclusively on the Synoptic Gospels to avoid debates about the Fourth Gospel. The *Gospel of Thomas* is in my estimation dependent on the canonical tradition (although not directly dependent literarily).

[8] Note Dale Allison's comment (Allison 1998:6), 'If our tools were designed to overcome subjectivity and bring order to our discipline, then they have failed.'

[9] See esp. Wright 1996:87–9, Allison 1998:1–77, and Dunn 2003b:174–254, to name the most obvious.

[10] Dunn 2003b:131.

[11] See Bauman 1985 on the lamentable history of interpretation of the Sermon on the Mount.

present a universal ethic, he did a poor job. He did not come with a new social agenda, even though his message is loaded with social implications and demands. He was not concerned merely that everyone get along; he did not fix the roads in Palestine,[12] attack patriarchy head on, achieve gender diversity at all levels, or address many of the ethical problems that have plagued humanity both before and after his ministry. Only by implication does he address racism. He does not condemn war, violence in general, or domestic violence. He says nothing about the evil of slavery, and he has very little that is practical for addressing the economic problems of the poor – other than that one must do so. He does not tell how to deal with extreme evil other than turning the cheek, which in many contexts – even today – means death. If we do not understand Jesus' gospel in his own time and in relation to Israel, we will not understand it at all, wonderful as some of his sayings may be.

Often in the past Israel and Judaism have been left out of descriptions of Jesus' message. One success of the so-called third quest for the historical Jesus is the insistence that Jesus' message is thoroughly Jewish and has to do with the restoration of Israel. Yet, what is striking – as much as Jesus' message of the kingdom *was* political and an implied rejection of the authority of the Herodian rulers and Rome – is that none of his sayings is *explicitly* directed against Rome and her agents.[13] The kind of national triumphalism one finds in *Pss. Sol.* 17–18 and other texts is totally absent with Jesus.

Further, Jesus – for all his statements about the temple – *says* little that is an attack on the cultic system or against priests. Only the temple 'cleansing' and the parable of the Good Samaritan give any explicit grounds for detecting conflict with the temple and its caretakers. A case can be made that Jesus opposed much of the temple system, but that case is indirect and implicit.

But can we speak of *the* message of Jesus? Should we speak instead of the messages of Jesus?[14] He did not say the same thing to all people. His message develops, even if we cannot trace the development. The message in Galilee is not merely repeated in Jerusalem. Some sayings are directed to the public and some to the disciples in private. The

---

[12] The complaint of Friedrich Naumann. See Bauman 1985:78–9.

[13] The closest Jesus comes is Luke 13.32, which seems more to brush Herod aside. I would add (contra Wright 1996:317, 342, 360–5) that the coming of the Son of Man cannot be reduced to a metaphor for Rome's destruction of Jerusalem.

[14] Meyer 1979:111–12 (and throughout) distinguishes Jesus' public and 'esoteric' teaching in his discussion of Jesus' aims.

private teaching is still part of the good news, as is obvious with such teaching as the new covenant language in the account of the Lord's Supper or Jesus' declaration that he would not drink from the fruit of the vine until that day when he drank it new with the disciples in the kingdom of the Father (Matt 26.29 par.).

Jesus' message does not conform to ancient or modern expectations, but it still has clarity and coherence and is capable of summation. Any comprehensive treatment of the gospel of Jesus should treat the following questions:

What was the explicit content of Jesus' gospel?

To what degree is the gospel of Jesus new?

To what degree is the gospel of Jesus eschatological?

What does Jesus' gospel have to do with Israel or other groups?

To what degree is the gospel of Jesus political?

To what degree is the gospel of Jesus focused on ethics?

To what degree is the gospel of Jesus focused on himself?

To what degree is the gospel of Jesus in line with the gospel of Paul and the early church?

Obviously these questions cannot be treated adequately in the confines of this chapter, yet daunting as the task may appear, four foci in Jesus' message account for the diversity of sayings and give them coherence: celebration (or joy); compassion; Israel; and kingdom. Other themes either provide the foundation for these four (such as the character of God) or are derived from them (such as repentance and judgment), but these four are windows through which the rest of Jesus' message may be understood. That these four are constituent features of Jesus' message is difficult to contest and can be substantiated from Jesus' direct teaching, from his parables, and from his actions. These four features are often discussed, but why they are constituent parts of Jesus' good news and how they relate to each other do not receive sufficient attention.

The theme of celebration is, at least as an entry point, the most instructive. Jesus thought that his message and mission created a context in which joy and celebration should rule. In effect, because of what he was doing, people should be dancing in the streets. They should be like one who found a treasure and for joy sold all he had to purchase it (Matt 13.44–5). Jesus' meals with sinners were clearly anticipations of the eschatological banquet of Isa 25.6–10 and allowed people proleptically to participate in such celebration. With parables like that of the Banquet (Luke 14.15–24) and of the Prodigal and Elder Son (Luke 15.11–32) Jesus in effect said, 'God is giving a party; are you going to come?' The lost were being found, and it was *necessary* to celebrate their return. Fasting was not appropriate, for the time of Jesus was a time of celebration (Mark 2.19 par.). The Beatitudes and other macarisms are calls to celebrate as well, but they are not general calls to be happy. In most cases they point to celebration that God's long-awaited promises are being fulfilled (e.g., Matt 13.16–17 par.). Other statements of privilege, promise, or the importance of Jesus' actions buttress the reasons for celebration.[15]

The image of dancing in the streets is, of course, from the parable of Children in the Market (Matt 11.17 par.) and merits reflection. Jesus said that 'this generation' is 'like children sitting in the markets calling out these things to others: "We played the flute for you and you did not dance; we sang a dirge and you did not mourn."' Regardless of how this debated passage is interpreted,[16] Jesus' application of the parable to himself and John the Baptist in 11.19 par. shows that Jesus thought his coming was an occasion for joy, for dancing in the streets. In effect, if you are not dancing, you do not understand what is happening with Jesus.[17] This is obviously a metaphor and a hyperbolical one at that, but it is a powerful image of the celebration attending Jesus' message. The focus on joy and celebration demonstrates that some explanations of Jesus are not adequate. It is hard to imagine people celebrating with such joy because a peasant Jewish Cynic had come or because someone urged a return to primitive communal values and equality.[18]

The second feature, the focus on compassion, is overwhelmingly characteristic of Jesus' teaching and actions. He voices his compassion for the crowds (Matt 15.32 par.), and compassion plays a major part in his parables. It is the motivation for the astounding forgiveness of the king in the parable of the Unforgiving Servant (Matt 18.27), for the actions of the Good Samaritan (Luke 10.33), and for the actions of the father of the prodigal (Luke 15.20). But the emphasis on compassion is not seen merely in places that use the word. Jesus' compassion dominates a great deal of the Gospels. His compassion, no doubt, is derived partly from his view of God and his conviction that the love commands are a summary of the

---

[15] E.g., Matt 9.6 par.; 12.6, 41–2 par.; Mark 3.27; Luke 10.18–20; 12.32.

[16] Are John and Jesus the ones calling, or are children of 'this generation' calling to their contemporaries, as Jeremias 1963:160–2 argued?

[17] A point made specifically by *Acts of John* 95.17 in dependence on Matt 11.17 par.: 'He who does not dance does not know what happens.'

[18] The views respectively of Crossan 1991:421–2, of Mack 1993:43, 47, 113–22, and of Horsley and Silberman 1997:51–60, 88, 97. Mack 1993:105 understands 'dancing to the pipes' as Q's challenge to readers to dare to dance to a different tune.

law,[19] but most importantly it is eschatologically rooted in the fulfilment of the OT promises, as we will see. Jesus' emphasis on mercy, his healings of the sick, his reception of outcasts and sinners, the forgiveness he offered, his beatitudes for and concern for the poor and mourning, his attention to individuals, and his treatment of women and children paint a compelling portrait. Whatever else Jesus' gospel is, it is good news expressing compassion.

Other Jews focused on compassion as well,[20] but nowhere is compassion so much a defining and regulating force as it was with Jesus. This focus appears to be a deliberate shift from the message of John the Baptist, who focused on coming judgment; Jesus emphasized the judgment theme even more, but he pushed the immediacy of judgment back (e.g., Luke 13.6–9) and shifted the focus to compassion. Love of enemies and forgiveness of others are not OT themes[21] and do not reflect the dominant attitudes of first-century Jews we know (and certainly not of the Qumran community). Purity concerns, sabbath, and separation from sinners were much more dominating forces in Judaism,[22] and it is just these concerns that created conflict when Jesus ate with tax collectors and sinners and took purity issues and sabbath less seriously. Marcus Borg argued that Jesus replaced the holiness code with the mercy code,[23] a statement that many find troubling, but at least the statement is a useful hyperbole.[24] Mercy governs Jesus' interaction with people. Jesus *did* care about holiness and avoidance of sin. Much of the holiness code he accepted, and he would have agreed with other Jews on cardinal issues of right living. In fact, his demands and his focus on judgment are often more stringent, but while not condoning sin, he did not think that righteousness meant avoidance of contact with

---

[19] Matt 5.43–8 par.; 7.12 par.; 22.36–40 par.; note the connection of the love commands and compassion in the parable of the Good Samaritan (Luke 10.25–37) and in Matthew's account of the rich young ruler (19.16–22).

[20] E.g. Sir 28.4; *Jub.* 36.4–8; 1QH[a] 6.3; *2 En.* 9.1; Ps.-Phoc. 1.19–29; *T. Zeb.* 5.1–9.9; *Jos. Asen.* 11.10–14; 12.8.

[21] The closest the OT comes to love for enemies is Prov 25.21. Scot McKnight drew my attention to the rarity of forgiveness of others in the OT. Only Gen 50.17, Exod 10.17, and 1 Sam 25.28 express the idea, but obviously Lev 19.17–18 is relevant.

[22] See, e.g., 1QS 1.4, 10; 2.4–10; 5.1–2, 10–18; 10.21; Sir 5.6; 12.1–14; 13.17; *As. Mos.* 7.9–10; Jdt 12.1–20, to list only a few obvious texts. The prevalence of *miqwa'ot* and stone vessels for purification give further witness to the concern for purification.

[23] Borg 1984:123–43; see also Caird 1994:392–3. Isa 52.11 is striking in this regard. For all that Isa 52 fits with Jesus' ministry, as the church was quick to recognize (Acts 10.36; Rom 10.15; Eph 2.17; 6.15), the view of purity in 52.11 is not his.

[24] The miracle accounts in Matt 8–9 seem intent on showing that Jesus substituted mercy for purity concerns since they recount Jesus touching a leper, a woman with a fever, and a dead girl, being touched by a haemorrhaging woman, and willing to go into the house of a Gentile.

those viewed as sinners. Rather, he viewed true holiness as stronger than sin, not needing protection from sin, and more contagious than sin. Mercy could be extended without sacrificing holiness. For Jesus' contemporaries, forgiveness was not extended until repentance took place; with Jesus, forgiveness seems to have been extended first with the expectation that repentance would follow.[25]

The OT and Jews of first-century Palestine knew celebration and God's compassion, but something different was happening with Jesus. Celebration and compassion receive the focus they do precisely because they are rooted in the fulfilment of the Isaianic promises. The significance of Jesus' gospel of compassion is evident in his use of Isa 61.1–2, most notably in Luke 4.18–21,[26] which is itself a summation of Jesus' gospel. Features of Lucan redaction are obvious, not least in this passage being placed at the beginning of Jesus' ministry, but Isa 61 was programmatic for Jesus' own sense of mission. It reappears in the response to the Baptist's query whether Jesus was the coming one (Matt 11.2–6 par.), and it lies behind the Beatitudes. The eschatological significance of Isa 61 is revealed by its use in *11Q Melchizedek*, where it is understood of the 'last days' and is connected to Isa 52.7 (the good news of God's salvation and reign) and the Jubilee of Lev 25, in effect pointing to the end time Jubilee.[27] Further insight is gained from Matt 11.2–6 par. and 4Q521 (*4Q Messianic Apocalypse*). The answer to the Baptist's query is that the blind are given sight, the sick are healed, the dead are raised, and the poor have good news proclaimed to them. The items listed reflect several texts: Isa 26.19; 29.17–19; 35.5–6; and 61.1.[28] Many of the same themes are listed in 4Q521: freedom for prisoners; sight to the blind; resurrection of the dead; and proclamation of good news to the poor. Jesus' compassion is not compassion in general, but the realization of the promises of Isaiah, promises understood by Jesus' contemporaries as the anticipated eschatological deliverance of God. No doubt, Jews looked for release from Rome and her agents, but this is precisely what is not *explicit* in Jesus' message. Certainly the coming of

---

[25] Jeremias 1971b:177; Meyer 1979:161. Sanders 1985:203–11 argued that Jesus accepted the wicked without requiring repentance, which is impossible, given the demands Jesus makes on his followers.

[26] Luke's form of the quotation of Isa 61 adds recovery of sight, apparently from Isa 42.7, an addition in the LXX as well. These words could come from Isa 35.5 or Ps 146.7–8. Luke's form also adds letting the oppressed go free (literally 'with release') from Isa 58.6.

[27] The tenth Jubilee according to the text. See Sanders 1975, esp. 90–1. Cf. 1QH^a 23.14–16; Bar 4.36–5.9. If Stuhlmacher 1992:157 is correct that Jesus interpreted Isa 52.7 of himself as well, the eschatological significance would be greatly heightened. Mark 1.14–15 is evidence for this view.

[28] In three of these texts judgment is also present, but that theme is conspicuously absent in Jesus' reference to them.

the kingdom would sweep away all claimants to power, but Jesus apparently had much larger concerns than the current regime.[29] For him, the release offered in his message was much more generally the release from the human plight of suffering, sin, and evil.[30]

Allusions to the Jubilee with Isa 61 draw attention again to the theme of forgiveness. Two parables are striking pictures of Jesus' gospel: the parable of the Unforgiving Servant (Matt 18.23–35) and the parable of the Two Debtors (Luke 7.41–2).[31] Both depict God's magnanimous forgiveness of sin as a cancelled debt and in doing so suggest that the end-time Jubilee is in effect. Debts are simply erased, even if they are incredibly large. These parables convey that with regard to forgiveness of sins God is like a loan manager who does not care about money. Both parables also stress the necessity of an appropriate response to forgiveness, but the first point in both is that the kingdom comes with limitless grace. It should be added that Jesus' granting of forgiveness, like the message of John the Baptist, implies at least a decentralization of the temple or an encroachment on the temple's functions.[32]

The focus on the Isaianic promises leads also to the third feature of Jesus' good news, the place of Israel, which has often been ignored or even suppressed, but Jesus was not preaching ethical generalities. He was calling Israel to be what God intended. The promises that were being fulfilled were promises to Israel concerning restoration. As numerous scholars have argued,[33] Jesus was reconstituting Israel under his own leadership, as is evident in his appointing twelve disciples to represent the twelve tribes (Matt 19.28; Luke 22.30). Jesus' use of Isaianic texts shows that he viewed himself as the eschatological prophet, whatever else we might say, i.e., God's agent putting the eschatological promises into effect. As prophets before him, he called Israel to repent and warned of judgment if people did not repent. The good news of Jesus was that the time for the restoration of Israel, the redemption for which people were waiting, was present and at work, even if a good deal of the expectation was still future.

Jesus' mission is formed on the promises of the restoration of Israel. He was reluctant to look beyond the borders of Israel (Matt 10.5–6; 15.21–8 par.), even

---

[29] This is not to deny the politically subversive implications of Jesus' message.

[30] Twice in Luke 4.18 the word *aphesis* ('release') occurs; in some contexts, of course, the word means 'forgiveness'.

[31] The narrative surrounding the Two Debtors heightens the understanding of Jesus' gospel by showing his compassion towards a woman known to be a sinner and his granting forgiveness to her.

[32] Jesus' relation to the temple is marked with tension and included both valuing and devaluing.

[33] They include Wright 1996:169, 173, 201, 477f., 651–3; Caird 1994:384; Dunn 2003b:506, 607; Jeremias 1971b:170; Meyer 1979:123, 133, 171, 198, 234; Sanders 1985, esp. 319–26.

though Israel was supposed to be a blessing to the nations. Most of his teaching about Israel comes indirectly in parables[34] or in warnings of judgment. The parables of the Fig Tree (Luke 13.6–9), the Banquet (Matt 22.1–14/Luke 14.15–24), the Two Sons (Matt 21.28–32), the Wicked Tenants (Matt 21.33–45 par.), and the Ten Pounds (Luke 19.11–27) are all specifically about Israel. The lament over Jerusalem (Matt 23.37–9 par.), the cursing of the fig tree (Matt 21.18–22 par.), the 'cleansing' of the temple (Matt 21.12–17), and the various statements about the destruction of Jerusalem all underscore how much Jesus' mission was centred on Israel.

What failure of Israel was being targeted by Jesus? This question creates serious debate, partly because the Gospels seem to take the answer for granted and partly because Israel was so diverse, indeed as all societies are. Of what was Israel to repent? Factionalism may have been part of the problem,[35] but Jesus does not address this explicitly. Sins in general made obvious by encounter with God may be intended, the kind of sins previous prophets denounced. Clearly the way Jesus' contemporaries observed Torah was not the way Jesus thought it should be kept. Much of his teaching and acts calls for a greater sensitivity to and care for people.[36] Revolutionary zeal and violent nationalism have been suggested as Israel's sins,[37] but this seems too narrow a focus. The teaching of Jesus (and John the Baptist) imply at least that Israel in large part had misunderstood the significance of election, which indeed led to nationalism and disdain for outsiders.[38] Election was not to be assumed as privilege; rather, it brings responsibility and requires conformity to God's will. Those who assumed that they would be at the messianic banquet may be excluded (Matt 8.11–12 par.; Luke 14.15–24). However the situation is described, with Jesus Israel faced a crisis. If the time of fulfilment was present, Israel was not ready, and Jesus sought to reorganize and redirect Israel, and in the end establish a new covenant. Jesus meant to gather a people and prepare them to fulfil the role Israel was supposed to accomplish for the nations. His new vision for Israel called for repentance and a righteousness that went to the core of one's being and did justice to God's intent for humanity.[39] It would require a

---

[34] Wright 1996 reads most of the parables as stories about Israel, but this is true only for some of them. See Snodgrass 1999:61–76.

[35] Dunn 2003b:265, 281–6, although he was not addressing this question.

[36] E.g., Matt 5.22–4, 39–47; Mark 3.1–6; Luke 7.36–50.   [37] Wright 1996:250, 317, 450.

[38] *Jub.* 22.16–22, *Let. Aris.* 139–43, and *Jos. Asen.* 7.1–8.7 are examples.

[39] McKnight 1999. Note, e.g., Matt 5.13–48, esp. the description of the disciples as the light of the world, surely drawing on Isa 49.6.

focus on the love command and a different understanding of what right-eousness entailed.

Without this focus on Israel and the conviction that God was fulfilling the promises to Israel, Jesus' call for celebration and his macarisms make no sense. To say 'Blessed are the poor' is not good news but mockery unless something is happening for the poor to change their situation.

The fourth feature of Jesus' message, the kingdom of God, is not the fourth of equals; properly understood, it is the foundation and driving force of the others. The kingdom of God is the central feature of Jesus' gospel, as nearly all acknowledge.[40] The problem is that many people know the centrality of the kingdom for Jesus but at best have only a vague idea what 'kingdom' really means. Scholars know what they mean with terms like 'reign' and 'realm', but many others do not grasp what is really at stake. Discussions of whether or how the kingdom is both present and future increase the confusion.

Jesus' language about the kingdom of God is unusual. The writers of the OT knew that God is king. While the exact equivalent of 'kingdom of God' does not appear in the OT, similar expressions such as 'kingdom of Yahweh' do, and various texts either assert that Yahweh reigns or look forward to the time when God truly will reign.[41] Judaism and particularly the Qumran materials acknowledged that God is king and also looked forward to the coming of his glorious kingdom.[42] Still, the language about the kingdom was not frequent prior to Jesus, especially the precise phrase 'kingdom of God', but any first-century Jew would recognize quickly the intent of the term. It meant that God alone was king and would one day fulfil his promises by establishing his reign – would actually be king – in Israel. But Jesus' language was unique in at least two respects: no one prior to Jesus spoke of the kingdom as already here and no one spoke of the kingdom with expressions such as having drawn near, as coming, or as being sought, entered into, or seized.[43]

[40] E.g., Matt 10.7 par.; 12.25–8 par.; 13.31–3; Mark 1.14–15 par.; 4.26–8; 9.47 par.; Luke 9.60–2; 17.21.

[41] Note among other texts Exod 15.18; 1 Sam 12.12; 1 Chron 28.5; Pss 10.16; 22.28; 29.10; 47.3, 7–8; 93.1–2; 95.3; 96.10; 97.1; 99.1–4; 103.19; 145.1, 13; 146.10; Isa 6; 40.10; 43.15; 52.7; 66.1; Jer 3.17; Ezek 20.33f.; Dan 2.44; 4.3; 7.13f., 27; and Obad 21.

[42] See, e.g., Pss. Sol. 5.19; 17.32, 46; Wis 10.10; T. Benj. 9.1; Sib. Or. 3.46f.; As. Mos. 10.1f.; 1QM 6.6; 9.1, 7–8; 4QFlor 1.10; and esp. 4QShirShabb^a.

[43] Jeremias 1971b:32–4, 108; also Stuhlmacher 1992:67–8; Dunn 2003b:386–7, among others. Meier 1994:244 suggests that Jesus may have been the first to forge and regularly employ the fixed phrase 'the kingdom of God' to evoke the OT mythic story. People both before and after Jesus did speak of the kingdom being established, revealed, received, accepted, set up, and of an exalted kingdom, an eternal kingdom, or the beauty and glory of the kingdom.

With the kingdom language Jesus tapped into the OT promises and the hopes of his contemporaries that God would redeem Israel. Certainly the focus is on the fact of God's kingship, his reign, but that does not exclude the idea of realm. Important as kingdom language is, however, the operative word in the expression 'kingdom of God' is *God.* Jesus proclaimed the good news *about God* (Mark 1.14). The kingdom of God means that *God is coming* with power and in fulfilment of the promises to set things right, to defeat evil and establish righteousness so that people live in keeping with his will and character.[44] Or as Ben Meyer put it, '" The reign of God" signifies "God" and signifies God precisely as Jesus knows him.'[45] This is why so much focus in Jesus' teaching is on the character of God, on God as a loving Father, Abba, who is full of compassion, who seeks to give people the kingdom (Luke 12.32), who knows how valuable people are (Matt 6.26; 10.31; 12.12), and who is 'for us' (Matt 18.14).

The celebration, the compassion, and the focus on Israel all make sense since God is coming to be king. Possibly the clearest picture is provided by Isa 40.9–11, which, although not quoted by Jesus, is among the texts determining 'Israel's larger story': the good news is that God is coming with might, his arm will rule, he will judge, and he will feed his flock and with tenderness care for the lambs and nursing ewes.[46]

Jesus asserted – audaciously to some – that this was already taking place in his own proclamation and acts. God has drawn near, and the kingdom is present.[47] Of primary significance is the claim that his exorcisms accomplished by the Spirit/finger of God show that the kingdom is present (Matt 12.28 par.; cf. Luke 4.18). On the one hand, the kingdom's presence is inauspicious, like a mustard seed or leaven;[48] on the other hand, it is obvious enough in Jesus' deeds that people should be celebrating with joy.

But the kingdom is also future in many sayings of Jesus. Consummation was still awaited, as is evident in the prayer 'Your kingdom come' (Matt 6.10 par.) and numerous other texts.[49] No larger disagreement exists

---

[44] Wright 1996 (pp. 204–6, 615–24) is correct to emphasize that the message is 'Yahweh is coming.' See also Beasley-Murray 1986, who uses 'the coming of God' as the rubric for framing his discussion of the kingdom, and Chilton 1996:10–12.

[45] Meyer 1979:137.

[46] The appearance twice of *mᵉbasseret* in Isa 40.9 (LXX: *ho euangelizomenos*) to designate the herald proclaiming good news connects this passage to Isa 52.7 and 61.1–2. Bar 4.36–5.9 appears to allude to both Isa 40 and 61.

[47] E.g., Matt 11.12 par.; 12.22–32 par.; Luke 17.20 –1; and parables such as the Mustard Seed, the Leaven, the Sower, the Tares, the Treasure, and the Pearl.

[48] McKnight 1999:95.

[49] Matt 7.21; 8.11–12 par.; 13.30, 39–43, 47–50; 16.28 par.; 18.3 par.; 19.23 par., 28; 25.34; 26.29 par.

among NT scholars than in explaining what Jesus meant with sayings about the kingdom as future. Did 'kingdom' mean the end of the space-time universe?[50] Was it only a symbol or metaphorical for happenings in this world?[51] Did Jesus anticipate an interval between his death and the kingdom? How soon did he expect that the kingdom would arrive? Clearly words like 'eschatology', 'end', and 'symbol' all become quite slippery. While these questions cannot be resolved here, at least several points are clear. With 'kingdom' Jesus did not mean 'going to heaven', although the future kingdom carried connotations of 'paradise', and he was not referring to the kingdom of God in human hearts.[52] He referred to specific events he expected God to perform for Israel and which included judgment,[53] and, therefore, he viewed those events at least as transcendent. While they took place in this world, they were not merely of this world, or the promise of many returning from the East and West to recline with Abraham, Isaac, and Jacob makes no sense (Matt 8.11–12 par.). Therefore, the attempt to have a non-eschatological Jesus will not work.[54] Jesus' message is highly charged eschatologically and focused on transcendent fulfilment of the promises to Israel[55] for the benefit of the nations.

With regard to the question of the relation of Jesus' ethical teaching and the kingdom, no separation can be allowed. All four features of Jesus' message are directly connected to ethics. Jesus' ethical teaching flows directly out of his sense of the character of the God who is coming and the expectation that people's lives will conform to their God. In the kingdom God's will is put into practice. The first three petitions of the Lord's prayer are all closely related. When God acts to sanctify his own name (i.e., demonstrates who God really is), his kingdom will be present, and his will accomplished. If the kingdom is God coming to put things right, ethics are not optional, and the prayer 'Your kingdom come; your will be done' may be synonymous parallelism.[56] Further, the ethical teaching of Jesus is not an add-on to

---

[50] Which seems to be what Bultmann 1951–5.1.4 presupposes and what Wright 1996:207 explicitly rejects.

[51] Borg 1984:250–63.

[52] The misinterpretation of Luke 17.21 as meaning that the kingdom is within you.

[53] Several of the parables include the theme of judgment or giving account. On judgment more generally see Matt 11.20–4; 12.26–7, 41–2 par.; 13.30, 47–50; 25.31–46; Luke 13.1–5. See Reiser 1997.

[54] Contra Borg 1986, 1987:8–17; Funk 1996:145, 254–5, 297–314; and Crossan 1991:243–92.

[55] See among many esp. Allison 1998, Meyer 1979, and Meier 1994.

[56] Granted, the first two petitions could be understood as parallel instead, but at least 'Your kingdom come' is the link between the first and third petitions. The proximity of kingdom and the will of God is attested by *m. Ber.* 2.2, which says that one first receives the yoke of the kingdom and then receives the yoke of the commands.

his gospel; as W. D. Davies said of Jesus' 'penetrating demands', the ethical teaching is part of the bright light of the gospel.[57] The ethical life Jesus called for was attractive good news. His good news proclaims that one finds life by losing it and thereby provides a way past the self-centredness of humanity. The ethic is all-encompassing, and no boundaries can be set beyond which one does not have to go in obedience. The kingdom comes with limitless grace, but with it comes limitless demand, a life conformed to the character of God.[58] Such a stance is obviously political. No earthly ruler – not the Roman emperor, not Herod, not a master of some sort – commands ultimate allegiance or determines identity; only God does that, the God described by Jesus.

Was Jesus part of his own good news? Some have opted for a brokerless kingdom,[59] but this does no justice to the data. If the evidence of the presence of the kingdom is in his own acts, if forgiveness is being granted by him, if people should be celebrating because of what is happening with him, if he is the one gathering a community, and if he saw himself performing the tasks of Isa 61, to mention only the most obvious, then he was not just part of his own good news but the key factor in what was happening, the God-appointed agent by which the promises were put into effect. (Note especially Matt 11.6 par.) Without him there would have been no present kingdom and no good news proclaimed. This kingdom has a broker.[60] The claim cannot be made that his death was part of his message generally, but it seems that Jesus saw his death as an integral factor in his identification with Israel and the means by which a new covenant would be established for his followers.[61] Obviously this is debated, but the Last Supper narratives urge such a conclusion.

Finally, the question of the relation of Jesus' message and that of the early church must be addressed briefly. While the church's message shifts the focus to the death and resurrection and their significance, that shift depends on and retains features of Jesus' message. A deep and enduring continuity exists between the characteristics of Jesus' gospel, including the four primary features identified above, and the church's message. Israel occupies centre stage in Jesus' gospel, which is not true of the church's message, but the NT writers stubbornly insist on Israel's foundational role

---

[57] Davies 1963:437.   [58] E.g., Matt 18.21–35.
[59] Crossan 1991:422; Horsley and Silberman 1997:72–6.
[60] If the question is 'Was Jesus the Messiah?', there were so many views of the Messiah that one must ask 'Whose Messiah?'.
[61] See, e.g., Wright 1996:553–611; Dunn 2003b:817–18.

in the past, present, and future of God's plan.[62] Kingdom language is not forgotten, even if it is less central. Acts often uses kingdom language to summarize the essence of the gospel, and the Pauline letters and Revelation both retain significant focus on God's kingdom (fourteen and five occurrences respectively).[63] The focus on both present and future continues as a constituent part of the Christian message, and in the Pauline material kingdom, language is used both of present fulfilment and of future expectation of the vindication of God. God is still addressed by Christians as 'Abba', even among those speaking Greek,[64] and God is still the God who is 'for us' in the church's message.[65] Identity is still determined by God and what God has done. God's grace and demand are constituent features in both the gospel of Jesus and that of the church. Jesus' teaching that one finds life by losing it reappears in the church, albeit with different language (such as dying and rising). The Spirit is even more important for the church and is explicitly connected by Paul to the kingdom and joy.[66] Paul shares Jesus' conviction that holiness is more powerful than evil and like Jesus rejects the notion that separation from sinners is the primary concern of God.[67] The love command and compassion continue as primary directives. The gospel of Jesus stays the gospel of the church, no matter how much it is augmented.

---

[62] In most of the NT, the relation of Israel and the church is a major theme. Romans, at least partly, was written specifically to address the issue.

[63] The Gospel of John has much less focus on the kingdom – only at 3.3 and 3.5 – but kingship ideas are still foundational and reappear significantly in 18.36 and the crucifixion narrative.

[64] Rom 8.15; Gal 4.6.   [65] E.g., Rom 5.5–8; 8.31–2.   [66] Rom 14.17; cf. 1 Cor 4.20.

[67] See 1 Cor 5.9–13; 7.12–16; 8.7–13; and 10.19–31. The discussion of separation is a much larger issue and must bring in texts like 2 Cor 6.14–7.1 and Eph 5.1–14.

CHAPTER 3

Q^I as oral tradition

James D. G. Dunn

The most influential study of Q in recent years has been that of John Kloppenborg, *The Formation of Q*.[1] Kloppenborg's analysis of the 'sapiential speeches in Q'[2] leads him to the conclusion that 'a collection of sapiential speeches and admonitions was the formative element in Q', a collection 'subsequently augmented by the addition and interpolation of apophthegms and prophetic words which pronounced doom over impenitent Israel'.[3] This 'formative stratum', which can be conveniently designated Q^I, consists of six 'wisdom speeches', 'united not by the themes typical of the main redaction [Q^2], but by paraenetic, hortatory, and instructional concerns'.[4] The six 'wisdom speeches' he lists as:[5]

1 Q 6.20b–23b, 27–35, 36–45, 46–9;
2 Q 9.57–60, (61–2); 10.2–11, 16, (23–4?);[6]
3 Q 11.2–4, 9–13;
4 Q 12.2–7, 11–12;
5 Q 12.22b–31, 33–4 (13.18–19, 20–1?);[7] and probably
6 Q 13.24; 14.26–7; 17.33; 14.34–5.

This chapter is dedicated to Graham Stanton, in token of long and much-valued friendship and as a far from adequate expression of deep appreciation for all that his scholarship on the Gospels has contributed to NT studies.

[1] Kloppenborg 1987; see also his masterful *Excavating Q* (Kloppenborg Verbin 2000).

[2] Kloppenborg 1987, ch. 5.   [3] *Ibid.*, 244.

[4] *Ibid.*, 317; Kloppenborg Verbin 2000:146.

[5] Kloppenborg 1987, ch. 5, summarized and amended in Kloppenborg Verbin 2000:146. That six collections of aphoristic sayings lie behind Q was already suggested by Zeller 1977:191–2 (Q 6.20–3, 31, 36, 43–6; 10.2–8a, 9–11a, 12, 16(?); 11.2–4; 12.2–3, 8–9, 10; Matt 6.19–21, 25–33; Q 12.35–37(?), 39–40). Piper 1989 identified five aphoristic collections: Q 11.9–13; 12.22–31; 6.37–42; 6.43–5; 12.2–9; to which he added Luke 6.27–36 and 16.9–13.

[6] Kloppenborg regards 10.23–4 as part of the secondary redaction of Q, along with 10.21–2 (Kloppenborg 1987:201–3), but with some qualification (Kloppenborg Verbin 2000:147 n. 63).

[7] In Kloppenborg 1995, he suggests that Q 13.18–21 (which was not treated in his analysis of Q^I in Kloppenborg 1987:223 n. 214) was perhaps added to Q 12.2–12, 13–14, 16–21, 22–31, 33–4, in the formative layer of Q (311).

Kloppenborg is clear that 'tradition-history is not convertible with literary history', and that his concern is only with the latter; the judgment that material is redactional, secondary, is a *literary* judgment and need not imply anything about the *historical* origin or emergence of the tradition in view.[8] So he certainly does not wish his analysis necessarily to imply that redactional material from the secondary compositional phase cannot be dominical. And by the same token, it need not follow that material from Q^1 is necessarily the oldest material in the Q tradition. On the other hand, the archaeological imagery of a *lowest* 'stratum', capable of being uncovered by 'excavation', almost unavoidably promotes the implication of an *earliest* stratum, a stratum which contains the earliest artefacts of the literary 'tell' known as Q.

More to the point here, Kloppenborg works essentially with a *literary* model for the history of the Q material. Not only is Q itself, or already Q^2, a literary document,[9] but Q^1 is conceptualized in the same way. He never explicitly examines the question, but his talk of Q^2 'interpolations' into Q^1 clearly imply an established script into which insertions can be made. And in *Excavating Q* he speaks of Q^1 as 'a good example of instructional literature' and as 'the product of scribes', 'a scribal accomplishment'.[10]

It is this assumption, that the earliest grouping of Q material (Q^1) was already a written text, which I wish to question. I have already raised the issue in a much more wide-ranging discussion (Dunn 2003a). And in *Jesus Remembered* I have expressed my doubts as to the character of the Q^1 material in a footnote,[11] with some comments on several of the passages designated as Q^1 scattered in a disjointed way through the following pages. What I would like to do in this chapter is to subject the Q^1 material as a complete whole to the same sort of analysis, to see what kind of collection it is and whether there are sufficient grounds for regarding it as a single, coherent collection or scribal composition. My hypothesis is (1) that the Q^1 material consists of groups of teaching material, clusters of wisdom sayings and exhortations, used by teachers in the early Christian communities in their oral teaching role within these communities; (2) that the use made of this material by Matthew and Luke attests the flexible or variable character of the oral tradition used in such teaching – hence the difficulty which the compilers of the Q document have typically experienced in reconstructing the Q text for this material;[12]

---

[8] Kloppenborg 1987:244–5. He has continued to make this point in subsequent writing – most recently Kloppenborg 2001.

[9] For Kloppenborg, Q is simply Q^2 with the temptation narrative (Q 4.1–13) and a handful of other brief passages inserted (e.g. Kloppenborg Verbin 2000:212–13).

[10] Kloppenborg Verbin 2000:197, 200, 209.   [11] Dunn 2003b:157 n. 82.

[12] *The Critical Edition of Q* (Robinson et al. 2000). I will refer to this by the abbreviation *CEQ*.

and (3) that it is very unlikely that the Q^I material formed a coherent unit or single collection used as such in the several communities which we can assume to have been familiar with the Q^I material.

I will proceed then by examining the six clusters of Q material identified above in sequence.[13] As in *Jesus Remembered* I will lay out the key Matthew/ Luke texts synoptically, along with *Gospel of Thomas* and other parallels where appropriate, and with the parallel (Q?) material indicated simply by underlining. To make the texts more accessible I will use English translation, but attempt to ensure as far as conveniently possible that the English translation and the underlining reflect the vagaries of the Greek.

I THE SERMON ON THE PLAIN — Q 6.20B–23B, 27–49

1.1   Matt. 5.3–6, 11–12/ Luke 6.20–3/ (*Gos. Thom.* 54, 69.2, 68)

Matt. 5.3–6, 11–12	Luke 6.20–23	*Gos. Thom.* 54, 69.2, 68
3 Blessed are the poor in spirit, for theirs is the kingdom of heaven. 4 Blessed are those who mourn, for they will be comforted. 5 Blessed are the meek, for they will inherit the earth. 6 Blessed are those who hunger and thirst for righteousness, for they will be filled.	20 Blessed are the poor, for yours is the kingdom of God.	54 Blessed are the poor, for yours is the kingdom of heaven.
	21 Blessed are those who hunger now, for you will be filled. Blessed are you who weep now, for you will laugh.	69.2 Blessed are those who hunger, that the belly of him who desires may be satisfied.
11 Blessed are you when they revile you and persecute you and utter all kinds of evil against you falsely on my account. 12 Rejoice and be glad, for your reward is great in heaven, for in the same way they persecuted the prophets who were before you.	22 Blessed are you when people hate you, and when they exclude you, revile you, and reject your name as evil you on account of the Son of Man. 23 Rejoice in that day and leap for joy, for surely your reward is great in heaven; for that is what their fathers did to the prophets.	68 Blessed are you when people hate you and persecute you, and no place will be found where you have [not] been persecuted.

In every case to be examined it is obvious that the sort of variation in the texts here presented could be explained by a process of editorial manipulation of a common written source. But it is at least equally possible to infer that each of the three texts has been derived from an oral tradition, or orally preserved memory

[13] Because of pressures of space I will have to bypass the items in Kloppenborg's list of six groups where he has put a question mark, and also those further passages which he now thinks may also belong to 'the earliest level of Q' – Q 15.4–7, 8–10; 16.(13), 16, 18; 17.1–2, 3–4, 6 (Kloppenborg 1995:314–15; Kloppenborg Verbin 2000:146 n. 62). The additional material does not make any real difference to the picture which emerges below; Luke 15.8–10 has no Matthean parallel.

of Jesus teaching the blessedness of the poor, the hungry and the persecuted.[14] Or to put the point more accurately, given that we are talking about a predominantly oral society as the context for this tradition, each of these texts can be seen as a typical performance of a shared oral tradition. The common features of the three texts are just what one might expect to have remained firm within such a tradition, and the variations between them are better explained as the variations deemed appropriate in performances of the tradition to different communities.[15] On a literary model the variations of Q 6.22–3 are hard to explain as editorial redactions: why such changes?[16] But on an oral model, such variations as part of a 'live performance' are what we should expect, without having to find a reason for them beyond the mood of the performative moment.

1.2   Matt. 5.39–47; 7.12/ Luke 6.27–35/ (*Did.* 1.3–5/ P. Oxy. 1224/ *Gos. Thom.* 95, 6.3)

Matt. 5.43–7	Luke 6.27–8, 32–5	*Did.* 1.3; P. Oxy. 1224; *Gos. Thom.* 95
43 You have heard that it was said, 'You shall love your neighbour and hate your enemy.' 44 But I <u>say to you</u>, <u>Love your enemies</u>	27 But I <u>say to you</u> that listen, <u>Love your enemies</u>, do good to <u>those who hate you</u>, 28 <u>bless those who curse you, pray for those who</u> abuse <u>you</u>.	1.3d Love <u>those who hate you</u>, and you shall have no <u>enemy</u>. 1.3b <u>Bless those who curse you</u> and <u>pray</u> for your enemies, and fast for those who persecute you.
and <u>pray for those who</u> persecute <u>you</u>, 45 so that you may be sons of your Father in heaven; for he makes his sun rise on the evil and on the good, and sends rain on the righteous and on the unrighteous. 46 For <u>if you love those who love you</u>, what reward do you have? Do not even the tax collectors do the same? 47 And if you greet only your brothers, what more are you doing than others? Do not <u>even</u> the Gentiles <u>do the same?</u>	. . . 32 And <u>if you love those who love you</u>, what credit is that to you? For even sinners love those who love them. 33 And if you do good to those who do good to you, what credit is that to you? For <u>even</u> sinners <u>do the same</u>. 34 If you lend to those from whom you hope to receive, what credit is that to you? Even sinners lend to sinners, to receive as much again. 35 But love your enemies, do good, and lend, expecting nothing in return. Your reward will be great, and you will be children of the Most High; for he is kind to the ungrateful and the wicked.	P. Oxy. 1224 . . . a]nd pray for your [enem]ies. *Gos. Thom.* 95 If you have money do not lend at interest, but give . . . from whom you will not get it (back).

---

[14]   Cf. Davies and Allison 1988–97:1.441.

[15]   For oral tradition as characteristically a combination of fixity and flexibility, of stability and diversity, of 'variation within the same', see Dunn 2003a:154–5.

[16]   Kloppenborg concludes that Q 6.23c is Q² redaction (Kloppenborg 1987:190).

Matt. 5.39b–42	Luke 6.29–30	*Did.* 1.4b, d, 5a
But whoever hits <u>you</u> <u>on</u> <u>your right cheek, turn to him the other also</u>; 40 and to the one who wants to sue you and take <u>your tunic</u>, let him have <u>your cloak also</u>; 41 and whoever forces you to go one mile, go with him a second. 42 <u>Give to</u> the one <u>who asks you, and</u> do not turn away the one who wants to borrow from you.	29 To the one who strikes you on the <u>cheek</u>, offer the <u>other also</u>; and from the one who takes away <u>your cloak</u> do not withhold <u>your</u> tunic also. 30 <u>Give to everyone who</u> <u>asks you; and</u> from the one who takes what is yours, <u>do not ask for it back.</u>	4b If someone gives <u>you</u> a blow <u>on the right cheek, turn to him the other also</u>, and you will be perfect. 4d If someone takes <u>your cloak</u>, give him <u>your tunic also.</u> 5a <u>Give to everyone who</u> <u>asks you, and</u> do not ask for <u>it back.</u>

Matt. 7.12	Luke 6.31	*Gos. Thom.* 6.3
Everything, therefore, whatever <u>you wish that people should do</u> <u>for you</u>, so also <u>do for them</u>; for this is the law and the prophets.	And as <u>you wish that people should do</u> <u>for you</u>, <u>do for them</u> likewise.	. . . [and what you ha]te do not do . . .

If the tradition used here was typical of Q, or to be more precise, typical of the material common to Matthew and Luke which provides the basis for the whole Q hypothesis, then it is doubtful whether the Q hypothesis would ever have emerged – that is, the hypothesis of Q as a written document known to and used as such by Matthew and Luke. The level of verbal agreement in the first two sections listed above is just too low to support the hypothesis of a literary document underlying both.[17] But equally improbable as an explanation of the character of the agreements and non-agreements of Matthew and Luke is the usual alternative, which dispenses with the Q hypothesis and argues instead that Luke derived his (Q) text by redacting Matthew (or vice versa).[18] Such hypotheses help make sense of some details, such as Matthew's introduction (Matt 5.43). But most of the other variations are inconsequential (e.g. Q 6.29–30),[19] and cause one to wonder why, on a literary hypothesis, the second author should have bothered to change the text of the first.[20] Much the more obvious explanation is that both Matthew and Luke knew a tradition about Jesus' teaching on love of enemies, and about generosity of attitude to the hostile and the poor; and that

[17] *The Critical Edition of Q* (*CEQ*; Robinson et al. 2000:58) has to opt for 'so that you may become sons of your Father, for he raises his sun on bad and [[good and rains on the just and unjust]]' for Q 6.35, drawn exclusively from Matt 5.45.

[18] Most recently Goodacre 2002.

[19] The *CEQ* version, without the double square brackets which indicate 'reconstructions that are probable but uncertain' (Robinson et al. 2000:lxxxii) – 'probable' seems too uncritical in most cases – reads '. . . you on the cheek, offer [opting for Matthew's *strepson* rather than Luke's *pareche*] . . . the other as well; and . . . your shirt . . . the coat as well' (Robinson et al. 2000:60).

[20] On Q 6.31 see Dunn 2003b:566–9.

either both knew the tradition in a form already diversely elaborated in performance and/or transmission,[21] or they on their own account produced their written text in the manner and with the freedom of an oral performance (in oral mode).

1.3 Matt. 5.48; 7.1–5; 10.24/ Luke 6.36–42/ (Mark 4.24/ John 13.16/ Gos. Thom. 34, 26)

Matt. 5.48; 7.1–5; 10.24	Luke 6.36–42	Mark 4.24; John 13.16; Gos. Thom. 34, 26
5.48 Therefore, be perfect, <u>as your</u> heavenly <u>Father is</u> perfect. 7.1 <u>Do not judge</u>, so that <u>you</u> may <u>not be judged</u>. 2 For with the judgment you make, you will be judged:	36 Be merciful, just <u>as your Father is</u> merciful. 37 <u>Do not judge</u>, and <u>you</u> will <u>not be judged</u>; do not condemn, and you will not be condemned. Forgive, and you will be forgiven; 38 give, and it will be given to you. A good measure, pressed down, shaken together, running over,	
and <u>with the measure you give it will be measured to you.</u>	will be put into your lap; for by <u>the measure you give it will be measured</u> in return <u>to you.</u> 39 He also told them a parable: 'Can <u>a blind man</u> guide <u>a blind man</u>? Will not <u>both fall into a</u>	Mk 4.24 <u>with the measure you give it will be measured to you</u> Th. 34 If <u>a blind man</u> leads <u>a blind man</u>, <u>both</u> of them <u>fall into a pit</u>.
10.24 <u>A disciple is not above the teacher</u>, nor <u>a slave</u> over <u>his master</u>. 25 It is enough for the disciple that he be <u>like his teacher</u>.	pit? 40 <u>A disciple is not above the teacher</u>, but everyone who is fully qualified will be <u>like his teacher</u>.	Jn 13.16 <u>A slave</u> is not greater than <u>his master</u>.
7.3 <u>Why do you see the speck which is in your brother's eye, but the log in</u> your <u>eye you do not notice?</u> 4 <u>Or how do you say to your brother, 'Let me take out the speck</u> from <u>your eye</u>', while <u>the log is in your</u> own <u>eye? 5 You hypocrite, first take the log out of your eye, and then you will see clearly to take out the speck from your brother's eye.</u>	41 <u>Why do you see the speck which is in your brother's eye, but the log</u> which is <u>in</u> your own <u>eye you do not notice?</u> 42 <u>Or how</u> can <u>you say to your brother</u>, 'Brother, <u>let me take out the speck</u> in <u>your eye</u>', when you yourself do not see <u>the log in your</u> own <u>eye? You hypocrite, first take the log out of your eye, and then you will see clearly to take out the speck</u> which is in <u>your brother's eye.</u>	Gos. Thom. 26 <u>The speck which is in your brother's eye</u>, you see, <u>but the log</u> which is <u>in your eye you do not see</u>. <u>When</u> you <u>take the log out of your eye, then you will see clearly to take out the</u> speck from <u>your brother's eye.</u>

[21] The parallels in *Did.* 1.3–5 (add in P. Oxy. 1224; also Rom 12.14, 1 Cor 4.12 and 1 Pet 3.9) increase the probability of an oral tradition, unless it is to be argued that 1.4b is drawn from Matthew, whereas the rest is drawn from Luke! See the discussion of the options in Niederwimmer 1993:95–100. See also Betz 1995:8–9: 'This wide distribution of similar but different elements points to oral tradition rather than to a dependency on written texts' (297). *Gos. Thom.*'s two parallels do not help much since they at best reflect traditions recalled with no great concern for any specific detail.

Unlike the first two (sets of) passages, the third gives more signs of literary dependence; the evidence suggests a transmission process more like copying than the inconsequential variations of tradition performed. The above synopsis shows it to be entirely plausible that there was a firm, written Q version (Q 6.37a, 38b–42, with a Marcan doublet at Mark 4.24), which Matthew and Luke have elaborated each in his own way, Matthew adding 7.2 and Luke adding 6.37b–38a (their performance variations). The closeness of verbal parallel in *Gos. Thom.* 26 (also 34) then invites a similar explanation. The synopsis also suggests the possibility, however, that Q 6.40 was known in an oral performance tradition, and/or in the double form of Matt 10.24–5a,[22] a possibility strengthened by the repeated emphasis on the latter part of the Matt 10.24b saying in John 13.16 and 15.20.[23]

1.4   Matt. 7.16; 12.35/ Luke 6.43–5/ (*Gos. Thom.* 45)

Matt. 7.16; 12.35	Luke 6.43–5	*Gos. Thom.* 45
7.16 You will <u>know</u> them by their <u>fruits</u>. Are <u>grapes</u> <u>gathered</u> from <u>thorns</u>, or <u>figs</u> from <u>thistles</u>? 12.35 <u>The good man</u> <u>out of his good treasure</u> brings <u>good</u> things, <u>and</u> <u>the evil</u> man <u>out of his evil</u> treasure brings <u>evil</u> things.	43 No good tree bears bad fruit, nor again does a bad tree bear good fruit; 44 for each tree is <u>known</u> from its own <u>fruit</u>. <u>Figs</u> are not <u>gathered</u> out of <u>thorns</u>, nor are grapes <u>picked</u> from a bramble bush. 45 <u>The good man</u> <u>out of the good treasure</u> of his heart produces <u>good</u>, <u>and</u> <u>the evil</u> (man) <u>out of evil</u> (treasure) <u>produces evil</u>; for it is <u>out of the abundance of the heart</u> that the mouth <u>speaks</u>.	1 <u>Grapes</u> are not <u>gathered</u> from <u>thorns</u>, nor are <u>figs</u> <u>picked</u> from <u>thistles</u>; for they give no fruit. 2 A <u>good man</u> produces <u>good out of his treasure</u>; 3 a wicked man <u>produces evil out of</u> <u>his evil treasure</u> which is in his heart, and <u>speaks</u> evil things; 4 for out of the <u>abundance of the</u> <u>heart</u> he brings forth evil things

It is quite feasible to envisage a text of Q something like Luke 6.43–5, and then to propose some substantial Matthean editing (omitting Q 6.43 and 6.45b, and separating 6.44 from 6.45a), with Thomas omitting Q 6.43–4a.[24] If we had only the Matthew/Luke parallels to work with, it would be easier to deduce an oral tradition which contained the recollection of two sayings of Jesus to similar effect. Moreover, the variations of grapes/thorns, figs/thistles (Matthew/*Thomas*) and figs/thorns, grapes/

---

[22] The *CEQ* version of Q 6.40 offers, 'A disciple is not superior to "one's" teacher. [[It is enough for the disciple that he become]] like his teacher' (Robinson et al. 2000:78).
[23] On the character of the interdependence of John on Synoptic-like tradition see Dunn 1991.
[24] Thus *CEQ* (Robinson et al. 2000:84–93).

bramblebush (Luke), as also question (Matthew) or statement (Luke/ *Thomas*), are more characteristic of oral performance than of literary copying.[25] But the *Thomas* evidence certainly strengthens the case for an established (written?) sequence consisting at least of Q 6.44b–45 – unless, of course, Thomas knew and used Luke!

1.5 Matt. 7.21, 24–7/ Luke 6.46–9

Matt. 7.21, 24–7	Luke 6.46–9
21 Not everyone who says to me 'Lord, Lord', will enter the kingdom of heaven, but only the one who does the will of my Father who is in heaven. . . .	46 Why do you call me 'Lord, Lord', and do not do what I tell you?
24 Everyone then who hears these my words and acts on them will be like a wise man who built his house on rock.	47 Everyone who comes to me and hears my words and acts on them, I will show you what he is like. 48 He is like a man building a house, who dug deeply and laid the foundation on rock;
25 Torrential rain fell, the floods came, and the winds blew and beat on that house, but it did not fall, for it had been founded on rock.	when a flood arose, the river burst against that house but could not shake it, because it had been well built.
26 And everyone who hears these words of mine and does not act on them will be like a foolish man who built his house on sand.	49 But he who hears and does not act is like a man building a house on the ground without a foundation. When
27 Torrential rain fell, and the floods came, and the winds blew and beat against that house, and it fell – and great was its fall!	the flood burst against it, immediately it fell, and great was the ruin of that house.

   In this case the indications point in the opposite direction.[26] We are back with a sequence of inconsequential variations: in particular, the 'wise'/ 'foolish' contrast and the contrast of sand with the rock are Matthew's alone; Luke fills out the story of the building of the house, and Matthew the picture of the elements battering the houses; likewise the different effects of the flood on the two houses look like free variation. These differences do not appear to be derived from an already-fixed text, but rather are just the sort of variations one would expect from story tellers painting a vivid picture for a spell-bound audience.[27] Or if we want to say that one or

[25] Cf. Davies and Allison 1988–97:1.706: 'Perhaps we are not dealing with Q but with variants from oral tradition.' The traditional example of what is contrary to nature (a vine does not bear figs, or an olive grapes) (Kloppenborg 1987:182 n. 52), as in Jas 3.12, is given a sharper twist (thorns, thistles, bramblebush).

[26] Morgenthaler 1971 notes that Matthew's and Luke's versions show only a 24 per cent verbal agreement.

[27] Cf. Betz 1995:559–60. Minor variations taken as evidence that Q was known in different versions (Q^{Mt} and Q^{Lk}) simply illustrate how well established is the literary 'default-setting' in modern analyses of the tradition history of such texts; but the facts which lend themselves to the hypothesis of multiple Qs are, in an oral society, more simply interpreted as evidence of a variably performed oral tradition.

other (or both) felt free to depart from an established text in this way, then it comes to much the same thing, for it means that however fixed in writing the tradition already was, the tradition thus written down was actually more fluid, as demonstrated by Matthew's and/or Luke's use of the tradition in oral or performance mode.

To sum up this far: it is likely that the Q material known usually as 'the Sermon on the Plain' (loosely speaking Q 6.20–3, 27–49) was already well established as a familiar and shared collection of material in the teaching resources of many early churches. Whether this was because Jesus was remembered as delivering some of his teaching in some such sequence,[28] or because the collection was the work of (an) early teacher(s) or apostle(s) whose grouping of the teaching set the pattern for other teachers,[29] it is no longer possible to tell. That some of the material was written down and known in that form is quite possible, though we must always recall that the society was predominantly oral, with only a small minority capable of *reading* any such text.[30] And the likelihood of more and more being written down (for convenient transmission) as the Jesus tradition spread ever more widely is strong. But even so, most of the 'Sermon on the Plain' was probably better known in oral form: the grouping could still be regular and firm – a standard repertoire for teachers;[31] but the variations still evident in the enduring form of most of the tradition bear the marks of a tradition variously performed in various churches, the substance stable, but the detail responding to the circumstances and the mood of the different occasions of celebration, instruction and performance.[32]

---

[28] Fitzmyer 1981: 'The similarities are such that they suggest that the tradition has preserved here something from an extended sermon delivered by Jesus toward the beginning of his ministry' (627).

[29] I use 'teacher' as shorthand to denote those in the various groups/churches/communities who were recognized by these groups/churches/communities, and perhaps even charged by them to be chiefly responsible for retaining and rehearsing the traditions shared by the groups/churches/communities.

[30] See, e.g., Dunn 2003a:148–9.

[31] 'A repertoire of sayings of Jesus originally spoken in other contexts' (Kloppenborg Verbin 2000:156). I cannot help asking whether the characteristics of the 'sermon' which Kloppenborg proceeds to describe as characteristics of Q (156–9) are better described as characteristics of Jesus' teaching preserved by the compilers of these repertoires.

[32] Contrast Vaage 1995: 'The composition before us could not reflect an antecedent "oral" work with sufficient stability to be identified as the "sermon", owing to the very nature of orality … The "sermon" would need to have been written down virtually at the very moment when it was first orally composed in order for the text that we now read in Q to represent the oral composition one might presume to posit' (92–3). This comment betrays the literary mind-set, where oral precedents relate to the Q text as earlier editions of the 'sermon', and fails to appreciate that the Q sermon can be seen as itself a performance of familiar groupings of teaching material.

2 ON DISCIPLESHIP AND MISSION – Q 9.57–62; 10.2–11, 16

2.6   Matt. 8.19–22/ Luke 9.57–62/ (*Gos. Thom.* 86)

Matt. 8.19–22	Luke 9.57–62	*Gos. Thom.* 86
19 A scribe then approached and <u>said</u>, 'Teacher, <u>I will follow you wherever you go</u>.' 20 And Jesus says <u>to him</u>, <u>'Foxes have holes, and birds of the air have nests; but the Son of Man has nowhere to lay his head</u>.'	57 As they were going along the road, someone <u>said</u> to him, <u>'I will follow you wherever you go</u>.' 58 And Jesus said <u>to him</u>, <u>'Foxes have holes, and birds of the air have nests; but the Son of Man has nowhere to lay his head</u>.'	1 [Foxes have] their [holes] <u>and birds have</u> [their] <u>nests</u>, 2 <u>but the son of man has nowhere to lay his head</u> and rest.
21 Another of his disciples said to him, 'Lord, <u>first let me go and bury my father</u>.' 22 But Jesus said to him, '<u>Follow me, and let the dead bury their own dead</u>.'	59 To another he said, '<u>Follow me</u>.' But he said, '[Lord], <u>first let me go and bury my father</u>.' 60 But Jesus said to him, '<u>Let the dead bury their own dead</u>; but as for you, go and proclaim the kingdom of God.' 61 Another said, 'I will follow you, Lord; but let me first take leave of those at my home.' 62 Jesus said to him, 'No one who puts a hand to the plough and looks back is fit for the kingdom of God.'	

It was to be expected that various sayings of Jesus about discipleship, or the call to discipleship, or the cost of discipleship would be located together in a pigeonhole of the memory of the typical teacher in early disciple groups. It was, after all, in response to such challenges that the members of these groups had become disciples. The fact that they are remembered as a cluster of 'discipleship sayings' distinct from the nearest equivalent cluster in Mark 8.34–8 pars., and that the latter are heavily marked by the lead saying on 'taking the cross' (8.34 pars.),[33] suggests that the former cluster (here being considered) reflects more the pre-Easter understanding of discipleship.[34] That is to say, the cluster may already have been in place before the events of Jesus' own passion. At all events, the three-fold tradition clearly indicates one or two sayings of Jesus which had bitten

---

[33] The Matthew/Luke parallels to Mark 8.34–9.1 are best explained as drawn almost entirely from Mark; the sequence is one of the best examples of literary interdependence between the three Synoptics. The Q material includes the parallels to Mark 8.34–8 of Matt 10.38/Luke 14.27, Matt 10.39/Luke 17.33 and Matt 10.33/Luke 12.9, so that there does not seem to have been such a widespread desire to retain them as a cluster, at least in performance. On Matt 10.38–9 par. see below, ##6.16–17.

[34] The *CEQ* reconstruction omits Luke/Q 9.61–2.

deeply into the shared memory of one or more disciple groups. At the same time, the different frameworks within which the sayings were presented indicate both the lack of concern to recall any precise context in which the sayings were initially delivered and the freedom of the different tradents to provide their own framework, as presumably was appropriate in the differing variety of circumstances in which the sayings were recalled.

2.7   Matt. 9.37–8; 10.7–16/ Luke 10.2–11/ (*Gos. Thom.* 73, 39.3, 14.2)

Matt. 9.37–8; 10.7–16	Luke 10.2–11	*Gos. Thom.* 73, 39.3, 14.2
37 Then he said to his disciples, 'The harvest is plentiful, but the labourers are few; 38 therefore ask the Lord of the harvest to send out labourers into his harvest'. …	2 He said to them, 'The harvest is plentiful, but the labourers are few; therefore ask the lord of the harvest to send out labourers into his harvest.	73 The harvest is plentiful, but the labourers are few; ask the lord to send out labourers into his harvest.
10.16 See, I am sending you out like sheep in the midst of wolves; so be wise as serpents and innocent as doves.	3 Go on your way. See, I am sending you out like lambs in the midst of wolves.	39.3 But you, be wise as serpents and innocent as doves.
9 Take no gold, or silver, or copper in your belts, 10a no bag for your journey, or two tunics, or sandals, or a staff. 11 Whatever town or village you enter, find out who in it is worthy, and stay there until you leave. 12 As on entering into the house, greet it. 13 And if the house is worthy, let your peace come upon it; but if it is not worthy, let your peace return to you.	4 Carry no purse, no bag, no sandals; and greet no one on the road.

5 Into whatever house you enter, first say, 'Peace to this house!' 6 And if anyone is there who shares in peace, your peace will rest upon him; but if not, it will come back to you. 7 Remain in the same house, eating and drinking | 14.2 And if you enter into any land and wander in the countryside, and if they take you in, (then) eat what is set before you. |
| 10b for the labourer deserves his food. | whatever they provide, for the labourer deserves his pay. Do not move about from house to house. 8 Whenever you enter a town and its people welcome you, | |
| 8 Cure the sick, raise the dead, cleanse the lepers, cast out demons. You received without payment; give without payment. 7 As you go, proclaim the good news, "The kingdom of heaven has come near". | eat what is set before you; 9 cure the sick who are here,

and say to them, 'The kingdom of God has come near to | Cure the sick among them. |
| 14 If anyone will not welcome you or listen to your words, as you leave that house or town shake off the dust from your feet. | you.' 10 But whenever you enter a town and they do not welcome you, go out into its streets and say, 11 'Even the dust of your town that clings to our feet, we wipe off in protest against you. Yet know this: the kingdom of God has come near.' | |

The tradition history of the mission commissioning of the twelve is particularly complex, since we have to include the further variants of Mark 6.7–13/Matt 10.1, 7–11, 14/Luke 9.1–6. Without attempting to unravel that complexity,[35] it is fairly clear that Matthew and Luke knew a tradition independent of Mark 6.7–13 but overlapping with it. The evidence presented in #2.7 is sufficient to indicate material that was used and reused in a variety of permutations. This is as might be expected in churches and communities of disciples/believers active in promulgating their faith, including the sending out of missionaries/apostles with a specific charge to evangelize. That is to say, the content and order of the material almost certainly reflects the diverse ways in which the tradition of Jesus' commissioning of the twelve was adapted and varied to suit the different circumstances of diverse contexts and situations. At the same time, there are certain recurring elements which could be included at different points as deemed appropriate. And the tightness of the strictures (no bag, no sandals) and the message of the kingdom's imminence (not attested in preaching after Easter) suggest elements given an enduring shape already in the pre-Easter context of Jesus' own mission.[36] At all events, the data are best explained as drawn variously from an oral memory of Jesus' own commissioning, as an oral resource from which differing (versions of) commission(s) could be constructed, rather than as a single established written text which the different Evangelists shredded and reconstructed at will.[37]

2.8 Matt. 10.40/ Luke 10.16 / (John 13.20; Mark 9.37 pars.)

Matt. 10.40	Luke 10.16	John 13.20
He who receives <u>you</u> receives <u>me</u>, and <u>he who</u> receives <u>me</u> receives <u>him who sent me.</u>	He who hears <u>you</u> hears <u>me</u>, and he who rejects you rejects me; but <u>he who</u> rejects <u>me</u> rejects <u>him who sent me.</u>	Truly, truly, I tell you, <u>he who</u> receives one whom I send receives <u>me</u>; and <u>he who</u> receives <u>me</u> receives <u>him who sent me.</u>

Matt. 18.5	Luke 9.48	Mark 9.37
<u>Whoever receives one</u> such <u>child in my name receives me.</u>	<u>Whoever receives</u> this <u>child in my name receives me</u>; and whoever receives me receives <u>him who sent me.</u>	<u>Whoever receives one</u> of such children <u>in my name receives me</u>; and whoever receives me receives not me but <u>him who sent me.</u>

Here is a typical example of a saying where the substance (*die Sache*) is consistent and constant while the wording (*die Sprache*) varies in content and

---

[35] See, e.g., the brief discussions in Fitzmyer 1985:842–3; Davies and Allison 1988–97:II.163–4.
[36] On Luke 10.4 and 7 see Dunn 2003b:505 and 601 respectively.
[37] The *CEQ* reconstruction is therefore remarkably bold – not only Q 10.2–3 (including 3a) and 9, but also 10.4 and most of 10.5–8, 10–11a (Robinson et al. 2000:160–79). Contrast Schröter 1997: 'Eine Betrachtung der verschiedenen Versionen, in denen diese Logien begegnen, erbrachte, dass der Überlieferungsprozess in diesen Fällen nicht nach dem Modell literarischer Abhängigkeit, sondern des Weiterfliessens des mündlichen Traditionsstromes vorzustellen ist' (211; also 236–7).

detail. This initial impression from the Q material is strengthened by the fact that Mark 9.37 has a different saying to the same effect, apparently followed/copied by Matthew and Luke, giving both Matthew and Luke an effective doublet of the saying. Rather than insisting that the Q material has to be explained in terms of literary dependence, in the same way that the 'child' version of the saying can be explained by literary dependence on Mark, it makes better sense of all the data to recognize something Jesus said, probably more than once, which was recalled in its substance and reused in varying forms in the course of performing and transmitting the Jesus tradition.[38]

The second block of putative Q¹ material (##2.6–8) therefore shares the characteristics of the first (##1.1–5), the last two units in particular (##2.7–8) indicating the likelihood of tradition widely and frequently cited and reworked. To conceptualize that reuse and reworking as a sequence of layers of tradition, equivalent to sequential literary editions, each subsequent edition redacting the written text of its predecessor, is hardly realistic in communities where literacy was at a premium. Much the more obvious explanation is that the tradition was known and used orally in various forms and combinations, and that the literary forms which have actually come down to us are actually frozen performances, normatively typical in their combination of stability and flexibility, rather than one or more fixed forms.

3 ON PRAYER – Q 11.2–4, 9–13

3.9 Matt. 6.9–13/ Luke 11.2–4 (*Did.* 8.2)

Matt. 6.9–13 (*Did.*) 8.2	Luke 11.2–4
9 Pray then in this way: Our <u>Father</u> who is in heaven, <u>hallowed be your name</u>. 10 <u>Your kingdom come</u>. Your will be done, on earth as it is in heaven. 11 <u>Give us today our daily bread</u>. 12 <u>And forgive us our</u> debts, as <u>we</u> also have <u>forgiven</u> our <u>debtors</u>. 13 <u>And do not bring us to the time of trial</u>, but rescue us from the evil one.	2 He said to them, 'When you pray, say: <u>Father</u>, <u>hallowed be your name</u>. <u>Your kingdom come</u>. 3 <u>Give us</u> each <u>day our daily bread</u>. 4 <u>And forgive us our</u> sins, for <u>we</u> ourselves also <u>forgive</u> everyone in<u>debt</u>ed to us. <u>And do not bring us to the time of trial</u>.'

[38] Dodd 1963:343–7: 'Any attempt, I submit, to account for these phenomena [variations] by a theory of literary dependence must be fruitless. The hypothesis that the evangelists drew upon different branches of a common oral tradition, and that the language they employ, within a form or pattern which remains largely constant, was in large measure determined by variations in that tradition, appears to me the hypothesis which best explains the facts' (347); see further Dunn 2003b:558.

These are the earliest forms of the Lord's Prayer known to us. There is nothing to suggest that the individual petitions of the prayer were known as having been used by Jesus separately, or that the prayer was the composition of some unknown disciple.[39] It is remembered only as a prayer taught by Jesus. On the 'default setting' of a literary mind-set the tendency is to think in terms, as usual, of literary dependency – of Matthew and Luke both having access to an established written text (Q), or, a minority would argue, of Luke copying from Matthew and thus producing his own version. But in either case one has to work hard to find reasons why either (or both) made the changes to the text which we find here. The case for transmission by copying is much clearer in *Didache*'s evident use of Matthew. But in the case of the Matthew/Luke parallel much the more obvious solution is that these were the forms of the prayer which were being used in the churches of Matthew and Luke respectively. In other words, the two forms exemplify a living liturgical tradition.[40] As still today, where among English-speaking churches there are three or four slightly different versions of the Lord's Prayer in use, so already in the earliest years of Christianity we can justifiably infer that regular congregational use of the prayer produced the variations which we see in Q 11.4 and the elaborations evident in Matthew's text.[41] This is not to deny that the Lord's Prayer may have been written down at an early stage. It is simply to observe that derivation of the prayer by Matthew and/or Luke from a written source is not the most obvious explanation for the character of the Matthean/Lucan versions.[42] The congregations served by Matthew and Luke almost certainly knew the prayer because they prayed it regularly, not because they read it, or because someone read it to them from a written document, Q or whatever.

---

[39] The two alternatives suggested respectively by Funk and Hoover 1993:148–50, and Crossan 1991:294. Crossan's assumption that a prayer taught by Jesus would have been more uniform in content (294) takes no account of the character of oral tradition, as well enough attested in the variations of the Synoptic tradition.

[40] See further Dunn 2003b:227–8, with bibliography.

[41] The trend continues with the subsequent but still very early addition of the final doxology (see again Dunn 2003b:228 and n. 232).

[42] Cf. Betz 1995:370: 'It is characteristic of liturgical material in general that textual fixation occurs at a later stage in the transmission of these texts, while in the oral stage variability within limits is the rule. These characteristics also apply to the Lord's Prayer. The three recensions, therefore, represent variations of the prayer in the oral tradition . . . (T)here was never only *one original written* Lord's Prayer.'

3.10 Matt. 7.7–11/ Luke 11.9–13/ (*Gos. Thom.* 92, 94, 2)

Matt. 7.7–11	Luke 11.9–13	*Gos. Thom.* 92, 94, 2
7 Ask, and it will be given you; seek, and you will find; knock, and the door will be opened for you. 8 For everyone who asks receives, and everyone who seeks finds, and for everyone who knocks, the door will be opened. 9 Or what person among you who, if his son asks for bread, will give him a stone? 10 Or if he asks for a fish, will give him a snake? 11 If you then, who are evil, know how to give good gifts to your children, how much more will your Father who is in heaven give good things to those who ask him.	9 So I say to you, Ask, and it will be given you; seek, and you will find; knock, and the door will be opened for you. 10 For everyone who asks receives, and everyone who seeks finds, and for everyone who knocks, the door will be opened. 11 What father among you who, if your son asks for a fish, will give a snake instead of a fish? 12 Or if the child asks for an egg, will give a scorpion? 13 If you then, who are evil, know how to give good gifts to your children, how much more will the heavenly Father give the Holy Spirit to those who ask him!	92 Seek and you will find. But those things about which you asked me during those days, I did not tell you on that day. Now I am willing to tell them, and you do not inquire about them. 94 He who seeks will find ... it will be opened. 2 He who seeks must not stop seeking until he finds; and when he finds, he will be bewildered; and if he is bewildered, he will marvel, and will be king over the All. (Similar in P. Oxy. 654.1 = *Gos.Heb.* in Clement, *Strom.* 2.9.45)

In this case one can readily envisage a written text copied quite faithfully for most of Q 11.9–11, 13, but with slight editorial redaction (addition or omission) in 11.11–12, and the interesting modification ('good things'/'Holy Spirit') in 11.13.[43] On the other hand, the variation in the illustration of a son asking of his father (bread/stone, fish/snake, egg/scorpion) is just the sort of elaboration which can be expected in oral performance, as the teacher/preacher presses home the point by multiplying examples. So, even assuming dependence on a written Q, here at least we could speak quite justifiably of both Matthew and Luke reusing the Q tradition in oral mode. The material can then count in part at least as a good illustration of the way tradition, including tradition already in writing, would be used in an oral society.

Given the amount of teaching Jesus presumably gave on prayer,[44] the slimness of the Q¹ collection (#3) is somewhat surprising. The evidence suggests, however, that no single collection of that teaching became dominant, or rather that his teaching on prayer (and example of

---

[43] Of course, the sayings of Q 11.9–10 and 13 could be sufficiently memorable to have retained a very stable form in oral performance and transmission. But Thomas indicates that only the 'seek and you will find' saying retained such stability over the years, though John 16.23–4 looks like an elaboration of the 'ask and it will be given you' saying (cf. Dodd 1963:351–2). For the debate whether Q 11.9–10 and 11–13 were two originally independent traditions see Kloppenborg 1987:204 n. 140.

[44] E.g. Mark 9.29; 11.24–5 par.; 14.32–42 pars.; Matt 5.44/Luke 6.28; Matt 6.5–7; Luke 5.33; 18.1–8, 10–14; 22.32.

prayer) was too pervasive in his mission and the resulting Jesus tradition to be restricted to specific collections and that his teaching (and example) served rather as a stimulus to further reflection (and practice).

4 ENCOURAGEMENT TO FEARLESS CONFESSION – Q 12.2–7, 11–12

4.11   Matt. 10.26–31/ Luke 12.2–7/ (*Gos. Thom.* 5, 6.5–6, 33.1)

Matt. 10.26–31	Luke 12.2–7	*Gos. Thom.* 5, 6.5–6, 33.1
26 So have no fear of them; for <u>nothing is covered</u> <u>that will not be uncovered, and nothing secret that will not become known</u>. 27 What I say to you <u>in the dark</u>, <u>say</u> <u>in the light;</u> <u>and what you</u> hear <u>into</u> the ear, <u>proclaim</u> upon <u>the housetops.</u> 28 <u>Do not fear those who kill the body</u> but cannot kill the soul; rather <u>fear him who</u> can destroy both soul and body in <u>hell.</u> 29 <u>Are not</u> two <u>sparrows sold for</u> a <u>penny?</u> <u>Yet not one of them</u> will fall to the ground apart from your Father. 30 And <u>even the hairs of your head</u> are <u>all counted.</u> 31 So <u>do not be afraid:</u> <u>you are of more value than many sparrows.</u>	2 <u>Nothing is covered</u> up <u>that will not be uncovered, and nothing secret that will not become known</u>. 3 Therefore whatever <u>in the dark</u> you have <u>said</u> <u>in the light</u> will be heard, <u>and what you</u> have said to <u>the ear</u> behind closed doors will be <u>proclaimed</u> <u>upon the housetops.</u> 4 I tell you, my friends, <u>do not fear those who kill the body,</u> and after that can do nothing more. 5 But I will warn you whom to fear: <u>fear him who,</u> after he has killed, has authority to cast into <u>hell.</u> Yes, I tell you, fear him. 6 <u>Are not</u> five <u>sparrows sold for</u> two <u>pennies? Yet not one of them</u> is forgotten before God. 7 But <u>even the hairs of your head</u> have <u>all been counted.</u> <u>Do not be afraid;</u> <u>you are of more value than many sparrows.</u>	5 Know what is before your face, and what is hidden from you will be revealed to you; for there is <u>nothing</u> hidden <u>that will not</u> become manifest. 6.5–6 For there is <u>nothing</u> hidden <u>that will not become</u> manifest, and there is nothing covered that shall remain without being revealed. 33.1 What you shall hear <u>into the ear</u> <u>proclaim</u> into the other ear <u>upon the housetops.</u>

The grouping here consists of three distinct units – Q 12.2–3, 4–5 and 6–7. The first (12.2) has parallels in Mark 4.22 and a doublet in Luke 8.17 (presumably following Mark), as well as the two *Thomas* versions (*Gos. Thom.* 5.2 and 6.5). To this have been added to form the Q cluster the second and third units (Q 12.4–5 and 6–7), which do not appear to be recalled anywhere else.[45] An interesting variation, however, is that the first unit (Q 12.2–3) has also been appended to a different saying about revelation, by both Mark and Luke (Mark 4.21/Luke 8.16). At this point the interest quickens further, since the same saying is also preserved elsewhere in Q material (Matt 5.15/Luke 11.33), as well as in *Gos. Thom.* 33.2.

---

[45] Some more detail is provided in Dunn 2003b:496–7, 552 n. 47.

Matt. 5.15	Mark 4.21	Luke 8.16	Luke 11.33	*Gos. Thom.* 33.2
Nor do they ignite a lamp and put it under a bushel, but on a lampstand, and it gives light to all in the house.	Is a lamp brought in to be put under a bushel, or under a bed? Is it not to be put on a lampstand?	No one lights a lamp and hides it under a jar, or puts it under a bed, but puts it on a lampstand, that those who enter may see the light.	No one lights a lamp and puts it in a hidden place or under a bushel, but on a lampstand, that those who enter may see the radiance.	No one lights a lamp and puts it under a bushel, or in a hidden place, but puts it on a lampstand that all who enter and leave may see its light.

So we have a fascinating sequence of permutations, where the same or similar material (Q 12.2/Mark 4.22/Luke 8.17) has been linked one way (#4.11 above), in another way with a different revelation saying (Mark 4.21/ Luke 8.16) and known in two versions (also Matt 5.15/Luke 11.33), with *Thomas* providing a further variation by linking the other variations together in *Gos. Thom.* 33 (33.1/Q 12.3; 33.2/Mark 4.21/Q 11.33).

All this indicates a motif in the remembered teaching of Jesus which provided stimulating teaching material for many of the early Christian communities, with the result that it has come down to us in multiplied and varied forms. The variations are hardly to be explained on a hypothesis of Matthew and Luke knowing such tradition in only two written documents (Q and Mark), as though tradition to be transmitted had to be written, and as written formed the only two streams of tradition of the material available. By far the more obvious explanation is that the tradition of the sayings was much used and reused, reflected on and discussed in the various disciple and early Christian groupings.[46] This is not finished tradition, already shaped into final canonical form. It is living tradition. In these passages the twenty-first-century reader is able to overhear the varied forms of the tradition as they were rehearsed and mulled over in the earliest Christian assemblies.

4.12 Matt. 10.19–20/ Luke 12.11–12/ (Mark 13.11; John 14.26)

Matt. 10.19–20	Luke 12.11–12	Mark 13.11	John 14.26
19 When they hand you over, do not worry how or what you will speak; for it will be given to you in that hour what you will speak; 20 for it is not you who are speaking, but the Spirit of your Father speaking in you.	11 When they bring you before the synagogues, the rulers, and the authorities, do not worry how you will defend yourselves or what you are to say; 12 for the Holy Spirit will teach you in the same hour what you ought to say.	And when they take you, handing you over, do not worry what you will speak, but whatever is given to you in that hour speak; for it is not you who are speaking, but the Holy Spirit.	But the Advocate, the Holy Spirit, whom the Father will send in my name, he will teach you everything, and remind you of all that I have said to you.

[46] Cf. Schröter 1997:369.

Jesus here is remembered as encouraging his disciples with the promise of inspiration in the hour of persecution (cf. Luke 21.12–15). A curiosity is the decision of most Q specialists to include the passage in Q.[47] For on normal reckoning of literary dependence and redactional modification, Matthew is more obviously explained as drawn directly from *Mark*. Consequently the basic agreement between Matthew and Luke (independent of Mark) on which the whole Q hypothesis is predicated ceases to exist; the indications that Matthew knew a second (Q) version of the saying are wholly lacking. None the less, the variations, including John, could be adequately explained on an oral hypothesis: Luke is demonstrating the kind of variation and elaboration which one might find in a particular performance of a familiar saying (whether known in written or only in oral forms); whereas in John the saying has been given a different direction to become the core or basis of a major strand of the extended discourses in John 14–16.

This fourth group of sayings (##4.11–12) hardly seems to form any kind of coherent unit. Quite why #4.12 should be separated from #5.13, which follows, or indeed why Q 12.6–7 has been held apart from Q 12.22–31, is not at all clear. Is it simply that some hortatory repertoires had linked sayings with slightly different purposes and the links were retained through the various transitions of the Q (and larger) tradition? In any case, the material in these sections evidently allowed a fair variety of ordering, probably typical of the permutations and combinations of many different teaching occasions rather than evidence of a careful composition.

5 THE RIGHT PRIORITIES – Q 12.22–31, 33–4

5.13   Matt. 6.25–33/ Luke 12.22–31/ (P. Oxy. 655/ *Gos. Thom.* 36)

Matt. 6.25–33	Luke 12.22–31	P. Oxy. 655/ *Gos. Thom.* 36
25 <u>Therefore I tell you, do not worry</u> <u>about your</u> life, what you will eat or what you will drink, <u>or about your body, what</u> <u>you will wear</u>. Is not life <u>more than</u> <u>food, and the body more than clothing?</u> 26 Look at the birds of the air; <u>they</u> <u>neither sow nor reap</u> nor gather into <u>barns, and yet</u> your heavenly Father <u>feeds them</u>. Are you not of <u>more</u> <u>value than</u> they? 27 <u>And</u> <u>can any of you by worrying add a single</u> <u>hour to your span of life?</u>	22 <u>Therefore I tell you, do not worry</u> <u>about your life, what you will eat,</u> or about your body, what <u>you will wear</u>. 23 For <u>life is more than</u> <u>food, and the body more than clothing.</u> 24 Consider the ravens: <u>they</u> <u>neither sow nor reap</u>, they have neither storehouse nor <u>barn, and yet</u> God <u>feeds them</u>. Of how much <u>more</u> <u>value</u> are you <u>than</u> the birds! 25 <u>And</u> <u>can any of you by worrying add a single</u> <u>hour to your span of life?</u> 26 If then you	Jesus said: <u>Do not</u> <u>worry</u> from morn- ing to evening and from evening to morning <u>what you</u> <u>will eat</u> or about your robe, <u>what</u> <u>you will wear.</u>

You are much better than the |

---

[47] Kloppenborg 1988:126; *CEQ* reconstructs the text on the basis of Luke's version – 'When they bring you before synagogues, do not be anxious about how or what you are to say; for [[the Holy Spirit will teach]] you in that … hour what you are to say.'

28 And why do you worry about clothing? Consider the lilies of the field, how they grow; they neither toil nor spin, 29 yet I tell you, that even Solomon in all his glory was not clothed like one of these. 30 But if God so clothes the grass of the field, which is alive today and tomorrow is thrown into the oven, will he not much more clothe you, you of little faith? 31 Therefore do not worry, saying, 'What will we eat?' or 'What will we drink?' or 'What will we wear?' 32 For it is the nations that strive for all these things; and indeed your heavenly Father knows that you need all these things. 33 But seek first the kingdom of God and his righteousness, and all these things will be given to you as well.	are not able to do so small a thing as that, why do you worry about the rest? 27 Consider the lilies, how (they grow): they neither spin nor weave; yet I tell you, even Solomon in all his glory was not clothed like one of these. 28 But if God so clothes the grass in the field, which is alive today and tomorrow is thrown into the oven, how much more will he clothe you, you of little faith! 29 And do not keep striving for what you are to eat and what you are to drink, and do not keep worrying. 30 For it is the nations of the world that strive for all these things, and your Father knows that you need them. 31 Instead, seek his kingdom, and these things will be given to you as well.	lilies which do not card or spin. And having one clothing ... you ... Who might add to your span of life? He will give you your clothing.

This is one of the better examples of the strength of the case for a written Q, a judgment which I have no wish to dispute.[48] Even so, the variations between Matthew and Luke are of no great weight,[49] apart from the final verse of each, and smack more of performance variation than of careful editing. It is possible that the tradition recalls a sustained sequence of teaching given by Jesus on one or more occasions and held in that shape in the tradition that was gathered by Q.[50] Alternatively, more disparate tradition was put into its present shape by Q or earlier, presumably to provide some teaching resource for church teachers.[51] This tradition continued to be known in oral form and in different sequence (P. Oxy. 655/ *Gos. Thom.* 36, paralleling Q 12.22, 27, 25).[52]

5.14 Matt. 6.19–21/ Luke 12.33–4/ (*Gos. Thom.* 76.3)

Matt. 6.19–21	Luke 12.33–4	*Gos. Thom.* 76.3
19 Do not store up for yourselves treasures on earth, where moth and rust consume and where thieves break in and steal; 20 but store up for yourselves treasures in heaven, where neither moth nor rust consumes and where thieves do not break in and steal. 21 For where your treasure is, there will be also your heart.	33 Sell your possessions, and give alms. Make purses for yourselves that do not wear out, an unfailing treasure in the heavens, where no thief comes near and no moth destroys. 34 For where your treasure is, there also your heart will be.	You also must seek for his treasure which does not perish, which abides where no moth comes near to eat and (where) no worm destroys.

[48] Other examples in Dunn 2003b:147 n. 29.

[49] Matt 6.31 sounds like the product of a more vigorous performance than Luke 12.29.

[50] In an oral community the transition from original teaching to well-formed and stable tradition would not require it to be written down, either to retain the impact of the original teaching or to ensure that the stability was retained in transmission.

[51] For the more common debate see Kloppenborg 1987:216–18.

[52] Cf. Betz 1995:466–8. For the debate as to whether P. Oxy. 655 or Q 12.22–31 is the earlier, see bibliography in Dunn 2003b:552 n. 45.

Here is a case, somewhat like #1.5 above, where some teaching has been preserved by Matthew and Luke attached to a proverbial saying of Jesus (Matt 6.21/Luke 12.34).[53] As is typically the case with such proverbs or epigrams, it has a stable form. The teaching which precedes the proverb has a common theme elaborated, and once again with the sort of variant illustrative detail which could be expected in a live performance (Matthew's 'rust', Luke's 'purses'). It is entirely possible that Jesus' teaching, perhaps on more than one occasion (why not?), provided the theme and the climactic proverb (cf. Mark 10.21 pars. – 'treasure in heaven').[54] The theme is retained (without the proverb) in *Gos. Thom.* 76.3, and Jas 5.2–3 reads like a further variant on the same theme.[55] Such variation has the character of an oral tradition played out with variations in the course of many performances more than of literary editing where the climactic punch-line has been dropped as a deliberate editorial decision.[56]

In this case (#5) one can readily see that two such themes of personal counselling might be grouped into a composite unit.

6 THE CHALLENGE OF DISCIPLESHIP – Q 13.24; 14.26–7; 17.33; 14.34–5

6.15   Matt. 7.13/ Luke 13.24

Matt. 7.13–14	Luke 13.24
13 Enter through the narrow gate; for the gate is wide and the road is easy that leads to destruction, and there are many who enter through it. 14 For the gate is narrow and the road is hard that leads to life, and there are few who find it.	24 Strive to enter through the narrow door; for many, I tell you, will try to enter and will not be able.

Once again we encounter a saying in which it is hard to envisage the thought processes behind a literary derivation. Why would Luke omit the bulk of a longer written text (= Matt 7.13–14)? Or why should Matthew

[53] The fact that there are partial parallels in contemporary Jewish exhortation (see Kloppenborg 1987:221–2 nn. 206–8) may only mean that Jesus was remembered as putting his own stamp on such a familiar theme.
[54] See further Dunn 2003b:521 n. 158.
[55] The discussion by Hartin 1991:179–81, assumes an 'original wording' of Q, that is, a tradition known only in a single fixed (written) form.
[56] Contrast the typical discussion of sources by Fitzmyer 1985:981, where the 'sources' assume a literary fixedness.

elaborate so extensively a shorter written text (= Q 13.24)?[57] The more obvious explanation is that a saying of Jesus about the challenge and difficulty of entering upon the way of discipleship, using the memorable imagery of a narrow entrance, has been variously formulated and used in different versions in the various congregations which cherished Jesus' teaching and reflected often on the traditions of that teaching. Matthew('s community) was familiar with one version, Luke('s) with the other. An identifiable Q version (= Luke 13.24) is quite possible, but an unnecessary hypothesis. And if Matthew did know a Q 13.24, he handled it with the liberty of a seasoned raconteur, free to elaborate as the dynamic of rapport with a live audience prompted.

6.16 Matt. 10.37–8/ Luke 14.26–7/ (*Gos. Thom.* 55, 101)

Matt. 10.37–8	Luke 14.26–7	*Gos. Thom.* 55	*Gos. Thom.* 101
37 He who loves <u>father</u> or <u>mother</u> more than me is not worthy of me; and he who loves son or daughter more than me is not worthy of me. 38 And he <u>who</u> ... <u>does not</u> take <u>his cross and</u> follow <u>after me</u> is <u>not</u> <u>worthy of me</u>.	26 If anyone comes to me and does <u>not hate</u> <u>his father and</u> <u>mother</u>, wife and children, brothers and sisters, yes, and even life itself, he <u>cannot be</u> <u>my disciple</u>. 27 <u>Whoever</u> ... <u>does not</u> <u>carry his</u> own <u>cross and</u> come <u>after me</u> cannot be my disciple.	Jesus said: Whoever will <u>not hate</u> <u>his father and his</u> <u>mother</u> ... will <u>not be able to be</u> <u>my disciple</u>; and whoever will not hate his brothers and his sisters and will not <u>carry</u> <u>his cross</u> as I have, will <u>not</u> be <u>worthy of me</u>.	Jesus said: Whoever will <u>not hate</u> <u>his fa[ther] and his</u> <u>mother</u> as (I do), ... will <u>not be able to be</u> <u>my d[iscip]le</u>. And <u>whoever</u> will [not] love his [father and] mother as I do, will not be able to be my d[isciple], for [my mother] ...

That Jesus was remembered as posing the challenge of discipleship in extreme terms (the disciple must 'hate his father and mother') is almost universally accepted.[58] Matthew's editorial hand is most evident in the softening of the saying's offensiveness ('love' less, rather than 'hate'), and in the insertion of the motif 'is not worthy of me' in verses 37 and 38.[59] On the hypothesis that the only forms of tradition available and known to Thomas were written, we would have to conclude that Thomas knew both Luke, or Luke's version of Q (not only the word 'hate', but also talk of 'carrying' his cross), and Matthew as well (Matthew's distinctive 'not worthy of me', possibly also the confused talk of 'loving father and mother' in *Gos. Thom.* 101.2). But it is more plausible that two sayings of Jesus, about the disciple hating his parents and about the disciple having to carry his cross,

---

[57] Davies and Allison 1988–97 (1:694) attribute 7.13–14 to M, Q^Mt, or Q + heavy redaction.
[58] Bibliography in Dunn 2003b:592 n. 217.
[59] *Axios* ('worthy') is a thematic term for Matthew in this chapter; note also Matt 10.10–13.

circulated orally in the early churches in various permutations, of which the four versions above are probably a fair sample.

6.17   Matt. 10.39/ Luke 17.33/ (John 12.25)

Matt. 10.39	Luke 17.33	John 12.25
He who finds his life will lose it, and he who loses his life for my sake will find it.	Whoever seeks to make his life secure will lose it, and whoever loses (it) will preserve it.	He who loves his life loses it, and he who hates his life in this world will keep it for life eternal.

The theme of discipleship and its cost evidently featured regularly in Jesus' teaching as it was recalled in disciple communities. We have already noted the collection of sayings in #2.6 above and Mark 8.34–8 pars. Now we add Q 17.33 as well as Q 14.26–7 (#6.16). Notable is the evidence of diverse selection and grouping from a larger resource of such sayings: in Matthew the last two/ three sayings are put together (Matt 10.37–9), whereas in Luke they are quite separate (Luke 14.26–7; 17.33); and the #6.17 saying has quite a close parallel in Mark 8.35 pars. ('Whoever wishes to save his life will lose it, but whoever loses his life for my sake . . . will save it'). In addition, John 12.25 indicates a wider knowledge of a saying of Jesus posing the same essential challenge (he who cherishes his life will lose it), once again indicating a Synoptic-like saying of Jesus used as a springboard for John's own reflections.[60] To explain all this in terms of literary derivation from one or two texts (Mark and Q) requires ingenuity of explanation for the variations in setting and inconsequential detail. It is much simpler to infer a flexible repertoire of teaching on discipleship[61] known to most teachers in the early churches and taught in various combinations and forms as occasion permitted, to which variety and flexibility the present state of the tradition bears ready witness.[62]

6.18   Matt. 5.13/ Luke 14.34–5/ (Mark 9.49–50)

Matt. 5.13	Luke 14.34–5	Mark 9.49–50
13 You are the salt of the earth; but if the salt has become tasteless, by what will it be restored? It is no longer good for anything, but is thrown out to be trampled under foot.	34 So salt is good; but if even the salt has become tasteless, by what can it be seasoned? 35 It is fit neither for the earth nor for the manure heap; they throw it out.	49 For everyone will be salted with fire. 50 Salt is good; but if the salt has become without content, by what will you season it? Have salt in yourselves, and be at peace with one another.

[60] See n. 23 above.

[61] The range of the repertoire could be easily extended; see, e.g., the material discussed in Dunn 2003b:425–6, 503–5.

[62] So Dodd 1963:338–43: 'The least difficult hypothesis to account for the likenesses and differences . . . is that this very fundamental saying had a place in many separate branches of oral tradition' (343).

The saying has the same character as we have already noted in ##1.2, 1.5, 2.8, 5.14 and 6.15. A tightly worded proverb has retained its essential point across the enduring strands of tradition, though the corollary has not been deemed so important as to be retained in fixed form. This suggests a proverb referred back to Jesus, but its corollary formulated and elaborated as individual teachers deemed appropriate.

In #6 as a group one can see some sort of link in terms of the challenges and responsibilities of discipleship. But to suppose that these four units formed a single group in Q¹ seems rather far-fetched, given the diverse locations of the material in Matthew and Luke. The middle two items (##6.16–17) would much more naturally have been linked with other groups, as in Mark 8.34–8 pars. That they formed part of a much wider repertoire of many early Christian apostles and teachers I have already suggested, and that is probably how the four units should be seen, not as a single cluster but as one permutation of elements from the larger resources of the widely known oral Jesus tradition.

To conclude: Kloppenborg suggests that the material reviewed above forms a coherent group and, in all likelihood, 'a discrete redactional stratum' = Q¹, 'the formative stratum' of Q. He offers two principal reasons for this conclusion. (1) 'These clusters share a common rhetoric – the rhetoric of persuasion, rather than that of prophetic pronouncement or declamation', in contrast to the rhetoric of defence or attack that characterizes the rhetorical strategy of the main redaction (Q²). (2) The subcollections display 'a common structure, beginning with program-matic sayings (6.20b–23; 9.57–60; 11.2–4; 12.2–3; 13.24), continuing with second person imperatives, and concluding with a saying that under-scores the importance of the instructions (6.47–49; 10.16, 23–24; 12.33–34; 14.34–35)'.[63]

As regards the first argument (1), 'the rhetoric of persuasion' is a very broad and indiscriminating category. It applies to a wide range of the teaching material in the Jesus tradition; indeed, it can embrace most of the material grouped by Matthew in his several collections (Matt 5–7, 10, 13, 18). What becomes clear from Kloppenborg's reasoning is that the decisive consideration for him is not the presence of rhetoric common to the Q¹ material, but the *absence* of the warnings of coming judgment,

---

[63] Kloppenborg Verbin 2000:144–5. It is not clear how the further material suggested by Kloppenborg for inclusion in Q¹ (nn. 7, 13 above) fits in with this analysis.

which he judges, not unfairly, to be evidence of Q^2 redaction (particularly Q 6.23c; 10.12, 13–15; 12.8–10).[64] But even on the hypothesis of Q as a written document, that hardly constitutes evidence of more than that the compiler of Q used the theme of coming judgment as a means of linking disparate teaching material which he may have been ordering into a whole for the first time. It is equally possible, on the Q hypothesis, that the compiler selected material and versions, or gave his own 'performance' of well-known material and themes in the oral Jesus tradition, drawing the material from a wider pool available in a variety of measures in the various churches known to him. It does not follow that the Q material shorn of its polemical and threatening elements[65] formed an already coherently organized single block of material, let alone that it was known in a single written form.[66]

The argument of a common structure (2) is rather tendentious. To describe ##1.1, 2.6, 3.9, 4.11, 6.15 as 'programmatic sayings' is a substantial overstatement (#5 apparently lacks such a saying). Almost any of the sayings in any of the sections could have been placed first and been designated 'programmatic'.[67] Likewise Kloppenborg's observation that the clusters conclude 'with a saying that underscores the importance of the instructions' (but ##3 and 4 apparently lack such a saying) is more in the eye of the beholder than in the text: the explanation works well with #1,[68] but in ##5 and 6, different sayings could have served that function.[69] The reality is that the groups for the most part are simply that, groups of sayings on a similar theme; and the two in #4 don't seem to form a particularly coherent unit anyway.

[64] Kloppenborg 1987:242–3; similarly, Q 13.25–7, 28–30, 34–5 and 14.16–24 are omitted from the #6 material because of its 'polemical thrust' (Kloppenborg 1987:235–7).

[65] Did teachers never utter threats and warnings to outsiders mixed with their exhortations to their communities? Kloppenborg's neat distinction between a tone which is 'hortatory and instructional' and one which is 'polemical and threatening', or between proverbs and wisdom sayings 'to reinforce ethical imperatives' and those 'to undergird the pronouncements of judgment' (Kloppenborg 1987:238–9) evokes more the clinical dissection of an anatomy class than the rhetoric of a fervent teacher.

[66] Tuckett 1996: 'It is not clear why the Q¹ layer should be considered as a unity at all ... it is a big step to jump from earlier (possibly disparate) material to a unified collection of sapiential speeches in a Q¹' (71; see further 71–4). The disagreements with Zeller and Piper (n. 5 above) also give cause for hesitation. Zeller 1992 gives a negative answer to his question ('Eine weisheitliche Grundschrift in der Logienquelle?'); see also those cited in Dunn 2003b:156 n. 80.

[67] Piper 1989 notes that each of his collections, which cut across Kloppenborg's, 'begins with a rather general aphoristic saying' 'usually followed by a general maxim in statement form which provides ostensible support for whatever is being encouraged' (61).

[68] Kloppenborg 1987:185–7.

[69] Note again Piper 1989:63 in regard to *his* collections: 'The final unit of the aphoristic collections always provides the key for interpreting the meaning.'

In short, then, the case for designating the material reviewed above as a discrete compositional unit or stratum is weak. Just as unconvincing is the hypothesis that this material was the formative stratum of Q, that compositional techniques can so readily be distinguished from redactional techniques.[70] Much the more likely hypothesis is that this material, both in the variation of individual content and detail and in the diversity of groupings of the individual units, reflects the pattern of oral tradition. That is, the material as we still have it reflects the flexibility of oral performance, of teachers drawing upon resources of Jesus tradition, much at least of it shared with other churches and teachers, and reteaching it with variant details and emphases which reflect their own idiosyncrasies, the vagaries of live performance and the needs of particular congregations. In a word, the so-called Q¹ material is best understood as oral tradition.

[70] See further Dunn 2003b:155–7, with bibliography.

CHAPTER 4

Eye-witness memory and the writing of the Gospels

Form criticism, community tradition and the authority of the authors

Martin Hengel

For the last several decades, Graham Stanton has worked primarily in Gospels and Jesus research.[1] Following in his footsteps, these reflections concentrate on how the 'history of Jesus', of which we have only fragmentary knowledge, is related to the four Gospels as the oldest narrative reports about him.

I

In studies of the Gospels, one often reads that they were not concerned to be 'historical narratives' (let alone 'biographies') but above all witnesses of faith and means of proclamation, so that questions of historicity completely miss their intention.[2] As a result of this judgment, Protestant Synoptic exegesis since ca. 1920 followed by its Catholic counterpart since ca. 1960 suffered *a certain loss of historical interest*; the individual Synoptic texts were often questioned only about the theology of their author or their narrative strategy and historical studies were often discredited as 'naïve historicism'. The one-sided flood of redaction-critical, linguistic, narrative and socio-rhetorical studies in recent decades has its source here. In reality, however, the Synoptic Gospels consciously intend to narrate *a temporally removed event of the past, i.e., Jesus' unique history, which, of course, has fundamental significance for the present time of the evangelists* and the communities addressed through them, indeed for all humanity, since what is narrated is already for Mark *euangelion* which wishes to convey saving faith in Jesus

---

[1] I thank Wayne Coppins for his translation. Literature: Jeremias 1971a:13ff.; Roloff 1970; Hengel 1971; Hengel 1984b; Hengel 1985a; Hengel 1993; Hengel 2000; Hengel 2002b; Hengel and Schwemer 2001; Riesner 1988; Stanton 1974; Stanton 2002; Stanton 1992a; Stanton 1995; Stanton 1997; Byrskog 2000; Dunn 2003a; Dunn 2003b. Translator's note: In order to remain faithful to Professor Hengel's citations of German texts, I have both drawn upon and modified existing translations. When possible I have consulted J. Bowden's translations in Hengel 2000.

[2] Marxsen 1969:131. See already Bultmann 1972:371–2: 'the *Gospels are expanded cult legends*'; 'there is no historical-biographical interest' in them.

as Messiah and Son of God. The closing statement of John 20.31 basically applies to all four Gospels.[3] All, however, even John, remain fully conscious of the difference between the time of Jesus and the later time of the church.[4] All emphasize that the disciples did not really understand Jesus' activity, dignity and way before Easter. They do not present a timeless cult-myth, but continue the Old Testament narration of the 'great acts of God'[5] towards his people in their history. These acts reach their divinely intended fulfilment in Jesus' activity, death and resurrection,[6] and the message of this event is to spread worldwide in the prophetically promised mission to the nations until the *parousia*.[7] Jesus and the salvation wrought through him thus appear as the unique and incomparable consummating act of God, that is, as an 'eschatological event', yet in space and time, i.e., in Galilee, Judaea and Jerusalem, in the time of John the Baptist, Annas and Caiaphas, Herod (Antipas), Pilate, and Tiberius Caesar;[8] one could also say: as the beginning of the end of history. In the Gospels, and especially in the Synoptics, history and eschatology are not perceived as absolute opposites. One could speak with some justification of an undue and goal-oriented *'end history', which had to be narrated* and has in view beyond Jesus' death and resurrection the real end of the 'old aeon' in the 'coming' of the Son of Man. For this reason, the 'apocalyptic' chapters of Mark 13, Luke 21 and Matt 24 and 25 stand between Jesus' activity and passion, and, at the end, the resurrected Christ refers to his presence in the church 'until the end of the world' (Matt 28.20). This view of the *parousia* and the *eschatē hēmera* even applies to the Fourth Gospel, whose future horizon may not be completely eliminated.[9] The Gospels are simply not understood if one fails to appreciate their fundamental *'salvation-historical'* direction, which presupposes the 'promise history' of the Old Testament, equally narrative in character.

---

[3] Mark 1.1; 14.9. The term appears seven times in Mark and is always redactional.

[4] Cf., e.g., John 17.20f. and 20.29 (cf. 1 Pet 1.8).

[5] Acts 2.11: *ta megaleia tou theou*. LXX: Deut 11.2; Ps 71.19 (LXX 70.19); 106.21 (105.21); Sir 18.4; 33.8 (36.7). Also, the narrative of the election of the patriarchs and the exodus was 'good news' for the Jews because these events established the salvation of Israel.

[6] Mark 1.14f.: *peplērōtai ho kairos*. Cf. Luke 16.16; Gal 4.4; Rom 8.3 and above all John 19.30: *tetelestai, hina plērōthē hē graphē*.

[7] Mark 13.10 par.; 14.9 par.; Luke 2.31; 24.47; Matt 28.18–20; John 17.20ff.; 20.21.

[8] Cf. Luke 3.1f. following Old Testament examples: see Jer 1.1–3 (LXX); Isa 1.1; 6.1; Ezek 1.1; Hos 1.1; Amos 1.1 etc. The historical date 'in the fifteenth year of Tiberius Caesar' (ca. AD 28) also follows prophetic examples. See the references to Augustus, King Herod and Archelaus in Luke 2.1, and Matt 2.1, 22; see also Ign. *Smyrn.* 1.2 (Herod Antipas) and 1 Tim 6.13. The fact that Pontius Pilate still appears in the Apostles' Creed should make those who despise all historical questions think again.

[9] Cf. John 5.28; 6.39f., 44, 54; 12.26, 31f.; 14.2f.; 15.6; 21.22f.; see Frey 1997–2000.

While the Gospels may not be 'biographies' in the modern sense, they are comparable, despite their unique eschatological determination, to ancient 'life descriptions' and were also understood as such in antiquity. This is shown by Justin's use of the term *apomnēmoneumata tōn apostolōn*, the 'memoirs of the apostles', which replaces for Gentiles the easily misunderstood term *euangelia*, and echoes Xenophon's 'memoirs of Socrates'.[10] This is valid, although in their intention they were and are texts *sui generis*. The parallels are undeniable. Even in Plutarch one sometimes looks in vain for a chronological ordering of the material, and for Suetonius this is the rule. There too, sayings and anecdotes are strung together and occasionally unbelievable miracle stories are narrated. Moreover, an interest in the psychological development of the hero is likewise absent. The focus is not on a hero's genesis or development but on the ideal type: every part has the whole in view. Plutarch also has at least two biographies that could be designated on the basis of their structure as 'passion narratives with extended introductions'.[11] An ancient biography comprising anecdotes and sayings that closes with the exemplary self-determined death of its hero is Lucian's *Demonax*, a portrayal of a respected cynic philosopher (ca. 70–170) who starved himself to death in old age.[12] The biographical Pythagoras tradition of the Hellenistic period and the later lives of Pythagoras by Porphyry and Iamblichus portray their hero as a unique, divinely gifted teacher, revealer, miracle worker and bringer of salvation for his followers. Philostratus' *Life of Apollonius* is a propagandistic novel for the truly divine Pythagorean form of life, which also indirectly opposes ascendant Christianity. The ancient Christians could not understand the Gospels in any other way than as wholly unique and Spirit-inspired 'biographies' of their Lord and redeemer.

From the beginning, the collection and transmission of the Synoptic tradition was motivated by the need for evangelism and catechesis to preserve the *unique words and deeds of the Messiah Jesus* including his atoning death on the cross and the miracle of his resurrection.

---

[10] Justin, *1 Apol.* 67.3. He uses *apomnēmoneumata tōn apostolōn* fifteen times, the singular *euangelion* twice (*Dial.* 10.2; 100.1) and the still uncommon plural once. See Hengel 2000.

[11] In *Cato the Younger* (95–46 BC) chapters 58–73 address his final residence and death in Utica (ca. 46/47 BC); in *Eumenes* (361/62–316 BC) chapters 10–18 concentrate on the final four-year defensive battle against Antigonus. In *Sertorius* Plutarch mentions origin and education (chapter 2) in only a few lines and passes immediately to his heroic deeds against the Cimbri and Teutones under Marius. For the Gospels and ancient biographies, see Burridge 1992; Frickenschmidt 1997. The quotation is an allusion to M. Kähler's provocative description of the Gospels. Cf. Kähler 1964:80.

[12] See Cancik 1984a:115–30 (with bibliography). Lucian probably already knew Gospel texts and mocked them; see Hengel 2003a:93f. See also Uytfanghe 2001:1088–1363 (citing additional literature).

This intention to narrate truly unique 'salvation history' says little, of course, about the historical reliability of what is narrated in detail. Here, an 'ugly ditch' has opened and grown ever deeper since the beginning of critical historical research in the seventeenth/eighteenth century. One should not, however, weaken – let alone deny – the evangelists' basic intention to report about a historical person in space and time.

2

We do not have any written material from Jesus himself or his immediate circle of disciples, i.e., no one from this circle wrote a 'Jesus biography' based upon eye-witness testimony. The ascriptions of the Gospels to authors from the circle of the twelve are not historical. This applies to Matthew, to John the son of Zebedee and, all the more, to the alleged apostolic authors of the later 'apocryphal' gospels. An exception is presumably 'John the Elder', whom the tradition of Asia Minor designates as a 'disciple of the Lord' and whom Justin, Tatian and Valentinus' pupil Ptolemaeus later identify with John the son of Zebedee. But this man of Jerusalem hardly belongs to Jesus' most intimate circle, and his picture of Jesus leaves the historical figure of Jesus far behind in favour of his decidedly high Christology, so that the question of the 'historical tradition' behind the work remains an insoluble riddle.[13] In John, the evangelist's own literary-theological share in the formation of the tradition is by far the strongest, and it has suppressed 'history' to a great extent.[14]

Thus, even the claim to eye-witness testimony does not yet mean reliability in the actual 'historical' sense. On the basis of the deepened, even radically changed Christological insight attained through Easter and the experience of the Spirit, also an eye-witness could sketch a picture of Jesus that, according to our modern understanding, no longer corresponds to the historical reality.

This absence of early literary witnesses is all too easy to understand: one who awaits the end of the 'old, evil world' in the near future is not at first interested in a literary consolidation of history for posterity. It is enough to proclaim orally what the disciples and he himself have from their experience with Jesus. It is therefore no coincidence that the summarizing narrative presentation of Jesus-history did not begin until the late 60s

---

[13] Here we have hardly come further than the great Cambridge work of Dodd 1963. The response of Haenchen 1968:346–8 shows only how little Dodd was understood in Germany.

[14] See Hengel 1993.

with Mark after the death of the first generation's great witnesses.[15]
Collections of Jesus' sayings or miracles could be many decades older,
and yet they were not closed literary works but texts that were open for
additions in notebook form,[16] i.e., texts whose history of development we
can no longer discern. Scholarship has invested far too much industry in
written sources *before* the Gospels, and despite great astuteness and effort, it
has obtained little more than hypotheses difficult to prove. Of lasting value
is that Mark was Luke and Matthew's main source (in this order). He is the
most important under the *polloi* of Luke 1.1. Beyond this conclusion, we
can at best suppose from the note of Papias that the oldest Aramaic
prototype of a sayings-collection was connected with the name of the tax
collector Matthew, which was then translated into Greek by various
translators, and that various collections were attached to it.[17] These written
collections were then used especially by Luke and Matthew, while the
latter, in my view, also made use of Luke.[18]

   On the other hand, *in the relatively short period of his public ministry,* Jesus'
word and deed *had already made a great impact,* which the leaders of the
people quickly judged to be dangerous, for otherwise they would not have so
promptly and resolutely disposed of him with the help of the Roman prefect.
That his followers were already spreading his words and deeds orally contributed to this impact.[19] Moreover, the Pharisees and scribes who, according
to Mark 7.1ff., came from Jerusalem to Galilee to sound out the Jesus-
movement, or also the 'false witnesses' in the process against Jesus, show that
this also happened among his opponents.[20] The accusations against Jesus
also had wider effects and presumably played a role in subsequent condem-
nations of Christians in Jerusalem through Jewish authorities up to the
persecution under Agrippa I[21] and the proceedings against James the brother
of the Lord and other Jewish Christians in AD 62.[22] The evangelists are
completely correct to stress the lasting impact of Jesus upon the people. This
is a prerequisite for the relatively quick spread of the Jesus-movement after
Easter outside Galilee, e.g., in Jerusalem. Therefore, it is reasonable, even
necessary, to join an account of Jesus with that of the primitive church and
not to make a sharp separation between them as has been common since

---

[15] James was probably stoned in AD 62 and Peter and Paul executed in the Neronic persecution in AD 64.
    In my view Mark originated shortly before AD 70. See Hengel 1985a:1–30.
[16] See Sato 1988; Hengel 2000:116ff., 174f.   [17] In Eusebius, *Hist. Eccl.* 3.39.16.
[18] Cf. Hengel 2000:169–207.
[19] Cf. Mark 1.28; 3.7f.; Matt 4.23–5; 9.26; 14.1; Luke 4.14, 37; 6.17f.; 24.19; Acts 2.22; 10.37.
[20] Mark 14.56ff. = Matt 26.60ff.; cf. Mark 12.13 = Luke 20.20 = Matt 22.15. See Schürmann 1968.
[21] Acts 12.1ff.; cf. 1 Thess 2.14.   [22] Josephus, *Ant.* 20.198–203.

R. Bultmann and his school. The first 'community' basically begins with the calling of the disciples to follow Jesus.

3

After Easter, Jewish Christian *missionaries* needed *concrete information* concerning the 'words and deeds of the Lord'[23] when they founded new communities, for they had to bear narrative witness to what this exalted, crucified Messiah had done and said. One can no more call for faith in a merely title-bearing but otherwise mute and deedless redeemer than for trust in an anonymously crucified man. The message they proclaimed was too uncommon, even offensive,[24] for them not to have to report something definite about Jesus, particularly as they were constantly and energetically resisted by their Jewish and later Gentile opponents. *Missionary preaching was only possible by argument*, and this required the narration of Jesus' words and deeds. As Justin and Celsus show, one argued not only about Old Testament 'prophecies', but also very concretely about Jesus' person and message. The Christians had to defend themselves against the accusation that he was an agitator, seducer, deceiver, magician, or one possessed, who was rightly condemned to such a shameful death. Therefore, Justin consciously appealed to the 'memoirs of the apostles'. This means, however, that the proclaimed Jesus Christ was more than a mere 'mathematical point'. One could not limit him to a 'historical' crucifixion and a 'mythical' resurrection and exaltation, i.e., he could not be reduced to Bultmann's 'mere fact of his coming'.[25] *Without the narration of Jesus tradition the stereotyped 'kerygma' would have*

---

[23] Papias according to Eusebius, *Hist. Eccl.* 3.39.15: *ta hypo tou kyriou ē lechthenta ē prachthenta.*

[24] Cf. 1 Cor 1.23; Gal 3.13; see also Hengel 1977:1ff.

[25] The formulation appears in Bultmann 1971:248 at 5.19: 'for his proclamation can only be the proclamation of the single fact of his coming, of the coming which is the eschatological event'. This is not even valid for the Fourth Gospel, which reports not a few 'facts'. See also Bultmann 1967:449f.: there, however, with the significant qualification on p. 454: 'the competence of the "Einleitungswissenschaft", i.e., the historical-critical analysis of the Synoptics with reference to the question of the objectively ascertainable Jesus history, reaches so far that it can confirm the "mere fact" claimed in the Kerygma against any scepticism towards Jesus' historicity and can also illustrate this to a certain degree with some probability'. The next sentence, 'what it, however, cannot do is provide proof that the historical continuity between Jesus and the kerygma is material correspondence', rests upon a fundamental error. The 'material correspondence' is grounded for primitive Christianity in the personal identity of the human being Jesus (as the Son of God who became human), who was crucified in Jerusalem, with the exalted Lord; this also included his *whole* 'prophetic-Messianic' activity, which was passed down as historical reality. What modern anti-historical scepticism wishes to separate was for them a unity. For the sake of this identity and continuity, which was foundational for the primitive church, the missionaries had to narrate the 'Gospel' as 'the history of Jesus' from the beginning, and Gospels were written later.

been incomprehensible to the church from the beginning. If he were to be proclaimed, the crucified Messiah Jesus of Nazareth had to be simultaneously 'painted before their eyes',[26] i.e., made present through the vivid narration of historical events. In all four Gospels there is, therefore, *necessarily* 'narration', whereby Mark and Luke stand closest to the historical reality. That there is little of this in the letters is related not only to the fact that they are largely occasional writings, but also to the 'letter' genre in which the narration of past events plays a secondary role, especially when these events were already well known to the community. In the letters of Paul, *the preaching at the founding of communities*, in which these 'original events'[27] were – necessarily – narrated, is only present in highly abbreviated form.[28] This means, however, that the primitive Christian messengers were dependent upon *memories* of Jesus from the beginning, first, as a rule, *also* upon *their own* experience with him. And yet they simultaneously began to exchange such traditions and presumably soon thereafter to preserve them in notebook form for personal and ecclesial use: thus one (or several?) basic form(s) of the passion story, but also a variety of Jesus' words and deeds. The material continuity between Jesus and the Greek-speaking missionary communities of Pauline (Galatia) and non-Pauline (Rome) character is visible, for example, in the unique, utterly uncommon Aramaic prayer 'Abba', Father, which goes back to Jesus and is rooted in the 'mystery of his sonship'.[29] The question is naturally how much the constant and varied kerygmatic and apologetic use of Jesus-memories shaped or reshaped the tradition in its selection and oral rendering. The changes – at first, above all, the *abbreviations and simplifications* – were certainly considerable. Of the abundant traditions available in the early period, the majority were lost in later decades. Moreover, as the Papias fragments, the *Gospel of Thomas* and similar texts show, the tradition gradually grew 'wild' in the course of time. Nevertheless, in the Synoptics, the overall impact of Jesus upon the tradition was remarkably maintained. This was possible because the tradition was at first secured by many witnesses.

4

Stimulated by the Old Testament scholar H. Gunkel and folklore research, the *form criticism* that arose with the end of the First World War attempted

---

[26] Gal 3.1; cf. also 1 Cor 2; 11.23f.; 15.3f. See Hengel 2004b.
[27] Cf. the *paredōka hymin en prōtois* at 1 Cor 15.3.   [28] See Wenham 1995.
[29] Gal 4.6; Rom 8.15; Mark 14.36; see Hengel 2004a.

to grasp the oral tradition before its written fixation. In the aftermath of
J. G. Herder and the Romantic Movement, it was concerned to work out
the forms of the pre-literary tradition and the 'laws' of its development
through an analysis of the Synoptic Gospels in order to unfold its *Sitz im
Leben* and often its secondary development. No longer was the bearer of
this tradition seen in the apostle, prophet or teacher who founded and *stood
over against the community as an authority*, but the community itself was
portrayed as a creative collective, which not only formed the tradition but
often also created it out of whole cloth. The much-used, but in reality
obscure and often vacuous, concept of *Gemeindebildung* (formation or
invention of the community) became dominant in Gospel criticism.
From the standpoint of the *Sache* (subject-matter) it is too vague insofar as
it tends to say little about what actually mattered, namely, when, where
and why a tradition was 'formed'. Here, the 'witness' (or 'assertion') of a
dominical tradition on the part of the Gospels is replaced by the rarely
verifiable hypothesis of a post-Easter fiction. Basically, the whole Jesus
tradition could naturally be designated as *Gemeindebildung*, for it was
'formed' by competent and authoritative members 'in contact with the
community', kept in memory, translated into Greek, shaped and narrated
into new situations and thereby proclaimed. But because it says too little,
one should either define this vague concept more precisely or abandon it
entirely. The simple opposition: authentic Jesus tradition–*Gemeindebildung*
greatly oversimplifies the complexity of the problem.

For the protagonist M. Dibelius, the point of departure was the identification of the Synoptic Gospels as *Kleinliteratur* (informal folk literature)
in which 'the personality of the author fades into the background'. As such,
they were largely assembled from anonymous 'collected material' that
originally appeared in 'small units' before being formed in the collective
of the community according to specific 'form-shaping laws'.[30] Bultmann
analysed all this material and classified it according to its 'forms' in the oral
tradition,[31] and yet his sometimes radical judgments concerning authenticity tended to be based *less on form than on content*. For example, he
identified as unhistorical *Gemeindebildungen* almost all the narrative material, including all miracle stories (assigned to the 'Hellenistic community')
and most controversy dialogues; the same applies to sayings in which Jesus
refers to his mission in the first person and those which indicate his
Messianic dignity. Here, Bultmann's approach characteristically indicates

---

[30] Dibelius 1919:1–4 = Dibelius 1933:1–8. See also Bultmann 1966:20.
[31] Bultmann 1995; Bultmann 1972.

that we are dealing with judgments that basically depend upon the 'pre-judgment' of the expositor.

5

The *narrative material was judged much more critically than the sayings tradition*, which shows itself to be more firmly fixed in a comparison of the Synoptics. Despite the variable narrative form, however, striking events are better kept in memory than the wording of oral proclamation – unless, of course, this was often repeated, a scenario that is not improbable for Jesus' preaching, but is widely underrated. Faithfulness to the wording of Jesus' message was made easier by its pictorial-graphic form in the approximately forty parables (ca. 29 per cent of the sayings material). A further mnemonic aid for the non-narrative spoken material was the poetic, Semitic form of the *parallelismus membrorum* and particularly the antithetical parallelism. Since this form was relatively uncommon for Greeks, it was partly weakened in translation. It probably characterized Jesus' original preaching more strongly and ensured that his words remained fixed in memory. In smaller parables I assume that word pictures and parallelism were combined as in the prophets.[32] It is completely incomprehensible that the passion, the event that must have impressed itself most deeply upon the memory, should have fallen victim to the knife of radical criticism, leaving only paltry leftovers.[33] This new rigorous perspective found enthusiastic support after the First World War and even more after the Second World War in Germany for the following reasons:

(a) The emphasis upon preaching and worship in the forming of the material resonated with the dialectical Word-of-God theology. One tended to emphasize that everywhere and always 'the resurrected one' spoke, whatever one wished to understand by this mythically conceived cipher. Not actual memory but, above all, 'the faith of the community' was at work here. The question is whether these may be played off against each other so fundamentally. One could object: without memory there can be neither faith nor Gospels.

(b) The liberal '*Leben Jesu* scholarship' of the nineteenth century, which had partly misunderstood the Gospels as 'biographies' in the modern sense and had wanted to build its 'modern' Christology of Jesus as a

---

[32] For the meaning of pictorial and poetic speech for memorization see, e.g., Riesner 1988:302–404 and Dunn 2003a:139–75.
[33] See Hengel and Schwemer 2001:45–63, 133–63.

'religious genius' upon the 'picture of Jesus' obtained through historical reconstruction, was thereby reduced to absurdity.[34]

(c) In the steps of J. Wellhausen and W. Wrede and still prior to Bultmann
and Dibelius, K. L. Schmidt had above all demonstrated *the unhistorical character of the redactional framework in Mark*, which, for him,
made every attempt at a 'life of Jesus' impossible.[35]

(d) Behind it, in connection with dialectic theology, stood a certain, and
for Bultmann obvious, lack of interest in historical realities, which as
'objectifying' and 'given' *bruta facta* could not be theologically relevant. This was strengthened by efforts to prove the scientific nature of
one's work by means of the most radical criticism possible, and thus to
avoid the appearance of apologetics that is presumed to underlie the
pursuit of historical questions.[36]

In itself the form-critical question was able to become fruitful for the
exegesis of the Synoptic texts because through it the development, formation and combination of individual text units became more transparent.
Making it absolute, however, was questionable, as were attempts to pass
fundamentally negative judgments on the age and authenticity of large
parts of the Synoptic tradition solely on its basis, judgments that give the
impression of prejudiced decrees rather than insights gained through
historical-philological arguments.

6

More recent research in literary studies has shown that the Synoptic
evangelists were by no means 'only to the smallest extent authors' and

---

[34] See, e.g., Bultmann 1969:28–52. As theological thinking after ca. 1980 turned again more positively
to the nineteenth century, historical Jesus scholarship accordingly attracted a renewed interest. Cf.,
e.g., Theissen and Merz 1998.

[35] Schmidt 1919. The individual observations of K. L. Schmidt are largely to be granted: 'But on the
whole there is no life of Jesus in the sense of a developing life story, no chronological outline of the
story of Jesus, but only single stories, pericopes that are placed in a framework' (317). On the other
hand, he must also concede that the remains of an itinerary are still present in the pericope
introductions of Mark (317). Unfortunately he does not inquire further about where Mark obtains
the geographical and material-historical information of his framework and the 'collected reports'
bound together with it. 'Memory' or 'tradition' is also involved in the 'framework' in a free manner.
On the whole, the 'rough framework' in Mark makes good historical-geographical and chronological
sense. The activity of the Galilean Jesus from Nazareth is connected with John the Baptist; it begins
after Jesus' baptism in the Jordan in Galilee with public preaching, healings and the calling of
disciples, and it ends with his crucifixion during the time of the Passover in Jerusalem. For critical
engagement with K. L. Schmidt see Hall 1998, and especially the five critical questions on 162f.

[36] With respect to the complete rejection of 'objectifying thinking' in favour of 'existentially interpreted *Geschichtlichkeit* (historical situation)' see Hengel 2002a:413ff.

'principally collectors, tradents and editors'.[37] The opposite is true: *Mark is already a dramatic narrator who works with great reflection and argues theologically through the ordering and forming of his material,* though recent attempts to make his work the first kerygmatic or mythical 'Jesus-novel' are equally misleading.[38]

Mark wishes to proclaim the Gospel through the narration of what he views as a genuine history of Jesus. At the same time, he also enters with his new, revolutionary work as *a known authority in the church,* and he was recognized as such by the communities that accepted, used in worship and handed on his Gospel and, all the more, by authors such as Luke and Matthew who intensively reused it. Therefore, his unusual work *cannot* have been circulated *anonymously* from the beginning, for that would have disqualified it from the start. Just as all the Old Testament writings had titles that were identified before they were read in worship, so also the new writings of the Messianic community had titles, whether apostolic letters or Gospels.[39] The community had to know *which* text was being read. As in the prophetic books, the title indicates the authority of the author. Both the letters of Paul[40] (the only written testimonies prior to Mark) and Acts stress emphatically and in various ways the elevated, authoritative position of individual apostles and teachers, and Paul especially underlines his own apostolic authority in the prescripts of his letters. The tradents and shapers

---

[37] Dibelius 1919:1.

[38] For Mark as a brilliant narrator, see the ancient philologist Zuntz 1984:205–22 (222): 'a ... masterwork ... of amazing originality' – in contrast to the judgment of the form-critical school that the author was a 'mere compiler'. For the 'mythical' Mark-novel, see, e.g., Mack 1988.

[39] For the Old Testament, cf. Luke 4.17; Mark 1.2; 7.6; 12.35; Luke 3.4; 20.42; 24.44; Acts 1.20; 8.28; 13.33; Matt 3.3 etc. Writings without titles were hardly usable in worship. See Hengel 1984a; Hengel 2000:38–54. The suppositions of Bovon 2003:2.12f. are misleading: 'The Gospel of Matthew could have been called "Origin" (*genesis*) or "Life" (*bios*), just as Luke–Acts could have borne the title "Narrative" (*diēgēsis*), or Mark that of "Memoirs" (*hypomnēmata*).' Bovon cannot distinguish between the almost unlimited 'possibilities' and that which can be made plausible through the sources. Moreover, he not only confuses general literary genre and unique title but also fails to recognize the liturgical *Sitz im Leben* of the Gospel reading. There, a title must give the hearer some idea of the specific content of the work. It could hardly be completely formal. As von Campenhausen has shown, this reading in worship is in no way identical to the later 'canonization' which gradually followed after the end of the second and the beginning of the third century. Moreover, as a rule, a title should contain a reference to the author, unless authorship was universally known, as in the case of the Pentateuch. Hebrews was only passed on because it was included in the collection of the Pauline letters, i.e., the question of authorship had already been raised in the second century. Finally, in addition to the manuscript tradition, which extends to the second century, we also have varied supporting evidence for the uniformity of the titles of the Gospels and their authors, while there are no indications of an earlier variety. Bovon's supposition concerning secondary ecclesiastical 'stabilization efforts' that are supposedly responsible for the titles is misleading. For the reading of the title see Melito of Sardis *Pasch.* 1: *hē men graphē tēs hebraikēs Exodou anegnōstai.*

[40] Cf. especially Galatians and 1–2 Corinthians, e.g., 1 Cor 1.12; 9.1ff.; 15.1–11; Gal 1 and 2.

of the Jesus tradition must also have belonged to this circle, i.e., those to whom the communities looked for guidance.

The Cephas party in Corinth, which, in my judgment, goes back to a visit of the apostle in the capital of Achaia, probably esteemed the first eye-witness of the resurrection not least as an authorized bearer of Jesus tradition. In my view, the Palestinian-Jewish messengers who cause Paul such difficulties in 2 Cor 10 and 11 and whom he calls *pseudapostoloi* in anger-filled exasperation because they preach 'another Jesus'[41] could be envoys of Cephas' mission. With a view to the Jesus tradition, the former fisherman, first disciple and first witness of the resurrection was far superior to the former Pharisee Paul. A good portion of the Jesus tradition in the West may go back to his person via Mark. The relative lack of concreteness with which Paul speaks in his toilsome defence against the message of his opponents is strange. It is as little concerned with 'Judaizers' who wish to introduce circumcision again as it is with Gnostics or *theioi andres* (Divine Men). The conflict, which is enigmatic to us, is concerned with the contesting of Paul's apostolic authority by greater authorities. The conflict of Gal 2.1–18ff. was not long past, and the tensions released by it were still active. All these texts[42] show the extent to which the history of the twenty to twenty-five years following the crucifixion at Passover and the influence of the great authorities were at once present and subject to debate in the communities.

Should this not also apply to the narrators of the 'Jesus-story'? The weight of tradition was particularly dependent upon the authority of the tradents or authors. This is also shown by the early rabbinic parallels, which B. Gerhardsson has intensively discussed.[43]

7

The *weaknesses of Bultmann's position* were exposed by none other than his form-critical comrade-in-arms Dibelius in his two reviews of *The History of the Synoptic Tradition*:

It must be said quite emphatically that B's scepticism in all questions of historicity is not necessarily connected with form-critical criteria but with his conception of

---

[41] 2 Cor 11.4, 13. It is striking that no more names are mentioned in 2 Cor 10–13. That Paul consciously keeps his opponents anonymous means that he is neither willing nor able to name them.
[42] Cf. Gal 1.15ff.; 2.1ff., 18ff.; 1 Cor 1.12ff.; 9.1ff.; 15.1–11; see also the individual names listed in Rom 16.
[43] Gerhardsson 1998.

the nature of the primitive Christian community as well as his emphasis upon the difference between Palestinian and Hellenistic Christianity.

This difference, indeed opposition, has been strongly relativized in the past decades. As Acts 6 shows, the 'Hellenistic community' had its origin in Jerusalem, and one could designate the numerous bearers of tradition (such as John Mark, Barnabas, Philip, Paul, Silas/Silvanus, Judas, Barsabbas, Agabus, the prophets in Antioch et al.) who had connections to Aramaic- and Greek-speaking communities or stood between them as 'Graeco-Palestinian'. As a result, as Dibelius rightly emphasized, the differences between the communities are

of little significance for the form-critical question. For the Gospels show most clearly how slight the influence of new theological notions on the Gospel material actually was; otherwise belief in the Kyrios and sacramental theology would have had made themselves felt much more strongly.[44]

This means that the Synoptic Gospels, which originated between ca. AD 70 and 90/100 in the order Mark, Luke, Matthew, have in comparison with the simultaneous theological development (Ephesians, Hebrews, 1 Peter, the Johannine Corpus, *1 Clement*, the Pastorals, the letters of Ignatius) a strikingly 'conservative' character that is still oriented on Jewish Palestine and the primitive community, regardless of whether they originated in Rome (Mark), perhaps in Greece (Luke),[45] or in southern Syria or Palestine (Matthew).

A typical example of this 'conservative' character is the fact that in Mark and texts dependent upon him, James the son of Zebedee, who was executed by Agrippa I in AD 43,[46] always stands first in the catalogue of disciples before John, although John outlived him and later became influential, while James did not thereafter have any more significance for the church. Luke first rearranges the names in three places; in other places, however, he leaves the old Marcan order.[47] For him, John the son of

[44] Dibelius 1932; see also Dibelius 1922: Dibelius's protest is directed against the 'overstepping of the limits of pure form-critical method' and against the radical scepticism in questions of authenticity behind which stands an 'unbounded subjectivism' resulting from 'a lack of sensitive empathy'.

[45] Thus the oldest Gospel prologue; see Aland 1997:549.

[46] Acts 12.1f.; cf. Mark 10.39.

[47] Mark 1.19, 29; 3.17; 5.37; 9.2; 10.35, 41; 13.3; 14.33; Matthew mentions them with their full names only three times and, also following Mark, places James before them: 4.21; 10.2; 17.1; he speaks three times of the 'sons' of Zebedee. Contrast Luke 8.51; 9.28; Acts 1.13, cf. 12.2; old order Luke 5.10; 6.14; 9.54. In Acts, he places John next to Peter: 3.1; 4.19; 8.14ff., and allows James to recede completely; but cf. 12.1f.: that Agrippa had James executed and Peter arrested indicates that they were initially the most influential disciples of Jesus.

Zebedee, who probably outlived his brother James by quite some time, had gained greater relevance as a tradition-bearer, a move that is confirmed by Gal 2.9, where John is named as the last of the three 'pillars' after James the brother of the Lord and Cephas-Peter.[48] That, conversely, the Palestinian community itself, which stood under the leadership of the brother of Jesus from the persecution through Agrippa I to the stoning of James in AD 62, had no more influence upon the Synoptic tradition from the beginning of the 40s is shown by the fact that James and Jesus' other brothers play no positive role in the Gospels.[49] The evangelists admittedly knew them, but in Jesus' lifetime his brothers were not yet among his followers.[50] In this essential point too, history was not falsified. Luke alone, with a view to the later significance of John, placed him in Acts at the side of Peter from the beginning.

This geographical and historical interest in Jewish Palestine still pertains even in the Gospel of John,[51] whose high Christology[52] goes far beyond the Synoptic tradition and fundamentally changes the portrayal of Jesus.

8

It can certainly be said that the whole Synoptic tradition as we have it in the Greek language first received its oral and then its final literary formation in the 'Greek-speaking communities', but that is not yet a judgment on the age and historicity of the tradition. We do not know exactly in which communities this translation of the tradition into Greek occurred. In my view it began already in the Greek-speaking community of the Hellenists in Jerusalem. The written Gospels are only the end points of a temporally limited development of ca. four to seven decades.[53] It is characteristic that in Bultmann's *History of the Synoptic Tradition*, with its formal-analytic approach, the historical lapse of time and the dating questions bound up with it play as minor a role as the geographical space and the

---

[48] See Hengel 1993:88ff. For the meaning of John in Acts, see chapters 3 and 4 and 8.14 as well as 12.2.

[49] In complete contrast to *Gos. Thom.* 12 or the fragment of the *Gospel of the Hebrews* passed down by Jerome concerning the protophany of the resurrected one before James; *Vir. Ill.* 2: see Aland 1997:507.

[50] Mark 6.3 = Matt 13.55; cf. Acts 1.14; 12.17; 15.13; 21.17: Luke met him during Paul's journey to Jerusalem.

[51] After the death of its author, pupils edited the Gospel of John around AD 100–5 in Ephesus.

[52] Hengel 1999:292–334.

[53] Wellhausen, who transferred the methods of his Old Testament criticism to the Gospels, failed to take into account that whilst he had to reckon with centuries, only decades were available in primitive Christianity.

tradition-bearing persons. When Mark wrote shortly before the destruction of Jerusalem, disciples were still alive as eye-witnesses according to Mark 9.1. John 21.20–4 wishes to refer to the death of the last eye-witness and author of the Gospel. According to the apologist Quadratus, people healed by Jesus lived until his time (under Hadrian, AD 117–38).[54] Dibelius refers in this context to a concession by Bultmann:

The individual controversy dialogues may not be historical reports of particular incidents in the life of Jesus, but the general character of his life *is rightly portrayed in them, on the basis of historical recollection.*[55]

In his review, Dibelius notes here that 'this judgment' must apply 'naturally also to other groups of material', and he explicitly names the miracle stories. Beyond that, the passion story should, above all, be mentioned. The memory of the last night with the Passover meal and the events in Gethsemane as well as Judas' betrayal, Peter's denial and the actual passion were burned into the hearts of the disciples.[56] One must go further than Dibelius and say that such *general* judgments as Bultmann (with his aversion to the concrete and contingent nature of historical processes) all too often makes are, as a rule, misleading. On the whole, he was mistaken about large sections of the history of primitive Christianity, and the effects of his sometimes blatant errors are still present today.[57] The problem is that because of the lack of comparable source material, we cannot *prove* the historicity of particular events in the strict sense, so that relatively great latitude remains for personal assessment. It is therefore all the more important to inquire about their plausibility or probability on the basis of concrete criteria. This presupposes *inter alia* a fundamental knowledge of the Judaism of the time and its social and political environment, an area in which Bultmann and most of the representatives of his school had basically little interest.[58]

9

An errant judgment that misled form-critical research from the beginning was the claim that there are unequivocal 'laws' for the oral (and written) folklore tradition,[59] which must have also determined the 'history of the

---

[54] Eusebius, *Hist. Eccl.* 4.3.2; cf. Papias according to Philip Sidetes frag. 11 in Funk and Bihlmeyer 1924.
[55] Bultmann 1972:50 (my italics).   [56] See Hengel 2004b; Hengel and Schwemer 2001:45–63, 133–63.
[57] See Hengel 2003b.   [58] See Theissen and Winter 1997; Dunn 2003b:970 (index).
[59] See Schmidt 1981:79, with reference to W. Bousset; Dibelius 1919:1ff.; Bultmann 1921:3: 'and attempt to recognize the laws of the passing on of tradition'. While he is somewhat more restrained in the second edition, pp. 1–8(7), his judgments are all the more confident.

synoptic tradition'. E. Fascher had already protested against this.[60] E. P. Sanders does this concisely and precisely:

There are no hard and fast laws of the development of the Synoptic tradition. On all counts the tradition developed in opposite directions. It became both longer and shorter, both more and less detailed, and both more and less Semitic … For this reason, dogmatic statements that a certain characteristic proves a certain passage to be earlier than another are never justified … For this reason, we must always give room for human differences and be alert to editorial tendencies of each particular writer.[61]

This means that form-critical judgments in the area of the pre-literary tradition mostly remain uncertain in terms of the historicity of traditions. For this point, we will limit ourselves to one example: Dibelius distinguished between the short anecdotal *Paradigmata* and the *Novelle*, a developed narrative tale. The first he considered to be more historically reliable than the latter. As a rule, however, Matthew changes Mark's 'tales' through abrupt abridgement into *Paradigma*. Here, historical reliability is precisely not discernible from the form.

We are on relatively secure ground only when we can compare written texts with each other. Therefore, it is also impossible to inquire about Mark's written sources, to work out a Proto- or Deutero-Mark or to reconstruct convincingly a 'Logia source', Q, with various levels. This applies all the more for the postulate of a Proto-Luke, which Marcion is supposed to have used, or the assumption of multiple redactors, who sinned against a 'theologically correct' version of the Gospel of John and falsified it 'in the interests of the mainstream church'. Here, the wish is all too often father to the thought. In this fashion scholars seek to obtain 'sanitized' primitive writings, e.g., a John without future eschatology or a Logia tradition without apocalyptic offences. All sorts of things may be supposed, but only a few can be convincingly grounded. The principle that 'we must give room for human differences' (Sanders) applies already to the primitive Christian teachers and tradents of the oral tradition. With them, it is not primarily a one-sided, collective, law-conforming event, but rather a relatively free, person-bound event, which is connected not least with

---

[60] Fascher 1924:25, 84, 142ff., 225: '(B)ut one will not be able to say that Bultmann clearly worked out and presented as the fruit of analysis "the laws of the passing on of tradition" as he names them in the introduction (Bultmann 1921: 3). He speaks of motives of every kind, which had an effect on the material, but they are not "the laws of the passing on of tradition". Where he speaks of laws … one has the impression of having rather a general rule of the analyst before oneself' (143).

[61] Sanders 1969:272.

theological competence, i.e., with the authority of the authors as teachers
and that of their tradents.

10

A further neglected factor in form criticism, therefore, is personal memory,
which can hold fast what is seen and heard for decades. It is closely
connected with the phenomenon of the 'eye-witness'.[62] To begin with,
everyone has individual memory. Particular 'eye-witnesses' may observe
the same process rather differently and often only in a limited way. Of
course, there was simultaneously a constant exchange, which was then
'institutionalized' in primitive Christian worship through the community
of witnesses, in that 'the memory of Jesus' from his baptism by John[63] to his
passion and its interpretation was narratively proclaimed. There arose thus
a 'treasure of memory', which could be supplemented but also controlled.
Naturally, this exchange probably influenced and changed the witnesses'
own perception, a truth familiar to every judge accustomed to the inter-
rogation of witnesses. On the other hand, memory lasts for years, and the
memory of ancient people was also better than that of people today who
suffer from constant information overload and stimulus satiation. Even
today, however, one often remembers after many years the person from
whom one heard a certain anecdote (for example, about a certain scholar).
Without being committed to writing, such anecdotes can be kept in the
memory for a lifetime; the wording can change slightly in the narration
with the point remaining the same. Also the names of tradition-bearers can
be kept in the memory.[64]

In Mark, there are some references to individual names as possible
guarantors of memory, e.g., Simon of Cyrene, the father of Alexander
and Rufus, who were evidently still known to the Roman community at the
time of Mark.[65] By contrast, Luke and Matthew omit the names of the two
sons. They no longer have any significance for them. Other figures are

---

[62] Luke 1.2: *kathōs paredosan hēmin hoi ap' archēs autoptai kai hypēretai tou logou.*

[63] Cf. Acts 10.37–41; 13.23ff.

[64] For example, characteristic anecdotes about A. Schlatter (1852–1938) are widespread. An anecdote
about the later career of F. C. Baur (d. 1860) was related to me by my teacher, O. Bauernfeind
(1889–1972); he heard it from his teacher Eduard von der Goltz (1870–1939), and he, in turn, from his
father Hermann von der Goltz (1835–1906), who attended Baur's Tübingen lecture on the book of
Revelation. He is reported to have commented with reference to the number 666 in Rev 13.17: 'And
Hengstenberg in Berlin [the leader of the strict conservatives, 1802–69] says that's me.' I could narrate
numerous anecdotes that reach back eighty to a hundred years and are based on controlled tradition.

[65] Mark 15.21; cf. Rom 16.13.

Joseph of Arimathea; Simon the leper in Bethany; the healed blind man Bartimaeus (and Luke's Zaccheus) in Jericho; the synagogue official Jairus and the tax collector Levi, the son of Alphaeus, in Capernaum et al.[66] The few names that Mark mentions outside the Twelve, especially in connection with the passion of Jesus, also point in this direction. Above all, we should not forget the three women named in Mark 15.40: Mary of Magdala, Mary the mother of James the younger and Joses, and Salome. They are individuals who are still known to Mark and the churches he addresses. As a rule, Mary Magdalene is first in the lists of women, and this indicates her significance, which is comparable only to that of Peter.[67] Where the additional female names vary in Luke and Matthew, this could be connected with conflicts over their 'authority' as guarantors of tradition. Where the disciples fail, they[68] and men such as Simon of Cyrene or Joseph of Arimathea enter. This state of affairs already makes it impossible to see pure fiction in the passion story of Mark.[69] In principle, one cannot always speak of fictional development in the mentioning of names. On the contrary, at first the tradition has a greater tendency to permit people and place names to vanish, since they were no longer significant for the content of the narrative or the tradition, e.g., in the Greek-speaking, predominantly Gentile-Christian communities.[70] This means that instead of 'oral poetry', which dominates the form-critical perspective, the related phenomenon of 'oral history', which is closer to the situation of Jesus' disciples as well as to the missionary churches of later decades, should be drawn upon more strongly for the understanding of the Jesus tradition.[71] In the Gospels, and especially the Synoptics, it is not primarily a matter of literary fiction; instead, they claim to describe a real event of the past, i.e., 'history' narrated in the form of 'stories' about Jesus' words and deeds, which are ultimately founded upon eye-witnesses and their memory, even

---

[66] Joseph of Arimathea: Mark 15.43 par.; Simon the leper: Mark 14.3 = Matt 26.8; cf. the Pharisee Simon, Luke 7.40; Bartimaeus: Mark 10.46ff.: Matt 20.30 (cf. 9.27) makes from this two anonymous blind men; Luke 18.35 also omits the names; see also Mark 5.22; Luke 10.38ff.; 19.1–10. Jairus: Mark 5.22 = Luke 8.41. Matt 9.18 deletes both name and title. Levi: Mark 2.14 = Luke 5.27 (without his father's name); Matt 9.9 makes from this a 'Matthew'. The otherwise unknown Salome in Mark 15.40; 16.1 is also removed by Matthew. Matt 27.56 interprets her as the mother of the sons of Zebedee: cf. 20.20. In Luke 'Maria and Martha' are added: 10.39ff.; cf. John 11.

[67] Hengel 1963:243–56.

[68] See Mark 15.40. That the names of the women vary somewhat only shows that there was a larger circle in which certain claims were later represented. Above all, Joanna, the wife of Chuza Herod's steward, may be seen as a tradition-bearer in Luke (8.3; 24.10).

[69] See Hengel and Schwemer 2001:45–63, 153–62.

[70] This is especially the case in Matthew, who generally tends to abridge.

[71] See Henige 1982, Vansina 1985 and the collection edited by Ungern-Sternberg and Reinau (1988).

if, time and again, they were newly shaped and changed by the tradition-bearers and authors for the purpose of effective missionary proclamation and teaching in worship.[72] In John, this occurred in a radical way, and yet the claim to eye-witness testimony is strikingly emphasized.[73] Also, the sentence in Luke 1.2, *kathōs paredosan hēmin hoi ap' archēs autoptai kai hupēretai genomenoi tou logou*, is to be taken seriously.[74] Because the *autoptai* are a reality for him, he does not need to invent any witnesses. Where names appear in Luke, they are based upon tradition.[75] Conversely, the figure of Damis in Philostratus' *Life of Apollonius* shows that a fictive eye-witness can play a central role as a guarantor of tradition in a work of literary fiction. Presumably, Philostratus knew the Gospels and authored his work as an account of the true Greek philosophical religion against the Christians' growing influence. Also, Celsus' Jewish informant is probably a fictive character. It shows, however, how well informed the anti-Christian author was about the Jewish polemic against Christians. The Synoptic Gospels are notable precisely for the absence of this strikingly *stereotypical* appeal to a permanent eye-witness as the guarantor of tradition. Their report does not need this. The uncommon reference in Luke 1.2 corresponds to the expectation of the high-standing recipient, and the much-debated report of the Presbyter John in Papias that Mark was based upon Petrine tradition has a genuine historical background. It is concerned here more with a criticism than a defence of the oldest evangelist.[76]

II

These objections against a radical anti-historical scepticism, which form criticism only appears to establish, do not, of course, gain for us 'historical certainty' in detail. Such certainty can hardly exist in this milieu of tradition. Here, relatively little permits itself to be really 'compellingly proven'.[77] The investigations of 'oral history' have shown that oral traditions

---

[72] See Byrskog 2000.   [73] John 19.35; 21.24.

[74] Cf. Heb 2.3. Luke and the author of Hebrews belong to the second or third generation. It is striking how naturally the eye- and ear-witnesses are spoken of. One knows that one is dependent upon them.

[75] Luke 1.5; 2.25, 36f.; 5.27; 6.14ff.; 7.40; 8.3, 41; 10.38f.; 19.1; 24.18. It is revealing that he does not add any names in the pericopes taken over from Mark. The same applies for Acts 1.13; 6.5; 13.1; 15.22; 18.2, 7f.; 20.4 etc.

[76] See Hengel 1985a:2ff., 47–50, 69–71; Hengel 1993:76–94; Hengel 2000:40–6, 52f., 57f., 65–76, 353 (index).

[77] The demand to 'compellingly prove' something appears all too often in New Testament literature and indicates a lack of historical consciousness. See Schlatter 2002:59: 'There is no completely accurate historical knowledge for any part of the course of history; we do not even have it for the course of our own life.'

based upon memory can often be flawed even for eye-witnesses. As a rule, they can only precisely order past events with difficulty, while information concerning places and people remains more firmly fixed in their memory. Particular episodes and brief scenes, anecdotes, parables and shorter units of sayings are therefore remembered and digested. This already applies to our own memory if we wish to date earlier events. The narrative-temporal frameworks of the Gospels *must* therefore be largely secondary and can only present a rough pattern. This does not mean, however, that temporal information is *always* non-historical. This is shown already by the passion story.[78] Even summarizing framework narratives can contain valuable facts and important general characteristics,[79] as so-called 'ideal scenes' often refer to historical events in that they summarize similar events in a paradigmatic scene.

12

A further problem is constituted by the gulf between the *Aramaic native language of Jesus and the Greek Gospels*. Since non-literary, simple Greek knowledge or competency in multiple languages was relatively widespread in Jewish Palestine including Galilee,[80] and a Greek-speaking community had already developed in Jerusalem shortly after Easter, one can assume that this linguistic transformation began very early. Also, the expansion of the new movement in the predominantly Greek-speaking cities of Palestine, Phoenicia and Syria took place with amazing speed and was only possible because missionaries, above all 'Hellenists' driven out of Jerusalem, soon preached their message in the Greek language. We find them in Damascus as early as AD 32 or 33. A certain percentage of Jesus' earliest followers were presumably bilingual and could therefore report, at least in simple Greek, what had been heard and seen. This probably applies to Cephas/Peter, Andrew, Philip[81] or John. Mark, too, who was better educated in Jerusalem than the Galilean fishermen, belonged to this milieu.[82] The great number of phonetically correct Aramaisms and his knowledge of the conditions in Jewish Palestine compel us to assume a

---

[78] Here even Paul provides exact temporal information in 1 Cor 11.23 and 15.3ff. Cf. Hengel 2004b.

[79] Cf. also Luke 8.1–3; 6.13–20; Acts 1.12–14; 2.42–7; 4.32–7; 6; 11.19–24 etc.

[80] For the linguistic situation in Palestine, see Hengel 1988:108–14, 191–5; Hengel and Markschies 1996.

[81] See John 12.20ff.: Greek pilgrims come to Philip in Jerusalem and wish to see Jesus; he tells Andrew, who like Philip has a Greek name, and the two of them take this request to Jesus. For John the first step towards the mission to non-Jews is suggested here, as already in chapter 4.

[82] Hengel 2002c; Hengel and Schwemer 1998:43–60.

Palestinian Jewish-Christian author. Also, the author's Aramaic native language is still discernible in the Marcan style. It cannot even be ruled out that some of the seven from Acts 6.5 heard and saw Jesus. We do not know to what extent any of them knew Aramaic, but it is certainly possible that they did. Perhaps Philip changed from the twelve to the 'seven'. This Galilean Jew from Bethsaida later worked in Caesarea before migrating to Hierapolis in Asia Minor.[83] Also later in AD 57, we still find some 'Hellenists' in Jerusalem, e.g., the Cyprian Mnason, a disciple from the early period (*archaios mathētēs*) with whom Paul stayed.[84]

13

The kerygmatic purpose, apologetic interest and the development of Christological thinking over many decades further determined the selection and formation of the gradually decreasing stock of reliable tradition. All the evangelists, and especially Mark and John, work eclectically and limit themselves to *paradigmatic* texts in a meaningful, even dramatically increasing order. *Scriptural citations* were an important apologetic supplement. One could only understand the activity of Jesus and the events surrounding his death as the fulfilment of prophetic promises, which were held before opponents in discussion. Through this process, differences must have become more and more visible, and secondary material could also have slipped in. Moreover, it made some difference whether a Gospel was written in southern Syria on the border of Palestine as with Matthew or in Rome as with Mark, and whether the community in which the author taught and wrote was primarily Jewish Christian or Gentile Christian. Similarly, it mattered whether (like Mark) it was composed under the immediate impact of either the Jewish war or the Roman civil war, or whether (like Luke) it looked back to the still recent destruction of Jerusalem and its terrible consequences as with Luke or whether it stood in bitter conflict with the reinvigorated Judaism under Pharisaic leadership in the mother country as with Matthew. Mark may reflect the terrors of the Neronic persecution and Matthew the dichotomy between love for one's own people and disappointment over rejection by one's kinsmen. All the more striking is the *agreement* of the three Gospels, which originated in very different places over a period of twenty to thirty years. A comparison

---

[83] John 1.44; Acts 1.13; 6.5; 8.3–4; 21.8ff.; Eusebius, *Hist. Eccl.* 3.31.3f. (the Montanist Proclus); 3.39.9 (Papias); 5.24.2 (Polycrates of Ephesus).

[84] See Acts 21.16.

of the Synoptics shows that the Jesus tradition was handled with relative care. As a result, in Mark, Luke and Matthew, we do not yet find a developed 'high Christology' with clear references to pre-existence and incarnation or a sacramental theology influenced by Hellenism, and there is a reserve in all four Gospels towards structures of office and hierarchical claims. On the whole, it is striking how Jewish the Gospels are. Dibelius had already drawn attention to this fact in his review of Bultmann's *History of the Synoptic Tradition*.[85] This even applies after AD 90 for Matthew, the most theologically profiled Synoptic author. With all his individual creative power, he preserved whenever possible the wording of his often greatly shorted Marcan material, and his handling of Luke or the material coming from the Logia tradition is similarly faithful. In addition to this conservative stance, the following factors gave the (later and, according to our modern understanding, 'pseudepigraphal') first Gospel apparently greater authenticity than the remaining Gospels: (1) its geographical proximity to Palestine, (2) its 'Jewish-rabbinic' character, (3) its strong Jewish-Christian influence and (4) the wrongly interpreted tradition about the 'apostle' Matthew as author and his 'primitive Hebrew Gospel'. This held true even in modern research until the end of the nineteenth century, i.e., until the demonstration of the priority of Mark.[86]

There is no reason to assume that Mark, for whom written sources have often been supposed but never yet convincingly demonstrated,[87] handled the tradition entrusted to him in a less 'conservative' way than Luke or Matthew. On the contrary, he was closest to the original event, and scarcely forty years after Christ's death, he certainly still had contact with eye-witnesses. This is true above all for Simon Peter, upon whose tradition he primarily drew according to multiple early ancient church accounts, and who suffered martyrdom in Rome only five or six years before the origin of the work. This is already shown by the unique, predominant role of Peter, who is highlighted by Mark in a striking way through a consciously formed *inclusio*.[88] The Peter tradition in the background gives this Gospel (which from a superficial perspective was relatively quickly outdated by Luke and Matthew) lasting authority. The claim that the author was an unknown

---

[85] See pp. 81f. above.

[86] For the particular theological accomplishment of the first evangelists see now Deines 2004.

[87] Naturally, Mark could have made use of 'notes', which he possibly produced for himself or took over from another. The history of the origin of his work is not clear to us, and we can only multiply hypothesis upon hypothesis concerning the question of written sources.

[88] Mark 1.16 and 16.7: he is deliberately named as first and last disciple. See Feldmeier 1985; Hengel 2000:78–89, 113f., 153–7.

Gentile Christian, i.e., an anonymous Mr Nobody without any authority, is absolutely absurd. Also, there is no evidence that it originated in Syria – the later home of Matthew. The numerous Aramaisms together with the Jewish milieu necessitate a close connection with Palestine; the striking Latinisms as well as church tradition suggest Rome.[89] Behind such a 'revolutionary work' *an authority must stand.* Only thus is it explained that Luke and Matthew relied upon it massively and that it was not lost despite the existence of more comprehensive Gospels such as Luke and Matthew and the 'apostolic' authority of the latter, which reused 80 per cent of it.[90]

14

Finally, the wishes, questions and impulses of the *hearers* (more than the readers) influenced the formation of the Gospels and their preceding tradition. Most Christians, who primarily came from the lower classes, were probably illiterate and were dependent upon hearing the report or reading in worship. The Gospels, at least Mark, Matthew and John, were written in the first place for worship. The hearers and – in the second place – the readers should place themselves in 'the story of Jesus', should become 'simultaneous' with it, should make his cause their own, although one always remained conscious of the uniqueness and singularity of Jesus and thus also of the historical distance.

Primitive Christian worship was also a lively affair; here there was discussion and questioning, and not just a monologue of 'preaching'.[91] Accordingly, Luke certainly responds in many cases to the expectations of the 'most worthy Theophilus' and his circle,[92] while Mark in Rome may still be influenced by the experience of the Neronic persecution, where we hear for the first time of the crucifixion of Christians for the sake of their faith.[93] The shock waves of the Jewish war and the Roman civil war also influenced him. This can still be felt in Mark 13. By contrast, Matthew after 90 stands in bitter conflict with the synagogue, which is completely reconstituting itself after the catastrophe of 70, in Palestine or southern Syria. The situation is similar for John in Asia Minor around AD 100,

---

[89] Hengel 1985a:1–30; Hengel 2000:35–40, 47, 51, 57, 107–10, 354 (index).   [90] Hengel 1985a.

[91] 1 Cor 14.29ff., 35; cf. Acts 19.9.

[92] Cf. Luke 1.1; Acts 1.1 and 10.24: the Gospel is written above all for him and 'his relatives and closest friends'. See also Acts 25.23; 26.24ff.; 13.12: 'Theophilus' could well be relatively highly placed in Roman society. We do not know whether he was baptized.

[93] Cf. Mark 8.34 and Tacitus, *Ann.* 15.44.4: *crucibus adfixi atque flammati.*

though of course with a different Christological background. In contrast to a predominantly 'formal' approach, we should make a greater effort to place the Gospels and their traditions as precisely as possible in time and space and be prepared to take note of clear indications lest the origin of the Gospels disappear into an a-historical fog in which only unverifiable literary-critical hypotheses are considered valid.[94]

We also regard it as fundamental that all the authors of the Gospels were already *experienced teachers with authority* and not *neophytoi*[95] or unknown 'Gentile Christians' riveted solely to their limited present and the acute problems of their community. The evangelists, each in his own way, all looked back. In doing so, they surveyed a great period of time and consciously intended to express *the fundamental salvation event that took place forty to seventy years earlier.* At the same time, they also introduced the rich experiences of their presumably decade-long mission and teaching activity, which were hardly separable in the first century.[96]

15

In the light of all these influences and changes of situation, the *possibilities for a historical reconstruction of Jesus' activity, his teaching, action and suffering remain limited.* We have only fragments from the abundance of the enormous events of that short period between ca. AD 28 and 30 enclosed in the golden frame of the primitive Christian proclamation through the disciples. They knew on the basis of the Easter events that the crucified Galilean Jesus of Nazareth was identical with the Lord exalted to the right hand of God. We do well, therefore, to remain modest. J. G. Droysen already objected to the misunderstanding that we could 'give a *depiction* [*Abbild*] of this or that past period'. 'For this could only be a *picture* [*Bild*] of *fantasy*, since what is to be portrayed is no longer available but can only be in our *imagination* [*Vorstellung*].' The task of a historian

---

[94] See Hengel 1985a:28ff., 45ff. for Mark and Hengel 2000:186–207 for Luke and Matthew.
[95] See 1 Tim 3.6.
[96] This means that long before the composition of the Gospels, their authors already stood in a continuity of teaching tradition, which at least in Matthew and John had the character of a school. Behind Mark and Luke, which were not attributed to apostles, stood the two outstanding teachers of the first generation, Peter and Paul. For all the evangelists it can be assumed on the basis of their longer activity as teachers that they possessed notes of their own and/or from others before the composition of the Gospels. Luke and Matthew made use of Mark. All three had collections of logia at their disposal that were in part almost identical and in part quite different. Their connection with the tradition could be based upon written documents as well as upon their own memory and oral tradition. Oral tradition and written materials influenced one another long into the second century. This applies all the more for the first century.

can only consist in *so understanding the memories and traditions, the remains and monuments of a past as the listener understands the speaker*, that from those materials still available to us, searching, we seek to understand what the (persons) thus ... acting ... wanted [*wollten*], what moved their ego, which they wanted to convey in such expressions and impressions of their being. From the ever-fragmentary materials, we seek to know them, their willing [*Wollen*] and acting, the conditions of their willing and the effects of their action.[97]

That is also the clearly delimitated task of the quest for the historical Jesus and his equally historical community of disciples on the basis of the four Gospels (here, above all, the Synoptics). In another context, Droysen stresses in a similar manner that

The *objective facts* ... *in their reality*[98] are *not at all available* to our research ... What happens is first *comprehended and united* through its *interpretation* as a connected process, as a complex of cause and effect, of purpose and realization, in short, *as a fact*, and these same details can be interpreted otherwise by others; they can be combined by others with other causes and effects or purposes.

Therefore, it follows that 'all sources, however good or bad they may be', are '*interpretations* of events' regardless of whether they were written down by an eye-witness or at a much later period. 'It is truly childish to think that what Diodorus narrates about the age of the Diadochi is the history of that period.'[99] Therefore, historical research must always also be critical research, which knows that direct access to past events is closed to it and that it has to take the 'interpretations' of the oldest authors and the sources used by them as its starting point. Fundamentalist polemic against the 'historical-critical method' does not understand historical perception. It can therefore also not perceive the *reality of salvation history*, because in its anxious rationalism, it cannot and will not grasp the true effects of God's action through his Word in history.[100] Droysen rightly warns against reading more from the sources than they can say, because they can never reproduce the whole event but only excerpts, and these also only in the form of conceptions (*Vorstellungen*). In the same way he warns against an overestimation of *eye-witness testimony*, since the eye-witness too only bears a 'conception' in him, but also against a false 'objective' understanding of

---

[97] Droysen 1977:26 (my italics).

[98] Archaeological discoveries *in situ* appear to constitute an exception, e.g., inscriptions and coins, but they too must be interpreted and placed within our overall historical interpretation.

[99] Droysen 1977:133f. (my italics). The way in which seemingly critical theologians disparagingly speak of 'objective historical facts' shows that they have not really comprehended the subject-bound manner of historical 'interpretations'.

[100] Fundamentalism is a form of 'unbelief' that closes itself to the – God-intended – historical reality.

facticity, in which the knowing and reporting subject is eliminated in favour of supposedly 'pure facts'.[101]

16

Jesus has left us no unmediated self-testimony of any kind; all we have is information about his impact upon eye- and ear-witnesses: what they heard from his mouth and observed from his action and how this was processed in Christian worship and missionary preaching and *came to be preached again as 'apostolic witness'*. Therefore, unmediated access to Jesus' thinking and self-understanding is unavailable to our historical work. With all caution we can only make grounded statements on the basis of the witnesses *about* him and must thereby consider that others may interpret the sources differently. The psychologizing access to the 'mystery of his person' that dominated Jesus research in the nineteenth century is closed to us. By means of history alone we cannot grasp the real 'inner life of Jesus' (W. Herrmann), the 'constant powerfulness of his God-consciousness' (F. Schleiermacher). We only encounter what is mediated through others, very fragmentary witnesses about his message, his activity and his suffering. Even his controversial Messianic claim to authority,[102] which I hold to be decisive, is disclosed only through these external witnesses. As a result, one should be careful with statements about Jesus' 'self-*consciousness*'. Certainly we cannot measure it with the criteria commonly employed today. Therefore, all attempts to produce a 'Jesus-psychology' must fail. As a rule, they lead only to banalities. Numerous questions that the curious historian would like to ask him remain unanswerable. The unanswered questions to which J. Bowden drew attention remain our fate.[103] Nevertheless, what is handed down to us in the refraction of the Gospels makes such a fascinating impression that one cannot avoid the question: 'Who (was and) is this one?': *tis ara houtos estin;* (Mark 4.41). The true answer is given to us by the early Christian proclamation, i.e., the 'apostolic witness' that recognizes and confesses the Galilean Jesus of Nazareth in paradoxical manner as the Son of God become human and as the resurrected Lord in the unity with the Father, a witness that John 20.31 formulated representatively for all the Gospels, indeed for the whole of

---

[101] Droysen 1977:133f. For the wrongly suppressed concept of 'salvation history', see Hengel 2003c. A biblical theology that is worthy of its name cannot do without the *Sache* (subject-matter) standing behind this concept.
[102] Hengel and Schwemer 2001.   [103] Bowden 1988.

primitive Christianity. The actual intention of the evangelists as narrators of history and as witnesses of faith is expressed there through the *hina pisteusēte*. This 'faith' is always also dependent upon historical tradition: 'the word became flesh and dwelt among us', and the Gospels intend nothing other than to bear narrative witness to this 'dwelling among us' and the 'beholding of his glory'.

PART II

Writing the four gospels

CHAPTER 5

Who writes, why, and for whom?

Richard A. Burridge

INTRODUCTION

Three basic questions arise with regard to any attempt at communication: Where does it arise from? Where is it directed? and What is being communicated? Such a model of communication theory, often associated with the name of Roman Jakobson (1896–1982), stresses the importance of analysing the transmitter, message and receiver for anything one person is communicating to another. Thus one can speak of a TV transmitter or station which sends out a broadcast which television sets (equipped with the right aerial, cable or satellite dish) can receive and decode so that the programme can be played. A troupe of actors who perform a play before a live audience are using the same process, albeit with a different medium.

For written communications, these three basic elements can be worked out in various forms around the model of author–text–reader, as when someone writes a letter for someone else to read. Naturally, this three-fold understanding applies much more widely than just to letters – it applies to poems, plays, books, stories: somebody has to produce them, and someone has to read them. Of course, the 'author' may involve a lot more than just the one who writes; there may be several authors or editors involved in the production of the text, and still others in its delivery or transmission. Meanwhile at the other end of the process, our use today of the term 'reader' must not blind us to the fact that personal, silent reading 'within the head' is relatively modern. In the ancient world, most people would read out loud, or under their breath – and very often would not be reading alone. The Roman writer Pliny describes the way his uncle, Pliny the Elder, would have a literate slave reading to him constantly around the house or in the bath or garden, while Uncle Pliny would just jot down notes on a wax tablet of things which he would later incorporate into his massive *Natural History* (Pliny the Younger, *Ep.* 3.5). Furthermore, many texts were received by being read or even declaimed by an educated performer to a group of people listening to them as after-dinner entertainment. Thus 'audience' is perhaps a better term than 'reader', with its modern quiet individualistic connotations.

Therefore these basic issues of author(s)/producers and reader(s)/audience lead to this chapter's questions of who writes, why and for whom? Indeed, they are the traditional questions usually tackled at the start of a commentary on any ancient text – who was writing what to whom, and why, where and when did they do so. For many Graeco-Roman works, such questions may be easily answered, sometimes from the texts themselves, which may begin with the author's name, and explanations and salutations to the audience. This is best illustrated from ancient letters, but such features also regularly occur in the prologue or preface to many other works.

Unfortunately this is not the case with the gospels: neither Luke's carefully crafted Preface (Luke 1.1–4) nor John's Prologue (John 1.1–18) gives us any of this information. Yet human beings are naturally curious animals, and this lack of hard information has never stopped interpreters, both ancient and modern, from speculating who wrote these books, where, when and to whom. On the one hand, this led to the various traditions in the early church about the apostolic authorship of the gospels and their possible churches, while most biblical commentaries over the last century or two include opening sections discussing authorship, date, provenance, readers, occasion and so forth. In such cases, the text is being used as a 'window' through which we look to that which lies 'beyond', 'behind' or 'the other side' of the text – namely the historical Jesus and the various early Christian communities. Yet despite two thousand years of tradition, research and speculation, it is important to stress at the outset that in fact we know practically nothing of who the original authors and audiences of these texts actually were.

1 SURVEY OF SCHOLARSHIP

(a) Early church traditions

There are various early traditions of the church which make suggestions about the composition of the gospels, their authors and their relationship to the apostles and connections with certain specific churches, and so forth. The earliest Greek titles are all variations upon the preposition *kata* plus the accusative, which, while indicating that the gospel is 'according to' the evangelist, does not mean the same as the normal genitive of the author, i.e. that it is 'by' him. Hengel argues that the unanimity of these descriptions implies an early date, perhaps even back well into the first century.[1] It was not long thereafter, however, that traditions start to emerge which link the 'who' of Matthew, Mark, Luke and John with our other questions of 'for whom' and 'why'. Some are derived from Papias, Bishop of Hierapolis, ca. AD 120–30, who wrote five volumes on the *Interpretation of the Lord's Sayings* which have not survived but are preserved in citations in Eusebius.

Papias (preserved in Eusebius, *Hist. Eccl.* 3.39.16) notes that Matthew collected Jesus' sayings 'in the Hebrew language' and interpreted or translated them 'as best he could'. Irenaeus adds that the gospel was composed while Peter and Paul were founding the church in Rome (*Haer.* 3.1.1), while Origen says that it was written for Jewish believers (Eusebius, *Hist. Eccl.* 6.25.4) and various other ancient authorities also suggest that it was composed in a Palestinian setting. As for Mark, Papias quotes from his source 'the Elder' that Mark was 'Peter's interpreter' who wrote the Lord's deeds and words which he had noted down (Eusebius, *Hist. Eccl.* 3.39.15); Irenaeus adds that it was written after Peter's death in Rome, ca. 64–5 (*Haer.* 3.1.1), although other writers disagree. Luke was a follower or companion of Paul according to Justin (*Dial.* 103.19) and Irenaeus (*Haer.* 3.1.1; 3.14.1); this tradition is also found in Eusebius, who notes that he came from Antioch (*Hist. Eccl.* 3.4.2). A very early tradition attributes the fourth gospel to 'John, disciple of the Lord, who leaned on his breast', who published it in Ephesus, according to Irenaeus (*Haer.* 3.1.1), who claims to have received this tradition from Polycarp. The purpose of the gospel is addressed in Clement of Alexandria's famous comment that John wrote a 'spiritual gospel' recognizing that the 'bodily facts' were in the other gospels (Eusebius, *Hist. Eccl.* 6.14.7).

(b)   *The rise of the historical-critical method*

These traditions about the authors and contexts of the gospels dominated most of their interpretation down the centuries and heavily influenced the first generations of critical commentaries during the nineteenth and early twentieth centuries as attempts were made to find supposedly medical vocabulary in Luke, or Petrine reminiscences in Mark.

However, all three aspects of authorship, purpose and audience of the gospels underwent significant changes with the development of form criticism. In 1882, Overbeck drew a distinction between the oral material

[1] Hengel 1985b:64–84.

of the primitive Christian communities (which he termed *Urliteratur*) and the later truly literary patristic writings; similarly, in 1919 Dibelius differentiated between formal 'literary' works produced by the conscious intention of an author (*Hochliteratur*), and the mere end-product of popular tradition and story-telling (*Kleinliteratur*).[2] Furthermore, K. L. Schmidt's analysis of the gospels' framework led to the conclusion that they were mere concatenations of individual separate units, *pericopae*, strung together like beads on a string.[3] These approaches thus get rid of any idea that the gospels are a single coherent narrative and make it impossible to ask our basic questions about the author. Furthermore, Rudolf Bultmann rejected any notion that the gospels were biographies: the gospels appear to have no interest in Jesus' human personality, appearance or character, nor do they tell us anything about the rest of his life, other than his brief public ministry and an extended concentration on his death.[4] Thus, the gospels were seen as popular folk literature, collections of stories handed down orally over time, a 'unique' form of literature, *sui generis*, and this approach dominated gospel studies for the next half-century or so.

This meant that the gospels were now less seen as windows onto the historical Jesus and more as windows onto the historical early church. One of the key arguments put forward by K. L. Schmidt was their community setting: the gospels are 'not the product of an individual author, but a folk-book, not biography, but cult-legend'.[5] A basic tool of the form critics was to seek to discover the *Sitz im Leben* of any saying or pericope – its setting within the life of the early Christian communities. At this point there was little attempt to define these early Christian communities; they were simply seen in a generalized or typical way.

The crucial implication for our study here is that the stress on the oral tradition meant that there was no author to speak of, no individual mind behind the text. The evangelists were seen as merely stenographers at the end of the oral tunnel, stringing together the pearls of wisdom composed by various early preachers. This is authorship by committee, with notes from a secretary. Finally, the purpose of the gospels is not to describe the life of Jesus, but rather to proclaim the kerygma, the preaching of the early faith of the church. Thus our three basic questions about the gospels of

---

[2] Overbeck 1882:417–72; Dibelius 1933, ET Dibelius 1971:1–2.   [3] Schmidt 1919.
[4] Bultmann 1972: see especially pp. 371–2.
[5] 'Nicht individuelle Schriftstellerleistung, sondern Volksbuch, nicht Biographie, sondern Kultlegende', Schmidt 1923:76.

author, purpose and audience can be answered as 'by committees, for communities, about the faith'.[6]

(c) *Redaction-critical approaches and the reinstatement of the author*

However, the rise of redaction criticism and the development of new literary approaches viewed the writers of the gospels as both theologians and conscious literary artists. This reopened the questions of the genre, purpose, authorship and audience of the gospels and their place within the context of first-century literature.

The pioneering work of Bornkamm on Matthew, Marxsen on Mark and Conzelmann on Luke directed attention to the particular theological interests of each evangelist in the light of the way each evangelist shaped and edited his material, seen especially in Matthew and Luke's use of Mark and their shared material, designated as 'Q'. Composition by committee was thus replaced by deliberate selection of material on the part of the gospel writers; once redaction critics attributed the overall shaping of the gospel to the evangelists as well, issues of authorship were bound to arise – and so we are back to our question of 'who?'.

This led quickly on to the question of the communities – 'for whom?'. If the form critics were interested in the general *Sitz im Leben* in which this or that kind of pericope might be used, the redaction-critical stress on the particular theology of each gospel led to an attempt to define the community interested in those aspects or affected by the situations envisaged to require that teaching. Thus the word 'community' itself begins to appear regularly in titles of studies which attempt to reconstruct the group or church behind each of the gospels – the so-called Matthean or Johannine community.[7] A good example is the way in which R. E. Brown and J. L. Martyn saw theological issues, especially that of Christology, as defining the various stages of the development of the Johannine community and the parallel multiple editions of the fourth gospel.[8]

Thus the gospel writers began to be seen as theologians, while the purpose and subject matter has moved from proclaiming the basic kerygma to the particular concerns of the writer's community; the audience is therefore defined very specifically as the church within which and for which this gospel was written. The text is thus a window for the modern

---

[6] Burridge 1998.
[7] See, for example, Brooks 1987; Balch 1991; Overman 1996; Kee 1977; Esler 1987; Brown 1979.
[8] Martyn 2003 (3rd edn; 1st edn 1968; 2nd edn 1979); Brown 1966, 1970; Brown 1979.

critic not just onto the early churches but onto certain specific, if hypothetical, ancient communities.

These approaches were refined still further by the development of approaches using the social sciences. In many respects, the search for the evangelists' communities followed the model of reconstructing the Pauline communities to which his various epistles were addressed. It is no coincidence that Wayne Meeks, who wrote the excellent introduction to sociological analysis of the Pauline churches in his *The First Urban Christians*, should also consider the question of Johannine sectarianism.[9] Over recent years, all four gospels have been subjected to such sociological analysis, and many different reconstructions of their communities have been hypothesized.

2   THE CURRENT STATE OF THE QUESTIONS

It might be thought odd that after two thousand years of intensive reading and study, such basic questions as who wrote the gospels, why and for whom should remain unanswered – or rather, have received such a wide variety of answers from the earliest traditions of the church through to the results of traditional historical and literary criticism. In such a fast-moving field, we can do no more than provide a mere snapshot, a 'freeze-frame' as we enter the third millennium.[10]

(a) Mark

We start with Mark as probably the first gospel to be written, then being used as a source by Matthew and Luke and sharing some traditions with John. Some scholars (such as Best) still hold to the traditional idea that Mark wrote his gospel in Rome as the 'interpreter' of Peter, while others have suggested places all over the Mediterranean: for one example, Kee reconstructs a missionary apocalyptic sect in 'rural and small-town southern Syria'.[11] Mark may have been prompted to write by the death of Peter, or of other eye-witnesses during Nero's persecutions, or by the Jewish revolt and/or the fall of Jerusalem, or by the delay of the Parousia or by his group's eschatological conviction of its imminence, or by some internal

[9] Meeks 1972; Meeks 1983.
[10] For a good treatment of all the various possible settings and communities proposed for the gospels, see Barton 1998.
[11] For discussion, see Pokorný 1983, especially pp. 2019–22; Best 1983:21–36; Kee 1977:77–105.

need of his community.[12] Alternatively, perhaps Mark was in dispute with other Christian groups: Weeden deduces from Mark's unflattering portrayal of the disciples that he was hostile towards the leadership of other churches, especially that at Jerusalem.[13] Given all this diversity, Guelich concludes that the internal evidence for authorship, date and place is simply insufficient for any decisions to be made.[14] A more promising direction has emerged with Beavis' attempt to outline Mark's 'audience' rather than reconstructing his community.[15]

(b) Matthew

Papias' suggestion that Matthew wrote down Jesus' sayings 'in the Hebrew language' is still debated today, but most scholars agree that this gospel is notable for its Jewish flavour because of its use of Old Testament citations for the fulfilment of prophecy and its regular concern for 'the law and the prophets'. However, the date, occasion and place of composition and its setting in relation to both contemporary Judaism and early Christianity are all issues over which scholars have argued greatly in recent years. Matthew's use of the Hebrew scriptures led Stendahl and Orton to talk of a 'school',[16] while Overman and Stanton reconstructed his community as typical of the 'sectarianism' of Jewish groups towards the end of the first century.[17] There has been debate about whether Matthew was written in response to external problems, especially in relation to the synagogue, or because of internal problems over things like false teachers. It is often dated around the time of the *Birkath ha-Minim* insertion into the Jewish liturgy and the supposed separation of church and synagogue about AD 85, but this date has waxed and waned along with the popularity of that hypothesis. Equally it is argued whether the debate with other Jews in the synagogue is still going on, or whether Matthew's community had already left, or been ejected.

The most common location involves a setting in Antioch,[18] though other major centres such as Caesarea, Tyre and Sidon, Tiberias or Sepphoris (Overman's preference) have been suggested, while others prefer somewhere east of the Jordan, such as Pella, where the Jerusalem church fled in about

---

[12] Best discusses these suggestions in Best 1983:21–36; Morton Enslin goes for the fall of Jerusalem (Enslin 1983:2363).
[13] Weeden 1971. [14] Guelich 1989: xxv–xxxii (xi–xliii).
[15] Beavis 1989; for a contrasting reconstruction, see Rohrbaugh 1993. [16] Stendahl 1968; Orton 1989.
[17] Overman 1990, which is then developed in his introduction and commentary, Overman 1996; Stanton 1992a, esp. pp. 85–107 and Stanton 1992b.
[18] See, for example, Schnackenburg 2002:5–7.

AD 66 (Eusebius, *Hist. Eccl.* 3.5.3).[19] As with Mark, more recent scholarship has begun to move away from attempting to define a particular community and location to sketching out the kind of group envisaged in the text.[20] For example, in 1994 Stanton warned against treating a gospel like a letter, and moved towards envisaging 'a loosely linked set of communities over a wide geographical area'.[21] In his most recent book, Stanton confesses: 'in recent years I have become increasingly uneasy about the constructs, "*the* Q community", "*the* Matthean community", "*the* Johannine community", and so on'.[22]

(c) Luke

The possible range of attempts to answer our basic questions of authorship, location and occasion can be seen in Orchard's suggestion that Matthew was the gospel of the Jerusalem church AD 30–44, Luke was the product of the 50s crisis over Paul's Gentile churches and Mark, the latest of the three, is based on lectures in Rome by Peter comparing Matthew and Luke![23] In contrast to that view, most scholars agree that a date of around 80–5 does seem likely for Luke, if one accepts the priority of Mark. Luke's account seems to imply a setting outside Palestine in a more Gentile environment; here too, a link with Antioch has been suggested, though other contenders include Achaia, Boeotia, Rome, Caesarea, the Decapolis – so it is not surprising that both Fitzmyer and Evans conclude that any suggestions are 'mere guesses'.[24]

The search for Luke's community has followed a similar trajectory to the search for that of others, though it never reached the specificity of Matthew's: in 1979, Johnson warned of the difficulties of identifying one community, followed by Allison's even more sceptical treatment. It is not surprising, therefore, that Moxnes has preferred to talk about the 'social context' of Luke in much more general terms.[25] As for its purpose and occasion, Luke–Acts has been seen as part of the brief for the defending counsel at Paul's trial (and hence why Acts finishes before Paul's death).[26] Other suggestions include the delay of the Parousia, internal debate about

---

[19] A full list of suggested locations is discussed by Davies and Allison 1988–97: I. 138–47 and in Brown 1997:208–17; see also Stanton 1983, esp. pp. 1941–3.

[20] See Aune 2001, esp. Richard S. Ascough's essay (Ascough 2001).

[21] Stanton 1994b, quotation from p. 12.   [22] Stanton 2004:193; his italics.

[23] Orchard and Riley 1987:229–79.

[24] Fitzmyer 1981:35–62, esp. p. 57; Evans 1990:1–15; see also Maddox 1982:6–15.

[25] Johnson 1979; Allison 1988; Moxnes 1994; see the discussion of all three by Barton 1998:186–9.

[26] Mattill 1970; see also Mattill 1975.

Paul in early Christianity, external debate with the Romans about the legality and acceptability of this new religion and many others.[27]

(d) John

The early church tradition that the apostle John, son of Zebedee, composed the fourth gospel at Ephesus towards the end of the first century has already been mentioned – and this tradition has continued to affect critical scholarship, with many commentators beginning their discussions with it, and allowing for some input from John at least into the early stages of the gospel. The multi-faceted nature of this gospel has led to swings of the scholarly pendulum between Hellenistic philosophical and religious influence and rabbinic or non-conformist Jewish ideas, between proto-Gnostic or naïvely Docetic understandings against Hebraic concepts, between mystical theology and eye-witness history – in fact, just about every aspect of the (pre-)history and theology of the fourth gospel seems to lead to polarized debate.

With regard to our questions of authorship, occasion and audience, the same redaction-critical processes which produced the ideas of the 'communities' behind the Synoptic gospels really found their zenith with John. Central to most reconstructions is the idea that the gospel can be read on two levels at the same time, namely the original story of Jesus and his ministry overlaid with the story of the development of the community which produced this book. This can be exemplified in the works already mentioned by J. L. Martyn and R. E. Brown.[28] Central to both is a reconstruction of the various stages by which the Johannine community came into being and developed, from the early Jewish disciples, through the addition of others such as Samaritans, to a crisis around expulsion from the synagogue in the mid 80s (as seen in the *aposynagōgos* material in John 9.22; 12.42; 16.22), followed by later periods of debate both with those who remained within Judaism and with heterodox believers who broke away from the community, especially over the reality of the incarnation, which led to the production of the Johannine epistles. Brown first works out the sequence of his reconstruction in the introduction to his Anchor commentary in 1966, which is then refined in his *Community of the Beloved Disciple* (1979); this is further revised in his *Introduction to the New Testament* in 1997 and finally in what would have been the introduction to his revised

---

[27] Maddox 1982; Gasque 1975; Fitzmyer 1981:8–11, 57–9.
[28] Martyn 2003 (3rd edn; 1st edn 1968; 2nd edn 1979); Brown 1966, 1970; Brown 1979.

Anchor commentary and was edited and published after his sudden death in August 1998.[29] Another good example of a sociological analysis of John's community is Meeks' important article arguing for 'Johannine Sectarianism'.[30]

It is notable that there has been more hesitation over the questions of authorship and audience in subsequent commentaries: thus Beasley-Murray talks of 'more caution' and maintains that such issues are 'less capable of precise determination than is frequently represented'.[31] Perhaps the best evidence for the recent shift away from such community reconstructions came in a Johannine Literature session at the annual conference of the Society of Biblical Literature (SBL) in 2002, where Robert Kysar gave a paper in which he outlined the 'rise and decline' of the expulsion theory and how it gave rise to the hypothesis of the Johannine community, which in turn was increasingly assumed to be an assured fact.[32] The responses from, among others, D. Moody Smith and J. L. Martyn were very salutary and reminded us that 'working hypotheses' need to be constantly re-evaluated.

In conclusion, therefore, such a wide variety of hypotheses about the authors and audiences of the four gospels inevitably means that they cannot all be right – and leads to the suspicion that probably none of them is all right! The only sensible conclusion to draw from this diversity is that the gospel texts themselves simply do not contain sufficient information for us to know the specific settings and occasions which prompted their production, or who produced them for whom, except for a general desire to tell others about Jesus, who he was, what he did and what happened to him in the end.

3   SOME CHALLENGES

(a)   Literary approaches and readers

Our analysis of the tradition-critical attempts to define the authors and audiences of the gospels has shown how these reconstructions have tended eventually to become self-refuting. In fact, this is exactly what the

---

[29] Brown 1997:368–78; Brown 2003:58–86, 189–219.
[30] Meeks 1972; see Barton's discussion (Barton 1998:189–93).
[31] Beasley-Murray 1987:lxvi–lxxxi, quotation from p. lxxviii; see also Witherington 1995:11–35 with its more tentative conclusions.
[32] R. Kysar, 'Expulsion from the Synagogue: A Tale of a Theory', Johannine Literature Section, Session S25-62, SBL Toronto, 25 November 2002.

development of more literary-critical approaches to biblical texts would lead us to expect. Rather than seeing the gospels as 'windows' through which we can look at what lies 'behind' the text in terms of authors and original communities, these literary approaches prefer to see texts as 'mirrors': readers can place their various concerns 'in front of' the text and gain some reflection upon them. In fact, such critics would argue that many of the community hypotheses are not windows onto the history of the early churches at all, but only mirror readings, reflecting the assumptions of those who composed them.

In its most extreme form, such an approach breaks down our communication-theory model completely: instead of an author communicating to an audience, there are just the text and the reader. Thus the structuralist Roland Barthes could speak of 'the death of the author' allowing us to concentrate solely on reader and text. He concludes, 'The birth of the reader must be at the cost of the death of the Author.'[33] The old model could use authorial intention as the criterion for determining what constituted a 'valid' reading – i.e. one which coheres with what the author meant to communicate in the first place.[34] Without such limitations, now any reading the reader finds helpful can be considered valid, for we simply cannot know what another person really intends. This is even more so for such ancient documents as the gospels, whose authors and original audiences are irredeemably lost to us.

Not all reader-oriented approaches need be quite so pessimistic, but the rise of reader-response criticism does stress the third element of our communication model – the person of the reader, who is active in the construction of the meaning of the text.[35] There is debate about the 'ideal' reader who can interpret the text perfectly, the 'real' or actual reader, and the 'implied' reader, a mediating concept of a reader with a certain amount of competence able to recognize the clues to the reading encoded in the text. Thus, the reader may be seen as completely 'in' the text, put there by the author, or 'over' the text and able to impose any reading he or she wishes upon it; a middle position envisages a dialogue between text and reader. Such approaches draw heavily on the work of Wolfgang Iser and Stanley Fish.[36] In response, Kevin Vanhoozer has attempted both to 'resurrect' the author and to 'reform' the reader.[37]

---

[33] Barthes 1968. [34] See Hirsch 1967, 1976.
[35] For a brief introduction, see Resseguie 1984; also Moore 1989 and Grant 1989.
[36] Iser 1974, 1978; Fish 1980. [37] Vanhoozer 1998.

Alongside such reader-based approaches has developed reception theory, which looks more at the history of the interpretation of a work than at the history of its creation. Gadamer introduced the term *Wirkungsgeschichte* for the critical history of the impact or effect of a text.[38] Especially for texts like scripture, their subsequent history and impact upon generations of believers may be more important than the original audience. Increasingly, biblical commentaries are including this aspect by looking at how the book or the passage has been received and interpreted, not just by scholars, but also in art, culture and music.[39]

(b)   The gospels for all Christians

Another challenge to gospel-community hypotheses came from Richard Bauckham in a paper originally given to the British New Testament Conference at Bangor in September 1995. It generated such interest that it, together with various papers reacting and responding to it, was eventually published as *The Gospels for All Christians*.[40]

A revised form of Bauckham's lecture opens the book by raising the question of who the gospels were written for – namely other Christians. Even Matthew and Luke's use of Mark implies that Mark was circulating outside any 'Marcan community'. Community hypotheses are often assumed, but never argued through. Their advocates read the gospels as allegories of hypothetical communities, and the sheer diversity of reconstructions calls the whole process into question. Such approaches confuse the gospels with letters which are written to specific groups; gospels, however, are a form of ancient biography and as such are meant to communicate widely. Furthermore, all the evidence about the early church is that it had good communications and frequent contact through highly mobile leaders. Therefore, Bauckham concludes that it is a mistake to give the hermeneutical key for the gospels to hypothetical communities: their audiences are much more indefinite than specific.

Other chapters in the book include discussions of the speed of ancient communications (Michael B. Thompson), methods of book production (Loveday Alexander), the implications of the biographical hypothesis

---

[38] Gadamer 1975.

[39] See, for example, Ulrich Luz's four-volume commentary on Matthew in German for EKKNT, now being translated and published in the Hermeneia series by Fortress Press, Minneapolis, or the development of the Blackwell Bible Commentary series, being edited by Christopher Rowland, John Sawyer and Judith Kovacs.

[40] Bauckham 1998b.

(Richard A. Burridge) and a theological reading (Francis Watson). It was never a unified project and we did not read each other's contributions or agree a common strategy – but we were united in opposing a hermetically sealed, or hermeneutically sealed, vacuum-packed community within which and for which the gospels were written.

Many of the critical reactions to the book seem to be misled by its title, ... *for ALL Christians*, into thinking that we underestimate the diversity of the early Christian movement. Perhaps the most thorough critique comes from Philip Esler, who began by stressing the element of cultural distance and the significance of such diverse gospels; in response to what he saw as our caricature of the community hypothesis, he proposed a 'third way' where the gospels were written for a local community but had the possibility of travelling further afield.[41] In his reply, Bauckham argued that this third hypothesis did not go far enough and reacted to the criticism that we did not take social anthropology sufficiently into account.[42] Sim's review article welcomed the book for forcing those who believed in community hypotheses to argue the case more than just assuming it. He criticized Bauckham for relying on 'circumstantial' evidence rather than using the texts of the gospels and argues against the idea that the gospels were for *all* Christians, 'any and every church'. Against this extreme representation of Bauckham, he quotes from other essays, particularly those of Alexander and Burridge, to argue for the diversity of gospels written for different groups.[43] Another review, from Wendy Sproston North, takes issue with Bauckham's other chapter, 'John for Readers of Mark'.[44]

The best indication of the debate stirred up by the book is that an entire session was devoted to it at the SBL meeting in 2003.[45] After Burridge presented the main argument of the book, responses were given by Mark Matson, Theodore Weeden and Loveday Alexander. However, the largest treatment came from Margaret Mitchell in her paper 'Patristic Counter-evidence to the Claim that "The Gospels Were Written for All Christians"'. Here she particularly fastened upon the idea of 'all' and for 'any and every', and counters it with detailed coverage of comments from early church leaders about the gospels, their authors and intended audiences or churches, amplifying the sorts of suggestions noted earlier in this chapter. In response, those of us involved in the book have welcomed her

---

[41] Esler 1998.   [42] Bauckham 1998a.   [43] Sim 2001: see especially pp. 9, 15, 19–20.
[44] Sproston North 2003.
[45] 'Gospels for all Christians? Rethinking Gospel Audiences', SBL session S22-118, Atlanta, 22 November 2003; papers are available on the Synoptic Gospels Section Website.

detailed survey of the fathers, but still do not consider that this evidence points to anything as definite or specific as the kind of separate communities envisaged by the reconstructions of, say, Brown or Weeden. Of course, we recognize that the four gospels are different and appear to be written for differing sorts of audiences; we are not trying to 'flatten them out'. But these are 'indefinite' audiences: Matthew indicating an audience of 'Jewish Christians' in general, rather than this particular church in Antioch, for example.

4 BIOGRAPHICAL GENRE AND TARGET AUDIENCES

If both ends of the communication model – the author/editor/producer(s) and original reader(s)/audience – are lost to us today, then we need to return to the actual text, as the message mediating between them and all that survives. Can it tell us anything about the nature of the communication? Contrasting the historical-critical approach to text as 'window' and the literary model of 'mirror' readings, we need to ascertain what kind of 'glass' we have here. In other words, we are back to the question of genre: if we discover that a message is in the form of radio waves of a certain frequency, then we can deduce that both the transmitter and the audience possessed wireless equipment of this kind. If, on the other hand, the message is in semaphore, then like the transmitter and receiver, we will need to acquire the proper flags and learn the code. This is why genre is so vital as the set of conventions and expectations mediating between authors and audiences, guiding both the production and the interpretation of texts.[46]

Graham Stanton pioneered this approach with his 1974 SNTS monograph, challenging Bultmann's assessment and comparing the gospels with contemporary literature, and he has continued this interest over many years.[47] My 1992 monograph in the same SNTS series built upon this work and argued from both genre theory and classical literature that the gospels are a form of Graeco-Roman biography and need to be interpreted accordingly. Although these conclusions ran counter to the prevailing scholarly consensus of the previous half-century, this approach has attracted increasing support in recent years. Therefore a second edition

---

[46] See Fowler 1982; Dubrow 1982.
[47] Stanton 1974, 2002 (1st edn 1989), 2004; Stanton also acted as external examiner to my own Ph.D. thesis, and commissioned it for the SNTS Monograph Series, so I am glad to acknowledge my debt to him here and gladly contribute this essay in his honour.

has now been published with a new chapter detailing how this change took place over the last decade and looking at the implications of the biographical hypothesis for narrative readings of the gospels, for their relationship to Jewish literature and for the results of sociological analysis by comparison with the authors and audiences of Graeco-Roman *bioi*.[48]

The traditional historical-critical method gives our three questions of author, subject/purpose and audience the answer of 'by committee, for communities about concepts'. However, the biographical approach stresses that such books as the gospels and ancient Lives are written 'by people, for people about a person'.[49] To return to the images of glass, the gospels are neither a window nor a mirror, but more like stained glass: of course, one can look 'through' them to what lies behind with the historical method and use them to reflect upon what is 'in front of' them – but the crucial element is the actual portrait of the person 'in' the glass. Given the constraints of space and materials, what is interesting is how the artist has portrayed the subject, what has been included or omitted, how it has been coloured and so forth. Similarly, given that the gospels, like ancient Lives, are only single-scroll works of 10,000–20,000 words, how the evangelist has focused upon the person of Jesus should be determinative of its meaning. This links this chapter's central question of occasion and purpose – why? – with that of the subject. Graeco-Roman *bioi* were written for variety of purposes, apologetic, polemic, didactic, etc., but central to them all is their focus on a person, and explaining their understanding of him. Similarly, therefore, the hermeneutical consequences of their biographical genre are essentially Christological. As a form of biographical narrative, the gospels tell us that their authors composed them to explain their understanding of the person of Jesus, and the original audiences would have interpreted them accordingly. This is the 'code' in which they were composed, transmitted and received.

Therefore we need a Christological hermeneutic where every passage and verse is interpreted in the light of that gospel's presentation of Jesus' teaching, life, death and resurrection.[50] Such a Christological approach can be illustrated by considering a notorious problem in gospel studies, namely Mark's depiction of the disciples as slow to understand and lacking in faith (Mark 4.40–1; 6.50–2; 8.14–21). The redaction-critical approach, which sees the gospels as written for specific communities, seeks to solve this

---

[48] Burridge 2004 (1st edn 1992), with a foreword by Graham N. Stanton.   [49] Burridge 1998.
[50] For such a narrative reading of all four gospels, see Burridge 1994, second edition forthcoming in 2005.

problem by relating it to certain groups in the early church. Thus, Weeden's account is actually entitled *Mark: Traditions in Conflict*; he sees the slow-witted disciples as standing for other leaders, particularly those with a *theios anēr* ('divine man') Christology to whom Mark is opposed.[51] Quite apart from the fact that there are problems over the concept of *theios anēr*, such an approach does not do justice to all the other positive material about the disciples in Mark. Once we stop seeing the gospels as written about certain problems for specific communities and read them instead as belonging to the genre of ancient biography, the Christological key can be used to interpret such passages. The point of each passage is not to tell us about the disciples, but to indicate something about the biography's subject – namely Jesus of Nazareth – in this case, that he is someone who is hard to understand and tough to follow. Given both the positive and the negative aspects of the disciples' portrayal, the readers should not be surprised if they find discipleship difficult; yet it is such struggling disciples whom Jesus calls and teaches, despite the difficulties.

This approach is confirmed by the absence of rabbinic biography. Many of the pericopes in the gospels can be compared to anecdotes within the rabbinic traditions about various teachers of the law, which also contain stories describing the death of the sage. Yet it is very significant that no one ever 'strung these beads together' to form an account of the life of Hillel or Shammai.[52] This is because the focus of each anecdote is quite properly upon the rabbi's understanding of the law; to string them together into a connected biographical narrative would be to replace that focus with the person of the rabbi himself. Thus the decision by the first evangelist(s) to write a gospel in a biographical genre for people to read about this person is itself a Christological claim – namely that it is in the person and work, life, death and resurrection of Jesus that God is now to be found.[53]

Thus viewing the gospels as ancient biographies helps with all three of this chapter's questions of author, audience and subject/purpose. It can liberate us from the circularity of deducing hypothetical communities from the text and then interpreting the text in the light of these (deduced) communities. Instead, this generic comparison provides some external evidence of some social groupings and ways in which *bioi* functioned. Rather than the very specific communities posited in recent decades, these comparisons suggest that our modern concept of 'target audience' or 'market niche' is better. Thus Tacitus writes his Life of Agricola for anyone interested in the events under Domitian, particularly as they affected his

---

[51] Weeden 1971.   [52] Neusner 1988:33–8 and Neusner 1993.   [53] Burridge 2000.

father-in-law, perhaps with half an eye on those who might criticize him for working with the tyrant. Such people may have come from the Roman ruling classes, but they do not comprise a 'Tacitean community'. The idea of the 'implied reader' of the gospels is thus more useful than speculations about their communities.

Such an approach suggests that Matthew has as his target audience Christians from a Jewish background who have a high regard for the law and who have suffered antagonism or persecution from other Jews, perhaps around the time of the separation of the church from the synagogue in the later years of the first century. On the other hand, Luke aims to explain Jesus' life and teaching for a Gentile market niche. Instead of looking at archaeological and literary evidence about Antioch or Ephesus and then interpreting the gospels in that light, we can picture people all over the Mediterranean world who would fit each evangelist's projected readership, rather than just a small group of people in one specific community. Matthew's and Luke's gospels could appeal to two Christians from different Jewish or Gentile backgrounds but who were still members of the same early church congregation – and who had friends who liked Mark or John!

In the absence of concrete evidence about the gospels' authors and audiences, we have turned instead to the biographical genre of the communication to answer this chapter's three basic questions. Through a generic comparison with other ancient biographies, we can see how the gospels were composed, circulated and received in a similar way, as they were written *by* some people to explain *to* others *why* Jesus of Nazareth is so important.

CHAPTER 6

How Matthew writes

Richard C. Beaton

What exactly did Matthew have on his table when he composed the gospel?[1] One wonders. Strewn upon his tabletop would no doubt have been a copy of some form of Mark, possibly another document or a collection of written traditions (Q), and papyri and other items upon which were inscribed bits of the Jesus tradition, sayings, miracle stories, parables, etc. Additionally, he would have had scrolls of OT texts (e.g., MT, Aramaic, LXX or some other Greek translation of Isaiah, Jeremiah, Psalms, etc.) or, at the very least, testimony collections.[2] But to limit his resources to texts alone is to bias Matthew's composition. As Ong, Kelber, Gerhardsson and, more recently, Dunn remind us, such a view results from the technologizing of the word that is the cultural residue of Gutenberg's press.[3] A purely textual focus is restrictive and misrepresents the culture of the first century. Of equal or, if Papias is correct, greater importance[4] would have been the communal Jesus narratives that were recounted as part of his community's corporate story (oral tradition). Furthermore, one wonders where the creative energy and impulse to write derived from and whether he wrote in isolation or others in his community somehow participated.[5] Would communal worship have affected his writing (e.g., the Lord's Prayer in 6.9–15)?[6] Furthermore, to what extent might the social

---

[1] This essay is in honour of one of those rare people who model what it is to be a distinguished scholar, teacher, supervisor and mentor, on the occasion of his sixty-fifth birthday.

[2] 4QTest and 4QFlor offer Jewish examples of the existence of collected testimonies. See Allegro 1956:174–87. Possible Christian testimony collections might include P. Ryl. 460; see Roberts 1936:49ff.; most recently, Stanton 1997:336–41 and Albl 1999.

[3] Gerhardsson 1961; Ong 1982; Kelber 1982; Byrskog 2000; Dunn 2003b. See also the discussion in a recent edition of the *Journal for the Study of the New Testament* between Dunn 2004, Byrskog 2004 and Holmberg 2004.

[4] Eusebius, *Hist. Eccl.* 3.39.4.

[5] One may not want to affirm the notion of a Matthean school (Stendahl 1968) or that documents are written by a community or committee; however, the degree to which a document is shaped by communal memory, interests and language is a more provocative topic.

[6] Luz 1992:77.

setting of the Matthean church have influenced the gospel's content and tone? All told, the question of how Matthew wrote contains within it a complexity that is staggering. It is a symbol of the intricate set of problems related to the preservation and transmission of the Jesus tradition among his early followers, and the composition and development of the gospels themselves.

TEXTUALITY, ORALITY AND MATTHEW'S COMPOSITION

The traditional manner of investigation has been to examine Matthew's sources, comparing and contrasting the original with Matthew's version. For obvious reasons of control and verifiability, the starting point has been located in Matthew's written sources. A guiding assumption in this regard is that the similarity between Matthew and Mark is best explained by Matthew using a copy of Mark as the basis for his new work. In fact, so striking is the resemblance at points that many have argued that Matthew is simply an expanded version of Mark. While this appears plausible initially, a close reading suggests otherwise. Matthew goes beyond Mark and composes a document that preserves the tradition while being wonderfully creative.[7] Matthew also shares the double tradition (material common to Matthew and Luke but not present in Mark), otherwise known as Q. Since the existence of a Q document remains a speculative hypothesis, it is difficult to assess fully the possible redactional modifications Matthew might have made.[8] Additionally, Matthew includes a great deal of material that is unique to his gospel (i.e., the so-called M material, as well as OT quotations).[9]

The Papias tradition of the penning of Matthew's gospel adds another layer to this description.[10] Eusebius records Papias as saying, 'Matthew collected the oracles in the Hebrew [Aramaic] language, and each interpreted [translated?] them as best he could.'[11] This notion that some early form of Matthew was originally composed in Hebrew also occurs in Irenaeus.[12] While one may not want to argue that the entirety of

---

[7] See especially, Stanton 1992a:326–45.

[8] On the issues related to Q and oral tradition, see the fresh assessment by Dunn 2003b.

[9] Given that there is no evidence that Matthew is working from a document, the usage of 'M' should probably be abandoned (so also Luz 1992).

[10] Note the cautious comments regarding the historical value of Papias in Luz 1992:94–5; Davies and Allison 1988–97:I.7–9; Hagner 1993:xliii–xlvi.

[11] *Hist. Eccl.* 3.39.

[12] Further, Irenaeus, Origen, Eusebius and Clement of Alexandria seem to think that Matthew was originally composed in Hebrew and translated into Greek. See the discussion in Davies and Allison 1988–97:I.8–9.

Matthew was composed in Hebrew,[13] a position seemingly untenable if Matthew employed a Greek Mark, the position that a collection or shorter gospel in Aramaic was used, along with other sources, to compose the gospel as we now have it has been gaining adherents.[14] If this is the case, then canonical Matthew is a Greek language production shaped by a Jewish follower of Jesus that is thought to have preserved the apostolic witness.[15]

An important issue that arises, however, is whether source-critical approaches are adequate to offer a full explanation of Matthew's work as redactor/author. More particularly, it is not immediately clear to what degree oral traditions that parallel the Marcan and Q materials influenced his composition. In the history of scholarship, form critics like Dibelius and Bultmann argued that Matthew was a mere redactor of the bits of tradition to which he had access.[16] The ultimate concern was the source and history of the traditions Matthew used, assuming that the author was temporally distanced from the events that surrounded Jesus and that he worked in isolation from those events. But it must also be noted that the early form critics and redaction critics were working with a text-based system. There was a considerable lack of sophistication and precision in describing the phenomenon of orality and textuality in the first century. The predominating fallacy was that oral tradition was a flexible and unreliable mode of passing on stories for simple, superstitious ancients. The community shaped the tradition; the tradition did not shape the community. By the time Matthew sat down to write, the traditions associated with Jesus had, according to this view, already undergone a radical theological transformation, and the written text served to codify the results. Matthew was a mere arranger of material that came to him, much of it having already undergone theological modification.

In contrast to such a position, however, Papias' general comments on the shift from what can best be described as the oral phase to written composition provide witness to the abiding vitality of the living testimony/memory that existed within the early communities.[17] Ong argues that the differences

[13] See Howard 1987, 1995, who argued for an original Hebrew version of Matthew but later changed his position. For a thorough discussion of the issue and the argument that there is likely no primitive Hebrew text in Ibn Shaprut's *Eben Bohan*, see Horbury 1997.

[14] It is at least possible that this shorter record was originally drafted by the apostle Matthew (so Hagner 1993:xlvi; Hengel 2000:177–8).

[15] There has, of course, been substantial disagreement over the Jewishness of the author of Matthew and the gospel itself. See most recently Foster 2004.

[16] Dibelius 1919; Bultmann 1921.

[17] Eusebius, *Hist. Eccl.* 3.39.4, 'For I did not consider that I got so much profit from the contents of books as from the utterances of a living and abiding voice' (*ta para zōsēs phōnēs kai menousēs*).

may be even more distinct than Papias suggests. Ong contends that Gutenberg's press gave birth to a revolution that served to technologize the word and that this technology (a text-based world) subsequently changed how humanity conceives of reality.[18] More importantly, the notion of oral tradition that the form critics and redaction critics employed is flawed because it presumes a text-based society. As is observed by Ong, Kelber, Bailey,[19] and Dunn, the gospel authors inherited a more stable core of oral tradition than is often assumed; discrepancies could be attributed to regional diversity.[20] Matthew, then, would have been intimately acquainted with the oral traditions/communal memory when he composed his gospel. Such an acquaintance with the tradition offers a different orientation or beginning point from those of the models constructed by the early form critics. One must offer a further qualification, however: Jewish society of the first century was both textual and oral.

An important implication of the recent studies on oral tradition is that the differences between Matthew and the sources he employed remain simply differences until an emphasis of the author, a pattern or a theme is distinguished within the book as a whole. A pattern or thematic development suggests a literary interest within the gospel. Further, each gospel is greater than the sum of its parts. The placement of each pericope and the inclusion, enhancement or diminishment of themes also serve to shape the narrative, as a viewing of Pasolini's *Gospel of St Matthew* will demonstrate in black and white.[21] Context does generally determine meaning. If in addition to the redactional adjustments one also keeps in mind Matthew's structure, literary features, and construction and development of theological motifs, it becomes evident that Matthew offers more than a mere history of Jesus' life and death, teaching and deeds, and establishment of a movement that would become Christianity. In his gospel, Matthew draws out the significance of the life of Jesus for the movement that he founded. By so doing, he is intentionally theological and historical. If this is correct, then Matthew is working on several levels simultaneously: while he provides a quasi-biographical narrative of the events surrounding the central character Jesus, he also includes and reshapes traditions in a way that offers

---

[18] Ong 1982:77–114. See also Goody 1986.   [19] Bailey 1976.
[20] One should note the earlier works of Gerhardsson 1961; Riesner 1981; and Riesenfeld 1970, which represent early attempts to address this issue. To the now burgeoning list of literature on this topic one might add the recent works by Baum 1998, 2003.
[21] Released in 1964; recently released in DVD format. What is fascinating about Pasolini's film is that it reproduces a great deal of Matthew verbatim, yet because the order of many of the pericopes is rearranged, the movie misses much of the gospel.

implicit commentary for the broader church while also raising complex issues about his own church's social location.[22]

This essay cannot begin to address the sheer quantity of data related to Matthean composition.[23] Rather than focusing upon minor adjustments, although necessary at points, it will briefly compare Matthew's use of Mark and stylistic features. More interestingly, however, it seeks to explore how the manner in which Matthew creates and shapes the narrative framework develops themes and emphases. This will serve as a springboard to the bigger issues of structure, thematic development and the use of the Old Testament, offering glimpses of Matthew's genius along the way.

Matthew and Mark

A careful comparison of Matthew with our version of Mark[24] suggests that Matthew is conservative in his treatment of his Marcan source. Matthew excludes only seven sections from Mark (1.23–8, 35–9; 4.26–9; 7.32–7; 8.22–6; 9.38–40; 12.41–4), thereby reproducing roughly 80 per cent of the gospel, much of it in close verbal agreement.[25] Further, Matthew follows Mark's order and narrative thread, maintains its geographical and temporal divisions of Jesus' life and ministry in Galilee and Jerusalem, and seems concerned to preserve the theological commitments found therein. It must be noted, however, that he uses considerably less of Mark in the first half than in the second, an oddity that has yet to be satisfactorily explained.[26] Matthew tightens passages where necessary, removing extraneous terms, phrases and details, and works at improving the language. Streeter, and most after him, suggests that Matthew greatly improves Mark's Greek. Matthew's Greek 'is more differentiated, polished and "elevated" than the popular Semitic Greek of Mark or Q'.[27] Whether it qualifies as polished may be questioned; Bacon's characterization of it as 'synagogue Greek' is perhaps closer to the mark.[28] Those more positively inclined might say that

---

[22] There is great debate on this topic. See especially Stanton 1992a and, most recently, Foster 2004.

[23] In addition to the numerous specialist studies, the three major commentaries of Luz, Hagner, and Davies and Allison provide lists and discussion. The older works of Allen 1912, Bacon 1930 and Hawkins 1909 remain very useful in this regard.

[24] See especially Allen 1912:xiii–xl, who offers a thorough comparison of the two. Note also Hawkins 1909:158–60.

[25] Of the 11,708 words in Mark, 8,555 recur in Matthew, with 68 expansions to the Marcan text.

[26] In 1.1–13.58 (= Mark 1.1–6.11), Matthew transposes five sections of Mark. From 14.1 onwards, he essentially follows Mark's order.

[27] Luz 1992:49.

[28] Bacon 1930; Moule 1982:67–74 suggests that Matthew is a secular, literate scribe.

the careful treatment of the material demonstrates that Matthew values Mark a great deal and is intentional about what is included in his document. The implication is that when Matthew adopts Mark, even though adjustments are made, he embraces the Marcan tradition and theological commitments.[29]

STYLISTIC FEATURES

Anyone who engages in even a cursory reading of the two gospels, however, cannot but notice substantive differences between them. A considerable divergence occurs in Matthew's opening, which consists of the birth narrative and a carefully constructed genealogy.[30] As one might expect of a well-crafted book, the opening section, here the birth narrative (chs. 1–2), introduces themes that are followed throughout the gospel. Notions of the coming of God, covenantal obligations, eschatological culmination, identity of Jesus and the people of God, conflict with the Jewish leaders and Jesus as the fulfilment of the OT and the bringer of the presence of God are all woven into a powerful narrative. Already, Matthew has set the reader on a very different course from that of Mark. By the conclusion, one discovers that the birth narrative is balanced both in length and complexity by the passion narrative.

Additionally, Matthew employs numerous formulae, temporal markers, *inclusiones*, and a penchant for triads and doublets,[31] all of which render attempts at establishing a definitive structure virtually impossible. The matter is further complicated by the collection of Jesus sayings crafted into five bounded, thematically controlled discourses. These include the Sermon on the Mount (5–7), mission discourse (10), parables (13), community life (18) and apocalyptic discourse (24–25). That they are Matthean constructs seems reasonable given that they incorporate material from Mark, Q and M. While the exact beginning of each discourse is not always

---

[29] Hengel 2000:177–8 speculates that the reason for the care afforded Mark by Matthew can be accounted for by a late dating (AD 90–100) and the elevated respect that Peter enjoyed within the community.

[30] Matthew's genealogy relies upon the LXX genealogies in 1 Chr 1.28, 34; 2.1–15; 3.10–15. In so doing, the gospel opens with a carefully constructed theological statement that is dependent upon the OT. Matthew employs the kingly lists to fashion a genealogy that places Jesus within the Davidic kingly line.

[31] Matthew doubles Mark's singular number in at least three places (so Davies and Allison 1998–97:1.87): Matt 8.28 par. Mark 5.2 one demonic = two demoniacs; Mark 10.46–52 par. Matt 20.29–34 one blind man = two blind men; and Mark 11.1–10 par. Matt 21.1–11 one ass = one ass and her foal.

clear,[32] they all conclude with the formula 'and when Jesus had finished' (*kai egeneto hote etelesen ho Iēsous*.[33] The final discourse culminates in 26.1 with 'when Jesus had finished saying all these things' (*kai egeneto hote etelesen ho Iēsous pantas tous logous toutous*), bringing to a conclusion not simply the discourse (24.1–26.1) but the entire series of discourses. Whether Matthew had the five books of Moses in mind, as Bacon thought, now seems doubtful,[34] but the collection of material in the discourses is striking. Each draws from various sources and is carefully arranged, structurally sophisticated and accentuated with recurring vocabulary and forms that facilitate easy memorization and produce audible rhetorical effect during public readings, much like the entire gospel. The discourses are a provocative block of material in which Matthew's compositional technique and theological interests are writ large. Through them one hears afresh the commands of Jesus for his community. Thus, one could argue they serve a catechetical function within the churches.[35]

The stylistic features of the discourses are consistent with the gospel itself, which uses repetition, formulaic language, thematic threads, and careful attention to characterization. These characteristics, along with the distinctive vocabulary and noted tendency towards Semiticisms and Septuagintalisms,[36] have lead many to the conclusion that the author of Matthew was Jewish[37] and that he exercised both deliberateness and creativity in his use of the tradition. Luz notes that Matthew's Greek occasionally betrays a 'clear relationship to the linguistic development in the rabbinic Judaism of the time'.[38] The Jewishness of the gospel may explain why it is replete with explicit quotations from and allusions to the OT. In many ways, the OT is the sub-text of the gospel itself: the events of Jesus' life represent the fulfilment of the purposes of God in history. Matthew's use of the OT reflects this profound awareness and develop-ment of the notion of fulfilment, which, although present in Mark, is more deliberately accentuated in this gospel. Others would include his

---

[32] For example, 12.22–50 seems to merge with 13 and 23 with 24–5. Further, while the discourse of ch. 10 clearly ends with the formula in 11.1, ch. 11 itself is primarily discourse material.

[33] 7.28; 11.1; 13.53; 19.1; 26.1.

[34] The primary critique objection to Bacon's position is the problem of the birth and passion narratives. In addition to this, there is the reality that the themes of the discourses do not parallel the Pentateuch. The strength of Bacon's proposal, however, is that Jesus' teachings represented by the five discourses offer authoritative teaching for the church (28.16–20), much like the books of Moses.

[35] So Kilpatrick 1946.

[36] Points of contact include frequent use of parallelism, the genitive, asyndetic *legei*, direct speech, repetition and numbers.

[37] Davies and Allison 1988–97:I.7–58; Hagner 1993:lxxvii (Hellenistic Jewish Christian).

[38] Luz 1922:50; Goulder 1974:116–20. See especially Schlatter 1947.

christology, theology, the law, righteousness, conflict with the Jewish leadership, the question of Israel and the definition of the people of God. Consensus has Matthew as a Jew,[39] writing for a broadly Jewish audience.[40]

ADJUSTMENTS, INTENT AND THEOLOGY

Matthew makes subtle changes to his sources that very often signal a thematic or theological emphasis. This is perhaps most evident in his christology, which is both higher and more textured than Mark's, and in his christological exegesis. He removes references to Jesus' emotions and ignorance,[41] apparently seeking to strengthen Mark's account. Nevertheless, Matthew's Jesus remains human and becomes more personal. He extends Mark's references to the messiah by adding *Christos* to the Marcan tradition at significant points. This is particularly obvious in the passion narrative (26.68; 27.17, 22). Taken on their own, these few changes may appear unremarkable, but they betray a more sustained explication of Jesus as the ideal Davidic messiah.[42] For Matthew, the coming of the messiah marks a definitive moment in Israel's history;[43] it is nothing less than the eschatological shift of the ages. In the opening section of the gospel (1.1–4.17), the author seeks to demonstrate that, above all, this one is the Davidic messianic king. Yet no one could have foretold that Jesus would die as the messiah (27.22), king of the Jews (27.37). Thus it is with great irony that the story brings to conclusion the themes with which it began.

Another provocative reference to the messiah occurs in 11.2 (Luke 7.18), this time within the double tradition (Q). In this example, the redactional inclusion occurs in a section that marks a key moment in the structure of the gospel. A brief overview of this double-tradition text suggests that Matthew follows the same source as Luke,[44] making few modifications. The alterations, however, reveal much about Matthew's compositional technique and skill.

---

[39] The position that Matthew is a gentile has had its adherents as well; see, e.g., Trilling 1961; Meier 1976.
[40] Cf. Stanton 1992a, who argues that Matthew's audience is no longer Jewish.
[41] Passages removed from Mark include 1.41, 43; 3.5; 5.9, 30; 6.6; 11.13.
[42] Of thirty-five uses of *Christos* in the Synoptics, sixteen occur in Matthew, seven in Mark and twelve in Luke.
[43] Note the divisions in the genealogy (1.1–6a; 6b–11; 12–16); Matthew measures fourteen generations from the Exile to the coming of the messiah.
[44] See Hengel 2000, who dispenses with Q and argues that Matthew used Luke.

Matthew 11.2–6[45]	Luke 7.18–23
2 When John heard about _the works of the messiah_[46] in prison, he sent word by his disciples 3 and said to him, 'Are you the one who is to come, or are we to wait for another?'	18 The disciples of John reported _all these things_ to him. So John summoned two of his disciples 19 and sent them to the Lord to ask, 'Are you the one who is to come, or are we to wait for another?' 20 When the men had come to him, they said, 'John the Baptist has sent us to you to ask, "Are you the one who is to come, or are we to wait for another?"' 21 Jesus had _just then cured many people_ of diseases, plagues, and evil spirits, and had given sight to many who were blind. 22 And he answered
4 Jesus answered them, 'Go and tell John what you hear and see: 5 the blind receive their sight, the lame walk, the lepers are cleansed, the deaf hear, the dead are raised, and the poor have good news brought to them. 6 And blessed is anyone who takes no offense at me.'	them, 'Go and tell John what you have seen and heard: the blind receive their sight, the lame walk, the lepers are cleansed, the deaf hear, the dead are raised, the poor have good news brought to them. 23 And blessed is anyone who takes no offense at me.'

Matthew's reading of 'the works of the messiah' (_ta erga tou Christou_, verse 2) is probably a modification of the tradition represented in Luke's 'all these things' (_peri pantōn toutōn_, v.18).[47] The question that arises concerns Jesus' identity. Clearly John is having serious doubts, presumably because Jesus' teaching and actions do not match his expectations for the 'coming one'. Matthew's phrasing explicitly links the deeds (teaching and miracles) with Jesus' identity, as 11.4 makes clear ('Go and tell John what you hear and see'). The reader is left to ponder what exactly it is that they have seen and heard, because there is no record of any specific healings or teachings that have occurred in the immediate context. The reference is to the litany of miracles and proclamation that follows in verse 5 ('the blind see, lepers are cleansed, good news is proclaimed to the poor') that presumably happened at some time in Jesus' ministry.[48] It is at this point that the complexity of Matthew's composition appears. Structure and literary motifs merge with theological commitments. Unlike the Lucan context, the command to tell John what they 'hear and see' finds its referent within the material that has preceded

---

[45] The translation is from the NRSV unless noted otherwise.

[46] My translation. The Greek here is _ta erga tou Christou_, which is better translated as 'works of the messiah'.

[47] Held 1963:251.

[48] Whether the various items in this listing derive from Isa 26.19; 29.18; 35.5; 61.1 or 4Q521 remains questionable. Nevertheless, Matthew is drawing upon the eschatological hopes of Israel and linking these hopes/expectations with the healing and teaching ministry of Jesus.

chapter 11.[49] Chapters 5–7 (the Sermon on the Mount) form the first major discourse, and ch. 10 comprises the second (the mission discourse). These four chapters of teaching presumably provide the content for 'what you hear', while the collection of miracle stories (chs. 8–9) forms the basis for 'what you see'. Thus, Matthew has structured the gospel in chs. 5–11 to concern the question of Jesus' identity, and the (Q) saying in 11.6, 'Blessed is the one who does not stumble (*skandalisthē*) on account of me', provides the climax and transition to the next section. Matthew, it seems, seeks to clarify that although Jesus remains enigmatic (this is expressed most eloquently in John's query (v.3), 'Are you the one to come or should we expect another?'), for the inquirer who has ears to hear and eyes to see, he is the messiah, the one to come.

A section like 11.2–6 is a fitting example of Matthew's approach to the tradition, since it maintains close verbal agreement with Q material. Yet the few minor redactional modifications allow the text to function as a mid-point climax and transition to the next section (cf. 4.12–17).[50] The force of the passage is similar to Luke's, yet the manner in which Matthew gets there is substantially different. One could offer similar explorations of the treatment of Jesus as the ideal Davidide, son of God, son of man, beloved, one to come, Moses, prophet, king of Israel, etc. Matthew employs a host of designations to create an especially rich christology as he weaves these various titles into the narrative. In so doing, he provides a thick description of Jesus that presents him as the expected messiah, the one towards whom the witness of scripture points. Yet at the same time John's disquiet (11.2–6), the lack of response to Jesus' works and teachings (11.20–4) and the focus of the entirety of chs. 1–11 upon the issue of identity all suggest that Matthew is aware that his presentation of Jesus as messiah is in some fashion controversial (cf. chs. 11–13; 12.22–50). Jesus remains enigmatic (11.6, 25–30).

THEMATIC CLUES

Numerous other themes are taken up and transmuted into new formulations. Matthew adopts the Marcan miracle stories, retaining their existential character,[51] yet his use departs from the context of Mark's cosmic battle. Instead, Matthew collects a larger group of miracle stories from his various

---

[49] Luke 7.21 has Jesus 'just then' healing people. Luke seems to represent Q at this point.
[50] Matt 11.4–6 is nearly identical to Luke 7.22–3; verse (= verse 23) *kai makarios estin hos ean mē skandalisthē en emoi* is the same.
[51] Mark's miracles are thus understood to provide a model or prototype for his audience. For example, Marshall 1989 suggests that they continue to call disciples to a life of faith.

sources and inserts them into a complex structure (chs. 8–9). The thematic diversity points in several directions, which includes the notion that Jesus, as the son of David, demonstrates the care and justice that mark the arrival of the kingdom of God within Israel.[52] From Matthew's perspective, the Jewish people were expected to recognize the eschatological days in which they lived and respond with repentance (11.20–4). As Held observes, however, the miracle stories are not simply historical accounts: they build upon the conception of Jesus' continued presence with the church and provide security that he is with them as he was in the past.[53] The treatment of the disciples provides a further case in point. Gone is Mark's presentation of the uniform lack of understanding of Jesus and his mission among the disciples. In Matthew, the disciples come to understand, albeit imperfectly (16.12; 17.13).[54] They also seem to take on a transparent character,[55] referring both to the historical disciples and to the church. Thus, as Luz argues, the term disciple (*mathētēs*) is used as an ecclesiological designation.[56]

The struggle with the Jewish leaders appears in all four gospels, but in Matthew the motif is intensified; the function changes. Matthew's characterization of the Jewish religious leadership is a sustained theme from the opening of the gospel (2.4) until its end (28.12–14). The Pharisees in particular are offended by Jesus, but the disputes are more than halakhic quibbles (cf. 12.1–8, 9–14). There seems to be a fundamental disagreement about God and life lived within his kingdom (11.25–30). The charges that Jesus' miracles are performed in league with dark forces expose the depth of the antipathy (9.32–4; 12.22–32). The text manifests an intense disquiet with the Pharisaic posture towards the law and the pharisees' expressions of how the people should live out the law's demands (23.4, 23). This in turn leads to the critique that the people are 'harassed and helpless, like sheep without a shepherd' (9.36). The reference to the Jewish leadership seems to include also broader Judaism. Matthew's penchant for using the designation 'their synagogues' (4.23; 9.35; 10.17; 12.9; 13.54) and 'the Jews to this day' (28.15) is suggestive of a broader interest. It is difficult, however, to know how much to read into these references. Are the references limited to the historical setting of the life of Jesus, which seems unlikely given that some positive interactions are recorded in Mark and Luke? Or are these issues also transparent, meaning that Matthew has taken historical

---

[52] Note the response of the crowds in 12.22ff. See Beaton 2002.   [53] Held 1963:165–210.
[54] Barth 1963:106ff.; Luz 1995a:119–21. The theme of understanding versus blindness is creatively employed especially throughout Matt 11–13.
[55] Luz 1995b:92–3.   [56] Luz 1995a:118.

material from the life of Jesus and developed it to address the situation that
has erupted between broader Judaism and the (Palestinian?) Jesus movement? Most recently, scholars have been confident that the Matthean
churches are either struggling within the synagogue (*intra muros*), or
have parted ways (*extra muros*).[57] There are good grounds to suggest that
an underlying *Sitz im Leben* exists that Matthew sought to address through
his composition.

One could also point to Matthew's construction of the Sermon on the
Mount (chs. 5–7), which has the law, ethics and the climactic nature of
the Christ event at its centre (5.17–20; 7.14–23) and ultimately seeks to
shape ideas of discipleship. Matthew's presentation of the law is one of the
more difficult topics in the gospel, in part because no clear position is
espoused. On the one hand, Matthew is a Jew for whom the OT and its
ethical demands remain in force (5.17–20).[58] This possibly led to his removal
of the phrase 'thus he declared all foods clean' (Matt 15.17 par. Mark 7.19)
from his Marcan source[59] and may suggest that Matthew, regardless of
the gentile mission, inhabited a Jewish world in which dietary restrictions
were still an issue. Similarly, the Matthean addition of 'nor on a sabbath' in
24.20 to the Marcan *Vorlage*[60] implies a community that faithfully kept
the sabbath. Jewish elements such as these permeate the gospel, leading
many to the conclusion that it finds its social setting within a Jewish framework and that obedience to the law mattered. On the other hand, Jesus'
teachings are considered the authoritative interpretation of the law for the
newly constituted people of God. The frequent disputes with the Jewish
religious leadership over issues of halakhah suggest as much (5.21–48; 12.1–14;
15.1–19).

MATTHEW'S USE OF THE OLD TESTAMENT

One of the fundamental themes in the gospel is Matthew's conception of
fulfilment and eschatology. Of the twenty-seven uses of the term *plēroō* ('to
fulfil') in the Synoptics, sixteen occur in Matthew, two in Mark and nine in

---

[57] Hagner 1996; Stanton 1992a; Stanton 1983; Overman 1996; Saldarini 1994; Carter 2000.
[58] Most would offer a moderating position, particularly in light of 5.21–48 (the so-called antitheses).
Perhaps as an indication of how one's position on one issue affects others, those who assume gentile
authorship (e.g., Strecker 1962) also assume that Israel is rejected and the law abandoned.
[59] This assumes that Matthew had access to a copy of Mark that included this reading.
[60] Mark 13.18 reads, 'Pray that it not be in winter.' Whereas many would argue that some members of
Matthew's group continued to keep the sabbath, Stanton 1989 maintains that a flight on the sabbath
'would provoke further hostility from the Jewish leaders'.

Luke. This simple comparison reveals Matthew's emphasis. Perhaps the best summary of Matthew's orientation is found in the two short sayings in 26.54 and 56, '⁵⁴But how then would the scriptures be fulfilled, which say it must happen in this way? . . . ⁵⁶ But all this has taken place, so that the scriptures of the prophets may be fulfilled.' Matthew writes from an eschatological vantage point that locates the Christ event at the centre of history.

Matthew contains more references to the OT than almost any other document in the NT; these serve primarily to validate events in Jesus' life and Matthew's theological understanding of Jesus. He incorporates quotations from Mark and Q. The text-form of these quotations is generally the LXX,[61] which he adopts virtually unchanged. Matthew also inserts allusions and explicit quotations into the narrative that are unique to his gospel; the best known of these are the ten formula quotations.[62] These theologically rich texts all serve to support Matthew's christology. They are also, unlike the inherited quotations, textually mixed. Their text-forms are at times closer to the Hebrew text or the LXX; at other times they are a combination of both the LXX and the MT, and sometimes completely unique. The question arises whether the unique text-forms are the result of Matthew's own translation work.[63] If that is the case, then one might expect the unique elements to evince Matthean theological concerns.

An example of the richness of these quotations is the use of Isa 7.14 in Matt 1.18–25. On the surface level of the narrative Isaiah validates the virginal conception, 'Behold the virgin will bear a son.' But the second part of the quotation points to a theological motif, '*they* will call his name Emmanuel, which is translated God with us'. Here the Matthean textual adjustment of 'she will call' to 'they will call' shifts the focus to a corporate affirmation. The motif of Jesus as the presence of God with his community is one of the most provocative themes in the book, particularly when one considers the various contexts in which Jesus finds himself throughout the gospel.[64] Further, the motif of Emmanuel both opens and closes the book

---

[61] The text-forms during the period that Matthew wrote were best characterized by fluidity and variety. On the Greek text, see Tov 1999 and Paul et al. 2003. On the Hebrew text, see Cross 1975 and Ulrich 1996 for two opposing positions.

[62] 1.23; 2.15; 2.18; 2.23; 4.15–16; 8.17; 12.18–21; 13.35; 21.5; 27.9–10.

[63] It is also possible that Matthew is working with a Greek text that is closer to the MT than the LXX– similar to Aquila, Symmachus and Theodotion.

[64] Landmesser 2001 explores the relationship between the presence motif and Matthew's soteriology.

(28.20, 'I am with you until the end of the age'), demonstrating once again the subtle literary and theological sophistication of the gospel. Other passages which seemingly include reference on two levels are Isa 8.23b–9.1 in Matt 4.16–17, where Jesus' move to Capernaum is supported along with a note on the inclusion of the gentiles (support for the gentile mission?), and Isa 42.1–4 in Matt 12.18–21,[65] where the focus upon Jesus' healing ministry is broadened to include notions of justice, gentiles and eschatology. These are examples of a use of scripture that cannot be reduced to simplistic proof-texting; rather, they are the deposit of the early exegetical enterprise that sought to locate the events of Jesus' life and the nascent movement within the purposes of God in salvation history.

A more complex usage of the OT occurs in Matthew when the author seems to weave motifs from scriptural passages into the fabric of the narrative itself to draw out the significance of an event. Some have argued that this is a form of midrash that betrays the gospel's Jewish provenance.[66] While many would view the notion of the gospel as midrash as overextending the categorical boundaries, midrash (as interpretation of scripture) is a sufficiently broad category to include these uses. A few examples include the arrival of the Magi in the birth narrative (Matt 2.1–3; Num 24.17); the Judas narrative (Matt 27.3–10; Zech 11.12–13; Jer 18.1–12; 19.1–15);[67] the events surrounding the resurrection (Matt 27.51–3); earthquakes (Isa 24.19; 29.6; Jer 10.10); raising of the dead (Ezek 37.13).

The episode involving the final days of Judas in Matthew (27.1–9) offers another specific situation in which to gauge Matthew's theological use of the tradition and the OT. When compared with the account in Acts 1.18–20, which seems the more historically plausible,[68] Matthew's technique seems to be to take an historical situation and tease out the significance of the event using implicit reference to scriptural passages. A comparison of the two accounts reveals Matthean interests for a broader section.

---

[65] Beaton 2002.   [66] See the overview in Hagner 1995:lviii.

[67] The account of Judas' death also occurs in Acts. See Hagner's discussion (Hagner 1995:814–15) on possible historical traditions behind Matthew's version and Brown 1994:657–60.

[68] Luke's account in Acts is seemingly included to mark the inclusion of the new member, Matthias, who plays no role in the narrative account from then on. Luke does not seem to derive any theological gains from the Judas narrative, which is quite the opposite from Matthew.

Matthew 27.3–9	Acts 1.18–20
3 When Judas, his betrayer, saw that Jesus was condemned, he repented and brought back the thirty pieces of silver to the chief priests and the elders. 4 He said, 'I have sinned by betraying innocent blood.' But they said, 'What is that to us? See to it yourself.' 5 Throwing down the pieces of silver in the temple, he departed; *and he went and hanged himself.* 6 But the chief priests, taking the pieces of silver, said, 'It is not lawful to put them into the treasury, since they are blood money.' 7 After conferring together, *they used them to buy the potter's field* as a place to bury foreigners. 8 For this reason that field has been called the Field of Blood to this day.	18 (Now *this man acquired a field* with the reward of his wickedness; and falling headlong, *he burst open in the middle and all his bowels gushed out.* 19 This became known to all the residents of Jerusalem, so that the field was called in their language Hakeldama, that is, Field of Blood.)
9 Then was fulfilled what had been spoken through the prophet Jeremiah, 'And they took the thirty pieces of silver, the price of the one on whom a price had been set, on whom some of the people of Israel had set a price, 10 and they gave them for the potter's field, as the Lord commanded me.'	20 'For it is written in the book of Psalms, "Let his homestead become desolate, and let there be no one to live in it"; and "Let another take his position of overseer."'

Three points of contact exist between the accounts of Matthew and Acts: (1) Judas dies; (2) the money paid to him is used to buy a field; (3) the field becomes known as the 'Field of Blood'. Similarities, however, end here. Davies and Allison postulate a pre-Matthean tradition that includes Judas' remorse and return of the money; his suicide by hanging; the purchase of a field referred to as the 'potter's field' by the priests with the money returned by Judas; and the field, now known as the 'Field of Blood', is used as a cemetery for strangers.[69]

It is also possible that Matthew's account was influenced by OT texts. In Matthew, Judas' suicide is less about Judas than it is about the Jewish leaders implicated in his death. In 26.14–16 we learn that the leaders, frustrated in previous attempts to seize Jesus, paid Judas thirty pieces of silver to betray him. In 27.3, Judas, filled with remorse, returns the silver to the leaders and declares, 'I have sinned by betraying innocent blood', which may be an allusion to Deut 27.25.[70] After casting the money into the

---

[69] Davies and Allison 1988–97:III.558. While there is no evidence for such a tradition, given the alternatives, it seems plausible.
[70] See also Jer 26.15; Ps 106.38–9; 2 Kgs 24.4.

temple, Judas hangs himself. The term Matthew uses, *apagchō* ('to hang oneself'), is unique to the NT and is only used twice in the LXX (2 Sam 17.23; Tob 3.10). The 2 Samuel usage refers to Ahithophel, David's counsellor who hanged himself after his betrayal of David.[71] The money trail leads back to the Jewish leaders, who implicate themselves by picking up the silver. The leaders' concern over the fact that the thirty pieces cannot be placed in the temple treasury, the Korban, because it is 'blood money' further implicates them. Instead they buy a field, which then becomes the 'Field of Blood'. The pericope closes with what is probably a composite quotation of Zech 11.12–13; Jer 18.1ff. and 32.6–9.[72] Thus, much as the narrative is concerned with Judas' ultimate end, it also exhibits several levels of textual awareness pointing to Jesus' innocence and the culpability of the Jewish religious leadership. As an example of Matthew's narrative technique, this passage, its OT quotation and differences in the oral tradition introduce themes that are adopted in the subsequent passages.

This episode is followed by the trial of the Sanhedrin (27.11–26), which Pilate's wife interrupts to warn Pilate not to have anything to do with that 'just man' (*tō dikaiō ekeinō*), because she was troubled in a dream (*kat' onar di' auton*) on account of him (cf. 1.20; 2.12, 13, 19). The motif of 'innocent blood' is developed further in the scene with Pilate, who, perhaps convinced of Jesus' innocence, attempts to distance himself from the actions of 'the crowds' and chief priests and elders by washing his hands while saying, 'I am innocent of this one's blood.'[73] The ritual of washing one's hands to acknowledge innocence was common in the OT (Deut 21.1–9; see also Ps 26.6; 73.13). For all Pilate's effort, the fact remains that he handed Jesus over to be flogged and crucified when he had the power to prevent his death. Again the two notions of the sense of inevitability and human responsibility collide. Pilate and the mobs of Jerusalem and the Jewish leaders are aligned in their rejection of Jesus.[74]

Finally, an inspection of a section of one of the discourses will provide one further example of Matthew's ability to collect, edit and create a distinctive narrative. In the table below, one can see the Synoptic parallels to Matthew 10.

---

[71] Whether the text generated the tradition or the tradition suggested an allusion to 2 Samuel is difficult to ascertain; the latter is perhaps more likely in this case. This may be an example of the phenomena of both orality and textuality within a narrative.

[72] Brown 1994:651; on Jeremiah in Matthew, see especially Knowles 1993. [73] Knowles 1993.

[74] On the problem of whether Matthew presents the rejection of all Israel or a segment thereof, see Kvalbein 2000 and Olmstead 2003.

Matthew	Mark	Luke
10.1–4	6.7; 3.13–19	9.1; 6.12–16
10.5–15	6.8–11	9.2–5
– 5–8	---	---
– 9–15	6.8–11	9.2–5
– 15	---	---
10.16–25	13.9–13	12.11–12; 6.40; 21.12–19
10.26–33	---	12.2–9
10.34–39	---	12.51–53; 14.25–27; 17.33
10.40–42	9.41	10.16(?)

An examination of one small section of the discourse (Matt 10.5–15 par. Mark 6.6b–13 par. Luke 9.1 – 6) clearly reveals Matthew's interests. The overall arrangement and the unique material is what puts Matthew's spin on the narrative. The three gospels contain a similar scene as twelve are commissioned on a short-term mission. What is odd is that Matthew includes a section of Mark's apocalypse (13.9–13) here.[75] Rhetorically, as in the other discourses, the Jesus sayings are transparent; they have a contemporary feel, as though they are timeless. The motifs in 10.5–15, however, are more related to the historical Jesus and the social setting of Matthew's audience.

Matthew 10.5–15	Mark 6.6b–13	Luke 9.1–6
5 These twelve Jesus sent out with the following instructions: *'Go nowhere among the Gentiles, and enter no town of the Samaritans, 6 but go rather to the lost sheep of the house of Israel. 7 As you go, proclaim the good news, "The kingdom of heaven has come near." 8 Cure the sick, raise the dead, cleanse the lepers, cast out demons. You received without payment; give without payment.*	6.6b Then he went about among the villages teaching. 7 He called the twelve and began to send them out two by two, and gave them authority over the unclean spirits.	9.1 Then Jesus called the twelve together and gave them power and authority over all demons and to cure diseases, 2 and he sent them out to proclaim the kingdom of God and to heal.
9 Take no gold, or silver, or copper in your belts, 10 no bag for your journey, or two tunics, or sandals, or a staff; for laborers deserve their food.	8 He ordered them to take nothing for their journey *except a staff*; no bread, no bag, no money in their belts; 9 but to wear	3 He said to them, 'Take nothing for your journey, no staff, nor bag, nor bread, nor money — not even an extra tunic.

[75] One could, of course, argue that Matthew simply relates the oral tradition with which he is familiar. This, however, does not account for the literary similarity with Mark. Further, if one assumes Marcan priority, then it seems we have Matthew weaving Marcan apocalyptic material (13.9–13) into his narrative.

11 Whatever *town or village* you enter, find out who in it is worthy, and stay there until you leave.		
12 As you enter the house, greet it. 13 *If the house is worthy, let your peace come upon it; but if it is not worthy, let your peace return to you.*	10 He said to them, 'Wherever you enter *a house*, stay there until you leave the place.	4 Whatever *house* you enter, stay there, and leave from there.
14 If anyone will not welcome you or listen to your words, shake off the dust from your feet as you leave *that house or town.* 15 *Truly I tell you, it will be more tolerable for the land of Sodom and Gomorrah on the day of judgment than for that town.'*	11 If any place will not welcome you and they refuse to hear you, as you leave, shake off the dust that is on your feet as a testimony against them.'	5 Wherever they do not welcome you, as you are leaving *that town* shake the dust off your feet as a testimony against them.'
	12 So they went out and proclaimed that all should repent. 13 They cast out many demons, and anointed with oil many who were sick and cured them.	6 They departed and went through the villages, bringing the good news and curing diseases everywhere.

Despite the similarities amongst the three gospels, Matthew's hand is noticeable. He includes unique material in verses 5b–8. Of particular interest are the explicit directions in verses 5b–6, 'Go nowhere among the Gentiles, and enter no town of the Samaritans, 6 but go rather to the lost sheep of the house of Israel.' This line echoes Jesus' statement about his own mission in 15.24 ('I was sent only to the lost sheep of the house of Israel'), a text absent in Mark's parallel (7.24–30). This taps a rich vein running throughout Matthew's gospel, namely, that in salvation priority, Jesus came first to Israel. The gospel would go to the Samaritans and then the gentiles, but not until the occurrence of the Jewish national response[76] (21.43; 27.25) and the events of the crucifixion and resurrection, which Matthew interprets eschatologically.[77] The acts accompanying the proclamation of the good news (verses 7–8) are also very unusual and mirror Matt 11.2–6 and other summaries of Jesus' works. The disciples are to perform the same works as Jesus. But unlike Mark and Luke, the disciples in Matthew never go out in mission. The text remains instructional. This is the power of this second discourse: while it

---

[76] Olmstead 2003.
[77] The significance and irony of the name of Jesus in 1.21, 'for he will save *his people* from their sins', is captured in this statement in 10.5 and looks ahead to 21.43 and 27.25.

may have begun as an instructional text for the disciples, it quickly expands to include the church. The inclusion of the apocalyptic material in verses 16ff. suggests that it offers missional instruction for a persecuted movement and a counterbalance to the potential triumphalism that verses 7–8 could engender.

These various uses of the OT demonstrate further Matthew's interest in presenting the significance of Jesus within the purposes of God. If the above analysis is in the ballpark, the details within the narrative that differ from the other Synoptic portrayals derive not simply from the fluctuations in oral tradition (as no doubt some do) but from the OT sources. For Matthew, the allusions to the OT within the narrative itself serve as pointers to the significance of a particular event for a thoughtful or informed audience. Admittedly, it is lost on those who do not know their OT. This suggests that, at least with the OT usage, Matthew was working within more of a textual paradigm than an oral one. This, plus the other literary and stylistic features, implies that the document was crafted with a sophistication and complexity that rewarded repeated performances or readings.

CONCLUSION

The obvious conclusion is that Matthew is one who is both very concerned to preserve the tradition and keen to reinterpret it for the church (13.52). This is evident on every level of the text. However one dissects Matthew, a comparison with the written sources to which we have access demonstrates that Matthew's interest is to compose a new gospel. While this may not be clear when examining the minute adjustments, it becomes evident when one considers the consistent thematic changes. Notions of messiahship, people of God, the law, conflict with Jewish religious leadership, ecclesiology and eschatology, the portrayal of the disciples, etc. display a concerted interest on the author's part to shape the narrative to produce a particular rhetorical result. In so doing, Matthew has produced a powerful narrative of the life of Jesus that is perhaps best described by the title of Graham Stanton's substantive contribution to Matthean studies, *A Gospel for a New People*.[78]

---

[78] Stanton 1992a.

CHAPTER 7

How Mark writes

Craig A. Evans

This chapter is concerned with *how* the Marcan evangelist wrote, not *what* he wrote.[1] The distinction is important. I am not directly concerned with genre, though the chapter may well have implications for understanding the genre of Mark. Rather, we are interested in the way that the evangelist puts his materials together, contextualizing them, and why – if it can be discerned – he did what he did. But our approach is limited, for we do not possess Mark's sources (as we do for Matthew and Luke), and so we often cannot distinguish between the evangelist's source and his redaction.[2]

The primary focus of this chapter is on how the evangelist arranges his material, especially that intriguing feature variously described as intercalation or 'sandwich'. A few other aspects of the evangelist's habits of arrangement will also be taken into account. The chapter is developed in three parts: (1) aspects of Marcan style, (2) the function of digressions and sandwiches, and (3) a proposal regarding Mark's bipartite structure.

ASPECTS OF MARCAN STYLE

Much has been said about Marcan style (Elliott 1993b; Turner 1976:11–30). It is Semitic.[3] It is unpolished.[4] It is stylistically and grammatically flawed.[5] We find examples of parataxis (as seen especially in frequent usage of *kai*),

---

[1] It is with pleasure that this chapter is presented in honour of Graham Stanton, who is held in the highest esteem by his students and colleagues.

[2] Today's scepticism stands in contrast to the older approach, as exemplified by a pioneer of Marcan redaction criticism, W. Marxsen (see Marxsen 1959). Contemporary scholars take a 'compositional' approach to Mark. On this, see Stanton 2002:38–9.

[3] Zimmermann 1979:83–96; Maloney 1981; Casey 1998. For vigorous but unpersuasive attempts to show that Mark's Greek Gospel is a translation of an Aramaic original, see Torrey 1912, 1933, 1937, 1941.

[4] For review of the evidence, see Pesch 1977, 1991:1:15–32; Peabody 1987.

[5] Trocmé 1975:68–86. Trocmé's judgment (esp. p. 72: 'the author of Mark was a clumsy writer'), however, is much too harsh.

redundancies (e.g., 1.28, 32, 35; 4.2, 39; 5.15, 19; 6.25; 7.33; 12.44; 14.61), pleonasm, and the historical present (some 150 in all), and on occasion use of the wrong word (e.g., *paiein* in 14.47, which should be *patassein*). Many of these infelicities are corrected by the Matthean and Lucan evangelists (which constitutes a major argument in support of Marcan priority).

Perhaps one of the most interesting and at times frustrating features of Marcan style is the evangelist's clumsy parentheses and delayed or misplaced qualifiers. This is especially noticeable in the use of *gar* clauses, which are almost always the work of the evangelist (Guelich 1989:173). Margaret Thrall comments: 'Writers who use *gar* frequently, as Mark does, are not always logical thinkers who develop an argument stage by stage . . . In the narrative they mention first the important or striking points in the story, and then fit in the explanatory details afterwards by using *gar*, whether or not these details should logically precede the main points' (Thrall 1962:47).

More often than not, the Marcan evangelist's use of his *gar* clauses is logical and appropriate (e.g., 1.16, 22, 38; 2.15; and others). But there are at least three examples where the evangelist misplaced the clause.

1.34. 'He would not permit the demons to speak, for (*gar*) they knew him.' Mark 1.33–4 summarizes Jesus' healing activity in Capernaum: 'And he healed many who were sick with various diseases, and cast out many demons; and he would not permit the demons to speak, for they knew him.' The impression the evangelist gives is that Jesus perhaps would have allowed the demons to speak had they not known him. But that, of course, is nonsense. It is *because* the demons know who Jesus is that they speak. We see this in 1.24 ('What have you to do with us, Jesus of Nazareth? Have you come to destroy us? I know who you are, the Holy One of God') and in 3.11 ('You are the Son of God'). Knowing the name of the demon gave the exorcist an advantage. He or she could then address the demon by name, inserting the demon's name in the exorcistic formula, and then command it to depart from the possessed person. Of course, if the demon knew the name of the exorcist, it might be possible to turn the tables. Declarations such as 'I know who you are' are threats (see the eerie account in Acts 19.13–17). That is, the demon tells Jesus that it knows who he is and therefore can speak directly against him, possibly harming him. Even the declaration, 'You are the Son of God' should be understood in this manner.

However, Jesus is unfazed. He commands the demon to be silent and to depart. Jesus does not need exorcistic paraphernalia, such as Solomon's ring, the baraas root, or magical formulae (as seen in the description of the exorcist Eleazar; see Josephus, *Ant.* 8.2.5 §§42–9). He merely commands the demon and it obeys, much to the astonishment of the onlookers. Accordingly, the point of the *gar* clause is that because the demons knew who Jesus was, they spoke; and they spoke in a desperate bid to thwart Jesus' attempts at exorcism. But Jesus had no intention of wrangling with these spirits, so he did not permit them to speak.

Recognition of Mark's misplaced *gar* clause in this case may well have implications for the so-called messianic secrecy motif in this Gospel. The point of Jesus' command was not to conceal his identity; it was to forbid them from arguing with him.

11.13. Mark's qualification 'for it was not the season for figs' has raised more questions than it has answered. Nevertheless, it offers another illustration of the misplaced Marcan *gar* clause. The strange episode begins with the cursing of the fig tree (11.12–14). The first two verses read: 'On the following day, when they came from Bethany, he was hungry. And seeing in the distance a fig tree in leaf, he went to see if he could find anything on it. When he came to it, he found nothing but leaves, for it was not the season for figs' (11.12–13). The placement of the *gar* clause suggests that the reason there were only leaves on the tree was that it was not the season for figs. Mark's narration makes Jesus' expectations and angry response seem ludicrous and capricious. But the *gar* clause is not intended to modify 'he found nothing but leaves' in verse 13, but 'he went to see if he could find anything on it' in verse 12. In other words, seeing the fig tree in leaf was not sufficient reason to believe that edible buds might be present; one had to examine the tree up close, 'for it was not the season for figs', which will appear later in the year. Leafy trees in the spring may indicate the presence of edible buds. But when Jesus examined the tree, he found none, despite the encouraging signs of the early foliage.

16.4. Mark's explanation 'for the stone was very large' is a classic. The evangelist's misplacement of the qualifying *gar* clause in this passage is so illogical as to be humorous. The relevant part of the passage reads: 'And they were saying to one another, "Who will roll away the stone for us from the door of the tomb?" And looking up, they saw that the stone was rolled back – for it was very large' (16.3–4). If this is taken literally, Mark seems to be saying that the stone was rolled back because it was very large (as though smaller stones were less likely to roll back!). Of course, this is not what the evangelist means to say. The *gar* clause explains the question of the women: 'Who will roll away the stone for us from the door of the tomb?' (verse 3). The women wonder at this, because the stone is very large and therefore they may not be able to roll it aside without assistance. Thus, Mark's *gar* clause belongs at the end of verse 3, not at the end of verse 4.

Three other awkward qualifying clauses may be mentioned briefly. In the passage about the Gerasene demoniac the evangelist inserts in 5.8 'for he had said to him, "Come out of the man, you unclean spirit!"' Jesus' command belongs earlier in the narrative, either in verse 6 or in verse 7. However, the misplacement of this clause, though somewhat awkward, does not create the confusion that we have seen in the first three examples. Another awkward *gar* clause is found in what is on the whole a very awkward passage. According to Mark 3.20–2: 'And the crowd came together again, so that they could not even eat. And when his family heard it, they went out to seize him, for people were saying, "He is mad." And the scribes who came down from Jerusalem said, "He is possessed by Beelzebul, and by the prince of demons he casts out the demons."' The awkwardness here is not so much due to the placement of the *gar* clause (delayed, as usual), but to the placement of the clause at the beginning of verse 21 ('when his family heard it'). As it stands, the evangelist seems to be saying that when Jesus' family heard that such a large crowd gathered that they could not eat, they went out to seize him. But that is not the reason, as is explained at the end of verse 21. What the family heard was not how crowded things had become, but that people were saying of Jesus, 'He is mad.'

And finally, we may consider one more example, one that does not involve a *gar* clause. According to Mark 4.35–6: 'On that day, when evening had come, he said to them, "Let us go across to the other side." And leaving the crowd, they took him with them in the boat, just as he was. And other boats were with him.' The 'just as he was' (*hōs ēn*) clause, alongside 'they took him with them', is quite awkward, leaving the reader wondering what is meant. It is not surprising that Matthew and Luke edit the Marcan introduction to this pericope. Matthew reads: 'And when he got into the boat, his disciples followed him' (Matt 8.23). Luke reads: 'One day he got into a boat with his disciples' (Luke 8.22). The problem in Mark is solved when one remembers that Jesus had earlier entered the boat, so that he could teach, undisturbed by the large crowd (cf. Mark 4.1). Accordingly, the evangelist's 'just as he was' means no more than that Jesus was already in the boat.

THE FUNCTION OF DIGRESSIONS AND SANDWICHES

Commentators and interpreters of Mark have from the very beginning observed Mark's digressions and clumsy order. It is not surprising that early in the second century Papias asserted that the evangelist did not in fact write in strict chronological or sequential order. In an oft-cited passage, the Father says:

And the Elder used to say this: 'Mark, having become Peter's interpreter, wrote down accurately everything he remembered, though not in order [*ou mentoi taxei*], of the things either said or done by Christ [*or* the Lord]. For he neither heard the Lord nor followed him, but afterward, as I said, followed Peter, who adapted his teachings as anecdotes [*pros tas chreias*] but had no intention of giving an ordered account [*ouch ... suntaxin*] of the Lord's sayings. Consequently Mark did nothing wrong in writing down some things as he remembered them, for he made it his one concern not to omit anything that he heard or to make any false statement in them.'(Eusebius, *Hist. Eccl.* 3.39.15)[6]

This famous passage has occasioned a great deal of discussion.[7] Although it is true that *taxis* and *syntaxis* do not necessarily refer to chronology, it is probable that Papias is saying that Mark's narrative is not tightly connected and that there are gaps in the narrative and some stories are simply out of place. The teachings of Jesus are presented as anecdotes (i.e., *chreiai*), not as an ordered, sequential account.[8] Study of Mark's narrative fully justifies Papias' description. It seems that the evangelists Matthew and Luke recognize this dimension in their Marcan source, as they edit, connect, and recontextualize some of these anecdotes and units of tradition.

One feature of Marcan narrative that has gained attention is the interrupted story, or 'sandwich', in which the evangelist begins a story, breaks away to tell another story, then resumes and completes the original story. These instances have been variously called interpolations, intercalations, and sandwiches. The last term seems to be in vogue these days.[9] They are presented as A + B + A structures.

Various explanations of this narrative feature have been offered. Most agree that the evangelist intends to heighten the drama of his story, calling attention to certain themes and theological perspectives. Tom Shepherd sees 'dramatized irony' in the Marcan sandwiches (Shepherd 1993:380, 384, and elsewhere). This seems correct in most instances. Gerald Downing

---

[6] The English translation is based on Lightfoot and Harmer 1989:316. For Greek text, see Lightfoot 1891:517; Lake 1926:296.

[7] For a representative sampling, see Westcott 1881:184–5; Schoedel 1967:105–19; Martin 1973:80–3; Hengel 1985a:47–50, 69–70; Gundry 1993:1026–45, esp. 1036–9.

[8] Some scholars render *pros tas chreias* 'as needed' (as in Lightfoot and Harmer 1989:316; Stanton 2002:55: 'to the needs'). See discussion in Kürzinger 1977. I follow Gundry 1993:1027, who translates 'with the anecdotes'.

[9] Studies of this phenomenon include Wright 1985; Edwards 1999; Van Oyen 1992; Shepherd 1993, 1995; Downing 2000. German terms include *Schiebungen, Ineinanderschachtelungen,* and *Verschachtelungen.*

finds somewhat similar patterns of digression and resumption in popular literature, especially the romances, of late antiquity, though he thinks that there are special features in Mark's employment of the technique.[10] Again, this seems correct. Probing for greater precision, James Edwards comments: 'The sandwiches emphasize the major motifs of the Gospel, especially the meaning of faith, discipleship ... the middle story' is the key (Edwards 1999:195).

Of these studies I find that of Edwards the most stimulating and compelling. His recent publication of a detailed commentary on Mark only further rewards review of his work (Edwards 2002). His work will be the point of departure for the rest of this chapter.

In most cases the middle component does seem to be the key, as Edwards has argued. But the interpretative function is reciprocal. We shall examine the most probable examples of Markan sandwiches: 5.21–43; 11.12–21; 14.1–11; and 14.53–72.[11] The story of the woman with the haemorrhage (5.21–43) may well exemplify the kind of faith that the frightened Jairus needs to have (so Edwards). The temple action (11.15–18) certainly clarifies the meaning of the fig tree (11.12–14, 19–21), as Edwards argues, but does not the fig tree shed far more light on the temple action? The anointing of Jesus is certainly the key element in Mark 14.1–11, but does not the devotion of the woman highlight the treachery of Judas (14.10–11) as much as his treachery highlights the faith and devotion of the unnamed woman? And finally, the sandwiched trials of Peter and Jesus at the home of the high priest – which Mark probably did not create but inherited from the tradition – mutually clarify: the courageous and unwavering Jesus stands in stark contrast to the faithless and cowardly disciple. But this pericope is more complicated than that, for the jeers hurled at Jesus that he 'prophesy' unwittingly remind Mark's readers that Jesus' earlier prophecy that Peter will fail is in fact being fulfilled at that very moment. (The prophecy, of course, falls outside the present passage.) Let us review these four passages in greater detail.

Mark 5.21–43. The combined stories of the healing of the woman with the haemorrhage and the raising of the daughter of Jairus have drawn a great deal of attention from redaction critics and interpreters of Mark. Some wonder if the number *twelve* drew the stories together

---

[10] Downing 2000:113–17. I have made a similar observation in my brief note, Evans 1982. The presence of Mark's insertions is often indicated by editorial seams, where a word or phrase at the point of breaking away is repeated at the point of resumption. For a list of Marcan seams, see Donahue 1973:241–3.

[11] Others have been proposed. See Edwards 1999:196–7. See also the list in Neirynck 1988:133.

(i.e., the number of years the woman suffered and the age of the daughter). Some think that the insertion of the material on the woman with the haemorrhage was intended to heighten suspense, to delay resolution of the major story, that of the dying daughter and her frightened father.

Edwards himself sees contrast in the principal characters in the stories. The unnamed woman has the kind of faith in Jesus that the prominent and named synagogue ruler should have. Her faith and her instantaneous healing should be a lesson to Jairus (Edwards 1999:204).

Edwards may well be correct in his analysis, so far as it goes. Contrast seems to play a role in all of the Marcan sandwiches. It may play a role in this passage too. But is the contrast between the two characters the evangelist's actual point? In my view the two stories teach Mark's readers that nothing is beyond Jesus' healing and redemptive power, whether it concerns a woman whose seemingly interminable condition has frustrated the best medical help that money can buy, or a prominent religious man whose daughter has died before the well-known healer could reach her. By combining these stories in the way he has done, the Marcan evangelist underscores this point.

This seems to be the principal point of these combined stories. Indeed, the contrast between the suffering woman and the anxious father contributes to this point. The woman with the haemorrhage had to endure the stigma of ritual impurity – perhaps we are to imagine that her friends and neighbours believed that this is why her prayers for recovery went unheeded. In her case – some of Jesus' contemporaries may well have thought – her problems reflected religious or spiritual shortcomings. In her case, perhaps, but surely this cannot be the explanation for the synagogue ruler, who by dint of office would have been viewed as a man unhindered in his petitions for heavenly mercy.[12] Alas, not so; even his piety and prayers (and those of his synagogue) could not save his daughter.

Thus, despite the obvious contrasts in the social standings of the two principals – the unnamed woman and the named synagogue ruler – in the end they are equals. They are equally desperate. Without Jesus there is no

---

[12] Admittedly I am assuming here a synthesis of Jewish ideas held by some in late antiquity, namely that God hears the prayers of only the righteous (cf. John 9.31) and that religious leaders were generally regarded as righteous (as implied in Mark 2.17 in context). These ideas provide an important part of the backdrop of Jesus' interview with the rich man (identified in Luke 18.18 as a 'ruler', probably meaning a religious ruler, possibly a synagogue ruler). When this man, who has kept the commandments from childhood, receives from Jesus no assurance of eternal life, the disciples ask in bewilderment, 'Then who can be saved?' (Mark 10.26). That is to say, if a religious leader cannot be saved, then can anyone? Building dedications and epitaphs also attest to the esteem, if not piety, in which rulers of synagogues were held.

salvation. Yet, despite the apparent hopelessness of their respective problems, Jesus is able to bring healing and restoration.

Mark 11.12–21. The intercalation of the cursing of the fig tree and the
action in the temple precincts is the most important of all the Marcan
sandwiches. Edwards, like others, assumes that the fig tree symbolizes Israel
(Edwards 1999:207; and it seems to in Hos 9.10). But most references to fig
trees in the Old Testament are not symbolic and do not represent Israel.

The only other occurrence of a fig tree in Mark (i.e., Mark 13.28) has
nothing to do with Israel. More importantly, in the context of Mark 11 the
fig tree is related to the temple establishment, not to the people of Israel.
The appeals to Isaiah and Jeremiah concern priestly failings, not national
failings. Moreover, in the parable of the Vineyard in Mark 12, it is not the
vineyard that is at fault (and in the Old Testament the vineyard sometimes
symbolizes Israel, as in Isaiah 5), but the ruling priests, who understand this
interpretative perspective and deeply resent it (cf. Mark 12.12). The same
seems to be the point in the sandwich under consideration. The fig tree,
which is fruitless and therefore judged, illustrates the temple establishment,
not the people of Israel.[13] Wrapping the fig tree story around the temple
action strongly recommends this interpretation. The fig tree helps the
reader understand why Jesus took the action he took. Indeed, without
the interpretative assistance of the fruitless fig tree and its subsequent
judgment, the reader would be left wondering why Jesus took umbrage
and acted the way he did. The action in the temple precincts itself clarifies
the significance of the fig tree: the fig tree does not signify Israel as a whole,
but the nation's religious leadership. The Marcan sandwich here must be
taken as a whole; neither part is fully intelligible without the other.

Mark 14.1–11. Contrast plays a significant role in this Marcan sandwich.
The perfidy of Judas Iscariot is sharply contrasted with the devotion and
extravagance of the unnamed woman. For reasons we can only imagine,
Judas gives up his loyalty to Jesus. Not so the woman, who despite the
danger, demonstrates her faith in Jesus as Israel's anointed. Death as theme
is accentuated by the evangelist when Jesus declares that the woman has
anointed his body beforehand for burial. Not only does this startling

---

[13] It has been suggested that the fig tree in fact represents the temple itself, not the ruling priests.
On this line of interpretations, see Ådna 2000. Admittedly, the fate of the temple is closely
bound up with the fate of the ruling priests (which is partly why I speak of the 'temple
establishment'). Destruction of the ruling priests will bring with it the destruction of the temple.
But Jesus' criticism is specifically levelled against the *priests* (Mark 11.15, 18), who have made the
temple 'a cave of robbers' (Mark 11.17, alluding to Jer 7.11). As the parable of the Vineyard makes
clear, the vineyard itself is not at fault. The fault lies with the hired servants. It is they who have
not allowed the temple to be the place of 'prayer for all the nations' (alluding to Isa 56.7).

remark reinterpret the act of anointing (from messianic faith to burial preparation), but describing the anointing as 'beforehand' may well darkly hint that in dying as a criminal (for whom the seven-day public funeral is not permitted), Jesus may not otherwise be anointed.

The contrast between Judas and the unnamed woman is rendered especially poignant by the evangelist when Jesus says, 'And truly, I say to you, wherever the gospel is preached in the whole world, what she has done will be told in memory of her' (14.9). Mark's readers will recall that Judas had originally been appointed as one of the Twelve, in order to proclaim the good news of the kingdom (Mark 3.14–19; 6.7–13). But wherever the gospel is proclaimed, the woman's act of devotion will be remembered and, by association, so will the act of villainy on the part of Judas – who was supposed to be a proclaimer of the gospel.

But the contrast is not only between the unnamed woman and the named disciple. There is an implicit contrast between the faith, love, and loyalty of the woman and the villainous intentions of the ruling priests who plot against Jesus. Instead of hailing him when he first entered the temple precincts, and instead of offering to anoint him as Israel's Messiah (as Samuel anointed David – the story of which is recounted in Aramaic Psalm 118, the Psalm to which appeal is made in the entrance narrative in Mark 11 and at the conclusion of the vineyard parable in Mark 12), the ruling priests seek to destroy him. The evangelist's sandwiches make the contrast between the opposing characters much more obvious to the Gospel's readers.

Mark 14.53–72. The contrast between the courageous Jesus inside before the ruling priests and the cowardly Peter outside before the servants has been a favourite among interpreters and preachers for centuries. In my view this sandwich pre-dates Mark, for the references to Peter 'warming himself' at the fire (14.54, 67) are also found in John 18.18, 25. For reasons that need not be rehearsed here it is improbable that the fourth Gospel is dependent on Mark.[14]

But even if the evangelist inherited this sandwiched material, this does not mean that it has any less significance than the other sandwiches that he constructed himself. Peter's miserable failure heightens the portrait of Jesus as one who does not quail in the face of intimidation and danger. The leading disciple has denied his master in the presence of a servant girl – socially

[14] As I argue in Evans 1982:249, which is accepted by Edwards 1999:211. See the summary in Stanton 2002:102–3. Stanton rightly views Johannine independence of the Synoptic Gospels as the majority view, though there are exceptions (among them C. K. Barrett, R. J. Bauckham, and F. Neirynck).

and politically the least powerful person in the Jewish world, whereas Jesus speaks the truth before the high priest – the most powerful person in the Jewish world.

But the contrast runs far deeper than that of faithless Peter on the one hand and faithful, courageous Jesus on the other. The sandwiched material calls the reader's attention to the person and identity of Jesus. In his climactic third denial, Peter asserts that he does not know Jesus (14.71). This flies in the face of the many confessions earlier in Mark, in which various characters do know who Jesus is (e.g., 1.24, 34; 3.11; 5.6–7; 10.47–8), including God (1.11; 9.7) and Peter himself (8.29). The identity of Jesus is also acknowledged at the end of the Marcan narrative by the Roman centurion (15.39).

The truthfulness of Jesus' identity – as God's Son who truthfully proclaims the rule of God – is underscored by the fulfilment of prophecy during the hearing before the Jewish authorities. Mark's readers know that earlier in chapter 14 Jesus prophesied that not only would all of his disciples fall away, but Peter himself would deny him three times before the rooster sounded (14.27–31). Sure enough, while Jesus is mocked and told to 'Prophesy!' (14.65), Peter is outside in the courtyard fulfilling Jesus' prophecy. Mark's reader marvels at how again and again Jesus cuts a striking figure, through whom God is clearly at work, no matter the dangers and difficulties. Others may fall away and prove cowardly and faithless; Jesus remains constant.

THE BIPARTITE STRUCTURE OF MARK

One may wonder if Mark's bipartite structure is in some sense cognate in structure and purpose to the sandwich structure that has been discussed. Many interpreters see Mark as breaking down into halves, approximately chapters 1–8 and 9–16. Most see at the end of chapter 8 and the beginning of chapter 9 something of a transition, a move from the Galilean ministry characterized by miracles to the journey to and ministry in Jerusalem characterized by the Passion.

What encourages this analysis is the appearance of the heavenly voice at the beginning of the two halves (i.e., 1.11; 9.7). That is, at the beginning of the Galilean ministry, the voice of God is heard saying, 'Thou art my beloved Son; with thee I am well pleased' (1.11). Then, after the announcement of the forthcoming Passion, the heavenly voice is again heard, 'This is my beloved Son; listen to him' (9.7). If this analysis is correct, then Mark's

Gospel as a whole may be a 'sandwich', with A = 1.1–8.26, B = 8.27–9.1, A = 9.2–16.8.

Of course, I am only suggesting an analogy, not an exact parallel. The sandwiches that have been reviewed above consist of two discrete units of material, with one inserted into the middle of the other. The whole of Mark appears to consist of two major parts, with the heavenly voice heard near their respective beginnings. What lies in the middle is not a block of material comparable in length, but rather a much smaller unit of tradition that functions as a hinge, linking the two halves. Although this macro structure is obviously different at points, the Marcan evangelist's use of sandwiches may aid in our attempt to understand better his composition as a whole.

The divine voice at the beginning of both halves underscores what is for the evangelist the most important element in christology: the divine sonship of Jesus. This feature coheres with his opening verse, the incipit of the Marcan Gospel: 'The beginning of the gospel of Jesus Christ, the Son of God' (1.1).[15]

The contents of the middle section, the B portion of our proposed outline, also contribute in significant ways to the christological thrust of the Marcan evangelist:

8.27–30. In this pericope the question of Jesus' identity is raised explicitly. 'Who do men say that I am?' Jesus asks his disciples. The various identities mentioned remind Mark's readers of the earlier speculation on the part of Herod, tetrarch of Galilee (6.14–16). It is significant that there Herod specifically wondered if Jesus might be John the Baptist raised from the dead, an idea that suggested itself because of the extraordinary power at work in Jesus. This identity is recalled in 8.28, which receives further significance in view of Jesus' first Passion prediction (8.31) and allusion to the fate of John (9.13). The identity of Jesus is boldly affirmed by Peter: 'You are the Christ' (8.29). This confession also recalls the Marcan incipit: 'The beginning of the gospel of Jesus Christ' (1.1) and anticipates the high priest's threatening question, 'Are you the Christ?' (14.61). Thus, Peter's confession, here at the centre of the Marcan narrative, welds together the beginning and ending of the two principal structural components.

8.31–3. The Passion prediction, which will be repeated in 9.31 and 10.33–4 and then acted out in chapters 14–15, qualifies Peter's messianic confession and sets the tone for the second half of the Marcan narrative. It is as though the evangelist has said: Yes, Jesus is the Messiah, but he is a

---

[15] On the originality of 'Son of God' in Mark 1.1, see Guelich 1989:6; Evans 2000.

Messiah who must suffer and die. Thus the B component in the Marcan structure does not *deny* the messianic identity of Jesus (as the miracles of chapters 1–8 support), but it does *qualify* it, preparing for the Passion narrative that will follow.

8.34–9.1. This pericope provides the next important, logical step for the evangelist. Not only is Jesus the Messiah – indeed, a Messiah who must suffer – but those who will follow him must be prepared to suffer the same fate: 'If any man would come after me, let him deny himself and take up his cross and follow me' (8.34). The pericope ends with the assurance that his followers will indeed see the rule of God come with power (9.1).

9.2–8. The B portion of the structure ends on a reassuring note. The announcement of suffering does not mean the withdrawal of divine approval. Jesus is still very much God's Son and still very much possesses the authority of heaven, on earth (cf. 2.10). Accordingly, the heavenly voice reassures the disciples: 'This is my beloved Son; listen to him' (9.7). The heavenly confirmation ends on a note of admonition, 'listen to him', which may well allude to the Mosaic command in Deut 18.15.

The elements that make up the transition, or B portion of the structure, do indeed appear to enhance and clarify the A halves. The first A half (Mark 1.1–8.26) dramatically illustrates Jesus' divine authority and power, thus justifying the bold assertion in the incipit that Jesus is the Son of God. The B portion recognizes this, concluding with Peter's confession that Jesus is indeed the Christ.[16] Of course, the B portion goes on to speak of suffering and death, which prepares readers for chapters 9–15 of the Marcan narrative.

Thus, the B portion of Mark's structure appears to function as a hinge or transition, linking the two halves of the Marcan Gospel. But at the same time this transitional unit also seems to play the role of the middle part of the Marcan sandwich, in that it clarifies and intensifies themes that are important to the evangelist. Christology, which includes suffering, is brought to the fore.

Mark's transitional unit also supplies an important element of contrast, which is often the case in B portions of Marcan sandwiches. The most obvious part of the contrast is seen in redefining Messiah in terms of suffering. Not only does this contrast with the power and authority seen in Jesus' ministry in the first eight chapters of the Marcan narrative, but it contrasts sharply with popular messianism in the first century. The Jewish

---

[16] Evidently the Matthean evangelist well understood the Marcan thrust at this point, astutely expanding Peter's confession to read: 'You are the Christ, the Son of the living God' (Matt 16.16).

Messiah was expected to defeat Israel's enemies (in Jesus' day this would have primarily meant the Roman Empire), not be executed.[17]

The structural analysis that has been proposed here is not a conventional Marcan sandwich by any means. The conventional sandwich comprises two stories combined. What has been proposed here is different, for it involves the whole of the Marcan narrative, which comprises many stories. But aspects of this structuring device seem to hold. Sandwiched in the middle of the two principal components of the Marcan narrative is a transitional unit that plays a vital role in relating the two disparate parts, making it possible for the one to lead to the other and for both to make sense in the light of the other. Indeed, each half deepens the meaning of the other, which would not have been possible without the B portion of the structure. The powerful, striking figure of Jesus in the first half is made all the more striking when the reader learns that he knows that death awaits him and he is willing to accept this fate. The second half of the narrative is also enhanced, for the reader knows that the betrayed, deserted, denied, and executed Jesus is indeed God's Son, who knowingly and willingly embraced his fate.

CONCLUDING COMMENTS

There are other features of Marcan style and compositional techniques that might be considered. The evangelist's adoption of Old Testament motifs that function as backdrops to the ministry of Jesus reveals more sophistication than some interpreters have allowed.[18] His opening verse, or incipit, appears to be an unmistakable allusion to the Roman imperial cult: 'The beginning of the good news of Jesus Christ, Son of God' (1.1). One thinks immediately of the Priene calendar inscription in honour of Augustus (*OGIS* no. 458; see also P. Oxy. 1021, in reference to Nero). Recently, it has been suggested that Mark incorporates themes and images from the Homeric epics (MacDonald 2000). Other points of contact with literary themes and traditions have been suggested.[19]

---

[17] The Davidic Messiah of *Psalms of Solomon* 17 and 4Q285 is expected to rout Israel's gentile enemies, even kill the Roman emperor. The awkwardness that the death of Jesus at the hands of the Roman prefect caused for early Christians is attested in John 18, where the Johannine Jesus informs Pilate that the latter in fact does not have the power to take Jesus' life, and in Justin Martyr (*Dial.* 89.1; 90.1), where Trypho protests that he finds the idea of Israel's Messiah dying a shameful death completely unacceptable: 'We cannot bring ourselves even to consider this.'

[18] For example, see Mauser 1963; Marcus 1992; Watts 1997. These studies call into question the conclusion that the Marcan evangelist had little interest in the Old Testament, which is argued by Suhl 1965.

[19] These suggestions are usually tendered in discussion of the question of Mark's genre. See Votaw 1970; Bilezikian 1977; Talbert 1977; Cancik 1984b; Guelich 1991; Burridge 1992; Stanton 2004.

We have found in Mark a thoughtful, even sophisticated ability to tell the story of Jesus by stringing together a series of anecdotes, yet without losing sight of important motifs and theological points. We are accustomed to the genre of the New Testament Gospels, taking them for granted. But Mark's effort was an attempt at something that in many ways was new. The Marcan Gospel is an instance of biography,[20] to be sure, but the crafting of this narrative from what were mostly loose and unconnected materials is a remarkable achievement.[21]

The Marcan evangelist found ways to arrange and connect his materials that would develop and advance a compelling plot and at the same time would instruct his readers in important aspects of christology, discipleship, and eschatology. For all the evangelist's shortcomings in matters of literary style and polish, it must be admitted that his literary achievement is nonetheless remarkable and should be viewed as successful. In that the Matthean and Lucan evangelists adopt approximately 95 per cent of the Markan text between them, it seems that they would agree with this assessment.

---

[20] With 'biography' here understood in the light of the qualifications argued in the learned works cited in the previous footnote (especially in Talbert and Burridge).

[21] Here I am assuming the basic insights of the classical form critics (Bultmann, Dibelius, and Schmidt).

CHAPTER 8

How Luke writes

David P. Moessner

'This Gospel is represented fittingly by the calf, because it begins with priests and ends with the Calf who, having taken upon himself the sins of all, was sacrificed for the life of the whole world.'[1] Thus Ambrose (333–97 CE) describes the 'Gospel according to Luke' which, in the subsequent years, has become one of the most beloved of the church's four Gospels. 'The most beautiful book in the world' was Renan's estimate.[2] Indeed, the Third Gospel portrays uniquely some of the most loved of Jesus' miniatures of the Kingdom of God in 'The Good Samaritan', 'The Prodigal (Lost) Son', 'The Friend at Midnight', 'The Persistent Widow'[3] et al., not to mention one of the most dramatically and beautifully narrated 'short stories' in all the Bible, the walk to Emmaus, where the suspense breaks only as Jesus 'is recognized' – finally – 'in the breaking of the bread'.[4]

Yet Luke's Gospel was not apparently the first to be recognized by the church in the second century when written 'gospels according to' an apostle or follower of an apostle first emerged.[5] But when the Third Gospel does emerge in the third-century commentary of Origen,[6] it has already established itself as foundational in the celebration of the church year and seems to be preferred for much of the church's admonitions for alms for the poor,[7]

---

[1] Ambrose, *Exposition of the Gospel of Luke* 1.4.7 in Just 2003:2.   [2] Renan 1877:283.
[3] Luke 10.25–37; 15.11–32; 11.5–8; 18.1–8 respectively.   [4] Luke 24.13–35.
[5] Papias (cited by Eusebius, *Hist. Eccl.* 3.39.14–16), conducting interviews towards the beginning of the second century of the first-generation apostles and their followers/acquaintances, cites 'John the Elder's' remarks on Mark and Matthew. The vocabulary used for Mark's alleged deficiencies, however, might suggest that Luke is the implicit standard of good narrative writing; cf. §15: Mark wrote not *in taxei* but nevertheless *akribōs*! (cf. Luke 1.1, 3); cf. Reicke 1986:166–7; Moessner 1999a:114–19.
[6] Origen, *Homilies on Luke, Fragments on Luke* (Origen 1996). The first explicit reference to Luke's 'gospel' among the 'Fathers' of the church is disputed, but appears to be Irenaeus towards the end of the second century in his *Against the Heresies*, 3.1.1, who aligns Luke's message with Paul's 'gospel'. See further, e.g., Fitzmyer 1981:37–41.
[7] Cf. the opening prayer for the Feast of St Luke in the *Sacramentary of the Roman Missal*: 'Father, you chose Luke the evangelist to reveal by preaching and writing the mystery of your love for the poor ... and let all nations come to see your salvation ... through our Lord Jesus Christ, your Son ... one God, for ever and ever.'

particularly as Luke's special material[8] matches catechetical emphases of the Lenten season.[9]

The topic of 'How Luke Writes' will be illuminated through 'What Luke Writes' (section I) and 'Why Luke Writes', (section II).

I WHAT LUKE WRITES (THE CHARACTER OF THE THIRD GOSPEL AMONG THE 'FOUR')

The Third Gospel distinguishes itself among the canonical four first of all through its connection to a second 'book' in a single two-volume work, The Gospel according to Luke[10] and the Acts of the Apostles, first referred to as 'Luke–Acts' in the post-war exegesis of the last century.[11] The church, however, never spoke of or even utilized, to our knowledge, 'Luke's' programme of composing one narrative movement in two parts.[12] Instead, Luke's Gospel was aligned alongside the other three, and among the varying sequences of canonical lists – even in one instance when Luke is listed last among the four – Acts never follows the Third Gospel![13] Beyond the necessary physical separation of two lengthy papyrus scrolls, the emerging church apparently was also forced to sift through a variety of 'Gospel' portrayals of Jesus to authenticate those accounts that squared with apostolic oral traditions, a process that Luke himself may be hinting at in its early stages in his Gospel prologue (Luke 1.1–4): (the) 'many [who] have undertaken to compose a narrative account of events come to fruition in our midst ... concerning those traditions (*logōn*) of which you have been instructed'. It is clear that what Luke had joined together formally and materially (Luke 1.1–4→Acts 1.1–2),[14] the church has rent asunder.

---

[8] The passages unique to Luke ('L'): e.g., Luke 12.47–8; 16.1–13, 14–15, 19–31; 17.7–10; 18.9–14.

[9] Just 2003, who cites *Augustine and the Catechumenate* (Harmless 1995) and Augustine's *Sermons on Various Subjects*, sermons 341–400, from Augustine 1995.

[10] For the emerging titles of the Gospels, cf., e.g., Reicke 1986:150–5; Hengel 2000:48–56; Lührmann 2004:29–47.

[11] For a brief survey of modern approaches to 'Luke–Acts', see Moessner and Tiede 1999; cf., e.g., the article title 'Luke–Acts, Book of' in *ABD* (Johnson 1992).

[12] Cf. the so-called 'Anti-Marcionite Prologue', ca. end of the second century: 'Luke was a Syrian of Antioch, by profession a physician, the disciple of the apostles, and later a follower of Paul until his martyrdom ... he was prompted by the Holy Spirit and composed this gospel entirely in the regions about Achaia ... Later the same Luke wrote the Acts of the Apostles'; see further, Fitzmyer 1981:37–41; Glover 1964–5.

[13] Cf., e.g., the 'Cheltenham Canon' (ca. 360 CE – northern Africa): Matthew – Mark – John – Luke – Paulines! – Acts; see Cadbury 1955:143–4.

[14] The arrows used with Scripture passages in this essay represent the dynamic within the narrative performance of auditors/readers recalling or anticipating the same or similar cluster(s) of phrases/

Nevertheless, it has become equally clear, given the passel of historical-critical and poststructuralist tools available to the (post)modern exegete, that the significance of events in Luke's Gospel is greatly enhanced through their construal in Acts and that, conversely, our understanding of Acts is 'significantly' impoverished without a fundamental grasp of its prequel ('all that Jesus began to do and to teach', Acts 1.1). Each volume completes as well as comments directly upon the other.[15]

1 Beginnings and endings

The very different beginning and ending of Luke's Gospel vis-à-vis the other three sets this volume apart in both scope and impact. Following his formal *prooemium* (see below), Luke places the action of John the Baptist's and Jesus' callings squarely within the history of Israel ('in the days of Herod, King of Judea', Luke 1.5) and its priestly orders at the centre of Israel's worship in the Jerusalem Temple ('a certain priest named Zechariah'). The choice of images and cadences of these first two chapters, in fact, echo Septuagintal (LXX) synchronisms,[16] as well as the stories of the callings of Abraham and Sarah (Gen 16.7–16; 17.1–22; 18.1–15), Manoah, his wife, and Sampson (Judg 13.2–25), Hannah and Samuel (1 Kgdms 2.1–10), and even Daniel (Dan 8.15–26; 9.20–7[17]) as the archangel Gabriel 'appears' (Luke 1.8–20, 26–38) to continue God's raising up of a prophet and a saviour to 'come to the aid of Israel, his [God's] servant' (Mariam, 1.54) and 'to visit and make ransom for the redemption of his people Israel' (Zechariah, 1.68b[18]).

---

themes/expressions in the rest of the narrative. The arrows 'take you back' or 'move you forward' as echo or flash forward. In both cases the word(s) or phrase(s) serve as 'metaleptic prompts' (my phrase).

[15] See, e.g., the volume of the 47th Colloquium Biblicum Lovaniense (1998) devoted to this issue (Verheyden 1999).

[16] E.g., the Septuagintal idiom: 'It happened in the day(s) of . . .' ([*kai*] *egeneto en tais hēmerais . . .*): Judg 14.15, 17; 18.31; 19.5; Ruth 1.1; 1 Kgdms 3.2; 4.1; 13.22; 28.1; 2 Kgdms 21.1; 3 Kgdms 9.9, *inter alia*; cf. several other analogous idioms.

[17] Gabriel appears to Daniel 'at the time of the evening sacrifice', Dan 9.22 – i.e., the same time as the *Tamid* offering in Luke 1.5–23 – and interprets to Daniel the vision of the 'seventy weeks of years' which climaxes in an 'anointed one' (*christos*) who 'is cut off' (9.26); cf. Exod 30.7–8.

[18] My rendering of the unusual phrase 'make redemption', which is not found in the LXX. But what is consistent from the LXX's usage of the verb *lutroō* and its noun *lutrōsis* is the requirement of either animal sacrifice or ransom money/goods (*lutron*) to *make* redemption a reality. In conjunction with God 'visiting' his people to effect release from slavery and/or sin (Luke 1.68b), 'make redemption' denotes the unspecified means through which God's presence for release is accomplished (cf. LXX Ps 110.9 ('send redemption')). Cf. Fitzmyer 1981:383: 'the combination of the noun *lytrōsis* with the verb *poiein* is strange . . . it describes Yahweh's activity on behalf of his people in terms of ransom or release'; cf. Johnson 1991:46: 'In contrast to the "liberation" of the people from Egypt under Moses, however (Acts 7.35), Luke here defines it in apolitical, cultic terms.' For God's visitation as gracious

But now it would appear that this 'coming of God' will enact something final and definitive 'forever' (cf. Luke 1.33, 55). John will be 'a prophet of the Most High' (1.76a) who will prepare a repenting people (1.16–17) and go before the Lord (1.76b), while Jesus will be 'Son of the Most High', 'the Savior, the Messiah, the Lord' ('angel/messenger of the Lord', 2.11) 'who will reign over the house of Jacob', 'on David's throne' 'forever' (1.32–3).

With these rich resonances of Israel's Scriptures it would thus appear that the promises to the ancestors of the 'Lord's Christ' like those to Hannah are on the verge of fulfilment when 'he will judge the ends of the earth' (cf. *krinei akra gēs ... christou autou*, 1 Kgdms 2.10 and Luke 2.26–32 – *christon kuriou ... phōs eis apokalypsin kai doxan laou sou Israēl*) as 'a light of revelation to the Gentiles and glory to your people Israel' (to Simeon (and Hannah!)).[19] Moreover, both Mariam and Zechariah prophesy of God's mercy executing great *reversal* in the socio-political bondage to oppressive 'enemies'. Patron–client relations will be reversed;[20] those of peasant-servile status like Mariam herself will be exalted over the proud and mighty;[21] the rich will be stripped of power and possessions;[22] and Israel will reign over all its enemies as in the glory days of David, with God's strength manifest in unprecedented 'peace and holiness',[23] just as God had promised Abraham and all the prophets had echoed in anticipating the time when God would fulfil 'His holy covenant'. Are these images of liberation and salvation to be taken literally?[24]

The *end* of Luke's Gospel certainly confirms a scriptural 'end'-scape of God's promises to Israel. The crucified but resurrected Jesus 'appears' to continue God's raising up of witnesses to the eschatological salvation of Israel that has been 'prepared' for all peoples of the world. But in Luke 24.44–9 the apostles' 'recognition' of Jesus can only ensue once they comprehend the *fulfilment of all that stands written* about him as 'the

---

deliverance, see esp. LXX Exod 4.31; Ruth 1.6; Pss 79.14; 105.4; for 'to redeem/make ransom' and its noun, see e.g., LXX Exod 6.6; 13.13, 15; 15.13; Lev 19.20; 25.25; 27.31, 33; Num 18.15, 16; Pss 48.7, 8, 9; 129.8 (from sin); Isa 63.4, *inter alia*.

[19] All OT citations are from the Old Greek (LXX); Hannah confirms the revelation to Simeon (Luke 2.36–8). Luke likes to use comparisons (*synkriseis*) in twos or threes in 'binding' (thickening) his plot (e.g., Luke 3.7–9; 3.10–11 with verses 13–14; cf. one male/one female with Acts 16.11–15, 25–34; passim).

[20] See, e.g., Moxnes 1991:241–68; Neyrey 1991; Green 1995:76–121; Esler 1987.

[21] See, e.g., Tannehill 1975. Though certainly not elevated to the authority of the twelve men, women are nevertheless promoted in Luke as disciples who along with males accompany Jesus 'from Galilee to Jerusalem' and receive the same mandate, 'at table', to be his witnesses (Luke 24.36–49; Acts 1.3–14); see, e.g., B. E. Reid 1996, esp. 21–54.

[22] See, e.g., Degenhardt 1965.   [23] See, e.g., Mauser 1992:83–103.

[24] See, e.g., the debate in Tyson 1988b; cf. esp. Tiede 1988 with Moessner 1988; Tannehill 1988 with Tyson 1988a.

Christ' (24.44b). Their minds have first to be 'opened' to understand (24.45) that the whole of Israel's Scriptures centres upon and points forward to Jesus as 'the Christ who suffers, rises from the dead on the third day, and through his name a release of sins is proclaimed into all the nations (*eis panta ta ethnē*)' (24.46–7). This dynamic goal of Scripture thus forms their new identity as 'witnesses'[25] (*martures*, 24.48) and transforms 'all that Jesus began to do and to teach ... until the day he was taken up' (Acts 1.1–2) into the continuing culmination of the one two-volume narrative. What is to be proclaimed to all peoples, beginning from Jerusalem (Luke 24.47), is this sweeping hermeneutic of Moses, the prophets, and the Psalms that finds its *telos* in Jesus as 'the suffering and raised up Christ' (cf. Luke 22.37b: *to peri emou telos echei*). It would appear that witness to this teleological centre of 'all that stands written' to all peoples forms the crux of what it means that Jesus 'will reign on David's throne' 'forever' (Luke 1.32–3).

Luke ends his Gospel volume with Jesus 'blessing' his disciples and 'being taken up into heaven' (Luke 24.50–1) along with their mirroring response of worship and joy and 'blessing God' continually in the Temple (24.52–3).[26] With this inclusio, Luke concludes his first 'book' where he began, at the centre of Israel's worship. Jesus has finished his 'exodus' journey of 'death' and 'taking up' from Galilee (Luke 9.31, 51) to Israel's central place and its 'place called "the Skull"' (19.41–4; 23.26–33) 'into his glory' to 'the exalted place' (24.26b→24.49b). Yet this concluding event of ascension and doxology does not conclude the one plot of the one unitary narrative.

Luke begins his second volume (cf. Acts 1.1) with extensive *synchronological* overlapping with the first (Acts 1.1–14). With such a 'linking' passage,[27] Luke reconfigures *chronologically* one day of resurrection (Luke 24.1–51) into forty days of teaching appearances of the resurrected Christ (Acts 1.3–14). 'Power from the exalted place' of the first volume is now

---

[25] On the importance of both 'witness' and 'eyewitness' in Luke–Acts see, e.g., Dillon 1978; cf. Byrskog 2000:228–53.

[26] Luke 24.50b–51, 52–3 (ab, b′a′).

[27] Cf. the 'linking passages' at the beginning of each new volume in Hellenistic general or universal histories such as Diodorus Siculus' *Library of History*, through which he ties disparate events of various peoples into one ongoing narrative as though they were the affairs of one great '*mētr-opolis*' (= mother-city) or global village (1.1.3; 1.3.6; 2.1.1–3; 3.1.1–3; 4.1.5–7; 5.2.1; 6.1.1–3; [7–10;] 11.1.1; 12.2.2–3; 13.1.1–3; 14.2.4; 15.1.6; 16.1.3–6 [cf. 15.95.4!]; 17.1.1–2; 18.1.5–6; 19.1.9–10; 20.2.3; [21–40;] [ ] indicate fragmentary books without extant linking passages. On fusing chronological and synchronological vectors to produce a narrative an audience can 'easily follow' (*eu-parakoloutheō*; cf. Luke 1.3), cf. 5.1.1–4 and 16.1.1–3, and see further, Moessner 2005.

rendered by the resurrected-crucified One as 'baptized by the Holy Spirit not after many days' (Luke 24.49→Acts 1.4b–5). In contrast to John, the characteristic mark of the twelve[28] apostles' witness will be a baptism *by* the Holy Spirit aligned with the living One's teaching – 'after he suffered' – about 'the Kingdom of God' (Acts 1.3–5). To be 'my [Jesus'] witness' in the 'power of the Holy Spirit' (Acts 1.8) encompasses the *resurrected, crucified* Christ's fulfilled presence in the Kingdom of God through his authoritative 'opening' of the Scriptures.[29]

Consequently in Acts the one who has proclaimed the 'Kingdom' in Luke does not become the 'proclaimed' but rather the 'proclaimed proclaimer'.[30] What is only provisionally anticipated in Luke 24.49 has been augmented into a leitmotif of the 'sym-phony' of both volumes. To 'recognize' Jesus as the resurrected, crucified Christ of God's reign must now entail the empowering presence of the 'Holy Spirit' as the Scriptures are opened to Jews, Samaritans, and all the nations of the 'end of the earth' (Acts 1.6–8).[31] It is not by accident that the giving of the Spirit at Pentecost by the exalted-crucified One attends Peter's witness of opening the Scriptures (LXX: Joel 3; Psalms 15(16), 109(110) in Acts 2.16–21, 25–8, 33–5) and crowns his explanation of just how it is that the resurrected-crucified Jesus of patriarch David's offspring 'reigns on David's throne, forever' as 'Lord and Christ' in God's comprehensive 'plan' (2.23–4, 33, 36). It is this overarching 'plan' or 'counsel' of God that binds Luke and Acts together as one plotted narrative in two parts.[32]

The resulting form and content of Luke–Acts comprises the single largest contribution of one author to the NT, ca. 28 per cent of the whole.[33] Together the Luke and Acts narrative configures the basis for the liturgical church year, binds the career of Jesus to his followers' subsequent movements, and engrafts many of the church's apostolic traditions of Jesus and the

---

[28] Acts 1.15–26; cf. Diodorus, in his short depiction of the 'Jews' in *Bib. Hist* 40.3.1–8, who finds it important to include the number of their tribes as *twelve* (regarded by them, he says, as a 'perfect' number and corresponding to the number of months of the year) as definitive of them as a distinct 'people'/'nation' (*ethnos*).

[29] For a fuller treatment, see Moessner 2004b, esp. 318–23.

[30] Cf. those passages where Jesus either as Lord and Christ or his 'name' is present and active: Acts 2.21, 24, 32, 33, 36, 38, 47; 3.6, 16, 20, 22, 26; 4.2, 7, 10, 12, 17, 18, 26, 30, 33; 5.14, 28, 40, 41, 42; 8.12, 16, 25, 35; 9.4–6, 10–16, 20, 27–8, 31, 34; 10.13–16, 43, 48; 11.20, 21, 23, 24; 13.10–12, 30–3, 34–9, 44, 47–9; 14.3, 23; 15.11, 17, 26, 35, 36, 40; 16.7, 14–15, 18, 31–2; 17.3, 7, 18, 31; 18.5, 9–10, 28; 19.4–5, 10, 13–14, 17, 20; 20.32; 21. 13–14; 22.7–10, 14–16, 17–21; 23.11; 26.14–18, 23; 28.23, 31.

[31] Note how Paul is described as continuing 'to open and lay out' 'from the Scriptures' that 'the Christ must suffer and rise from the dead, and that this Christ is Jesus . . . ' (Acts 17.2–3; cf. Luke 24.26–7, 45!); see further, Moessner 1996b.

[32] *Contra* Parsons and Pervo 1993.

[33] Luke the longest book, ca. 31–2 ft, 1,151 verses; Acts second, ca. 31 ft, ca. 1,006 verses. See esp. Aland and Aland 1989:26–31; Cadbury 1955:138–46.

church more integrally into the *history* of God's dealings with Israel and the Jewish peoples than any other book(s) of the NT.

2 *The journeying framework of Luke's Gospel*

When viewed in the light of its *canonical* character, however, the Gospel of Luke stands out from Matthew and Mark through its structure of a Jesus who journeys. Luke divides his material into five such journeys, although only two represent Jesus' own decision to move towards a determined goal (=*):

(1) Luke 2.22–40. Jesus' parents fulfil 'the law of Moses' for 'the purification' of a mother and 'sanctification of the firstborn' à la Lev 12.2–4 and Exod 13.1–16 respectively (Luke 2.23–4). The entire encounter with the pious worthies Simeon and Hannah, however, mimics more the 'presentation of Samuel' in Eli's temple at Shiloh than straightforward fulfilment of *halakah*.[34] Does the sacrifice of redemption of the 'firstborn' in Exodus 13 which recalls Israel's redemption through the Passover, together with Zechariah's prophecy of 'making redemption' (*poiein lutrōsis*) in the 'Lord's' 'visitation of his people' in Luke 1.68b, adumbrate perhaps Jesus' self-sacrifice when he will signify his voluntary death 'for them' as the sealing of a 'new covenant' at the Passover with his 'apostles' (Luke 22.19–20 in 22.14–38)?[35]

(2) Luke 2.41–52. Jesus journeys again to the Temple under the tutelage of 'his parents' (2.41), this time as a boy (*pais*) of twelve for the Passover. Jesus' questions and answers to the 'teachers' of the Temple 'astound' 'all' as well as confound 'his father' and 'mother' (2.47–8, 50–1). Might the greater tutelage and 'concerns of his Father' (2.49) point forward to a future Passover when Jesus in the Temple will again teach and 'astound the teachers'[36] of Israel (cf. Luke 19.47–21.38)?

(3) Luke 4.9–14. Jesus is 'led' by 'the Devil/Slanderer' into Jerusalem and onto the pinnacle of the Temple even though the Holy Spirit has been leading him in the wilderness since his baptism in the 'region of the Jordan'[37] (4.1; 3.3). The Slanderer casts doubt whether Jesus could be 'my

---

[34] See esp. LXX 1 Kgdms 1.24–2.10, 20; cf. Luke 2.22b – 'to present him to the Lord'.

[35] Cf. n. 18.   [36] E.g., Luke 20.26, 39–40.

[37] Though this 'third' temptation, similar to the second, would seem to transcend normal notions of time and space and thus not be a journey like others, still Jesus is presented as allowing himself to be transported by the Devil from one temporal-spatial moment to another, and in 4.14 Jesus 'returns', again in the 'power of the Spirit' (cf. Luke 4.1), to Galilee.

Son' or 'please' his 'father' – like Abraham's Isaac or the Lord's 'servant' (*pais*) in Isaiah – just as the voice from heaven has echoed (3.22[38]) and as Luke's narrator re-echoes immediately in Jesus' genealogy ('son of Adam, son of God', 3.23–38). If so, the Devil reckons, Jesus' privileged status must be showcased in a Psalm of trust like LXX Ps 90 'concerning' the 'you' whom 'the Lord' will not allow to be harmed (Ps 90.11–12).[39] Does the Slanderer's 'logic' anticipate here an even greater temptation which Jesus will undergo in Jerusalem when the 'chief priests and scribes' will 'lead' him into their 'council' to challenge his identity, 'So you, then, are the Son of God!' (22.66, 70)? Does the Devil's subsequent reappearance 'at an opportune time' (4.13b) foreshadow the more humiliating taunts against Jesus' 'Sonship' (22.63–5; 23.11, 18–23, 35–9; cf. 22.3!) when, from the cross, Jesus will cry the lament of a 'suffering righteous' as he 'entrusts' his spirit to his 'Father' (23.46 (LXX Ps 30.6))? In any case, Luke's reconfiguring of 'every temptation' of Jesus (4.13) as Israel's 'son',[40] who must re-enact the wilderness trials of Israel's exodus[41] before the 'conquest' of the land of inheritance[42] is climaxed in true worship of the Lord at the 'central place' (cf. Deut 26.1–11; diff. Matt 4), prefigures Jesus' great journey from Galilee to Jerusalem to 'cleanse' 'my house' (Luke 19.46) and become the 'head stone which the builders have rejected' (20.17 (Ps 118.22)).

(4) *Luke 9.51–19.44. Luke's great journey of Jesus from Galilee to Jerusalem, occupying nearly 40 per cent of the Gospel narrative,[43] stands in singular relief to the short journey of Mark 10.1–11.10 and the slightly extended version of Matt 19.1–21.9.[44] Consequently, much of the material that Matthew and Mark place in Galilee Luke places in this journey.[45] What is Luke trying to signify?

First, the sonorous solemnity of Jesus' decision in Luke 9.51 strikes a contrasting chord to his 'being led', previously, by others. Now

---

[38] Cf. Gen 22.2 ('your [Abraham's] beloved son') with Isa 42.1, '[Israel] my servant, my chosen/elect [son], in whom my soul [I /Yahweh/the Lord] delights. I have put my spirit upon him'.

[39] Ps 90.11: 'concerning you' (sing.), i.e., the psalmist who trusts in the Lord; the LXX title attributes the psalm to David.

[40] See n. 38 above on Gen 22 and Isa 42.

[41] Deut 8.3 recited by Jesus in Luke 4.4; cf. Deut 6.13 and 10.20 in Luke 4.8.

[42] Luke 4.5: Jesus has been 'led up' to view 'all the kingdoms of the world' under the Devil's 'watch' on a scale grander than 'all the lands' from Mt Nebo that Moses is shown as the fulfilled promise to 'Abraham, Isaac, and Jacob' (Deut 34.1–4).

[43] That is, when the journey's introduction (Luke 9.1–50) is included; see Moessner 1989, esp. 46–79.

[44] John's Gospel divides Jesus' public ministry into four journeys to Jerusalem, which in its overall form as well as its emphasis upon Israel's feasts is closer to Luke's portrayal but still quite divergent in content and tone from the 'syn-optic' construal.

[45] Cf., e.g, Moessner 1989:1–20; Reicke 1986:63–5, 171–3.

re-sounding the resolve of Ezekiel – priest, 'son of man'[46] – to declare God's judgment against an idol-sated Jerusalem, and the flint-like purpose of the prophet-'servant' (*pais*) of Isa 50.4–11[47] to accept humiliation from his own people as he announces good news, Jesus himself exhibits 'unbending determination' to complete his 'taking up' by moving resolutely towards Jerusalem. He now unflinchingly embraces the journey of his 'exodus/death/departure', discussed by Moses and Elijah and Jesus on a mountain with lightning and cloud and voice from heaven (Luke 9.31 in 9.28–36) (cf. 10.38;[48] 13.22, 31–3; 14.25; 17.11; 18.31; 19.11, 28, 37, 41).

Second, though Luke provides no itinerary or map of Jesus' journey, or any geographical locale for the vast array of 'Q' and 'L' sayings of Jesus, the number of references to his being received in towns and inns along some 'way', his own 'receiving tax collectors and sinners' or, alternatively, acting as host when invited by others to a meal, parables which reflect a journeyer and hospitality, and the 'notices' that Jerusalem is still the destination 'in mind' all create a journey or 'travel narrative' unparalleled by the other three Gospels.[49] Passages like 13.31–3, 34–5 undertone the whole of the journey with the certitude that Jerusalem is the most fitting, indeed, God-ordained, scripturally intended destination for Jesus,[50] since he journeys as a prophet who must be pressed with the fate of the long line of prophets sent, rejected, and even killed by their own people in Israel's central place (cf. esp. 11.47–51; 19.41–4). Whether primarily through Samaria, the Trans-Jordan, or even Galilee,[51] Jesus journeys as a persecuted prophet from the 'Horeb' mountain of theophany to his 'departure', like Moses,[52] and to his 'taking up', like Elijah,[53] in order to fulfil in Jerusalem the scriptural mandate of 'Moses and/ or all the prophets' (Luke 16.29, 31; 18.31; 24.27, 44; cf. Acts 26.22; 28.23).[54]

---

[46] See esp. LXX Ezek 21.2; cf. the 'setting of the face' or unbending resolve of Ezekiel, 'son of humankind/mortal' to declare judgment in Ezek 6.2; 13.17; 20.46; 25.2; 28.21; 29.2; 38.2; cf. 14.8; 15.7 of God's 'face'.

[47] Isa 50.4: 'set the face as a solid rock'.

[48] For the emphasis upon *poreuomai* and cognates as the linking vocabulary of 'the journey notices', see, e.g., Gill 1970.

[49] See Moessner 1989:91–288.   [50] See esp. 13.35 with LXX Ps 117.26 and Jer 12.7; 22.5.

[51] In Luke 17.11 Jesus is 'passing along corresponding to the middle of Samaria and Galilee'; it is not clear whether this is through the middle of the land between Samaria and Galilee, or along the boundary of the two regions outside the two in the Decapolis. Commentators are likewise divided regarding whether from 9.51 Jesus is presented primarily in Galilee and/or Samaria or in the Trans-Jordan (the Decapolis and Perea).

[52] Moses 'is completed/dies' 'through the word of the Lord', Deut 34.5; cf. 'this word' in Deut 1.37; 3.26–7; 4.21–2.

[53] 4 Kgdms 2.1, 11 (2.1–14).

[54] Cf. Luke 1.70; 4.24; 6.23; 9.8, 19; 10.24; 11.47, 49, 50; 13.28, 33, 34; 16.16; 24.25; Acts 3.18, 21, 24, 25; 7.42, 52; 10.43; 13.15, 27, 40; 15.15; 24.14; 26.27; cf. Moessner 1989:47–56.

Third, as Jesus progresses towards his goal, more and more of the throngs of Israel press upon him and join him in his journey (11.29; 12.1; 13.34; 14.25). Accordingly Jesus intensifies his warnings to a people (*laos*) he perceives to be an increasingly 'faithless generation' who, like the synagogue congregation of his home town, Nazareth (4.16–30), demand 'a sign' of his authority ('evil generation', 11.29; 'killers of the prophets', 11.49–51; 'hypocrites', 12.56; 13.15; 'workers of iniquity' who indulge Jesus' 'eating and drinking and teaching in their streets', 13.26–7). These prophetic rebukes are laced with pronouncements of judgment upon a 'hardened', intractable folk (10.12, 14–15; 11.31–2, 42–52; 12.45–8, 57–9; 13.3–5, 24–30, 35; 14.24; 16.27–31; 17.26–30, 19.27, 41–4), 'on account of whom', like Moses in Deuteronomy,[55] Jesus must die. Indeed, as Jesus presses on towards the city that stones the prophets, his anointed consciousness of the 'divine necessity'[56] to be delivered over to death (3.22; cf. already 5.35) comes more and more to expression (12.49–50; 13.33–5; 14.27; 17.25; 18.31–3; 19.42; cf. 9.22, 23–4, 44). Gazing down from the Mount of Olives upon the city of Israel's destiny, Jesus weeps for a nation that has failed to recognize its 'exodus visitation' of deliverance from God (*episkopes*, 19.44; Exod 3.16!; 13.19; cf. Gen 50.24). Thus, Luke's great journey plots Jesus' journey to receive the 'prophet's reward'.[57]

But as Luke's fifth and final journey of Jesus suggests (below), the death of the prophet in Jerusalem ushers in a new, eschatological release from Israel's 'interminable' disobedience of God's life-giving words through Moses and its violent rejection of God's mediators of redemption. Though the relation of a journey 'form' to sayings 'content' in Luke 9.51ff. remains disputed,[58] it may just be that Luke was inspired by Deuteronomy's retrospect of Moses' 'words', framed by Israel's exodus

---

[55] Deut 1.37; 3.26–7; 4.21–2.

[56] Cf. the impersonal verb *dei*, 'it is necessary', as expressing a divine point of view or plan that Jesus must die, in 9.22; 13.33; 17.25; cf. 9.22; 22.37; 24.7, 26, 44.

[57] Conzelmann 1960 stressed that Luke's 'journey' was a portrayal of Jesus' 'consciousness' that he must suffer; because Conzelmann's development of 'redaction criticism', however, relied too heavily upon modern conceptions of an individual author, working with discrete written sources and with Mark as a definitive template, Luke's 'own' emphases resemble more the 'Gospel according to the Changes of Mark', rather than the poetics of a Hellenistic narrative *oikonomia* epistemology. Hellenistic convention for utilizing sources, oral or written, dictates that the author rewrite the material in order to produce a 'seamless' narrative; see esp. Polybius, *Hist.* 1.4.1, 4.3, 4.10, 12.5, 13.9, 14.1, 14.5, 14.8, 15.13; Dionysius of Halicarnassus, *Dem.* 51; *Thuc.* 9–20; Lucian, *Hist. Conscr.* §§41–55; cf. Josephus, *Ag. Ap.* 1.10 (§54;) Cadbury 1927, esp. 155–83, 215–30; Plümacher 1972:32–79; Drury 1976:46–81, 185–6, and my *Ancient Narrative Hermeneutics and the Gospels*, in preparation. On the role of oral traditions and 'composed orality' making it impossible to determine Luke's *motives* when his text varies from the parallels in Mark (or Matthew), see, e.g., Lord 1978; Reicke 1986, esp. 1–23; Achtemeier 1990; Dunn 2003a.

[58] See, e.g., Denaux 1997; cf. Foreword (Hays 1998) and Preface (Moessner 1998) to the paperback edn of Moessner 1989, pp. xi–xxxi.

journey and 'travel notices' of the unfinished journey, and by Moses' prospect for the Israelites' life once they have crossed over the Jordan into the promised inheritance. For Moses foresees that the Israelites will continue to disobey God's commands even after they have established a central place of worship and will be judged by God into exile, but will ultimately return through a journey that consummates their first exodus[59] and features a 'prophet like me' to whom Israel must 'hearken' (Deut 18.15–19). It is telling that Luke introduces Jesus' 'exodus' with the voice from heaven at the Horeb mountain, 'hearken to him' (Luke 9.35b), and, after Jesus has crossed over the Jordan, climaxes this journey with 'this generation' not recognizing the fulfilled time of their 'exodus visitation' from God.[60]

(5) * Luke 22.54–24.51. At the Passover meal in the 'guest room' with his apostles (Luke 22.11–14) Jesus declares that a betrayer 'at table' will 'deliver over' 'the Son of man' 'to go (*poreuomai*)[61] just as it has been ordained' (22.22). But before he embarks on this journey he also indicates he will go willingly to 'suffer' and 'give' his 'body' and 'pour out' his 'blood' 'for their sake' (22.15–20). Such suffering he will undertake 'in order that you might eat and drink at my table in my kingdom and sit upon thrones, judging the twelve tribes of Israel' (22.30). Through this sealing of a 'new covenant', Jesus will already be bequeathing the apostles 'the kingdom' which 'my Father' had already 'bequeathed to me' (22.28–30). What is more, this time his apostles will not be able to 'go' (*poreuomai*, 22.33) with him since they will betray, deny, and all fall away so that 'this that stands written should come to its finale with respect to me (*touto to gegrammenon dei telesthēnai en emoi*), "he was reckoned among the lawless" (Isa 53.12); for indeed, what is written concerning me is now coming to its intended goal' (*gar to peri emou telos echei*). Like the 'servant' of Isaiah, Jesus must suffer *alone* the fate of those 'without law'.[62]

From the Mount of Olives Luke now describes Jesus, once again, 'being led' by others – 'into the house of the chief priest', to 'the council chamber', 'to Pilate', to 'Herod',[63] and to 'the Skull' 'with two evil doers'.[64] But now

---

[59] E.g., Deut 29–30, et al.   [60] Cf. the retrospect in Acts 7.37–8.   [61] See n. 48 above.

[62] Note how the 'servant' of Isaiah 40–55 is both all Israel (Isa 41.8, 9; 42.1, 19; 43.10; 44.1, 2, 21, 26; 45.4; 48.20; 49.3; cf. Luke 1.54) and a part of Israel portrayed esp. in the fate of an individual symbolic of the latter (Isa 42.7; 43.10; 44.26–8; 49.4–6(7); 52.13–53.12). For the plot of Luke–Acts enacting the fulfilment of all three representations of the 'servant' mission in Isaiah, see Moessner 2004a :193–221.

[63] Only Luke attributes some participation of Herod in effecting Jesus' death; this Herod is the Antipas who 'beheads' John the Baptist (Luke 9.9), and is said by Pharisees to be out 'to kill' Jesus (13.31). Pilate and Herod become 'friends' after their collusion in Jesus' execution (23.12; cf. Acts 4.27!). For the view that Herod was a prime instigator of Jesus' death à la Luke's presentation, see Parker 1987.

[64] *Ēgagon, anēgagon,* and *apēgagon*, Luke 22.54, 66; 23.1, 26, 32; cf. Luke 4.1, 9; cf. 2.22; 4.5, 29; 21.12.

Jesus actively embraces this humiliation as his divine calling and utters one final judgment upon an unrepentant Israel before he is crucified and 'laid' by others in a tomb (22.42; 23.28–31, 52–3). His journey, however, is not over. In fact, when the 'women from Galilee' are perplexed to find the tomb empty, they are reprimanded by two 'men in white' for not 'remembering' that they could not find the 'living one among the dead', since Jesus had told them that he would 'rise up on the third day' (24.1–7). Jesus is still actively journeying ahead with the scripturally 'scripted' plan of his 'Father' (Luke 3.22; 9.22–6, 31–5, 44; 22.29, 42; 23.34, 46; cf. 18.31–4). As he continues (*poreuomai*, 24.13, 15) 'on the way',[65] he (again) scolds two of his disciples for 'not believing' what 'Moses and the prophets' had declared that he as 'the Christ had to suffer (*edei pathein*) before entering into his glory' (24.25–7). And after 'appearing' and 'opening' 'the law of Moses, the prophets, *and* the Psalms' to his authenticated 'witnesses' (Luke 24.36–43→Acts 1.3–5), Jesus, the crucified *and* living Christ, completes his great journey from a mountain in Galilee (9.51) by 'being carried up' but *also* by actively 'journeying into heaven'[66] – but not before he discloses the promise of his 'Father' for his continuing witness among them (Luke 24.49→Acts 1.4–5, 8).

In sum, these journeys[67] organize Jesus' public career into three main divisions (Galilee 'Release', 4.1–8.56;[68] 'Exodus' Journey, 9.51–19.44; 'Lord' of the Temple, 19.45–21.38) with the births of John and Jesus and John's baptism introducing (1.5–3.18) and the final journey of the passion and his 'taking up' consummating Jesus' calling (22.54–24.51). Jesus' anointing[69] and genealogy (3.19–38), his appearing 'in glory' on a mountain[70] (9.1–50), and his 'last' Passover meal and 'temptation' on the mountain (Olives) (22.1–53) form watersheds in the developing plot. Together these major sections 'divide' the narrative into a five-fold 'arrangement'.

In short, through the intertextuality with Israel's Scriptures and the intratextuality of Luke and Acts, Luke's narrative configures a trans-historical 'plan of God' enacted through the history of Israel as promised and

---

[65] Cf. Luke 24.32, 35.

[66] *Anapherō* (Luke 24.51); *anelēphthē* (Luke 9.51; Acts 1.2, 11); *eperthē* (Acts 1.9); *hypolambanō* (Acts 1.9); *poreuomai* (Acts 1.10, 12).

[67] See, e.g., Marguerat 1998; Alexander 1995.

[68] Fourteen miracle stories are located in this Galilean section, Luke 4.16–8.56, whereas the great journey primarily summarizes Jesus' 'mighty deeds': e.g., Luke 10.13 (flashback); 11.20; 19.37; but cf. Luke 11.14–15; 13.10–17; 14.1–6; 17.11–19; 18.35–43.

[69] Cf. Acts 10.38.   [70] Cf. Exod 24.16–17; Deut 5.24–5; Luke 9.31–2; 24.26; Acts 7.22, 55; 22.11.

provoked by those Scriptures and re-enacted[71] and consummated in the witness of Israel's Messiah.

(1) Accordingly, the Third Gospel *cannot* be adequately construed as 'biography', since all the emphasis upon Jesus' character is subsumed and integrally, intertextually!, interwoven with the characters and events of Israel's past and future hopes of God's reign. Though thoroughly biographical,[72] as indeed are many biblical and Graeco-Roman histories, Luke is intent to signify the interconnections, including cause and effect,[73] of Jesus' 'words and deeds' with the events and mediators of God's interactions for salvation in Israel's Scriptures, as well as with the extension of that salvation through the Messiah's witness-mediators in Acts.[74] To be sure, Graeco-Roman multi-volume succession narratives display the continuing influence of a famous person;[75] yet, the dense intra-text of Acts with Luke and Acts' continued intertext with the Scriptures[76] transcend in form and content any extant exemplars.[77] The closest parallel, rather, would appear to be the biblical succession of the Deuteronomistic history, with its singular focus upon Moses (Deuteronomy) – prophet unlike any other (Deut 34.10–12) – succeeded by Joshua and a long host of judges, kings, and prophet-mediators, who

[71] Cf. Green 1996; Trompf 1979, esp. 116–78.

[72] Cf., e.g., Momigliano 1993, esp. 101–4; Alexander 1996; Daryl D. Schmidt 1999; Pervo 1999; Dihle 1987, esp. 7–22, 64–80; Aune 1987:29–31; Unnik 1979; Plümacher 1979; Moessner 1991; *contra*: biography, e.g., Burridge 1998.

[73] E.g., Luke 11.29–32; 12.57–9; 13.1–5, 34–5; 17.1–3; 18.9–14; 19.41–4; cf. Polybius, *Hist.* 1.4–5; 3.6.7; 4.28.3–4, passim; Diodorus Siculus, *Bib. Hist.* 5.1.1–4; 16.1.1–3; Dionysius of Halicarnassus, *Thuc.* 10–11; Lucian, *Hist. Conscr.* §55; cf. Allen 1997; Marguerat 2002:85–108.

[74] In Acts 2–5 Luke presents the first Jesus-Messiah believers as indeed fulfilling certain scriptural injunctions and promises of future life together (e.g., Deut 15.7–11; 30.1–10). While these fulfilments do not result in any great reversal within society itself according to the literal referents of, e.g., Mariam's prophecies (Luke 1.46–55), for Luke there are clearly more subtle ways in which society is being confronted/transformed at every level (cf. Acts 17.6).

[75] See esp. Talbert 2003; Talbert 1977; cf. Moessner 1993.

[76] For 'the end of the earth' symbolizing the nations controlled by a great pagan empire used by God to judge/destroy Israel, see Isa 5.26 (Assyria); Jer 6.22 (Babylonia); Isa 48.20 (Persia). In *Pss. Sol.* 8.15 that great power is Rome! The end of Acts may just portray the 'end of the earth' (Acts 1.8) now receiving the 'witness' of the servant mission, since Cyrus (the Lord's 'anointed', Isa 45.1) is to liberate Israel (Isa 45.13; 48.20; cf. 52.9–10) so that all the nations at 'the end of the earth' may 'turn to the Lord' through the 'witness' of the 'servant' (Isa 45.22). For the 'servant's' mission as 'witness', see Isa 43.10, 12; 44.8; 55.4; as God's 'plan', see Isa 42.21; 44.26; 46.10; 51.13; 53.10–11; 55.7–8; cf. 40.13; 41.21; 45.20; 47.13; see n. 62 above.

[77] Talbert 1977 singled out Diogenes Laertius' *Lives of the Philosophers* as a close parallel to Luke–Acts; but the successor volumes lack a continuing narrative plot with the great 'founder' of the first volume; successor lists and anecdotes portray the 'succession' very differently from the one 'plan of God' plotted in Luke–Acts in which the founder continues to act through his witness-*agents*. Talbert treats 'plot' only as a formal or generic category (Talbert 2003, esp. 50–5).

act out the continuing impact of God's words and actions through Moses in Israel's exodus (Joshua – 2 (4) Kingdoms).[78]

(2) None the less, Luke's moulding of both volumes to 'the plan of God' as an epitome of the whole of Scripture's fulfilment in Jesus 'the Christ' (*hē boulē (tou theou)*, Luke 7.30; Acts 2.23; 4.28; 5.38 (ironically); 13.36; 20.27; cf. 27.42–3) indicates that Luke is also following the pattern of Hellenistic historians who encompass the rise and fates of peoples under a grand control or influence of the divine, such as *pronoia* (e.g., Josephus, *Ant.* 2.332; 4.47, 114, 128, 185; 5.277; cf. 3 Macc 4.21; 5.30; 4 Macc 9.24; Wis 6.7; 14.3; Diodorus Siculus, *Bib. Hist.* 1.1.3); *gnōmē* (e.g., Josephus, *Ant.* 1.14, 46; 2.174, 209; 5.277; 10.177; 11.327, etc.); or *tychē* (e.g., Polybius, *Hist.* 1.4.1–5; 1.7.4; Diodorus Siculus, *Bib. Hist.* 1.1.3; 13.21.4–5; 18.59.6; 26.15.3; 34/35.27.1, etc.; Dionysius of Halicarnassus, *Ant. Rom.* 1.4.2; 1.5.2; 3.19.6; 8.32.3; 11.12.3, etc.; Josephus, *J.W.* 3.387–91; 4.238; 5.78, 120–2; 6.14, 44, etc.; Arrian, *Anab.* 5.1.2 ('the divine principle')).[79] Except for the Jewish historian Josephus – who provides the closest parallel of God's 'will' as pervasively programmatic – the 'Sicilian' Diodorus is probably the most vocal in insisting that apart from such interweavings of divine and human agencies, history cannot be adequately recorded and thus serve as inspiration and direction for future generations.[80] He even devotes the first six of his forty books to the 'deeds and myths of the earliest times',[81] since for Diodorus, a nation's cultic-religious life provides the most telling template for many of its later achievements and cultural characteristics.[82]

(3) God's 'plan' is expressed and summarized in a variety of ways, including (i) 'the divine necessity' (*dei*) that Jesus journey to his death

---

[78] See, e.g., Moessner 1989:325; note how Luke and Acts portray Moses, all the prophets, righteous sufferers of the Psalms (David et al.), Jesus (Luke 3.21; 4.42; 5.16; 6.12; 9.18, 28; 10.21–2; 11.1; 22.39–46 (23.34); 23.46), Peter (and the eleven), Stephen, and Paul as mediators on their knees before God on behalf of Israel; see Moessner 1993:216–22.

[79] For 'fate'/'chance'/'necessity' (*heimarmenē*/*peprōmenē*/*anagkē* (*inter alia*)), cf., e.g., Diodorus Siculus (*Bib. Hist.* 3.15.7; 10.21.3; 15.63.2 etc.); Josephus (*Ant.* 16.397–8; *J.W.* 2.162–4, etc.); Dionysius of Halicarnassus (*Ant. Rom.* 3.5.2; 3.11.1; 5.8.6; 9.8.1; 10.45.4, etc.); Lucian of Samosata (*Zeus Catechized*). See also Squires 1993:15–77, 164–71.

[80] Good historiography must conjoin vertical divine dimensions with horizontal cultural forces as though they were the interlocking affairs of 'one human city' (*Bib. Hist.* 1.2.2). The narrative itself functions as the 'herald of the divine voice' (1.2.1, 3), and a good historian serves as a 'minister of divine providence (*pronoia*)' (1.1.3); see n. 27 above.

[81] *Bib. Hist.* 4.1.1.

[82] 'For very great and most numerous deeds have been performed by the heroes and demi-gods ... who, because of the benefits they conferred which have been shared by all men, have been honoured by succeeding generations with sacrifices which in some cases are like those offered to the gods ... and of one and all the appropriate praises have been sung by the voice of history for all time' (4.1.4) (LCL; trans. C. H. Oldfather).

and taking up in Jerusalem, and that 'release of sins' be proffered in Christ's name beginning *from* Jerusalem,[83] as well as through (ii) *scriptural citations, allusions,* and *re-enacted plots* of OT divines figured as 'fulfilled' at some stage in the calling of Jesus and/or the church,[84] or 'the Day of the Son of man'.[85] (iii) Luke's ascending *genealogy* (Luke 3.23–38; cf. Tob 1.1) imitates both Jewish (LXX) and Hellenistic convention:[86] Jesus is descended from David (through some rather obscure and lowly offspring) and Abraham, and yet is God's 'son', analogous to 'Adam, son of God' (Luke 3.38) and thus crowns the whole human race as 'God's offspring' (e.g., Paul in Acts 17.28 (Aratus, *Phaen.* 5); cf. Luke 1.32, 35!). As Moses' calling to liberate the people (Exod 3) is grounded in the genealogies of God's previous working (Exod 6.14–27) before Moses leads out the Israelites (Exod 7–12), so Jesus' calling as obedient 'Son and Servant' (Luke 3.21–2) will span all of God's dealings with the world through Israel (3.23–38) as Jesus is poised to bring 'release' to Israel's 'captives' and announce liberation for the whole human race (4.16–30 (24–6)).[87] (iv) *Synchronisms* likewise combine both Hellenistic and Jewish historiographical practice.[88] Similar to the synchronisms of 'multiple accessions and deaths' or 'sea crossings' or 'auxiliary events' featured later in the narrative which for Polybius illustrate 'Fortune's' unprecedented intertwining of world events to effect the rise of Rome,[89] is Luke's joining of Roman hegemony to the birth, calling, and expansion of the messianic witness of Israel to demonstrate its unparalleled, recurring, and far greater significance for the whole of humankind (Luke 1.5; 2.1–2; 3.1; Acts 11.28; 18.2, 12; cf. 'this did not occur "in a corner"', 26.26!). At the core of this plan is the systemic conviction that 'the Christ' of Scripture is Jesus, that Jesus himself interpreted the whole of the Scriptures in relation to himself as the suffering and raised Messiah, and that thus he promulgated the apostolic witness for all times and places.

Consequently the Gospel of Luke can be read like no other. There is no indication that 'what' Luke wrote, according to his *prooemium* to both

---

[83] The 'thus' (*houtōs*) of Luke 24.46 is the epexegetical link with the *dei* of 24.44; cf. n. 56 above.

[84] See esp. Tiede 1980.

[85] Luke 17.30; 21.27, 36 *inter alia*; see, e.g., the imaginative interpretation of OT passages in Luke–Acts in Drury 1976:44–81.

[86] Kurz 1984.   [87] See Sanders 1993.

[88] Of special interest in Luke–Acts are the 'completions' of a period of time which themselves introduce a new stage of fulfilment in Israel's festal calendar or Torah observance or promises of the prophets: e.g., Luke 2.21, 22–4, 34; 3.3–6, 15–16; 4.16–21; 9.28–31, 51; 10.23–4; 12.49–53; 13.31–5; 17.22–35; 18.31–4; 19.41–4; 22.14–18, 28–30, 35–8; 24.25–7, 44–9; Acts 1.20–2; 2.1; 3.22–6, etc.; cf. Kurz 1999.

[89] Polybius, *Hist.* 1.3.3–4; see Scafuro 1984:155–204.

volumes (Luke 1.1–4),[90] was to be anything other than what the church would eventually entitle 'the Gospel according to . . .' (see further below). The Christ of volume one remains instrumental through the second; the church exists and thrives only from the 'witness' of the risen-crucified One, empowered by the Holy Spirit. Church and Christ are inseparable; thus Acts is the only book of the NT that 'narrates' the continuing presence of Christ in God's church and world.

II WHY LUKE WROTE (THE DISTINCTIVE AIMS OF THE AUTHOR 'LUKE')

1 The primary prooemium (Luke 1.1–4) and Luke's new narrative configuration

In one short but balanced Atticizing period,[91] Luke demonstrates that he is thoroughly familiar with the standards of good Hellenistic narrative production:

(1) Three pairs of balanced clauses link 'Luke' with the 'many' others and their dependence upon 'eyewitness and attendants' traditions, while simultaneously distinguishing his 'narrative' (*diēgēsis*) from theirs. The dependent clauses of the protasis (a, b, c = verses 1–2) are 'answered' by the main, dependent participial, and final clauses of the apodosis (a′, b′, c′ = verses 3–4):

(a) <u>Since many</u> *have undertaken to compile* a narrative (verse 1a)
    [causal clause]

(a′) *It seemed good* <u>to me also</u> . . . *to write* in sequence (verse 3a, b)
     [main clause]

  (b) <u>Concerning the events/matters which have come to fruition</u> *in our midst* (verse 1b)
    [participial clause as object of preposition]

  (b′) *To one who from the beginning/top has followed/been steeped in* <u>all these events/matters</u> *carefully/with understanding* (verse 3b)
    [participial clause dependent on indirect object of main verb of main clause]

    (c) <u>Just as</u> *those from the beginning eyewitnesses and attendants of the word delivered over* to us (verse 2)
    [secondary adverbial clause dependent on causal clause]

---

[90] It is pure speculation whether Luke 1.1–4 was 'originally' written as the preface only to volume one or to both volumes; as it stands, the preface functions, by convention – de facto – as the *prooemium* to all the following volumes; cf. the multi-volume Hellenistic historians and esp. Diodorus' 'linking passages' following the secondary *prooemia*; see n. 27 above.

[91] See Alexander 1993:102–46.

(c′) <u>So that</u> you *may gain a firm grasp of the true significance of the traditions in which you have been instructed* (verse 4).
[secondary final clause dependent on main clause]

(2) Luke's new 'narrative sequence' (*kathexēs*[92]) would seem to indicate that he is not fully satisfied with the narrative accounts of the 'many', especially since his own enterprise should produce a 'firmer grasp of the true significance' (*epignōs … tēn asphaleian*)[93] of those 'from the beginning' (*ap' archēs*) traditions 'delivered over to us' (*paredosan hēmin*) (verse 2a→v. 4).[94] As neither 'eyewitness' nor 'attendant/servant' (*hypēretēs*) of these traditions – and absent the stereotypical critiques of previous attempts[95] – Luke appears unconcerned to present his[96] own qualifications to undertake such a project. By what standard can Luke reinterpret 'eyewitness tradition'?

(3) With *parēkolouthēkoti*, however – the pivotal, balancing participle of the two halves of verses 1–4 – we do have Luke's distinguishing credential. Contrary to the *idola theatri* of its usual rendering, *parakoloutheō* does *not* mean 'investigate', 'go back over', 'do research', 'figure out', etc.[97] Its sense, rather, is to 'follow', 'stay abreast' with something *as it develops*, whether physically or 'with the mind', whether the referent be persons, historical events, teachings, habits, or documents, etc.[98] 'Habitual following' of teaching or a 'school of thought' can refer to one who 'has been steeped' or 'trained' in those particular traditions, as Timothy is so described in 1 Tim 4.6[99] and 2 Tim 3.10. For Luke, therefore, 'as one who has followed [perfect tense] from

---

[92] *Kat-* 'corresponding to' *hexēs*, 'the next', i.e., the 'sequence', but with respect to the whole (2 volume-) narrative; approaching the 'narrato-logical sense'; see Moessner 1999a:98–114, esp. p. 98 n. 44 (eleven exegetes' renderings).

[93] Cf. Acts 2.36: the adverbial sense in the *peroratio* of a suasive speech, 'Let the whole house of Israel know therefore with *clear certainty* [*asphalōs*] that God established him as both Lord and Christ, this Jesus whom you crucified'; adjectival senses which are linked with verbs of 'understanding' and 'writing' just as with 'His Excellency, Theophilus' in Luke 1.3 (e.g., Acts 25.26 – Festus ('His Excellency',! Acts 26.25) does not have anything 'firmly grasped' about the accusations against Paul (*asphales ti … ouk echō*) 'in order to write' (*grapsai*) his superior. He therefore needs further illumination from those who are competent to judge Paul's case; cf. Acts 21.34 (*gnōnai*); 22.30 (*gnōnai*)). *Asphaleia* thus combines both the *senses* of 'clarity' (*saphēneia*) and 'security' (*asphalēs*); cf. literal referent, Acts 5.23 – 'prison gates'.

[94] Cf., e.g, Shellard 2002:261–88: 'a "corrective" Gospel' (p. 261).   [95] See Rajak 1987:81–94.

[96] *Parēkolouthēkoti* (masculine perfect participle, Luke 1.3) indicates a male author, inscribed by a 'me' (Luke 1.3), who came to be identified in Christian tradition as 'Luke'.

[97] The third edition of Bauer, Arndt, Gingrich, Danker (BAGD; Bauer et al. 2000) has correctly dropped the earlier sense of 'investigate', 'research', and now, for Luke 1.3, refers to Luke's 'thorough familiarity'.

[98] H. J. Cadbury maintained against the stream that 'going back over' something after the fact was contrary to the meaning and not attested anywhere in the literature: see Cadbury 1922b; Cadbury 1922c; Cadbury 1922a; Cadbury 1956–7; similarly, Trocmé 1957:122–9; Moessner 1999b.

[99] In 1 Tim. 4.6, parallel to the perfect participle *parēkolouthēsas* with the referent 'teachings' is the present participle 'being nourished' with the referent 'words/traditions (*logoi*) of the faith'! Like Timothy, Luke is one who has been 'steeped' in these traditions through his 'following'.

the top/beginning' can mean that he had been trained in 'all' (*pasin*, verse 3) the traditions which are being characterized by their 'starting point' (*anōthen*, verse 3; cf. *archē*, verse 2).[100] Luke may provide a clue to his own background of training when he later identifies Paul as a *hypēretēs* (Acts 26.16)[101] who, though not an 'eyewitness from the beginning', is portrayed as an authoritative 'servant' of the traditions 'from the beginning', whose pedigree of comprehension is confirmed through the 'apostles'.[102]

(4) In his two short *prooemia*, Luke divulges his familiarity with the convention of 'arrangement' (*oikonomia*)[103] of Hellenistic narrative poetics described in Polybius and developed into a 'system' by the time of Diodorus Siculus and Dionysius of Halicarnassus.[104] Luke's mention of his: (i) 'scope' (cf. *syntaxis*[105]) – namely, 'all' the 'matters/events' (Luke 1.3→1.1)→'all ... until the day he was taken up' (Acts 1.2); (ii) 'beginning point' (*archē*) for the 'narrative ordering' (*kathexēs*) – namely, 'those from the beginning eyewitnesses' (Luke 1.2)→'all that Jesus <u>began</u> to do and to teach' (Acts 1.2→1.22); (iii) main 'divisions' (cf. *diairesis*)[106] – namely, 'in the first volume, all that Jesus began ... until ... he was taken up ... power from the Holy Spirit shall come ... and be (my) witnesses (to me) in Jerusalem ... all of Judea and Samaria, and to the end of the earth'

---

[100] For comparison with Josephus' use, see Moessner 1996a.

[101] In tandem with 'witness' to and for the resurrected Christ, including 'all the things which I [Jesus] will reveal to you', Acts 26.16b.

[102] If it is argued that Luke must be a 'third-generation' believer who had no direct contact with the 'eyewitness' apostles and/or 'attendants' 'from the beginning' (e.g., Conzelmann 1966), then this must be based on evidence other than the prologue, where *parēkolouthēkoti* does *not* indicate a distanced 'investigation' but rather its opposite, a 'close familiarity' with the traditions directly communicated/'handed over to *us*' (Luke 1.2–3).

[103] The 'eco-nomics' of narrative 'arrangement' and/or 'management' of meaning *for the audience*, derived metaphorically from 'household management/home economics' (cf. esp. Xenophon, *The Estate Manager* (*oikonomikos*)); see esp. Polybius, *Hist.* 1.1–15; Diodorus, *Bib. Hist.* 1.3.1–8; 5.1.1–4; 15.95.4; 16.1.1–3; Dionysius of Halicarnassus, *Thuc.*, esp. 9–20; *Gn. Pomp.* 3; Lucian, *Hist. Conscr.* §§49–50, 55.

[104] Meijering 1987, esp. 171–225; R. S. Reid 1996; Reid 1997; Moessner 2002.

[105] Cf. Papias (see n. 5 above), citing 'John the Elder's' reference to Matthew, in juxtaposition with the Elder's comments on Mark (§16): 'Matthew composed a narrative of the traditions (*ta logia synetaxato*) [Jesus' sayings and deeds] in Hebrew/Aramaic, and each one translated/interpreted (*hērmēneusen*) them as each was able' (in contrast to Mark, who did not produce a literarily acceptable narrative account (*syntaxis*), yet was Peter's own (hence, trustworthy) 'translator/ interpreter' (*hermēneutēs*) of his teaching and preaching).

[106] Cf. the threefold taxonomy of narrative 'arrangement' – *diairesis, taxis, exergasia* ('division', 'order', 'method/effectiveness of development') – in Dionysius of Halicarnassus, *Thuc.* 9–20; according to Dionysius, without the proper 'beginning' and 'ending' points in the 'division', no adequate 'order' or 'sequence' can be produced to create a sufficient 'continuity' of plot (*to dienekes*); when both the 'divisions' and 'ordering' are inadequate, 'effective development' of the plot through speeches, dramatic scenes, synchronisms, etc. to produce the intended audience comprehension is impossible.

(Acts 1.1–2→1.8); and (iv) general 'purpose'[107] (cf. *telos*) for composing yet another version of a 'narrative' already 'at hand' – namely, 'a firm(er) grasp of the traditions' (Luke 1.1a→1.4) – all indicate Luke's intent to write proper Hellenistic narrative, inclusive of Hellenistic auditors' expectations.

One such expectation for multi-volume productions is a well-defined 'beginning point' from and because of which the rest of the volumes are 'ordered'[108] (*taxis*, *anataxasthai*, Luke 1.1!) and configure the author's over-all understanding (cf. *dianoia*[109]) and purpose for writing. In the opening episode of volume two, Luke, with the help of Scripture! (LXX Pss. 68 and 109 in Acts 1.20–1), delineates this 'beginning' as 'from the baptism of John' and the 'ending' scope for volume one as 'the day he was taken up' (Acts 1.22). 'Apostleship' and 'witness' are thus defined as 'eyewitness' to this whole period, and Judas' replacement for the 'apostolic service' of the 'twelve' must meet this criterion. But in Acts 11.15 through Peter's justifica-tion of 'lodging and eating with the uncircumcised', Luke defines another 'beginning', the 'falling' of the Holy Spirit upon the believing circumcised at Pentecost (Acts 2; see also Peter in Acts 15.7–9). Moreover, by threading the two 'beginnings' together via the 'linking' *prooemium*, Peter in effect aligns them with the narrative beginnings of each volume. 'The word of the Lord' of Acts 11.16 echoes Jesus' words in Acts 1.5, which in turn point back to the overlapping passage at the 'end' of volume one and to the 'promise of the Father' of Luke 24.49; but this 'promise' through Jesus' words at the end is already re-sounding John the Baptist's 'word(s) of God' precisely at the 'beginning' of volume one, that is, 'from the baptism of John' (Luke 24.49→3.16→3.2b!). These beginning points thus 'partition' the narrative for the proper emplotment and, hence, for his audience, ensconce the authorially intended comprehension of the whole two volumes.[110]

2 *The scriptural mandate of God's 'plan' 'to the nations'*

The rich polyvalencies of narrative combined with their interplay with other texts would seem to defy any 'reading' which could elucidate what the author intended for his audience to grasp. Yet the poetics of Hellenistic

---

[107] Cf. esp. Diodorus Siculus, *Bib. Hist.* 16.1.1–2.

[108] Polybius, *Hist.* 5.1; 12.5; 13.9; Diodorus, *Bib. Hist.* 15.95.4; 16.1.1–2; Dionysius of Halicarnassus, *Thuc.* 11; *Gn. Pomp.* 3; Lucian, *Hist. Conscr.* §55.

[109] Cf. Aristotle's broader sense for *dianoia* as the author's overall orientation and thus rhetoric of the text through the author's control of the intermeshing actions, characters, and characters' under-standings of the events themselves; see *Poet.* 19.

[110] For fuller treatment, see Moessner 1999a:100–5.

narrative had built into its epistemology a tria-lectic hermeneutic in which certain of the (i) audience's understandings are the result of (ii) the author's 'management' (*oikonomia*!) of the reading (iii) through the form or *poiēsis* of the text itself. Thus, while an assortment of purposes undoubtedly motivated Luke 'to set to hand' (Luke 1.1), he does provide clear markers for a number of significances which 'manage' his readers to a 'clarity of understanding' of the 'words and deeds' of the two volumes. One such example is the unusual appearance of *kathexēs* in Acts 11.4 (Luke 1.3!), which, through Peter's eyes, leads Luke's audience to a new viewing and – hence – new comprehension of Jesus' practice *at table* in the first volume.

(a)   Jesus' 'eating and drinking' – acted parables of God's 'plan'
for the 'unclean' peoples of 'the nations'
Criticism of Peter's 'lodging' and 'eating with' the uncircumcised Cornelius leads intriguingly back to similar criticism of Jesus (Acts 11.3→Luke 24.36–49→15.2→7.34). *Kathexēs* in Acts 11.4 signals a reconfiguring by Peter of his own experiences of the 'vision' in the light of his new understanding of the 'plan of God' (Acts 10.39–43). Such rehearsing *kathexēs* will place the significance of the Cornelius 'visit' in the more comprehensive narrative of God's intention through the 'apostolic witness' of Scripture to extend the 'release of sins' through the 'suffering-raised Christ' to the 'unclean' peoples of the earth (Luke 24.46–8). For Peter to recount *kathexēs* means for the audience to 'get God's story straight', to plot the Cornelius and Peter 'turnings' in their proper 'arrangement' within the *oikonomia* of God's 'plan'.

(b)   The 'today' of salvation
But to be 'rehearsed back' from the middle of Acts to Jesus' eating and drinking with 'tax collectors and sinners' via Jesus' own words in Luke's linking prologue (Acts 1.4b–5→Luke 24.36–49) is to be thrust also into the 'release of sins' which Jesus offers most palpably 'at table' (Luke 24.47→15.1–32→7.31–50→5.17–39). In the apostolic assembly of Acts 15, Peter again rehearses how 'God bore witness' (*emartyrēsen*) 'from the days of the beginnings' 'by cleansing' the Gentiles' 'hearts' 'through the grace of the Lord Jesus', while James reinforces Peter's explanation by 'opening' Amos 9 and Isaiah 45 to illuminate how 'the words of the prophets' pointed forward to God's 'visit' of Cornelius 'at the first' 'to take out a people (*laos*) for his name' 'upon whom my name is called' (Acts 15.14–18→Amos 9.11–12; Isa 45.21→42.4, 10→41.25). It is Israel as the 'Lord's' 'servant' (*pais*) who will 'shine out' 'so that the nations will trust in his *name*' (Isa

42.4).[111] At the same time, Peter stresses the 'same basis' upon which both Jews and non-Jews 'are saved', with the incredible admission that God made 'no discrimination between' them, even 'saving' Jews 'just *in the same way* that they [Gentiles!] are saved' (Acts 15.9, 11). Hence both Peter and James point to the mandated *witness at table* (cf. Acts 10.41) in which Jesus reveals his raised up 'broken body' and 'shed blood' on their behalf for 'the release of sins' *'in his name (the Christ) to all the nations'* (Acts 15.8–11, 14–18→11.16–17→10.40–3→1.4–5→Luke 24.40–9→24.30–5→22.19–20). Truly to recognize Jesus as 'the Christ' of Scripture who 'releases sins' is to recognize him 'in the *breaking* of the bread'.

But this recognition means that 'the today' of salvation announced by the rejected prophet-servant of Isaiah 61 in Nazareth (Luke 4.16–30) and which climaxes with Jesus 'broken' on the cross, uttering release to his executioners and the 'today' of 'paradise' (Isa 51.3!) to the 'turning' 'evil doer' (Luke 23.34, 42–3) is tied directly, *organically* to the death of Christ in Scripture's plan, as well as to his 'raising up'. The 'Christ' who pronounces 'release' to the 'poor', who 'eats and drinks' and releases the sins of the 'captive' Israel, who pronounces the 'today of salvation' to those who 'turn' and 'receive' him in their houses and alley ways as he journeys to Jerusalem is the same 'Christ' about whom Scripture 'bears witness'[112] that 'he must be reckoned with the lawless' – *by his own – at table!* (Luke 22.37→Isa 53.12). It is only as Peter 'remembers' and 'turns' from his 'denial' of *Jesus' voluntary death* that his own 'faith' is reconstituted and enabled to 'strengthen' his 'brothers' (the twelve) (Luke 22.19–20 (*anamnēsis*), 31–3→60–2 (*hypemnēsthē*)!). The (post)-modern notion, fuelled largely by redaction criticism,[113] that Luke attributes no atoning significance to Jesus' rejection and death[114] has bypassed the Hellenistic epistemology of narrative arrangement and thus also severed the intricate lacing of Jewish Scripture that bears added witness to Luke's fundamental portrayal of Jesus, the suffering, righteous, and raised up 'Christ of God'.

(c) The 'today' of Luke: Evangelist of God's Christ, historian of Israel's legacy
Luke writes, then, to expound the 'plan of God' at a time of 'engaged disengagement' between Jews who believe and those who cannot be

---

[111] See n. 62.   [112] E.g., Acts 10.43.
[113] Cf., e.g., Conzelmann 1960:9–17; Perrin 1969, esp. 29–31.
[114] E.g., Conzelmann 1960:201; Wilckens 1974:216; Haenchen 1971:91–2; Kümmel 1975:134, 138; Marshall 1971:172; Käsemann 1964:92; Green 1995:124–5; Buckwalter 1996:231–72; Doble 1996:235–7. Some notable exceptions to this 'reading': e.g., Fitzmyer 1989:212; Neyrey 1985, esp. 184–92; Karris 1986; Ford 1983; cf. Moessner 1990.

persuaded, when the vast majority of Israelites are not turning to Jesus the Messiah and growing numbers of the 'uncircumcised' are embracing the Christ of Israel's Scriptures. Luke addresses his narrative of 'events come to fruition' to both Jew and Gentile, all who need a 'firmer grasp' of how Israel could reject its own 'Lord and Christ', how Gentiles can worship the God of 'this people Israel', how God himself could appear impotent to save his own 'people'. Luke shows how the Scriptures are rife with promises, prophecies, adumbrations, and hopes which choreograph the Israelites' final salvation and 'glory' by their rejection of their 'servant' calling which simultaneously extends this life 'to the end of the earth'.

Luke thus lays claim to Israel's scriptural heritage. Separated or read together, Luke and Acts bridge the fourfold portrayal of the Christ to the heart of the church's life and theology. 'Luke' functions therefore as the first of biblical-theological historians whose overarching 'plan of God' lays the foundation upon which the early church will rehear and refigure 'Moses, the prophets, and the Psalms' as Christian Scripture. The theory of Luke and Acts' formative role in the process of NT canonization, though unproven, has much to commend it.[115] Moreover, the *oikonomia* of Luke–Acts will inspire later meta-narratives of God's universal salvation through Israel in such schemas as Irenaeus' *recapitulation*, or Eusebius' 'apostolic tradition' within the 'history of the church'. Certainly Luke's depiction of Paul as possessing an omniscient-like grasp of 'God's plan' plants Paul deeply, richly into the apostolic soil of the emerging 'ecumenical' church.[116] But above all else, Luke broadcasts the 'good news' of how 'God was with Jesus', 'who went about doing good and healing all who were oppressed by the Devil' (Acts 10.38), who willingly gave himself over to the suffering death of 'the lawless' and to the 'the authority of all the kingdoms of the earth' in order 'today'[117] to seal the release of sins for Israel and the whole world.

It is most fitting that this attempt to summarize the 'today' of Luke's 'good news' be offered to honour one whose expositions of the Gospel narratives and whose teaching and lecturing to the end of the earth have indeed promoted the 'clear certainties' of the finest of Gospel scholarship.

[115] E.g., Harnack 1925; cf. J. Knox's adaptation of Harnack in arguing that Marcion's Gospel was a shorter form of Luke before Luke was expanded and aligned alongside Matthew, Mark, and John, and also Acts was enlarged as an introduction to the 'apostles' (Peter, James, John, and Jude) who were added alongside Marcion's Paul to create, ca. 150 CE, an expansive alternative to Marcion's Luke–Paul 'canon' (Knox 1987). Cf. Barrett 1996; Hengel 2000:31–3.
[116] See esp. Acts 20.17–38; 21.1–14, where Paul's outline of the 'plan of God' (cf. 20.27) trumps inspired prophets like Agabus (21.10–14) and 'disciples' (21.4–6) who try to prevent Paul from proceeding on to Jerusalem.
[117] Luke 4.5–6→22.37→23.43.

CHAPTER 9

How John writes

Judith Lieu

> Last of all, John, perceiving that the bodily facts had been made plain
> in the gospel, being urged by his friends and inspired by the spirit,
> composed a spiritual gospel.
>
> (Clement of Alexandria in Eusebius, *Hist. Eccl.* 6.14.7)

Clement was not the first to recognize the distinctive character of the
Fourth Gospel: his words were designed to set at rest the anxieties of
those for whom that distinctiveness threatened to split the harmony of
the Gospel witness:[1] properly understood, he suggests, the four Gospels,
John included, speak with a single voice, inspired by the Spirit and by the
consensus of apostolic testimony. Yet, it may be said, the dilemma he
betrays and the answer he gives have continued to dog the Gospel throughout its subsequent history. Clement's claim, then, and specifically the
epithet 'spiritual', may still provide a guide for asking 'how John writes'.

We may begin by asking whether 'spiritual' is a description of Johannine
distinctiveness or an explanation. As a description it might be replaced by
other terms; so, some have held the Gospel to be more 'theological',
perhaps an epithet supported by the title 'the theologian', which at an
early date was bestowed upon its putative author, the apostle John.
'Theological' in turn could direct our attention to its apparently more
developed Christology, for its Jesus engages in long monologues and can
claim, 'I and the Father are One', and 'Before Abraham was I am' (10.30;
8.58); pursuing this particular track might return us to 'spiritual', for some
find the Johannine Jesus to be more spiritual and less fleshly, at least
verging on the docetic, for this is a Jesus who also suffers no agony in the
Garden, or dereliction on the Cross, but can at the moment of his arrest fell
his opponents to the ground with a theophanic 'I am' (18.5–6).[2] This may
echo Clement's contrasting 'bodily' and direct us gently towards the

---

[1] See Nagel 2000 and Hill 2004 for the early reception-history of the Gospel.
[2] Käsemann's (Käsemann 1968) 'God striding across the earth'.

question of history, for did the 'historical Jesus' ever speak so? In the same vein, those who point out that in John the Cleansing of the Temple happens at the beginning of Jesus' ministry (2.13–22), whereas in the Synoptic Gospels it provides the climatic event that will seal Jesus's fate, are apt to comment that John was not so much interested in the How of what happened but in the meaning it held. Yet matters cannot now be so simply stated: redaction criticism has shown that the other evangelists are also driven by theological concerns, and the single visit made by the Synoptic Jesus to Jerusalem may be less historically persuasive than the repeated visits he makes in John.[3]

John's 'spiritual' Jesus might also direct us to the distinctive world-view of this Gospel. Its dualism of light and darkness, truth and falsehood, from above or below, of God or of the world, was at one time attributed to its Hellenistic background, contrasted with the 'Hebraic' realism preserved by the Synoptics. Some would go further and locate it in the world of incipient gnosticism, pointing also to the importance of 'knowledge' in the Johannine goal (8.31; 17.3) (although the verb and not the noun is used); Clement's defence was, it seems, inspired by the attraction that the Gospel held for those of 'gnostic' inclination, among whom was the first commentator on the Gospel, Heracleon. Doubts as to the existence of 'gnosticism' prior to or even contemporaneous with the Gospel have been succeeded by a dismantling of the category, which then allows the question of John's location in the contemporary maelstrom of ideas to be reopened.[4] At the same time, that it stands diametrically opposed to the Hebraic thought of the origins of Christianity has been undermined by a very similar dualism within the Dead Sea Scrolls (1QS 3.15–4.20). Against older views that John – and gnosticism – stand at the opposite end of the spectrum to apocalyptic, whose failure they respond to, some would now recognize the fundamentally apocalyptic structure in John's presentation of Jesus as revealer of the heavenly world.[5]

Yet 'spiritual' as a description of this Gospel has also suffered a more direct offensive. For some, indeed, this Gospel is 'spiritual' because it presents them with the Jesus in whom they believe, the 'beloved Son' sent by 'God (who) so loved the world' (3.16); the 'Lamb of God who takes away the sin of the world' (1.29); the 'good shepherd' who 'lays down

---

[3] For a defence of historical tradition in John, see Robinson 1985.
[4] Some still find a gnostic or gnosticizing tendency in its thought (see Schotroff 1970), whereas more recently the possibility of shared traditions with some of the Nag Hammadi texts has been raised.
[5] For the older view, see Barrett 1975:66–7; see now Rowland 1992:227; Ashton 1991:383–406.

his life for the sheep' (10.14–15) and whose 'kingdom is not of this world' (18.36). But in recent decades it has also become the Gospel of anti-Judaism which assigns 'the Jews' to a father, the devil (8.44), denies their claim 'to be of God' (8.46), charges them with plotting to kill Jesus almost from the start (5.19), gives voice to their cry, 'we have no King but Caesar' (19.15), and projects the spectre of believers living in 'fear of the Jews' (9.22; 19.38; 20.19) – and which, by at each point speaking univocally of 'the Jews', resists the newly rediscovered place of Jesus with his followers as Jews among Jews (Bieringer et al. 2001; Reinhartz 2001). How can such a Gospel, whose rhetoric was to be taken up by subsequent Christians with devastating consequences, be allowed the sobriquet 'spiritual'?

'Spiritual' as a description of how John writes may, then, prove decep-tive. Will it serve as a guide to why John writes as he does? John's Gospel, perhaps more than any of the others (although cf. Luke 1.1–4), betrays some reflection on the nature of its own undertaking, although the reflection might appear inconsistent. On the one hand, there is the explicit testimony of 21.21–4, where an anonymous 'we' guarantee 'the beloved disciple' who 'wrote these things'. For some, and for the tradition, a straight line runs from here to authorship by the apostle John, son of Zebedee; a reading of the Gospel then becomes a matter of negotiation between the authority of eyewitness and the freedom of mature insight, which only an eyewitness could claim, to express 'what it meant'. In practice that straight line encounters a number of obstacles: the uncertain referent of 'these things' (verses 15–23, ch. 21, or the whole Gospel); whether 'who has written' might mean 'who has authorized' or 'who has originated the writing of . . .' (cf. John 19.22); whether chapter 21 and, therefore, the claim it makes, is original to the Gospel or is a later attempt to authenticate and incorporate it amongst other church forms; and, perhaps most importantly, on what grounds we are to believe the anonymous 'we' (or the 'I' of the final verse); internally, there is that circular a priori alternative, whether the ('spiritual'/ unhistorical) content of the Gospel undermines any eyewitness claim, or whether the eyewitness claim authenticates the ('historical') content of the Gospel. Some more recent approaches have preferred to ask how that claim, and its subject, the Beloved Disciple, functions within the Gospel as a textual construct or might have functioned in the circles among whom it circulated (Lincoln 2002).

On the other hand, precisely at the misplaced(?) Cleansing of the Temple John distinguishes clearly between the words that Jesus then spoke (2.20), their meaning with which the ('omniscient') narrator privil-eges readers (verse 21), and the 'remembering' which the disciples attained only after he was risen from the dead but which, by leading to belief both in Scripture and in Jesus' word, is given unequivocal authentication (verse 22). 'Remembering' encompasses, in particular, Scripture as the hermeneutical key, again provided for readers by the narrator, but so woven into the narrative that there can now be no other reading of it (2.17; 12.14–16) (Lieu 2000). While these two passages alert the reader to the process at the beginning and end of Jesus' public ministry, many would associate with them the promise given to the disciples of the Spirit who will bear witness alongside their future witness, and who will not only remind them of all Jesus has said, but lead them into all truth, receiving from Jesus and proclaiming to them (14.26; 15.26–7; 16.13–15). If even the disciples could not bear all that Jesus has to say, and if all Jesus' address to them counts merely as 'parables', to be surpassed only in the future when he will speak 'plainly' or 'openly' (16.12, 25), should we find in the Gospel the exercise of the promised (in the text itself!) Spirit-inspired openness superimposed on a narrative and tradition whose resonances were opaque even to those most closely involved (see Hoegen-Rohls 1996)? Given the inconsistency in John's appeal to the Spirit in chapters 14–17, and its absence from the earlier passages quoted, it would be wrong to speak unilaterally of a prophetic consciousness, although the promise of witness (15.27) is anticipated by the 'we' sayings that punctuate the text (1.14, 16; 3.11; 6.69). However, this self-conscious awareness of the gap between event and witness or proclamation, coupled with the conviction that the latter is not one possible reading of those events to be laid alongside other readings but carries the absolute authority of their subject, challenges the reader, and so the modern interpreter, to assent or to protest.

On the other hand, that gap between event and witness, between the presence of Jesus and his absence from them, is already within the Gospel both embedded and transcended in the Farewell Discourses: these unfold under the shadow of Jesus' knowledge that 'the hour has come' (13.1). Although there is still the 'little while' of his presence, the same moment is the 'now' of the Son of Man's glorification (13.31–3). The mix of present and future tenses (e.g. 14.17–24; 15.18–27) in which the events of Jesus' ministry and his time with his disciples move into the past and the conditions of their life in the light of his 'glorification' move into the present challenges the historiographical conventions of the *bios* genre with which the Gospels are now frequently aligned. The reader of Jesus' final prayer to his Father knows not only that Jesus' subsequent arrest, trial, and death do nothing to undermine the successful completion of his task, but also that his disciples for whom he prays are already in possession of a fullness of knowledge, and are already the object of that hatred by the world whose outworking against Jesus will shortly be narrated (17.6–8, 14–16). Here even subsequent generations find in Jesus' words their present (17.20–3), and are assured that there can be no disjunction between their own experience and what Jesus achieved in his ministry, or between their own celebration of divine unity and that which was already manifested there.

There have been a number of responses to this textually inspired invitation to discover in the Gospel the adoption of a lens or screen through which the events, or earlier traditions concerning them – on which more below – have been refracted. The importance of Scripture has already been signalled; although John uses far fewer explicit citations of Scripture than does Matthew, and although those he does use are concentrated in the second part of the Gospel, the influence both of Scripture and of contemporary exegetical traditions is pervasive (Oberman 1996). Exemplary here is the Bread discourse (6.26–59), which redefines each element of its lead Scripture (verse 31 = Ps 78.26; Exod 16.4, 15?) as it moves towards a prophetic companion passage (verse 45 = Isa 54.13), and which has been compared in method with (synagogue, cf. verse 59) homilies (Borgen 1965). Yet alongside this explicit exegesis, 'the Jews' by their murmuring recall those who 'murmured' in the wilderness and so did not live to enter the promised land (verses 41, 49; Num 14; Lieu 2000). In a very different way, any understanding of 1.51 presupposes knowledge not only of Gen 28.12, which it quotes, although without acknowledgement, but also of contemporary exegetical debates about what, or who, it was upon which the angels ascended and descended. So embedded is Scripture, and so often implicit rather than explicit, that tracing its limits becomes a matter of scholarly subjectivity and we are left wondering just how much was, or needed to be, patent to the earliest readers in order for them to understand the message of the Gospel. If Scripture has helped shape the murmuring Jews of chapter 6, where else has it exercised its creativity? Has the early Christian conviction that Christ died 'according to the Scriptures' provided the licence for the portrayal of a Jesus whose words as well as whose deeds take their script from those Scriptures (Hanson 1991)?

A similar difficulty in tracing limits and in determining the extent or necessity of authorial intention and readerly apprehension emerges in relation to the Gospel's undoubted use of symbolism. Water as a symbol of the spirit or of life (7.38–9; 4.10–15), or the night into which Judas departs as belonging to the powers of evil (14.30) are relatively unproblematic; but is the night when Nicodemus visits Jesus (3.2) equally redolent of a meaning that must determine the rest of their conversation, and does the water that will be changed into wine, together with the six jars, one short of the completeness of seven, serve only to convey the meaning of all Jesus' activity as a transformation if not replacement of 'Judaism' (2.6–10)? Do readers need to recognize in a man's thirty-eight-year-long illness Israel's wandering in the wilderness, or in the pool's five colonnades the books of Torah which could not offer wholeness (5.2–5; Deut 2.14)? Experience has demonstrated that, once unleashed, readers' capacity to discover layers of symbolism in the Gospel appears uncontrollable, and, importantly, that the text itself apparently offers little unequivocal control. So understood, any surface reading is inadequate; the disciples' 'remembering' that revealed the Temple as a symbol of Jesus' body (?or his body of Temple: 2.21), it might be argued, can or even must be replicated by the reader at every point.

One objection would be that 'John' chose to write a narrative of the words and deeds of Jesus; why do this if they were not important in and of themselves? Another would be to point to 1.14, the centrality of the 'becoming flesh' as the medium of revelation, which might militate against treating mundane details as only ciphers for another level of meaning. Although in an important debate Ernst Käsemann argued that the climax of that verse was 'we beheld his glory', signalling a 'docetic' Christology,[6] these objections, together with the Gospel's emphasis on seeing, do demand a more sustained account of 'the interplay of form and meaning' (Lee 1994; see also O'Day 1986). Whereas the search for coded meanings in arbitrary words and details ignores the careful literary construction of Johannine narrative, a more satisfying approach recognizes that the way in which the author writes as well as the content of what he writes work together in the unveiling of meaning. Such well-known *topoi* as misunderstanding, irony, and double meaning, as well as echoes of Scripture or the use of language and imagery laden with potential significance (blindness, light) mean that narratives such as Jesus' well-side encounter with a Samaritan woman (4) or the giving of sight to a man born blind (9) can and must be read on two levels at once, so that the reader, like the participants, is forced to come to a decision; only within these broader structures can one safely locate the symbolic reading of specific details.

Such a reading evidently draws on the development of recent literary approaches to the Gospels in which the reader is an ever-present part of the search for meaning (and so invites discussion of the relationship between how John writes and how John is read). It might be argued that the Fourth

[6] Käsemann 1969 in opposition to Bultmann's emphasis on the offence of the word-become-flesh.

Gospel, most of all, is a congenial host to such a reading with its explicit appeal to its readers, 'that you might believe/ maintain your belief' (19.35; 20.31).[7] While narrative-critical or literary readings have been applied to all the Gospels, they work particularly well with the narrative parts of John which are notable for their sustained story-line and characterization, for the interplay of participants and possibility of speaking of 'plot', as well as for the techniques already noted, such as irony, anticipation, and misunderstanding (e.g. 9; 11.1–44; 18.28–19.16).[8]

However, a sensitivity to the potential of Johannine narratives to be read as transparent of another story has provoked other analyses of the double layer of reference. Particularly influential has been that associated with J. Louis Martyn (Martyn 2003 (1st edn 1968); 1978). Here the story of Jesus becomes a mirror of, or a window for viewing, the story of the Johannine community. Paradigmatically, the story of the Johannine Christian(s)' own experience is told in/through the story of the man born blind who receives his sight and is cast out by 'the Jews', who had determined to exclude from the synagogue all who confessed Jesus to be the Christ. Searched for and found by Jesus, he confesses his faith (9): the choice is unequivocal – to be disciples of Moses or of 'that person' (9.28) – as too may be the dangers that await (16.2). The story may be extended, back to the roots of the community in one-time followers of John the Baptist (1.35–40), to the incorporation of heterodox Jewish and Samaritan elements (4.4–42), and to a heightening Christology which incurs the charge of blasphemy against those until then still part of 'the synagogue' (5.17–18), and so offers the impulse to the 'exclusion from the synagogue'; it extends, too, to internal conflicts over the language to be used of Jesus, and to schism (6.60–71), to recognition of and hope for unity with other followers of Jesus (10.16), despite their differing structures of authority or tradition-claims (21.15–23), and even into the schism and other conflicts reflected in the Johannine Epistles (1 John 2.18–19; 3 John) (Brown 1979). There are those who are secret disciples 'for fear of the Jews' (19.38) or who, despite a commitment to faith, are unable to follow where a Johannine confession will lead (8.31), while the mission to the Gentiles may hover in the shadows (12.20). Perhaps most importantly and influentially, within this reading John's antagonism to 'the Jews' becomes ameliorated, directed only to 'the synagogue' whose rejection of his community (9.22) has led to deep pain

---

[7] Depending on whether an aorist or present tense is read.
[8] See, for example, Stibbe 1992; Segovia 1996. For a commentary which exploits John's narrative skill see Moloney 1998.

and to the need for sharp self-definition. The Johannine world-view with its sharp antitheses has then invited comparison with the sectarian mentality demonstrated so often among groups which have broken abruptly away from their parent body, the Jesus who has no true belonging here (3.31–6; 8.23) mirroring and legitimating the bewildering experience of multiple alienation (Meeks 1972). From another perspective, the prominent role played by women, including the 'Petrine' confession of Martha (11.27) and the dominical sending of Mary Magdalene as 'apostle to the apostles' (20.17), can be read either as a rebuke to the Johannine community's conventionalism or (more commonly) as a celebration of their egalitarianism against other 'church' models (4.27). Some have rejected such 'history-of-the-community' readings as 'allegorical' or as implying that John is writing 'allegorically' (Watson 1998); these labels are unhelpful, not only because of the imprecision with which the term 'allegory' is used, but because it underplays the integral and causal relationship that is being claimed by interpreters between the story of Jesus and that of those who believe in him. This same claim may also provide a partial answer to the question (again) why John should write 'a Gospel' if his concern was with the past experience of his community. More fundamental is the objection that, although sometimes identifying external points of reference and often couched in a rhetoric of historical certainty,[9] all such reconstructions can only be extrapolated from the text which they are then used to explain. However internally persuasive, and even theologically valuable (e.g. against the charge of anti-Judaism), the story of the Johannine community may be, this may still be the plausibility of well-crafted fiction. Moreover, however likely it is that any text reflects the conditions of its composition and needs of its audience, and however well tested this is through redactional-critical techniques, the Fourth Gospel gives no hint that it is telling the community's own story.

Both narrative and community-history readings find themselves most comfortable with the narrative parts of the Gospel.[10] This may sometimes reflect a perplexity as to what to do with the discourse material and how to root it in a historical context and process, or how to interpret it without adopting the categories of the later theological formulations to which it

---

[9] Particularly the identification of 9.22 with the *birkat-hamminim* or 'benediction against the heretics' conventionally dated to the mid 90s. However, it is now widely acknowledged both that the Johannine references do not match that tradition and that the traditions about the benediction, which would in any case not have functioned outside Palestine, are unreliable: see Kimelman 1981, followed by many since.

[10] Although see Moloney 1998; Segovia 1991.

contributed. What does it mean for the Jesus of the Gospel narrative to say, 'I and the Father are one', or what does the commentator say about that account without becoming mired in the categories of priority or truth?[11] Answer can be made via a history of the community or by appeal to the hermeneutical lens of Scripture; reference has been made above to the debates as to whether the Gospel reflects the Hellenistic transformation of the earliest ('Hebraic') belief in Jesus. The pendulum has swung decisively against this model, although largely alongside a recognition that the two categories cannot be set antithetically against each other. The 'Logos' of the Prologue may best be understood within the framework of Jewish wisdom-speculation, and the figure of wisdom may then suggest how, even within a Jewish context, the dilemmas of unity and multiplicity in divine revelation and mediation could be articulated (Scott 1992). The pervasiveness of 'sending' in the relationship between Son and Father leads away from closed categories of ontology towards Jewish conceptions of agency and activity, which can better accommodate the accompanying assertions of dependency and subordination (5.19–20). Some would even argue that the Gospel may rather be evidence of what was possible within Jewish thought than the clearest articulation of a Christian (= non-Jewish) belief in Jesus (Boyarin 2001). Implicated in such views is that the boundaries between the different thought patterns which we choose to label 'Christian', 'Jewish', and also 'gnostic' were fluid, a fluidity to which John bears particular witness, rather than, as in older formulations, concretized by the Gospel. These views also encourage us to see the discourses of the Gospel as representing a story (to avoid earlier controversies over 'myth'), that of the sending of the Son by the Father, and of the Son's return to the Father, and not as static theological formulations.

Some would also set them within another story: although often mined for such formulations, and sometimes exegeted as a series of them, for the most part the discourses take the form of argument and demonstration. The normal designation 'discourses' masks the importance of Jesus' interlocutors, the appeal to evidence, and the repeated challenge to decision or judgment on both sides (e.g. 5.31–40); all this invites the language of 'trial', although whether the discourses thus pre-empt the trial of Jesus before the Jewish authorities, not described in this Gospel, or deliberately echo the deutero-Isaianic trial motif is a matter of dispute (Lincoln 2000; Asiedu-Peprah 2001).[12] An interpretation along these lines holds together the deeds of Jesus

---

[11] Robinson 1985; Casey 1996.   [12] For the influence of Deutero-Isaiah on John see also Ball 1996.

and his words, for the former represent the evidence to which Jesus appeals, being not his own achievements but those given him by God (5.36; 10.25).

This provides a positive answer to another frequently asked question, that concerning the origins of the discourse material and its relationship with the narrative within which it is set. Although the discourses regularly take their starting point from the actions of Jesus, they can also be read independently of these; whereas the miracles of Jesus, taken on their own, present a wonder-worker of dramatic power who out-classes the Synoptic Jesus,[13] the discourses give us a revealer whose word is the source of life and whose mission is to bring knowledge of God. Rudolf Bultmann's identification of the discourses as revelatory – albeit only of the 'that' of Jesus as revealer – and as best illumined by Mandaean traditions has largely been abandoned, but his separate identification of a 'signs source' has had a longer life, aided by the numbering of the first two signs (2.11; 4.54), by the final summary (20.30–1), and by the Gospel's own ambivalence towards faith based on signs (2.23–4). Reconstructions of this signs source, sometimes (unpersuasively) pursued with the same precision that accompanied older pentateuchal criticism, produce what might be seen as a thoroughly 'un-Johannine' substratum – in Clement of Alexandria's terms, 'bodily', not 'spiritual' – although one that has been located in the earliest stage of the Johannine community by those who adopt such a trajectory (Fortna 1970, 1988).[14] Levels of editing and, most important, the interpretative addition of the discourses are what then render these 'Johannine', divesting them of inappropriate emphasis (6.63) and pointing towards their true meaning (11.23–6). Whence, then, the discourses? Bultmann's solution, mentioned above, assigned them an origin outside an exclusively Johannine context but also saw in them the core of the characteristically Johannine understanding, albeit crucially embodied in the offence of the word-made-flesh. Others have suggested that they have grown out of homiletic or sermonic material based either on the signs or perhaps on earlier, Synoptic-like traditions, such as the parable of the apprentice son in 5.19.[15]

This has brought us to the point where some would start their inquiry into how John writes. What sources were at his disposal, and what degree of creativity did he exercise over them? Our postponement of this until the end may be justified by the image of the seamless robe (19.23) that many

---

[13] An excessive abundance of water into wine, a man born blind, a man whose corpse will already have begun to putrefy.

[14] Similarly, some would posit an earlier Passion Narrative source.

[15] Lindars 1992 includes a number of examples.

have applied to the Gospel; what will now emerge are the multiple breaks in the thread that are revealed under the microscope if not to the naked eye. The hypothetical signs Gospel is prior to any form of the Gospel accessible to us, betrayed only, for example, by the Synoptic-like structure of the miracle of 5.2–9a, which only by stages becomes the object of a sabbath controversy and then the impulse to Jesus' christological claims (verses 17–47), which are pursued without reference to the incident that initiated them. More obvious are disjunctions such as those between 14.31 and 15.1; 20.30–1 and 21.1; and the geographical incoherence that would be avoided were ch. 6 to follow 4.54.[16] The first two of these have given rise to theories of the subsequent redaction of the Gospel (ch. 21), and of the possible circulation of variant forms of the same tradition (chs. 15–16 alongside 13.31–14.31, possibly with ch. 17, lacking any reference to the Spirit Paraclete, as a third variation). Alongside these textual seams there have been detected theological seams, such as the apparently literalistic future eschatological hope of 5.28–9 after the realized eschatology ('and now is') of 5.25, or the crude and perhaps sacramental language of chewing flesh and drinking blood (6.51c–56) which clashes with a 'logocentric' reading of the bread from heaven of the preceding discourse, or even the paraenetical interpretation of the foot-washing which itself rather represents the unrepeatable death of Jesus into which believers are incorporated (13.12–17; contrast 13.1–11). In each case the first of these has been dubbed 'more ecclesiastical' and has been assigned to a redactor seeking to assimilate the Fourth Gospel to the normative tendencies of the wider church; chapters 15–16 with the image of the vine and call to demonstrate love by a Christ-like self-giving (15.1–8, 11–17), and chapter 21 with its concern to acknowledge Petrine pastoring, may appear to demonstrate a similar tendency.[17] This model tends to treat the redactional process antithetically, as one of intentional balancing and even correction; implicitly the label 'ecclesiastical' can be derogatory as signalling a decline from the essential Johannine vision, although some, even before narrative emphases on the final form of the text, have preferred to see the final editor as the true Johannine author (Thyen 1977). More recently there have been attempts to see in the redactional process a process of 'relecture', a rereading of existing traditions to address new contexts that is predicated on continuity, not on correction,

---

[16] For an attempt to reorder the Gospel see Bultmann's commentary (Bultmann 1971).

[17] We might also add the question whether the Prologue (1.1–18) had an independent origin and/ or was added after the composition of the main Gospel. Richter 1977 and Thyen 1977 represent such an approach particularly well; see also Ashton 1991:76–90, 160–6, 199–204.

on affirming the earlier tradition, not on seeking to qualify it (Scholtissek 2000; Zumstein 1996).[18] One may be forgiven for suspecting that both approaches reflect prior understandings of the nature of tradition, of the church, and of the essence of 'the Gospel message'.

Of necessity all such theories have only the Gospel text to work on, and so arise out of the interpreter's close attention to the text and her sense of its consistency. Whether or not the Epistles of John can help is contested: the majority view still holds that they are subsequent to and presuppose the Gospel, although a minority would argue the reverse; a third view is that they represent an independent articulation of a shared tradition. If either of the last two positions is found persuasive, then we might use the Epistles to detect core Johannine tradition and its reworking, but the findings are meagre and the principles likely to remain disputed (Sproston North 2001). Underlying the debate are some important questions: did the tradition only become 'Johannine' at the hands of the evangelist, or did it already bear the distinctive characteristics that we recognize when it came to him? For those who accept the hypothesis of a Johannine community this means, did the community create the Gospel, or the Gospel the community, at least as a *Johannine* community?[19] It is in line with wider New Testament study that the pendulum is again swinging towards the creativity of the Johannine author, although now decisively anonymous.

If this has returned us to Clement of Alexandria's claim, albeit with a carefully qualified 'spiritual', the last question he provokes is where the Gospel stands in relation to the Synoptic Gospels. Evidently there is no relationship such as that which connects those three to each other, and yet without the model of at least one of them would 'John' have written a Gospel in the form and with the basic structure that he did? Although there are links between John and Luke, for example, in traditions about Martha and Mary, or a figure who dies named Lazarus, Mark has best claim as a source for John, supported by fine details of language.[20] John's positioning of the Cleansing of the Temple at the beginning and not the end of Jesus' ministry, his failure to provide an 'institution narrative' at a Last Supper, or his dating of Jesus' death as prior to the Passover and not

---

[18] This is much more theologically nuanced than Raymond Brown's (Brown 1966, 1970) theory of five stages in the development of Johannine tradition. All the approaches referred to in this paragraph are frequently co-ordinated with theories of the history of the Johannine community.

[19] The latter position would also be favoured by those who see all constructions of the past as textual constructions.

[20] E.g. the rare word *pistikos* at John 12.3; Mark 14.3, or the reference to the grass in John 6.10; Mark 6.39. See Smith 2001, and the variety of views in Hofrichter 2002.

following its celebration (John 18.28; 19.14; contrast Mark 14.12) then fall into stronger relief.[21] Is this the deliberate correction of a tradition he understood to be wrong, a conscious ('spiritual') reinterpretation,[22] or a lack of concern for such details? Abandon Johannine acquaintance with one or more of the Synoptic Gospels and these questions disappear, although we may still have to decide on the implications of the different accounts of the shape and length of Jesus' ministry. It is difficult to see how the question can be conclusively answered, and the pendulum again continues to swing with reputable weight on both sides (Smith 2001). Perhaps of equal interest is the effect of John's canonical positioning alongside the other three Synoptics; although this may be deemed to fall outside 'how John writes', it allows some reflection on its implications.[23] Many modern scholars share Clement's apparent sensitivity to the dangers in taking John on its own, whether because of a fresh acknowledgement that his Jesus does not always convincingly appear as one like us (although see Thompson 1988), or more particularly because it can be read in ways that would deny the inescapably Jewish roots of Christian faith, and the continuing need for Christians to affirm God's covenantal promises to Israel. To wrestle with how John writes is to wrestle with the particularity of the claims to universality (1.1–18) in early Christian thought.

[21] The list could be continued at length.

[22] Hence some suggest that the transfiguration is omitted because Jesus' glory is seen throughout; others debate whether the absence of the Last Supper meal reflects anti-sacramental tendencies or a desire to tic the sacrament to Jesus and his word (ch. 6).

[23] And an appropriate point at which to express deep gratitude to and respect for Graham Stanton as a colleague at King's and as a friend.

CHAPTER 10

Beginnings and endings

Morna D. Hooker

Where the beginning is, there shall be the end.

(*Gospel of Thomas*, Logion 18)

In recent years, New Testament scholars have become increasingly aware of the significance of beginnings and endings for their understanding of the Gospels.[1] The beginning and ending of any literary composition are both important – not simply because the beginning provides a way of attracting the reader's attention, the ending a way of rounding things off – but because each provides important clues about the meaning of the material that lies in between. If these clues were, for many centuries, for the most part ignored, this was largely because the Gospels tended to be broken up into lectionary readings, rather than being read as wholes. Short passages read in this way make a very different impact from that which they have when read as part of a larger story: heard out of the context given them by the evangelist, they become once again independent pericopes, functioning as entities rather than as elements of something larger.

The Gospels are themselves part of something larger, however. Unlike the so-called 'Gospel of Thomas', which is a collection of sayings, our canonical Gospels are all narratives, and all narratives have to begin and end in particular places and at specific moments in time. Beginnings and endings provide ways of getting into and out of a sequence of events that begins long before and continues long after the story that is being told. Like a mother at an airport, guiding her children on and off a moving walkway, the narrator takes us with him from the starting point to the conclusion, and needs to assist us in getting on and off. But when the travellers leave the walkway, the rolling metal continues to move unseen; without it, they would have been unable to make that short journey. So, too, for the story-teller, his narrative is the crucial section of a bigger narrative which may or

---

[1] On beginnings, see Smith 1991; Hooker 1997; on endings, see Kermode 1967 (on endings in general); Hooker 2003.

may not be of interest to him. In the case of the traditional fairy-story, the opening phrase 'Once upon a time...' and the conclusion '...and they lived happily ever after' are ways of focusing on the particular events that take place in between, emphasizing their significance in contrast to whatever happened before and after: the story is self-contained, and has no need of a wider narrative to understand it. For our evangelists, in contrast, this underlying narrative is, as we shall see, of vital importance, for the story each of them tells needs to be seen in the context of God's plan for humankind.

Ancient writers were clearly aware of the important role of beginnings and endings. Those who were trained in rhetoric knew that it was essential, in composing a speech, to gain the audience's attention by giving some indication of the purpose and importance of what was about to be said. In written works, too, similar rules applied. In the introduction – the *prooimion* or *exordium* – an author would give some indication of the purpose or contents of the book. Some genres of literature – history, biography, scientific, medical or technical works – begin with a formal preface, indicating the author's purpose and method.

Of our four evangelists, only Luke begins with a preface of this kind. His formal address to Theophilus is in fact a literary device indicating that his book is intended, not for Theophilus alone, but for public distribution. Theophilus is mentioned again in Acts 1.1, and since Acts is clearly the sequel to Luke's Gospel, we need to consider them together. In Acts, too, Luke follows contemporary literary convention by beginning with a brief secondary preface which makes reference to the previous volume and indicates the content of this one. Since Acts was intended to be a continuation of what Luke had begun to write in the Gospel, that means that Luke 1.1–4 can be understood as a preface to the whole work. What is *not* clear, however, is whether Luke already had a second volume in mind when he wrote those verses,[2] or whether they were originally intended to refer to the Gospel alone.[3]

Although Luke's prefaces conform to contemporary literary conventions, this does not immediately identify the genre to which his two books belong. Traditionally, Luke was regarded as an historian, and it is hardly surprising if his prefaces were compared to those found at the beginning of historical works:[4] in particular, parallels to Luke 1.1–4 can be found in Jewish Hellenistic writings such as 2 Macc 2.19–32. Formal

---

[2] See Cadbury 1927:344; Higgins 1970.
[3] Alexander 1993: 146 suggests that this must at least be acknowledged to be 'a possibility'.
[4] Cadbury 1922a. Earl 1972 compares the opening lines of *The Iliad* and *The Odyssey*.

prefaces could also be found at the beginning of biographies,[5] however, and
indeed at the beginning of a wide range of literature dealing with various
technical and academic subjects.[6] A close parallel to Luke's preface is found
in Dioscorides' first-century treatise on medicine:

Although many reports have been made, not only in the past, but also recently,
about the production, effects, and testing of medicines, I nevertheless intend to
instruct you, dear Areios, about them: the decision to undertake such a thing is
neither needless nor injudicious, for some of my predecessors have not completed
their works, and others have written most things down from hearsay.[7]

Luke's preface indicates that he was writing a serious literary work, which
presented 'the truth concerning the things about which' his readers might
have heard. It does not identify his Gospel as 'history' or 'biography'.

PROLOGUES

Following this formal preface to his Gospel, Luke offers us another
introduction, which spells out the significance of the story that he is
about to tell. In this he is at one with the other evangelists, for they all
provide us with introductions that not only explain the importance of their
narratives, but give us the key information that will enable us to understand
them. If it is remembered that the Gospels were written to be heard, rather
than read privately, and that they are all essentially narrative in format, it is
hardly surprising if these introductions are reminiscent of the openings of
classical dramas. It was customary for the Greek dramatist to introduce the
theme of his play in a 'prologue', which provided members of his audience
with the vital information that would enable them to comprehend the plot,
and to understand the unseen forces – the desires and plans of the gods –
which were at work in the story.[8] The prologue might be delivered by one
of the characters in the play,[9] but was often spoken by the chorus,[10] who
would continue to comment on the action of subsequent scenes; at other
times it was delivered by a god or goddess.[11] Sometimes the prologue would

---

[5] Burridge 1992:109–13.
[6] Alexander 1986 termed these 'scientific', a term that covered topics such as medicine, philosophy,
mathematics, engineering, rhetoric and astrology (57). For a detailed discussion, see Alexander 1993.
[7] *Peri hylēs iatrikēs* (*Mat. Med.*)1.1. Cf. also Josephus, *Ag. Ap.* 1.1 and 2.1.
[8] Aristotle, *Poet.* 12 (1452b); *Rhet.* 3.14.6 (1415a).
[9] E.g. a nurse in Euripides' *Medea*, and a peasant in his *Electra*.
[10] E.g. the chorus of Persian Elders in Aeschylus' *The Persians*.
[11] See Euripides' *Hippolytus*, where the opening words are spoken by Aphrodite, and *Ion*, where they are
found in the mouth of Hermes.

take the form of an opening scene which introduced the audience to the chief characters in the story and gave them some understanding of its importance. Nor was this dramatic method confined to the classical stage, for there is an excellent example of an introductory scene functioning in this way in the book of Job, where chapters 1–2 explain to the reader (but not to Job himself!) why he is overtaken by so many afflictions.[12]

The fact that our evangelists are all following the same pattern is not immediately obvious to us, because each of them does it in a very different way. Mark, almost certainly the first of our Gospels, begins with what is possibly a title (1.1),[13] followed by a quotation from scripture (1.2–3), and three short scenes (1.4–8, 9–11, 12–13), all of which are set in 'the wilderness'. Matthew begins with the genealogy of Jesus, followed by stories about his conception and birth. Luke, after his formal preface, also follows this up with stories about Jesus' conception and birth, but they are completely different from Matthew's, and set out the link between John the Baptist and Jesus, which was the theme of Mark 1.4–8. The Fourth Gospel, distinctive as always, opens with a magnificent theological prologue about the Word of God, now made flesh in Jesus Christ.

John

To modern readers, John 1.1–18 is most clearly recognizable as a 'prologue', and we therefore begin with this Gospel. Like Luke 1.1–4, these verses stand apart from the rest of the book, which has a narrative structure. Their purpose is plainly theological: to make sure that the reader understands that Jesus Christ is 'the Word' made flesh. This message is, of course, in keeping with the purpose of the rest of the Gospel, which is to make plain who Jesus is. Nevertheless, this introductory prologue sets out Jesus' relation to God and to his work in the world in a unique way; without it, the reader would find it difficult to understand *how* Jesus is able to do the 'signs' that he subsequently performs, or *why* he makes the claims he does.[14] Readers – and hearers – of the Gospel who have studied John 1.1–18,

---

[12] For the theory that Mark, in particular, was influenced by Greek tragedy, see Bilezikian 1977. It is not necessary to suppose that the evangelist *read* the plays, since theatres were found throughout the Hellenistic world, and the stories would be familiar. The fact that theatres were located at shrines and that the plays told of the involvement of the gods in human affairs suggests that the evangelist might well have been influenced by the dramatic format in presenting his own story of the good news of God's salvation through Jesus.

[13] The words 'the beginning of the gospel' could be understood to refer to the key events described in 1.1–13, but it is more probable that they are intended as a heading to the entire narrative.

[14] Cf. Hooker 1974–5.

however, will have learned that the creative purpose and power of God – the 'Word' – which was at work 'in the beginning' and which was revealed to Moses on Sinai is now made fully known in the person and work of God's Son, Jesus Christ, and they will therefore be able to comprehend the significance of John's story. It is because the Word was with God in the beginning (1.1–2) that Jesus, the Word made flesh (1.14), declares 'before Abraham was, I am' (8.58). It is because all things were made through him (1.3) that the works he performs are the works of God (10.37–8). It is because life was in him (1.4) that he is the resurrection and the life (11.25), and because that life was light (1.4) that he is the light of the world (8.12). These positive statements are tempered by the warning that the world, which was made by him, did not know him, and that his own people did not receive him (1.10–11), so preparing us for the narrative that follows. At the same time, there is the assurance that some will receive him and believe in his name, and so become God's children (1.12–13).

So far, however, John's prologue has not named Jesus. In verse 14 we are told that the Word was made flesh: but who was he? The answer to that question is provided by the witness of John the Baptist (1.6–8, 15), and the narrative proper will begin with John's witness to the one who follows him, whom he identifies as the Son of God (1.19–36).[15] Now, however, he is named by the evangelist himself: the Word made flesh, whose glory has been revealed (1.14), and who has brought grace and truth, is Jesus Christ (1.17), Son of the Father (1.14, 18). The evangelist compares this revelation with the revelation made through Moses – i.e. the Torah, or law (1.17) – but he does not denigrate the law, for it bears witness to Christ (1.45; 5.39, 46). Nevertheless, the full revelation of God can be made only through the Son, who reveals God's glory, a glory that is revealed in the cross (12.23, 28; 13.31–2; 17.1).

John's prologue begins and ends with references to the wider narrative: the story he is about to tell has its origins 'in the beginning', and it is the crucial turning point in the continuing story of God's dealings with the world which he has made. Within that wider narrative, God's self-revelation to his people Israel is a vital factor; how, then, does the story the evangelist is about to tell relate to the Torah, and to the promises made to Israel? John's answer is that Jesus Christ is the fulfilment of those promises because he is the fulfilment of the Torah itself – the true embodiment of God's self-revelation which was glimpsed by Moses on Sinai.

---

[15] See Hooker 1969–70.

The relevance of John's prologue to the rest of his Gospel is clear, but it nevertheless stands apart from it, and it is precisely because it stands apart from it that commentators have sometimes argued that it is a later addition to the Gospel.[16] This over-analytical approach overlooks the purpose and necessity of a prologue for a narrative of this kind.[17] John's prologue is no more an addition to the text than were the prologues to Shakespearian plays, which were intended to enable the audience to comprehend the plot. Once you know the story, of course, the need for a prologue is not so obvious.

Mark

Mark's prologue is far less distinctive than John's. Apart from the first four verses, it appears at first to be simply part of the narrative. Indeed, even after scholars recognized the existence of the Marcan prologue, arguments continued as to where it ends: does it consist of verses 1–8, 1–11, 1–13 or 1–15? If it ends at verse 8,[18] then the story proper begins when Jesus appears on the scene. But verses 9–11 reveal important information about Jesus to the reader – information that is concealed from all the characters in the story except for Jesus himself – and this suggests that they are part of the prologue. Similarly, verses 12–13 give us the key to understanding some of the events that follow.

Mark 1.1–13 provide the theological explanation of the subsequent narrative, and permit the reader to see it from the divine perspective: here the forces that are at work in the ministry of Jesus are revealed, but elsewhere they are only glimpsed. The clear testimony of scripture, of John the Baptist, and of the heavenly voice distinguishes this section from what follows, as do those who are named as participants in the story – the Holy Spirit, Satan, wild beasts, angels. In a few short verses, Mark provides us with a great deal of theological information: scripture is being fulfilled, the expected prophet has prepared the way of the Lord, Jesus has been identified as God's Son by a heavenly voice, God's Spirit is at work, and Jesus has confronted Satan in the company of wild beasts while angels lent him support. In the light of these insights, readers will be able to comprehend the rest of Mark's story, and they will understand why Jesus acts with

---

[16] E.g. Robinson 1962–3.
[17] Barrett 1971:28 (Barrett 1972:48): 'the Prologue is necessary to the gospel, as the gospel is necessary to the Prologue'.
[18] Westcott and Hort placed a gap after verse 8, marking these verses off from what followed.

such extraordinary authority when he arrives in Galilee, even though those present at the time, who are unaware of who he is or of the source of his power, are either bewildered or hostile.[19] As with John's prologue, the language and explicit statements set this passage apart from the rest of the Gospel, even though there are clear links with the subsequent story. These are found in the echoes of scripture in the passion narrative, John's role as Jesus' forerunner in death as in life (6.14–29; 9.11–13), and Jesus' identification as the Son of God (9.7; 15.39); to those in the know, moreover, the significance of Jesus' words about the Holy Spirit and about Satan (3.22–30) is plain.[20]

Mark's prologue and John's, though presented in very different ways, have a common purpose: they provide the reader with information that is concealed from the characters in the story that follows. Moreover, there is remarkable agreement in the *content* of that information. Both point to the fact that what takes place in Jesus is the fulfilment of God's purpose set out in scripture: Mark begins with an Old Testament quotation,[21] while John begins with the opening words of Genesis – 'In the beginning' – and offers us a midrash of Gen 1.1–3 and Exod 33.[22] Both evangelists tell us of the special relationship between Jesus and his Father, describing Jesus as the 'beloved' or 'only' Son, and both term him 'Christ', i.e. 'Messiah'. Both refer to the work of John the Baptist as the witness to Jesus, and stress the latter's superiority. Both describe Jesus' confrontation with evil: in Mark this is termed 'Satan', in John, 'darkness'. Both indicate the source of the power with which Jesus is to work: in Mark, this is expressed in terms of the Holy Spirit; in John, Jesus is said to be the Word made flesh.[23]

Matthew

Like Mark, Matthew and Luke choose to convey the essential information about Jesus in the form of narrative, and once again, these opening narratives are distinguished from the subsequent story because the truth

---

[19] Those who argue that the introduction continues to the end of verse 15 point to the use of *euangelion* in verses 14–15, and suggest that this forms an *inclusio* with verse 1. They also understand the reference to John the Baptist's 'handing over' to be a theological statement: John is handed over by God himself. See Keck 1965–6. These verses are better understood as the first scene in the narrative proper, however, since they refer to events that were common knowledge. See Hooker 1993. The NRSV places the break after verse 15, the REB after verse 13.

[20] There is a further echo of 1.12–13 in 8.33.

[21] This is the only place where Mark himself quotes scripture, though there are allusions to it in the course of the narrative, and Jesus and his opponents both appeal to it.

[22] Borgen 1969–70; Hooker 1974–5.

[23] The word 'Word' implies action, since for God, to speak was to act: the world itself was created by his Word.

about Jesus' identity is spelt out openly. One crucial difference, however, is that in Mark, only Jesus is aware of his identification as God's Son: there is no hint that even John the Baptist recognizes him as the one whose coming he had foretold. In Matthew and Luke, on the other hand, some of the human participants in the story are told something of the true significance of events, and so become witnesses to their truth. Remarkably, however, they show no hint of this in the subsequent narrative.

In Matthew, an angel explains to Joseph how Mary has conceived a child, who will be called 'Emmanuel'. The angel instructs Joseph to name the child 'Jesus', because he will save his people from their sins (1.21, 25), and subsequently instructs Joseph about where he is to take Jesus in order to save him from Herod (2.13). The magi come to Jerusalem, seeking the child who is born to be 'king of the Jews'. Yet the truth is far greater than any of them guess; for the name 'Emmanuel', though it means 'God with us', was a name – like 'Jesus' – that might well have been understood as no more than an expression of the piety of the child's parents, and 'king of the Jews' suggests simply a descendant of David. As Matthew's story progresses, his readers discover that both these terms have a far deeper significance than they might at first suppose.[24]

Remarkably, we find that there is a close correlation between the key information provided by Matthew and that which we are offered in Mark and John. In Matthew, also, God's purpose as it is revealed in scripture is fulfilled, but this theme is set out in Matthew's own distinctive way; first, in the genealogy, which traces Jesus' legal ancestry back to Abraham, the father of the nation; the four women who are mentioned – Tamar, Rahab, Ruth, and Bathsheba ('the wife of Uriah') – underline the fact that God's purpose is sometimes worked out in unorthodox and surprising ways, and prepare us for the apparent scandal surrounding Jesus' birth;[25] and secondly, in the frequent editorial comments that what was happening was taking place in order 'to fulfil what the Lord had spoken by the prophet' (1.22; 2.5, 15, 17, 23).

Like Mark and John, Matthew tells us that Jesus was in a special sense God's Son – a relationship to which Israel had been called[26] – and terms

---

[24] For Jesus' kingship, see Matt 21.1–9; 25.31–46; 27.11–44. For the idea that Jesus is 'God with us', see 14.22–7; 28.16–20 (see p. 197 below).

[25] Tamar disguised herself as a prostitute in order to seduce her father-in-law (Gen 38.1–26); Rahab was a prostitute (Josh 2; 6.22–5); David and Bathsheba engaged in an adulterous relationship (2 Sam 11); even the virtuous Ruth (already an 'outsider' as a foreigner) made risky sexual advances to Boaz (Ruth 3).

[26] Matt 2.15, quoting Hos 11.1. Cf. the Old Testament allusions behind Mark 1.11 (Gen 22.12; Ps 2.7; 44.3 (LXX 43.4), etc.), which also suggest that the origin of the idea of Jesus' sonship is to be found in God's special relationship with his people.

him 'Christ', i.e. 'Messiah' (1.1, 18; 2.4). Jesus is said to have been conceived by the Holy Spirit (1.18, 20). The attempt of the powers of evil to destroy God's plan begins with Herod's reaction to the news of a rival's birth, and his slaughter of the innocent children in Bethlehem.

Matthew's narrative hints at other significant ideas. By placing Jesus' birth in Bethlehem, he underlines his credentials as Messiah, something already spelt out in the genealogy. The story of the magi, who bring gifts to the child and fall down in homage before him, not only echoes Old Testament prophecies (Isa 60.6; Ps 72.10) but foreshadows the future worship of Jesus by the Gentiles: those who come looking for 'the king of the Jews' are acknowledging him as their own ruler. The statement that all Jerusalem is troubled by the announcement of a king's birth, together with the account of Herod's attempts to kill him, prepares us for what happens when Jesus arrives in Jerusalem at the end of the story. Finally, the story of the slaughter of the children and of Jesus' flight to Egypt are reminiscent of Pharaoh's attempts to destroy all the male children born to the Israelites and the remarkable escape of Moses. Jesus is marked out as the successor to both David and Moses, and will prove to be greater than both, since he is the fulfilment of God's promises.[27]

Luke

Luke chooses to begin his narrative with traditions concerning the birth of John the Baptist. Zechariah, the faithful priest, is fulfilling his duties in the Temple when he is apprised by an angel that he and Elizabeth are about to have a son. The role of John as the forerunner of Jesus, already central in Mark 1.4–8, and important also for John (1.6–8, 15), is here elaborated, and taken back to their remarkable conceptions. The birth of Jesus to a young virgin (1.34) is extraordinary, but so also is the birth of John to a woman who is old and barren.[28] Both events are announced by Gabriel, and both Zechariah and Mary express disbelief (1.18, 34); since Zechariah's response leads to his temporary dumbness, it is Zechariah's wife Elizabeth who sums up what the Lord has done for her (1.25) and pronounces the blessing on Mary (1.42–5), while Mary herself is able to acknowledge the truth of what is to happen (1.38). John himself bears witness to Jesus even before he is born (1.44). Mary's song (1.46–55) is balanced by that of Zechariah when,

---

[27] For Jesus as greater than David, see Matt 12.1–8; 22.41–6; as greater than Moses, Matt 5.21–48; 17.1–8; 28.16–20 (see p. 197 below).
[28] Cf. Hannah, mother of Samuel, 1 Sam 1.1–2.11.

his speech restored, he praises God for what is happening (1.68–79); although the final verses of Zechariah's song refer to John's role as the forerunner of the Lord, most of his words refer to Jesus.

These various poetic utterances, found in the mouths of angels (1.15–17, 32–3, 35; 2.10–14) or those inspired by the Holy Spirit,[29] provide information about both John and Jesus. As in Mark, John is portrayed as the prophet who prepares the way of the Lord, announcing the salvation of God's people from their sins (1.16–17, 76–9). Jesus is the Son of God (1.32, 35), and the descendant of David (1.32–3, 68–9), i.e. the Messiah and Lord (2.11). His coming is the fulfilment of the promises set out in the scriptures, promises that go back to Abraham (1.55, 73), for he brings the promised salvation, the deliverance of God's people (1.49–55; 1.68–79), which is hailed by Simeon as bringing enlightenment also to the Gentiles (2.29–32). The similarities with the key themes in the Marcan, Matthean and Johannine prologues are striking.

Unlike Matthew, Luke does not quote explicitly from the Old Testament, but the style of these first two chapters is remarkable, soaked in Old Testament allusions and full of echoes of Septuagintal phraseology. It is Luke's own distinctive way of reminding his readers that the story he is telling is part of a story that commenced long before 'the fifteenth year of the emperor Tiberius' (3.1). Luke's insistence that the Holy Spirit is at work – in John (1.15,17) and in Jesus (1.35), as well as those who declare his significance (1.67; 2.25–7) – ensures that we understand that God himself is at work in the Gospel story.

Luke's first scene is set in the Temple, and his Gospel will end there (24.53). Two more incidents in the Temple (2.22–38, 41–51) describe how Jesus' parents obey the Torah's commands (2.21, 22–4, 41), and hint at Jesus' own righteousness.[30] But there is an ominous hint that God's purpose will be achieved only through suffering (2.35).

The style as well as the contents of these two chapters marks them off from the rest of Luke's Gospel. As a result, they have sometimes been treated as an addition to the Gospel and ignored.[31] To do so, however, is to ignore the vital clues they provide for understanding Luke's narrative.

---

[29] Elizabeth, 1.41, and Zechariah, 1.67, are both described as filled with the Holy Spirit, as is Simeon, 2.27. Mary, too, may be assumed to be so, 1.35.

[30] Cf. also the stress on the righteousness of John's parents in 1.6, and the divine favour in which Mary (1.28–9) and Jesus (2.40, 52) are held.

[31] Notably by Conzelmann 1960.

We have already seen that there is disagreement about the ending of Mark's beginning. So, too, with Matthew and Luke. Are Matt 3.1–4.11[32] and Luke 3.1–4.13, which are parallel to Mark 1.1–13, part of the Matthean and Lucan prologues?[33] The action appears to be taking place on a wider stage, involving Pharisees and Sadducees (Matt 3.7–12) and the crowd (Luke 3.7–17), but alongside this we have scenes in which the truth about Jesus is made clear – but not in public (Matt 3.13–4.11; Luke 3.23–4.13).[34] This is perhaps one more piece of evidence that it was Matthew and Luke who used and adapted Mark, rather than the reverse. By the time they wrote, the stories about John's preaching and Jesus' baptism had been absorbed into the narrative about Jesus' ministry. They chose different material to convey to their readers certain insights into the significance of Jesus' ministry, death and resurrection – insights hidden from Jesus' contemporaries during his lifetime, but considered by the evangelists to be essential for understanding their story.

Although our four Gospels begin in totally different ways, there is remarkable agreement between them concerning the key information they feel they should impart to their readers. While they stress the link between scripture and the story of Jesus in very different ways, their common theme is that Jesus is the fulfilment of God's plan for his people. This suggests that in searching for the genre of the Gospels, we should look to the accounts of God's dealings with his people in the past, since the evangelists relate the continuation of that earlier story.

ENDINGS

If beginnings are important, so too are endings. In a speech, it is necessary to end in a way that will inspire the audience to respond. In a story, it is necessary to round things off. According to Aristotle, an ending was that 'from which nothing else follows'.[35] Outside the fairy-story, however, this is impracticable: novels frequently leave us wondering 'and what happened next?'. In classical times, The Iliad and The Odyssey and Virgil's Aeneid all left their hearers in suspense, and the same is true of many biblical

---

[32] Kingsbury 1988:43–58 sees 1.1–4.16 as the introductory section.

[33] Luke seems to have multiple openings: 1.1; 1.5; 3.1; 3.23; 4.14.

[34] Remarkably, there is no indication in Luke that John recognized Jesus (3.21–2), in spite of 1.41: the unborn baby acknowledged Jesus, but now, in the story proper, he does not recognize him; cf. 7.19 and Matt 11.2–3. Similarly, in neither Matthew nor Luke does Mary show any recollection of the events related in the so-called 'birth-stories'.

[35] Poet. 7 (1450b).

narratives. The most obvious example is the book of Jonah, the final sentence of which is a question: readers are left wondering what Jonah did next, but more significantly, they are left pondering the moral of the story – can it really be true that God is concerned about the salvation of the Gentiles?[36] Even the book of Revelation, presenting a vision of the final completion of all things, necessarily ends on a note of eager expectation, with the fervent prayer: 'Come, Lord Jesus.' The reader is left in suspense, waiting for his coming. It is precisely because the story told by the evangelists is only a part – though the crucial one – of a continuing narrative which began with the creation of the world and will end with its final restoration that the Gospels all end by pointing their hearers forward to what follows.

Mark

The most obvious example in the New Testament of what has been termed a 'suspended ending'[37] is found in Mark, and we shall therefore begin this time with his Gospel. Following his account of the death and burial of Jesus, Mark describes the visit of a group of women to the tomb, and their subsequent flight: his final words are 'for they were afraid' (16.8). This abrupt conclusion emphasizes both the women's terrified reaction to the young man whom they encounter at the empty tomb and the message to the disciples to return to Galilee: if they obey, they will see Jesus there. Galilee was the place where Jesus had first summoned them to follow him, and the disciples, who had fled from danger in the garden of Gethsemane, need to learn once more what discipleship means. The brief reference to Peter hints at the significance of Jesus' death and resurrection. Peter, who denied that he was Jesus' disciple (14.66–72) and who had therefore forfeited the right to be called a disciple, is specifically included in the invitation. The two words 'and Peter' are thus a message of forgiveness, offering him the chance to begin again on the path of discipleship.

But was the message ever delivered? Did the disciples go to Galilee? And did they see Jesus there? Later scribes clearly felt the need to round the story off with accounts of appearances of Jesus to the disciples.[38] It used to be

---

[36] Cf. also Deuteronomy, which ends with Moses' death, but with the hope of entry into the Promised Land still unfulfilled. It is clear that this is not the end of the story. To a lesser or greater extent, this sense of expectation is common to the endings of all the Old Testament books.

[37] See Magness 1986.

[38] Two attempts to 'conclude' Mark were included in different manuscripts – the 'shorter ending' and the 'longer ending' of 16.9–20. The vocabulary and syntax of both are clear evidence that neither of them was written by Mark.

assumed that Mark could not have meant to conclude so abruptly, and that he himself wrote (or intended to write) more after 16.8.[39] Although some commentators still argue for one or the other of these possibilities,[40] most now argue that the sudden end is deliberate. An abrupt ending of this kind forces readers to continue writing the narrative for themselves:[41] the message to the disciples is in effect an invitation to Mark's hearers to 'go to Galilee' with the disciples, and a promise that those who retrace Jesus' steps and who follow him in faith will see him. The command to return to Galilee and the reference to what Jesus had previously told his disciples suggest that if we want to understand Mark's story we should turn back to the beginning of the Gospel and begin rereading it, looking once again at what Jesus did and said in Galilee. In the light of the death and resurrection of Jesus, we find that we are now in a better position to understand his narrative: as happens when one rereads a detective story, vital clues now reveal their significance. The ending of Mark, like its beginning, illuminates what comes inbetween.

On turning back to the beginning, we recall that Mark headed his narrative 'The beginning of the Gospel', and we realize that the story he tells is indeed only the beginning of the good news about Jesus, since the story is continued in the lives of those who are prepared to become disciples of the crucified and risen Jesus.

Matthew

Matthew and Luke both felt it necessary to 'complete' their narratives with stories about appearances of Jesus, but their two endings, like their intro- ductory birth-narratives, are very different. Matthew describes the removal of the stone from the tomb by an angel (28.2), who gives the women the message that was entrusted to them in Mark (28.7). The women, running from the tomb, encounter Jesus and so become the first witnesses, not simply to the empty tomb, but to the Risen Lord. Jesus repeats the message for the disciples, and the Gospel ends with an account of how the eleven disciples go to a specific mountain in Galilee, where they meet Jesus. Jesus' final words are a claim to have been given all authority in heaven and on earth, a command to the disciples to make disciples of all the nations, and a promise that he will be with them, to the end of time.

---

[39] For discussion of the problem of the abrupt ending, see Lightfoot 1938:10–15; Lightfoot 1950:365–7; Horst 1972.

[40] See Gundry 1993:1009–21; he is followed by Evans 2001:538–40.

[41] Petersen 1980:153: 'the reader is compelled by the narrator to respond'.

Although Matthew has provided his readers with what Mark's story lacks – accounts of appearances – his ending is also somewhat abrupt, and equally forward-looking. The disciples have obeyed the command to go to Galilee, but that is only the first stage in their journey; now they are to go into the whole world, making disciples of all the nations. This story cannot have an ending until everyone recognizes the authority of Christ.

Matthew's conclusion is far more impressive than Mark's: Jesus speaks of his own authority, and commissions his disciples: he promises to be with them. Yet strangely, Matthew breaks off without explaining what happened next. There is no account of Jesus' departure or ascension into heaven. Matthew seems to have deliberately chosen to end by pointing forward – to the mission of Jesus' followers to make disciples of all nations – rather than trying to bring Jesus' own story to any kind of conclusion. Indeed, such a conclusion is clearly impossible, since Jesus promises to be with them till the end of time.

Although Matthew's conclusion points forward, it also contains significant echoes of his prologue. We are not told where 'the mountain to which Jesus had directed' the disciples (28.16) was located, but the words are reminiscent of the story of Moses (Exod 3.12), who was a significant (if concealed) figure in Matt 2.13–19. Once again, Moses is not named, but readers who picked up the echoes of the story of Moses' call will recognize that something very significant is being said about Jesus: for while Moses was commissioned by God, it is Jesus himself who sends the disciples to the mountain, who commissions them to go out in his name, and who reveals himself to them as 'I am.' His final promise, 'I am with you always, to the end of time', not only reminds us of the name of God revealed to Moses, but takes us back to the name 'Emmanuel', meaning 'God with us', which was applied to Jesus in Matt 1.23. Finally, Jesus' claim to earthly authority, and his command to make disciples of all nations, reminds us that Jesus was acknowledged as 'king of the Jews' and worshipped by Gentile kings in Matt 2.1–12. These final verses point back to some of the important truths spelt out in the prologue to the Gospel. In the light of what they were told there, and what is revealed now, readers of the Gospel are in a position to comprehend the story that has been unfolded inbetween.

Luke

Luke was a more skilled literary writer than either Mark or Matthew, and he provides us with a more polished ending. He, too, begins with the story of the women's visit to the tomb, but the message they are given refers to what Jesus told the disciples when they were in Galilee, and contains no command to return there. The women's account of the empty tomb is confirmed by Peter, but it is two travellers to Emmaus who are the first to see Jesus. Rushing back to Jerusalem, they are told that the Lord has also been seen by Simon, and a few minutes later, Jesus himself appears. It is noteworthy that both in Emmaus and in Jerusalem, seeing Jesus is associated with eating together. Significant, too, is Luke's emphasis on what has been said and written in the past: the angels at the tomb remind the women of what Jesus had said in Galilee (24.6); Jesus himself points to 'everything that the prophets have declared' about himself, 'beginning with Moses and all the prophets' (24.25–7). Back in Jerusalem, he reminds the disciples of his previous teaching, which had pointed to what the law of Moses, the prophets, and the psalms had said about his suffering and resurrection (24.44–7).

We need not consider here the historical questions raised by these statements: it is clear that they reflect the growing awareness of the Christian community that the story of Jesus' life, death and resurrection corresponded to particular passages in scripture. For Luke, they confirm the truth that he signalled to his readers in his opening chapters, and that has underlain his narrative ever since:[42] the story of Jesus is the fulfilment of the promises set out in scripture.

The story itself has not yet come to an end, however! Scripture also promised, we are told, that forgiveness would be offered, in Jesus' name, to all the nations (24.47). Luke's Gospel ends with Jesus' promise to the disciples to send 'what my Father promised' (24.49), and a brief account of his ascension (50–1). Then the disciples 'returned to Jerusalem with great joy, and were continually in the Temple, blessing God'. The need for a sequel is clear.

And Luke did indeed write a sequel – the Acts of the Apostles, which continues the story of what 'Jesus began both to do and to teach'.[43] There is no space here to consider Luke's second book, except to make two brief comments. First, we note that Acts is deliberately linked to the Gospel with a brief summary of Luke 24 and a second, fuller, account of the ascension (1.2–11), followed soon after by an account of the pouring out of the Holy

---

[42]   A good example of this is seen in the quotation of Isa 61.1–2 in Luke 4.18–19. Jesus reads the passage and announces that the scripture has been fulfilled (4.21). In the next chapters (until 7.23) we see the 'programme' set out in these verses being fulfilled. Unlike Matthew, Luke does not keep reminding us that what the prophets had written was being fulfilled, but Jesus' answer to John the Baptist's disciples in 7.18–23 makes it plain that it was.

[43]   This interpretation of Acts 1.1 is supported by Barrett 1994:66–7.

Spirit (2.1–36; cf. Luke 24.49). The disciples now embark on the mission to preach to all nations (Luke 24.47; Acts 1.8). Jesus' commission at the beginning of Acts (1.8) not only repeats the stress at the end of the Gospel (24.48) on the role of the disciples as his witnesses, but reminds us of the opening words of the Gospel (Luke 1.2).

Secondly, the sudden ending of Acts is one of its most remarkable features. It seems extraordinary that a writer of Luke's calibre should conclude with an ending almost as abrupt as Mark's. Did he perhaps intend to write a third volume? Did he deliberately stop where he does in order to avoid telling the story of Paul's death? That can hardly be the explanation, since he did not shrink from describing the deaths of Jesus and of Stephen. Closer examination suggests that Luke's ending is not as feeble as has been suggested. With a neat piece of *inclusio*, we are reminded of the themes at the beginning and end of the Gospel and at the beginning of Acts – the fulfilment of scripture, the establishment of God's Kingdom (28.23), the recognition of Jesus as the Christ (28.23, 31), and the fact that God's salvation includes the Gentiles (28.28). For Luke, the fact that the Gospel had reached Rome and was being proclaimed there was a triumph: 'Paul lived there for two whole years ... proclaiming the Kingdom of God and teaching about the Lord Jesus Christ quite openly and without hindrance.' Even this was not the end of the story, however – but if more was to be written it must be written by others, including those who were inspired by Luke's words to carry on the task.

We are not surprised to find Luke using *inclusio*, for it was a recognized literary device in the ancient world. Matthew, too, as we have seen, has echoes of his opening words in his final verses. Echoes of a book's opening lines at its end make a satisfying conclusion, but they are not mere artistry; rather, they are reminders of the particular point of view from which the author has attempted to make us see his narrative.

Mark's ending also, in its own way, serves to take us back to the beginning of his narrative. If we are looking for *inclusio* in Mark, however, we should perhaps go back to the centurion's astonishing declaration that Jesus was 'Son of God' in 15.39, or to the intriguing reference in 15.34–6 to Elijah (identified by Jesus as John the Baptist in 9.11–13) and the rending of the Temple curtain in verse 38.[44]

If there is no certainty about where beginnings end, there is similar uncertainty when it comes to deciding where endings begin. In Matthew, it seems to be the final five verses of the Gospel, the scene in which Jesus

---

[44] Many commentators note the use of the verb *schizō* in both 1.10 and 15.38.

commissions his disciples, which forms an *inclusio* with the beginning, whereas Luke seems to use all the material in his final chapter to point back to the beginning of his story and so remind his readers of its significance. It is John, however, who is the most problematic.

John

Mark has appeared to many to be half-finished; the Fourth Gospel, in contrast, provides us with two endings, and with two statements about John's purpose in writing. Unlike the synoptic evangelists, John rounds off his Gospel with an editorial comment explaining the purpose of his book. This follows the stories of the finding of the empty tomb and of the appearances of Jesus to Mary, to ten of the disciples, whom Jesus sends out in his name, and finally to all eleven. In 20.30–1, a brief epilogue explains that the Gospel is written so that its readers may 'come to believe that Jesus is the Messiah, the Son of God', and so 'have life in his name'. With its statement of intent and its reference to the other material which could have been used but has not been selected, this epilogue serves the same purpose as Luke's literary preface in Luke 1.1–4. Moreover, these verses contain echoes of some of the themes set out in the prologue: Jesus is Messiah, the Son of God (cf. 1.14, 17), and those who trust in him receive life in his name (cf. 1.4). Once again, we have *inclusio*.

Many commentators believe that John's Gospel as we have it today is the final version of a text that evolved over a period of time, and that 20.30–1 originally formed the conclusion of the book. If they are right, the Gospel ended with a challenge to believe the good news about Jesus – a demand for a response that is as challenging as the ending of Mark. Moreover, although the final words of the chapter seem to give us closure, they tell us that Jesus did many other signs which could have been described, reminding us that what we have been given is by no means the whole of the story.

It is hardly surprising, then, if a later editor added an account of yet another sign (21.1–14). This takes place when Jesus makes another appearance to his disciples, this time in Galilee, and is followed by the commissioning of Peter. The conversation between Jesus and Peter picks up themes found earlier in the Gospel (chapter 10). Like Mark 16.7, this passage indicates that Peter has been forgiven and restored, but it also points to his significant role in the early church. A second epilogue, in 21.24–5, identifies 'the disciple whom Jesus loved' as the one who witnessed what happened and wrote it down, and makes a further reference to the 'many other things that Jesus did' which it has been impossible to include. Like Luke (1.2; cf. 24.48;

Acts 1.3, 8, 22), the fourth evangelist insists that the source of his material was an eye-witness to events. This second Johannine conclusion is not merely a neat literary device to bring the book to an end, but the authentication of what it contains. At the same time, it affirms that, though the book is now concluded, the story of Jesus can never be fully told: it is a story that has no end.

Just as their introductions showed interesting similarities in spite of their differences, so too with their endings. Three of our four Gospels contain scenes of commissioning in their final chapter. In both John 20 and 21, the disciples are commanded to continue Jesus' work (20.21–3; 21.4–21), while Matthew, as we have seen, chooses to use Jesus' commissioning of the disciples as his conclusion. In doing so he, too, gives his book an open ending. Jesus' final words to his disciples – the promise to be with them to the end of the age – are linked with the command to go into all the world, making disciples. Like Mark and John, Matthew reminds us that the story of Jesus is not yet at an end. Luke's last story of an appearance by Jesus also takes the form of a commissioning (24.44–9), but he does not conclude there, because he wishes to provide a link with the next part of the story. He describes how Jesus takes leave of his disciples, after promising that he will be sending the gift of the Holy Spirit. So the disciples return to Jerusalem, where they spend their time in the Temple, and wait for what will happen next. It is a neat ending, and a neat piece of *inclusio* (cf. 1.8–9), but most important of all, it is an open ending, which indicates clearly that the story will continue.

Another common theme – and a surprising one – is that of disbelief or doubt. We might expect the evangelists to provide compelling evidence to persuade their readers that Jesus really had been raised from the dead. Yet they seem deliberately to emphasize the doubts of their witnesses. In Mark, of course, we have only the story of the women – who fled from the tomb in terror, saying nothing! In Matthew's final scene, he tells us that the disciples, seeing Jesus, worshipped him – but some doubted (28.17). In Luke, we are told that the disciples thought that the Risen Lord was a ghost (24.37), while John includes the story of doubting Thomas, who insisted that he would not believe until he saw Jesus for himself (20.24–9). It would seem that all the evangelists are urging their readers to trust in the good news that Jesus has been raised, in spite of their fears and doubts. They can believe, even without seeing Jesus. Like the disciples in Mark, who cannot see Jesus unless they believe and go to Galilee, Mark's readers will not 'see' Jesus unless they respond in faith. John's readers are invited to believe *without* seeing and touching – unlike Thomas, who refused to believe the good news – with the promise that 'those who have not seen and yet have come to believe' are blessed (John 20.29). Those who do so can rely on the reliable witness of those who *did* see (John 19.35; 20.8; 21.24; cf. Luke 1.2).

The fact that all our Gospels conclude with open endings is hardly surprising, for it is in keeping with their message. Their final chapters all deal with the resurrection, which brings new life, not just for Jesus, but for all his followers. If the story the evangelists have been telling is not at an end, that is because, in Mark's words, the story of Jesus' life, death and resurrection is for *all* of them only 'the beginning of the Gospel'. In very different ways, therefore, they all conclude with a challenge to their readers to continue the story for themselves.

PART III

After writing

CHAPTER II

The Four among Jews

James Carleton Paget

THE DIFFICULTIES OF THE TASK

Attempts to reconstruct Jewish opinion about Christianity in antiquity are dogged by a number of problems. These mainly arise from the character of the available sources. On the one hand we lack any substantial Jewish source on Christianity, and the fragmentary extant material is not without difficulty. On the other hand the Christian sources which apparently give us Jewish opinion about Christians are polemical in tone, and often repetitive and stereotypical in content. It has long been noted that to read off Jewish opinion from such texts is either misguided (see Taylor 1995) or at best a complex and nuanced task, involving the realization that such sources contain a difficult-to-decipher mixture of image and reality (see Lieu 1996).

These remarks are obviously relevant to the subject of this chapter, the Jewish knowledge of and interaction with the canonical Gospels. In this more limited context there are grounds both for pessimism and for optimism. Pessimism emerges from the limited character of the source material available. Interestingly, if we examine the Christian material which is termed 'adversus Judaeos', it is striking that it concerns itself much more with arguments about the scriptural (in Christian language, Old Testament) justification for Christian claims[1] than with a defence of 'ad hominem' assertions against the figure of Jesus as he is recorded in the canonical Gospels. Why this might have been the case will be examined briefly below. On the other hand there are grounds for some optimism. First, insofar as we have any Jewish material from antiquity which concerns itself *explicitly* with Christianity, this relates to Jesus. Although fragmentary and contested, at least such material exists. Secondly, in the Christian sources, we are better served than might at first seem the case. Some of the relevant texts have a high claim to reflect actual Jewish comment on

---

[1] See Bammel 1966–7:221–2.

Christianity. In addition to Celsus' Jew there are potentially helpful sources elsewhere, and it is precisely the limited and exceptional character of this material which means that we should take it seriously as a source of information for Jewish opinion. Yet none of this optimism should disguise the difficulties we face in addressing the question set; and what follows will be necessarily tentative in the claims it makes.

THE GENRE, AUDIENCE AND LANGUAGE OF THE GOSPELS

To some, questions relating to the genre, audience and language of the Gospels may appear irrelevant to the task which lies before us. But a *prima facie* case in favour of a known Jewish genre, an intended Jewish audience on the part of one or more of the evangelists, and a possibly semitic Vorlage for a Gospel would give our case for Jewish knowledge of the Gospels a good start.

Scholars have long debated the question of the genre of the Gospels. For some they should be considered 'sui generis'; for others, it is clear that they bear a close relationship to certain known literary genres. Recently there has been a tendency to see their closest literary parallel in the form of the 'bios', or life, which begins to emerge in the third century BCE in the Greek world (see Stanton 2002:13–18). For Gerd Theissen such a generic definition of the Gospels renders them in some sense 'alien to Jewish literature' (Theissen 1999:169), for in Judaism the only comparable parallel lies in Philo's *Vita Mosis*, which is itself addressed to Gentiles (*Mos.* 1.1f.). In Theissen's view, then, the very fact of the existence of the Gospel form indicates a desire to demarcate the evolving religious community from its Jewish root.

Theissen's point is overplayed. The decision to write a *bios*-like account of Jesus' life may have arisen as a consequence of the early Christian conviction of the centrality of the figure of Jesus, rather than as the result of any desire on the part of the authors concerned to participate in an act of demarcation. Moreover, it is quite wrong to set up as strict a distinction as Theissen does between the Gospels and any known genre of writing engaged in by Jews. Philo, for instance, does not present his decision to write a life of Moses as eccentric and requiring justification. And Josephus' *Life*, while not straightforwardly a 'bios', is close enough to render Theissen's comments too absolutist.

Theissen's observation, by implication, raises the old problem of Gospel audiences. In this context we can only be brief. At the most general level we should note that the world the Gospels describe is a Jewish one and that they assume a knowledge of the Jewish scriptures. Moreover, all of the

Gospels give evidence of what could be construed as Jewish objections to Jesus and his preaching (see, for instance, Matt 28.13), and in the case of the Fourth Gospel, they do this in an intense and highly polemical manner. None of these observations prove a Jewish audience, and other evidence may serve to count against such a conclusion, not least places in the Gospels where distinctive Jewish practices are explained, or where an apparent separation from the non-Christian Jewish community is assumed. The best case for something approximating to a Jewish audience can be made for the Gospel of Matthew. In making such a case we might combine the external testimony of Origen that the Gospel was written for Jews who had come to believe (*tois apo Ioudaismou pisteusasin*: Eusebius, *Hist. Eccl.* 6.25.4), which itself may reflect an old tradition, emerging from the view that Matthew was originally written in Hebrew or Aramaic (of which more below),[2] the fact that, in whatever form, groups described as Jewish Christian possessed copies of Matthew, and certain internal indicators (Matthew's apparently more conservative attitude to the Jewish law, for instance). Such a case assumes Jewish Christian rather than non-Christian Jewish readers, but we should not hold to such a clear division between the two in the first century. If Jewish Christians were the intended audience of some Gospels, then we should assume that they would have spoken to unconverted Jews about them.

Any case for a Jewish audience for the Gospels would be stronger if we were able to prove the existence of a Hebrew Matthew. Reference to this phenomenon is found in Papias, who says that Matthew brought together in writing the sayings of Jesus *hebraidi dialektō* (Eusebius, *Hist. Eccl.* 3.39.16), in Irenaeus (*Haer.* 3.1.1), in Eusebius' statement that the apostle Bartholomew took Matthew, written in Hebrew characters, to India (Eusebius, *Hist. Eccl.* 5.10.3), and in the repeated view, expressed in Epiphanius' account of the Ebionites that the fourth-century Jewish Patriarch Joseph of Tiberias had available for use Matthew in Hebrew, as well as John and the Acts of the Apostles (*Pan.* 30.3.8–9; 30.6.9; 30.12.10). But attempts, notably by George Howard, to prove the existence of an ancient Hebrew Matthew have generally met with scepticism,[3] not least because it is unclear, certainly for the first and second centuries, that Jews would have preferred Hebrew rather than Aramaic to Greek. But the opposite might be said to be supported by the Aramaic terms found in

---

[2] Origen refers to the fact that Matthew was originally written in Hebrew in the same passage. See also *Hist. Eccl.* 3.24.6 for Eusebius' view that Matthew originally preached to the Hebrews.
[3] See Horbury 1999:128–9.

Philo, Josephus and the New Testament, and the lack of evidence for the use of Hebrew in that period.[4] This has led some to countenance the possible existence of sayings material in Aramaic, even if not a full Gospel.

EVIDENCE FOR KNOWLEDGE OF THE GOSPELS AMONGST JEWS

(a) Direct Jewish references to the Gospels

There are few direct references to Jewish use of the Gospels. Two of these occur in rabbinic sources and one in a Christian source.

(i) b. Šabb. 116a–b

In this passage we read of an anonymous 'philosoph', who had a reputation for incorruptibility. Wishing to expose him as a fraud, Imma Shalom, R. Gamaliel's sister, the wife of R. Eliezer (b. Hyrcanus), brings him a golden lamp and states that she wishes to share in the inheritance of her father. Her brother notes that such a thing is not possible, for it is decreed that where there is a son, a daughter shall not inherit. The 'philosoph' denies the validity of this law, stating that 'since the day that you were exiled from your land the law of Moses has been superseded and the *'awon gilyon* given, wherein it is written, "a son and a daughter inherit equally"' (Num 27). But in order to contradict him and expose him as a fraud, R. Eliezer says: 'I have looked at the end of the *'awon gilyon*, wherein it is written, I, *'awon gilyon*,[5] came not to destroy the law of Moses nor to add to the law of Moses, and it is written therein, a daughter does not inherit where there is a son.'

The authorities mentioned in the passage, R. Eliezer and R. Gamaliel, hail from the first century, but most scholars assume a later date, perhaps no earlier than the beginning of the third.[6] With one notable

---

[4] Note that the only possible quotation of a gospel verse in rabbinic literature occurs in Aramaic (*b. Šabb.* 116a–b: see the discussion below).

[5] Maier 1982:89 argues that *'awon gilyon* is a gloss here. See Kuhn 1960:54 n. 109 for a defence of the reading.

[6] In defence of a first-century date see Herford 1903:146–54. For a date no earlier than the beginning of the third century see Kuhn 1960:55. He mentions in particular the fact that the passage is preserved in Aramaic, that it is un-attributed and that it assumes things that seem unbelievable (Christian judges adjudicating in Jewish disputes, the Mosaic Torah as less authoritative than the Christian Gospel etc. – but note how at *Eccl. Rab.* 1.8.3, a passage parallel to *t. Hull.* 2.24, a piece of Christian halakah is accepted, albeit temporarily, by R. Eliezer). He argues that the characters mentioned in the passage were chosen because both were known to be associated with Christianity, Gamaliel as the drafter of the Birkath ha-minim and Eliezer as someone who flirted with Jewish Christianity (see *t. Hull.* 2.24 and parallels).

exception,[7] most scholars who have examined this passage argue that the anonymous 'philosoph' is a Christian and that it should be read, therefore, as a sharp attack upon the Christianity in which the fraudulence of one of its followers and the contradictory character of its Gospel are exposed.[8] Three principal observations support this. The first relates to the reference to the apparent redundancy of the Jewish law;[9] the second to the threefold mention of the *'awon gilyon*, taken by most to be a reference to the *euangelion*;[10] and the third to a possible allusion to Matt 5.17 in the words, 'I came not to destroy the law of Moses nor to add to the law of Moses', interestingly quoted here in Aramaic. Admittedly, these words do not constitute a precise reproduction of Matt 5.17,[11] and they do not appear at the end of the Gospel as the passage implies – in this respect one should also note that the passage falsely attributes to a Gospel a statement about a son and daughter inheriting equally – an observation which might lead one to the view that the reference here is to a collection of sayings rather than to any known Gospel.[12] Even if we are left to accept this rather muted conclusion, we still have a text in which, in close proximity to each other, we have an allusion to a dominical saying and the word 'gospel'. To deny any Christian association to the passage, as Maier does, seems a little extreme.

(ii) The 'gilyonim' and the books of the heretics

At *t. Yadayim* 2.13 we read: 'The Gospels (*gilyonim*) and the books of the heretics (*sifrei minim*) do not defile the hands.' And at *t. Šabb.* 13 (14).5 we read: 'The Gospels (*gilyonim*) and books of the heretics are not saved but are left where they are to burn, they and their sacred names.' The association of the term *gilyonim* with the Gospels has not gone undisputed and the term has also been understood as referring to apocalypses or the margins of biblical scrolls.[13] Identification with the canonical Gospels arises precisely from its linguistic proximity to the term used in *b. Šabb.* 116a–b, where it seems certain that the reference is to something approximating to a

---

[7] Maier 1982:76f. His discussion contains a detailed bibliography.   [8] See Kuhn 1960:56.

[9] Maier 1982:86 relates the statement not to a Christian argument about the abrogation of the law, but to a realization that since the disastrous Jewish wars against Rome, the Jews had lost their legal autonomy.

[10] For scepticism on this point see Maier 1982:81f.

[11] See Davies and Allison 1988–97:1.485 n. 8. They reject Jeremias' suggestion that the additional words 'nor did I come to add to the Law of Moses' were Jesus' original.

[12] Maier 1982:90 argues strongly that the passage has nothing to do with Matt 5.17 and is in fact closer to Deut 4.2; 13.1 and a passage like *b. Ḥull.* 63b.

[13] For a bibliography and a delineation of the alternatives see Kuhn 1960:33–4.

Christian Gospel. Kuhn argues that such reasoning is spurious as the passage from the Talmud is clearly later than these passages from the Tosefta and that the transcription of the Greek word *euangelion* as *gilyonim*, that is, a transcription of only the second half of the word, is odd practice when we consider other transcriptions of Greek words in rabbinic material.[14] For Kuhn the term should be understood as marginalia cut off from biblical books and *sifrei minim* as Bible scrolls that belong to communities thought to be heretical by the rabbis (see *b. Gitt.* 45b), as opposed to other Christian books or Christian Torah scrolls.[15] While none of Kuhn's points strikes me as conclusive, they warn us against a straightforward acceptance of the passages as referring to Christian books.[16] But if we do render *gilyonim* as 'Gospels', while these references furnish us with little information about how the Gospels were read by Jews, it might be taken to imply an attempt by some Jewish Christians to pass these texts off as canonical within the synagogue, and, perhaps more interestingly, presents the possibility that these texts were read in Hebrew.[17]

(iii) Joseph and the Hebrew Gospels of Tiberias

At an early point in his lengthy discussion of the Ebionite heresy, Epiphanius, as noted above, mentions the fact that members of the sect use a Hebrew version of Matthew. Mention of this translation leads Epiphanius to state that the Gospel of John was also translated from

[14] Kuhn 1960:34–5. He also argues that if the Tosefta is second century, it would seem odd to have a reference to 'Gospels' in the plural from this time. But Kuhn fails to mention the evidence for Gospels in the plural before Irenaeus, not least Justin, *1 Apol.* 66.

[15] Ginzberg 1922:122–3 n. 19 accepts a translation of these passages as 'Gospels', arguing that the interpretation of the term as margins as we appear to have in *b. Šabb.* 116a (a different section from that discussed above) arose from the fact that defilement would only be connected with a document where eighty-five letters or more of scripture were continuously quoted. This doesn't occur in the Gospels, hence the interpretation. For a detailed discussion of the references to *gilyonim* and *sifrei minim* see Maier 1982:28f. He shares with Kuhn a scepticism about identifying these references with anything Christian but disagrees with Kuhn's understanding.

[16] Some might want to refer to *b. Sanh.* 106b, where the nameless heretic, in discussion with R. Hanina, states that he has read a book he calls 'The chronicle of Balaam' which states that Balaam the lame was thirty-three years old when Pinhas the Robber killed him. For a discussion of the passage see Herford 1903:72–5. It is quite uncertain whether the reference to Balaam here is a reference to Jesus. G. F. Moore's view that we should read the 'Books of Ben-Laana' at *y. Sanh.* 10.28a as a reference to the Gospels seems far-fetched. On this see Ginzberg 1922:121 n. 18.

[17] This point is made by Philip Alexander (2005 (forthcoming)). While noting that it is possible that there is a reference here to Greek Gospels read in the Greek-speaking Diaspora, he argues that '(t)he question as to whether one should save gospels and other books of the minim [he understands *gilyonim* and 'books of the *minim*' as non-contrastive] from destruction could only arise if those texts were *in Hebrew* and contained divine names *in Hebrew*. This text may point, then, to Hebrew Gospels circulating among Jewish Christians in Palestine, and to attempts by Jewish Christians to read some of these texts publicly in synagogue.'

Greek into Hebrew and that this translation is to be found in the Jewish treasuries together with a copy of the Acts of the Apostles. Epiphanius reports that he has been told this by a number of Jewish converts, in particular Joseph of Tiberias, whose story he then goes on to relate, repeating the claim about the Gospel translations (see *Pan.* 30.3.8–9; 30.5.3; 30.6.9; 30.12.10).

It is difficult to assess the historical value of this tradition concerning the existence of Hebrew translations of the Gospels secretly retained in a Jewish genizah. The assertion might be dismissed because (a) the claim about the Acts of the Apostles and John is found nowhere else; and (b) the account of Joseph as found in Epiphanius is uncorroborated and contains much that might be considered highly questionable.[18] But in relation to (b) we should note that there are elements of the story that seem to ring true,[19] and that it would not seem a wholly peculiar thing for Jews to have Hebrew copies of the Gospels for the purposes of disputation, not least at a time when Christianity had become the favoured religion of the Emperor (note *b. Šabb.* 116a–b above).[20] We should also note that it is precisely the fact of the existence of these translations that leads Epiphanius to tell the story of Joseph and that he repeats the tradition about these translations on a number of occasions in the same section. But beyond that we can say very little in support of this uncorroborated assertion.

(b) *Indirect evidence*

(i) *Josephus*
Ant. 18.63–4
The authenticity of few passages has been the subject of so much discussion as this one, and to try, therefore, to establish the degree to which it may betray knowledge of the Gospels on the part of Josephus is a probably futile task. Moreover, even if one accepts that some parts of the text are authentic, determining influence from the Gospels is almost impossible.

---

[18] For some of these see Goranson 1999:340 and Stemberger 2000:73f. We should note that Epiphanius met Joseph in 353 but that he wrote his *Panarion* in 375, twenty-two years later. More specifically we might refer to the legendary character of stories such as Joseph's healing of a naked maniac and his magical contests with Jews in Tiberias and the baths at Gader (7.5f.). Most doubt has been cast on the story of Judah Ha-Nasi III's death-bed conversion to Christianity (4.5).

[19] See Thornton 1990:60f.

[20] Avi-Yonah 1976:168 makes a similar point. Thornton 1990:55 n. 2 sounds a more sceptical note, stating that Syriac versions of the Gospels and Acts existed 'and that the original language of the versions was not accurately remembered'.

Ant. 18.113f.

This passage shares a number of things in common with the Gospels. In both, Herod kills John; in both, John is a preacher; and in both, baptism is an action subsequent to an inner change, and crowds flock to hear John. But there are also significant differences: in Josephus it is John's popularity and fear of an uprising that lead to his death; in the Gospels it is his criticism of Herod's marriage which leads to his death. Different locations for John's death are presented; and in Josephus, John's preaching is meant to lead to a virtuous life, in the Gospels, to repentance. Moreover, the failure of Josephus to associate John in any way with Jesus, a point to which Origen will allude (*C. Cels.* 1.48), would seem strange if he knew any of the Gospels.[21]

(ii) Justin Martyr

On a number of occasions in his *Dialogue* Justin refers to Jewish accusations against Jesus. At 69.7 he states that the Jews (here he is referring to Jesus' contemporaries but also probably aping current accusations) call Jesus a magician and a deceiver of the people, an accusation that we find in broadly the same form in some rabbinic texts (see below). Further on in the *Dialogue* he states that Jews have sent out messengers who proclaim Jesus to be a Galilean deceiver who was crucified, whose body was stolen from the tomb by his disciples and about whom a number of false claims are made (108.2f.). Accepting these two passages to be genuine reflections of Jewish opinion, might we take them to imply Jewish knowledge of the Gospels? Graham Stanton thinks not, at least in relation to the passage at 69.7 (Stanton 1994a:168). Certainly it is difficult to prove. In this respect we should note two things. First, all of the information above could have been gleaned from independent Jewish tradition about Jesus, for broadly it reflects Jewish opinion about Jesus found in the Gospels themselves. Secondly, it is striking to note that Justin Martyr, who appears to quote Gospel material and is possibly the first Christian author to show knowledge of the fourfold Gospel, never makes Trypho engage in argument about these sources, although we should note that at *Dial.* 18.1 Justin states that Trypho has read the doctrines taught by Jesus. Such a statement, which one assumes possesses some verisimilitude (Justin knows of Jews

---

[21] See Mason 1992:155. He points to the presence of apologetic motifs in Josephus and argues that some of these might account for some of the differences cited above. A similar point is made by Meier 1992, esp. 234f. He shows how in his presentation of John, Josephus plays down the eschatological content of John's message and that this makes John's baptism unintelligible.

who did such things), should make us wary of exploiting silence too much. Absence of straightforward argument about the content of the Gospels might be best explained by noting that the central concern of the *Dialogue* is Jewish and Christian contention over the Old Testament, for those were the texts that both parties acknowledged (see *Dial.* 120.5).

(iii) Celsus' Jew

Much has been written about Celsus' Jew.[22] A tradition deriving from Origen has questioned the genuineness of the opinions attributed to the Jew, seeing him as a constructed figure. Another tradition has in broad terms argued the opposite case. A simple either/or on this matter is probably not possible. Bammel, amongst others, has shown that Origen's objections, which broadly reflect those of later scholars, are not valid, especially when one assumes, as Origen seems unable to, that the Jew concerned was hellenized.[23]

Interestingly, almost all of the argument offered by Celsus' Jew is directed against the person of Jesus and his followers.[24] He is described as the son of an adultereress, Mary, and a Roman soldier, Panthera (1.28, 32); he is said to have gone to Egypt when a young man to earn a living but ended up becoming a magician and returning to Palestine to declare himself the Son of God (1.28);[25] and he is associated with John the Baptist, whom he appears to dupe into becoming his follower and who ends up being crucified with him (2.4; 1.41).[26] In line with the claim that he learned magic in Egypt is the assertion that his miracles are the work of a sorcerer, that is, they have an impure origin, a point which receives particular emphasis (1.68; see also 1.71; 2.3, 48–9 for the claim that Jesus is a *goēs*). While Jesus can be portrayed as a pious person living in accordance with the law (2.4, 5), such praise is merely there to make more telling the accusation that he went on to abandon the law and mislead

---

[22] See Bammel 1986a:265–6. [23] See Bammel 1986a:267–83 and de Lange 1976:42–3.

[24] See Lods 1941:5. Origen notes that the Jew is introduced by Celsus in dialogue with Jesus (*C. Cels.* 1.28).

[25] Note that at 1.66 the Jew is made to refer to Jesus' flight to Egypt when still an infant. Lods 1941:9 notes that this story is irreconcilable with the story of the visit to Egypt when Jesus was older. The latter story should probably be attributed to Jewish tradition.

[26] At 2.4 John is introduced as a Jew, 'our prophet, the prophet of our God'. This seems to be a polemical ploy to make it plain that Christianity's founder began life as a Jew and that, therefore, Christian movement away from Judaism is equivalent to desertion. In the second reference to John, which is not explicit, but plain from the context, Celsus' Jew attacks the veracity of the account of the events accompanying Jesus' baptism by noting that the only witness to it was someone punished with him. Again we seem to be in the presence of two mutually contradictory accounts of the same person's activities.

the people. In this context Jesus is described as if he were the leader of a political party, intent upon insurrection rather than religious renewal (2.12; see also 2.44). His pitifully small number of followers (1.62; 2.46) emerge poorly from this. Duped into following Jesus (2.12), they are described as 'infamous men, the most wicked tax collectors and sailors', who collected 'a means of livelihood in a disgraceful and importunate way' (1.62).[27] Celsus' Jew takes particular pleasure in depicting Jesus' passion negatively. Rather than accepting that he has to die, Jesus is depicted objecting strongly to his death (2.24), even trying to hide and escape (2.9, 70), and his cry for sustenance on the cross is presented as greed (2.37). He is justly condemned as an impostor and false messiah and he dies a shameful death (2.35, 44 (a death fit for a robber), 47), hated by God (1.71). The account of his resurrection is assailed from a number of angles, not least the lack of reliable witnesses to Jesus' appearances (see 2.55, 63, 67 and 70) and his failure to appear in public or to those who convicted him (2.63).

This unremittingly negative picture of Jesus is striking in its detail relative to the other relevant material we possess. Its claim to reflect genuine Jewish opinion is strengthened by the fact that we find parallels to some of the assertions, particularly those which are not found in the Gospels, in independent Jewish and Christian sources.[28] Much of the material attributed to the Jew could, however, be said to have emerged from a negative reading of the Gospels, and it is *Contra Celsum* above any other extant text which betrays evidence for Jews reading the Gospels, at least before the writing of the *Toledot Yeshu*. This much is implied in the Jew's comment, found at 2.74, that his assessment of Jesus emerges from a reading of the Gospels themselves. The point, as Origen notes, is a polemical one, but it does not misrepresent much of what we find in *Contra Celsum*, some of which centres on interpretations or particular readings of words or events found in the Gospels.[29]

---

[27] See also 2.22, where they are described as 'traitors and impious men'.

[28] On the questionable activity of Jesus' mother see Tertullian, *De Spect.* 30.5 (on which see below), as well as the *Toledot*; on Panthera see *b. Sanh.* 67a; 104b, and esp. *t. Ḥull.* 2.22f., although here it is written in the form 'Pandira' (on this see Maier 1978:264f.; N.B. in the *Toledot* it is Joseph, not Jesus, who is associated with Panthera); on the political overtones of his ministry see Lactantius, *Div. Inst.* 5.3.4, probably reflecting Jewish opinion, discussed below; for the accusation that he was a magician see Justin, *Dial.* 69.7 as discussed above, *b. Sanh.* 67a and Arnobius 1.43, where Jesus' magical knowledge is explicitly associated with Egypt; on his execution with John the Baptist see a tradition in *Toledot* found in the Cairo Genizah, and discussed by Bammel 1968:194–5.

[29] See, *inter alia*, 1.58, 65; 2.24, 32, 37. In each of these instances Origen speaks of a distortion of Gospel material. Note how the Jew accuses the Christians of distorting their own Gospels (2.27), though precisely what he is referring to is unclear. See Chadwick's note on p. 90 of his translation.

(iv) Some rabbinic texts

In discussing relevant rabbinic material, I do not wish to examine in any detail many of the passages that scholars have claimed refer to Jesus. There is not sufficient space to do such a thing, and in any case very few of the relevant passages are germane to the present subject.

One potentially significant passage is found at *b. Sanh.* 43a. The passage in question states that Jesus was hanged on the eve of Passover, that a herald went forth forty days before announcing that 'Yeshu the Nazarene goes forth to be stoned because he has practised magic and led Israel astray' and that anyone who has anything to say in his favour should step forward. It is then stated that Jesus was a deceiver and that according to Deut 13.8 he should not be spared. Although some have claimed that only at a very late date was the passage made to refer to Jesus, most have argued for its relative earliness.[30] The passage has seemed important to some as witnessing to pre-Gospel tradition favouring a Johannine (John 18.28) date for the crucifixion,[31] but it looks more like an attempt to show that Jesus was rightfully convicted. On the question which principally interests us, namely the extent to which the passage reflects any dependence upon the Gospels, we should note that the passage attributes responsibility for Jesus' death exclusively to the Jews. Given the apparently apologetic motifs which it is claimed form a part of the passage, failing to mention Roman participation might seem odd, and point away from the idea of knowledge of the Gospels. Moreover, the accusation laid against Jesus, also found at *b. Sanh.* 107b, and similar also, as we noted, to that found in Justin, could have derived from non-Gospel traditions about Jesus.[32]

In relation to the same passage, *b. Sanh.* 43a, we should note the reference which follows to Jesus' five disciples, Mattai, Nakai, Nezer, Buni and Todah. Originally thought to be an addition to the text, it is now generally acknowledged to be original. It bears no clear relationship to

---

[30] For the view that the passage did not originally refer to Jesus see Maier 1978:219–37, and Horbury's response in Horbury 1998a:104–7 (1982 original). Maier argues that Jesus fits uneasily in the original Talmudic context (a discussion of an halakhic debate in the Mishnah), that the list of charges against Jesus (found also at *b. Sanh.* 107b) were probably not uncommon in the rabbinic period and that the original story would have been told of a magician, ben Pandera, who is explicitly mentioned in *b. Sanh.* 107b. Horbury responds by stating that Maier too easily sets up a distinction between a Palestinian lack of interest in Jesus and a western Diasporan interest in him. For Horbury there is far too much evidence in favour of Palestinian interest in Jesus for such a distinction to be justified. He argues strongly that the passage can be read in such a way as to see the reference to stoning as an intrusion which was added in accordance with the halakah. The reference to the herald also accords with *m. Sanh.* 6.4 and is placed there simply to indicate that Jesus was 'guilty peradventure'.

[31] For a sceptical assessment of the historical value of the passage, see Catchpole 1971:5–6.

[32] On the apologetic motif of the passage, see Catchpole 1971:4.

any known list of Jesus' disciples, but in naming just five followers, rather than the somewhat more significant twelve, it may have an indirectly polemical tone. But again this need not betray actual knowledge of the Gospels, but rather traditions associated with Jesus.[33]

The other passage to consider is *y. Ta'an.* 65b. Here it is reported that R. Abbahu, a third-century authority, said: 'If a man says to you: "I am God", he is a liar. If [he says, "I am] the son of man", in the end people will laugh at him. If [he says], "I will go up to heaven", he says, but shall not perform it.' To some this clearly refers to Jesus, a point that might be supported by the fact that elsewhere we hear of R. Abbahu interacting with Christians.[34] Whether the references to the divine identity of Jesus, the 'son of man' and 'going up to heaven' imply knowledge of John's Gospel is another matter. Travers Herford, for instance, denies this possibility, noting that 'it is enough to admit a general knowledge of what Christians alleged concerning Jesus from the Rabbi's own discussions with them'.[35] But the three assertions together, in particular the somewhat heightened use of the term 'son of man', make one think immediately of John and might allow one to assert something more specific than the above statement would allow.

But none of the above demonstrates any knowledge of the Gospels on behalf of the Rabbis.[36]

(c) Early evidence for the existence of a Jewish anti-gospel

The earliest unambiguous evidence we have for the existence of a continuous account of Jesus' life written by Jews comes in the ninth century with the mention of the *Toledot Yeshu* by the well-known anti-Jewish writer the archbishop of Lyons, Agobard.[37] But is there evidence for a possible Jewish anti-gospel from an earlier period? What has been written above indicates the fragmentary character of the evidence for non-Christian Jewish

---

[33] I have failed also to discuss *t. Hull.* 2.24 and its parallels. What is interesting here is that in one of the parallels, *Eccl. Rab.* 1.8.3, we have words attributed to Jesus not found in the Gospels. This seems to imply some interest in Jesus' words only hinted at in the extant rabbinic evidence. On this see Bauckham 1990:106f.

[34] See *b. 'Abod. Zar.* 4a.

[35] Herford 1903:63. For a non-Christian reading of the passage, see Maier 1978:76f.

[36] Even the possibly credulous Travers Herford agrees with this conclusion. 'If the summary of the Jesus-Tradition, given above be examined, it will be found to contain little, if anything, which would imply the knowledge of a Gospel or Gospels, on the part of the Rabbis' (Herford 1903:357).

[37] See Agobard, *De Judaicis Superstitionibus* 10 (CCCM 52, 206–7). The work is dated to 827. For an introduction to the complex collection of texts called the *Toledot Yeshu* see Di Segni 1985.

interaction with the Gospels, and from this some have wanted to argue that insofar as Jews engaged in writing against the figure of Jesus, this was of a piecemeal kind and did not lead to the writing of a continuous narrative about him.[38] I wish to conclude this piece by noting some of the evidence that might indicate a position somewhat different from that just expressed.[39]

(i) Contra Celsum

Contra Celsum gives evidence of a wide-ranging set of assertions about the life of Jesus, stretching from his birth through to his death and resurrection. It is not easy to determine the extent to which such material is taken from a source which looked something like an anti-gospel. Certainly the Jew goes on to claim that what he has written is no more than an account of the contents of the Gospels (2.74; see also 2.13). But such an assertion need not tell us anything about whether the material was originally in a written form or constituted sections of a continuous polemical account of Jesus' life rather than disjointed responses to different Gospel passages.[40] No such Jewish source is ever explicitly referred to,[41] an interesting point given that Origen does on at least one other occasion refer to a source related to the Jewish-Christian controversy.[42] But at *C. Cels.* 1.28 there may be some evidence for a source that may have looked a little like an anti-gospel. Here we read of the adultery of Jesus' mother, his birth, his learning of magic in Egypt, return, and self-proclamation as Son of God. Lods argued that such a set of assertions might be read as a summary of a longer account, although he was unclear as to the extent to which such a longer account might be evidenced elsewhere in *Contra Celsum*.[43]

(ii) Tertullian, De Spectaculis 30.5–6

At *De Spectaculis* 30.5–6 Tertullian speaks of Christ's return to earth, mentioning in an accusatory way the opinions of those who were opposed to Jesus: 'This is the carpenter's or hireling's son', I shall say, 'that sabbath-

---

[38] Bauer 1909:452–86, although keen to collect together a lot of anti-Christian Jewish material relating to Christ (he was keen also to show how it converged with pagan material), argued for the view that this early material would have been more in the form of 'disiecta membra' than a continuous narrative, not least because he could not see the need, either pagan or Jewish, for such a thing. Individual incidents from the life of Jesus would have been discussed as the need arose.

[39] See Horbury 1970:354f. for a presentation of the relevant primary material. He argues for a third-century date for a Jewish anti-gospel. See also Horbury 1998b.

[40] See Bammel 1986a:274–82 for a discussion of the apparent differences between the material in *C. Cels.* 1 and 2.

[41] Although at one point (2.10) Origen vaguely refers to material taken *ek diēgēmatōn ioudaikōn*, nothing more is said about these 'tales'.

[42] See *C. Cels.* 4.52 and the reference to the *Dialogue of Jason* and *Papiscus*. [43] See Lods 1941:31–2.

breaker, that Samaritan and devil-possessed. This is he whom you purchased from Judas! This is he whom you struck with reed and fist, whom you contemptuously spat upon, to whom you gave vinegar and gall to drink! This is he whom his disciples secretly stole away so that it might not be said that he had risen again, or the gardener removed so that his lettuces might come to no harm from the crowds of visitors.' The attribution of the opinions expressed to Jews has been widely accepted, mainly on the grounds that they appear compatible with Jewish opinion about Christ expressed elsewhere. What is most interesting about the passage for our purposes is that amidst its straightforward repetition of observations gleaned from the Gospels, there also appear allegations not found there. The first of these concerns Jesus, being a hireling's son; the second, the claim that he is a Samaritan, and the third, the claim that he was abstracted from the tomb by a gardener to stop people treading on his lettuces. All three of these assertions are found in a variety of forms in the *Toledot*,[44] as, incidentally, are the other claims witnessed in the Gospels. Indeed, Krauss saw the passage as containing most of the contents of the *Toledot*, even though he was not himself willing to countenance the existence of a Jewish anti-gospel much before the fifth century.[45] Krauss' caution should be heeded, not least because no source for Tertullian's statement is explicitly mentioned. But the passage, especially on account of its containing extra-Gospel material compatible with the contents of *Toledot* and material covering the different facets of Jesus' life, is suggestive of the existence of an anti-gospel.[46]

(iii) Lactantius, Divine Institutes 5.3.4

Something similar to *C. Cels.* 1.28 might be found in Lactantius' *Divine Institutes.* At 5.3.4 he states that an anti-Christian writer had asserted that Christ, driven out by the Jews, gathered a band of nine hundred men and committed acts of brigandage (*latrocinia*).[47] Nothing more is quoted from the source, which was probably authored by the vehemently anti-Christian Hierocles against whom Eusebius wrote. The view that Hierocles' source for the allegation may ultimately have been Jewish emerges from parallels in Jewish sources to the three assertions of the passage, namely that Jesus was driven out by the Jews, gathered a large band of followers and committed acts of brigandage. Two of these statements are probably

---

[44] For a discussion of the *Toledot*'s relationship to the story about the gardener, see Newman 1999.
[45] Krauss 1902:3.   [46] See Maier 1978:258–9; and Horbury 1970:455–6.
[47] On this whole passage, its background and implications, see Horbury 1998b.

derived from the Gospels, while one, that relating to brigandage, probably is not. What is important in relation to our present discussion is that what we find cited by Lactantius via Hierocles could be taken to be a fragment from a longer story in which Jesus is defamed.

(iv) The Martyrdom of Conon

The first possibly clear reference to a Jewish anti-gospel source appears in *The Martyrdom of Conon*. Ostensibly this is the account of the death of a Christian, Conon, at the time of the Decian persecution (250), but for a variety of reasons some have wanted to date it considerably later.[48] While addressing Conon, the unnamed governor of Magydus states that he has learned accurately from the Jews what Jesus' family was, the works he showed forth to his people and how he died on the cross. He asserts that the Jews have brought his (*autou*) accounts and read them to him (see 4.6). The term for accounts (*hypomnēmata*) is a known and possibly early way of referring to Gospels,[49] and the accusations made against Jesus are again well evidenced in a number of Jewish sources or sources claiming to represent Jewish opinion.

(d) Some concluding observations

There does seem to be some direct evidence for Jews possessing copies of the Gospels. Which of the canonical Gospels, in what form and in what language is not clear. In the one place in Talmudic literature where we appear to have a quotation from a Christian Gospel, it could be argued that it comes from a collection of sayings of Jesus influenced by Matthew, possibly in Aramaic. The one reference to the existence of copies of Matthew and John in Hebrew which were kept in a Jewish genizah remains uncorroborated. Unfurnished references to *gilyonim* in the Tosefta, whose meaning is in any case disputed, do not help us any further on this point.

Where we have evidence of Jewish attacks upon Jesus, it is sometimes unclear whether these derive from a reading of the Gospels, from oral tradition or from Jewish anti-gospels. This is particularly the case when we are dealing with short accusations against Jesus such as the claim that he is a magician and a deceiver of the people. In the case of Celsus' Jew, we have an apparently clear admission that he has read the Gospels and that many

---

[48] For a discussion of the reasons for a date later than the third century see Horbury 1970:383 n. 1; and for a defence of the plausibility of the story in a third-century setting see Lane Fox 1986:483.

[49] See Eusebius, *Hist. Eccl.* 2.15.1; 3.24.5; 3.39.15, here referring to Papias's description.

of the negative things he says against Jesus derive directly from that source (such an admission may also be witnessed in *Dial.* 18.1). This assertion is partially confirmed by the fact that Origen speaks on a number of occasions of the Jew's distortion of Gospel material.

Insofar as we can reconstruct it, the Jewish response to the Gospels was broadly negative. Attacks upon Jesus tended to concentrate upon his origins and the origins of his parents, his activity as a miracle worker/ magician/deceiver, the shameful character of his disciples and their and Jesus' possible involvement in politically seditious activity, events surrounding his crucifixion, and his resurrection. In the main, traditions about Jesus in this material which are not found in the Gospels can usually be explained as originating in a reaction to, or exploitation of, material found in the latter.

The phrase 'broadly negative' in the preceding paragraph should be taken seriously. In the story of Joseph of Tiberias, as found in Epiphanius' *Panarion*, Joseph is depicted as reading Gospels in Hebrew and responding positively to them. *b. Šabbat* 116a–b could be taken to imply respect, or at least neutral interest in, Gospel material insofar as it is assumed that consultation of a Christian on a legal matter could take place.[50]

There are some grounds for thinking that Jewish anti-gospels existed from perhaps the third century onwards, although apparently unambiguous evidence for their existence is first found in *The Martyrdom of Conon*, a text that purports to come from the third century but may be later. It is certainly striking that a number of traditions parallel to those found in the *Toledot Yeshu*, the first Jewish anti-gospel for which we have unambiguous evidence, are found in material dating from the second century onwards.

Some have noted that there is an uneven geographical distribution of the material under discussion (there is much more from the West than from the East), and have wanted to deduce from this that while in the West there was a greater need for Jews living in close proximity to Christians in a Diaspora setting to respond to Christian claims, the Rabbis were only really forced to enter into debate with Christians after the fourth century and in particular in the early Islamic period.[51] But while such a view picks up on a genuine absence of substantial Jesus material in rabbinic texts, it too easily assumes a lack of interest in Christians on the part of Jews in Palestine and

---

[50] For other rabbinic material implying positive responses to the figure of Jesus see *b. Sanh.* 107b, at least part of it, as discussed by Catchpole 1971:1–4; and *t. Ḥull.* 2.24 and its parallels.
[51] Maier 1978:254.

the East, and makes too much of a near-silence which need not be reflective of what was really the case.[52]

There remain some outstanding questions which we have not addressed. One of these was alluded to, namely the almost complete lack of references to arguments against Jesus as he appears in the Gospels in material 'adversus Judaeos'. Was this because Christians saw such arguments as considerably less significant than the arguments about the right interpretation of scripture which dominate this material?[53] Or were they simply uninterested in allowing many of the blasphemous claims against Jesus to see the light of day? And another relates to the almost complete failure of any Christian writing after *Conon* and before the *Toledot* to refer to Jewish anti-gospels. Again, if we are not to take the sceptical line and assert the non-existence of such material, then embarrassment might be a possible explanation.

---

[52] Amongst a number of cautionary phenomena relevant to the above observation, we should note the almost total absence of references in rabbinic literature to apocalypses.

[53] See the interesting comments made by Augustine in *Epistula ad Catholicos* 50 (xix), where, referring to Luke 24.4–7, he states that the Lord expected the disciples to be convinced not by his resurrection appearances but by the fact that the sequence crucifixion–resurrection had been predicted in the Prophets and the Psalms. My thanks for this reference to Professor W. Horbury.

CHAPTER 12

The Four among pagans

Loveday Alexander[*]

Round about 175 CE, an otherwise unknown Platonist philosopher named Celsus wrote a hard-hitting polemical tract against the Christians which he modestly entitled *The True Logos*.[1] Whether Celsus' polemic had any impact on pagan opinion is unclear. But it must have survived, and worried at least some Christians enough to consider that it needed answering, because some seventy years later Origen was asked to provide a systematic refutation of Celsus' tract; and it is because of this that Celsus' polemic survives, in the form of embedded quotations within Origen's reply. In this chapter, I shall focus largely on pagan[2] reception of the gospel story up to and including Celsus, concluding with a brief survey of third- and fourth-century developments in the pagan–Christian conversation. Since my concern here is with pagan reception of the gospels, I have not included writers like Pliny, Fronto or Suetonius, who deal with Christianity as a social phenomenon.[3] Nor have I sought to unravel the pagan testimony to the historical Jesus, which raises a different set of questions.[4] Instead, I have tried to build up a picture of the gospel story as viewed by second-century pagans, asking the question, What did pagans know of the Christian story of Jesus, and when and how did they know it?

Celsus' polemic marks a watershed in the process of pagan engagement with the gospels. Up to the end of the second century, the spread of Christianity was largely a popular phenomenon, barely noticed by the writers of elite literature. For Tacitus and his contemporaries,

---

[*] It is a great pleasure to contribute to this well-deserved tribute to Graham Stanton. I first contacted Graham when, as a very new doctoral student, I was told that his just-completed thesis on the gospels might have implications for my own work. It did; and, typically, he was generosity itself in sharing his research, and has remained a friend and offered encouragement ever since – as he has to hundreds of others in the UK and round the world. Happy Birthday!

[1] Origen, *C. Cels.* (cited throughout from Chadwick 1953) 1.40.

[2] I use the term 'pagan' here without pejorative intent, simply as a means of distinguishing writers from the Late Antique world who are neither Jewish nor Christian.

[3] Surveys in Benko 1980; Wilken 1984.   [4] See Harris 1985; Evans 1994; van Voorst 2000.

Christianity can be contemptuously dismissed as a degraded *superstitio*. Mass conversions relied on the spectacular effects of healing and exorcism, and the conversion of the philosophically inclined individual like Justin is comparatively rare.[5] Before Celsus, it is hard to be sure that any pagan writer has first-hand acquaintance with the gospel as text. What the second-century writers do testify to, in differing degrees, is a widely diffused knowledge of the gospel as story, of the story that lies behind the sect that bears the name 'Christian'. The gospel story they know is the story as mediated to pagan society via the social phenomenon of the local Christian community and its activities. Tertullian complains, probably justly, that 'no-one turns to our literature who is not already Christian'.[6] For most second-century pagan writers, the gospel story is projected onto a screen whose underlying shape and colour are determined by the writer's perception of contemporary Christianity.

With Celsus, the level of engagement changes.[7] Celsus clearly has a detailed knowledge of at least one gospel text, probably (as Origen surmises) Matthew (*C. Cels.* 1.34).[8] He quotes verbal details which he could not have learned except from the gospels; but, Origen complains, his reading is a highly selective one (2.11, 24, 34). He knows of a genealogy which traces Jesus' descent 'from the first man' (2.32), which sounds Lucan; and he has some Johannine allusions (2.31; 1.67). But his canon is wider than Origen's: he cites texts which Origen labels as heretical,[9] and he claims to have access to rival accounts of Jesus – a claim, as Origen points out, which is never substantiated (2.13). He refers to the accounts of the life of Jesus written by his disciples (e.g. 2.13, 16, 26); but he never refers to any of the evangelists by name. In this he is closer to second-century Christian practice than Origen, writing seventy years later: Helmut Koester reminds us that second-century Christians normally refer to 'what the Lord says in his gospel' rather than to what was said by Matthew or Luke: 'The "Gospel" to which appeal is normally made, remains an elastic concept, designating the preaching of Jesus as a whole in the form in which it lives on in church tradition.'[10]

Celsus also stands as a potent reminder of the dialectical nature of pagan–Christian polemic in this period. None of the pagan texts attacking Christianity survive unmediated; the opinions of pagan writers have to be gleaned at second hand from the quotations of the Christian apologists

---

[5] MacMullen 1984, esp. 256–42; Nock 1933.   [6] Tertullian, *Test.* 1.4, cited from Cook 2000:17.
[7] On Celsus see further Chadwick 1953; Benko 1980:1098–1118; Wilken 1984:94–125; Frede 1999; and Cook 2000:17–102, with the literature there cited.
[8] Cook 2000:25–6.   [9] *C. Cels.* 2.27; 5.61–2; 5.54; 6.53; 6.74.
[10] Koester 1990:29, citing von Campenhausen 1972:129.

who respond to them. But equally, pagan polemic is itself a reaction against earlier forms of Christian self-presentation. Whether or not Celsus is writing in conscious response to earlier Christian apologetic,[11] he is responding to the challenge of Christian activity in his own world. For Celsus, the challenge may not be too serious: Simon Swain describes him as 'an establishment figure picking holes in the views of an idiot minority' (Swain 1999:157), and his contemporary, the fashionable doctor Galen, treats Christianity with tolerant condescension. Yet both testify in different ways to a faith that is making an increasingly significant impact on pagan society, and the 'heavy-weight anti-Christian tracts' of the third century, in Swain's words, 'show clearly that Christianity could not be ignored' (Swain 1999: 158). Thus it is important to remember that the pagan writers cited here cannot be taken in any simple way as representative of all pagan reaction: 'paganism' is no more monolithic in this period than 'Christianity' (Swain 1999:193). The texts quoted by the apologists come from an educated elite, and one that increasingly sees its own cultural identity under threat.[12] We have very little access to popular pagan opinion, hostile or otherwise – though the hostile reactions of the polemicists may itself be seen as an index of Christianity's popular success.

THE CRUCIFIED SOPHIST

Probably the earliest surviving visual representation of Christ by a pagan artist is a third-century graffito found on the Palatine hill in Rome. It is a crude scratched image of a worshipper beside an ass-headed figure on a cross, with the inscription 'Alexamenos is worshipping his god.'[13] A century earlier, Tertullian saw a similar graffito, 'a picture with this inscription: "The God of the Christians, ass-begotten". It had ass's ears; one foot was a hoof; it carried a book and wore a toga.'[14] These images neatly encapsulate both the challenge and the dilemma of presenting the gospel story in the pagan world. At the heart of the gospel is an intolerable paradox. Christians offer worship, assign divine honours, to a human being[15] – and not merely a human being, but one who suffered the ultimate degradation of a criminal's death. Already in the second century, popular gossip accused Christians of worshipping the wood of

---

[11] Cook 2000: 7.   [12] Swain 1999; Young 1999.
[13] Walsh 1986:62. The charge of worshipping an ass-headed figure is made against Jews as well as Christians: Tacitus, *Hist.* 5.3–4; Minucius Felix, *Oct.* 9.3.
[14] Tertullian, *Apol.* 16.12.   [15] Pliny, *Ep.* 10.96: *carmen Christo quasi deo dicere.*

the cross;[16] and in many ways the dialectic of Christian and pagan apologetics in the first three centuries can be read as a moving battle-line of charge and counter-charge around this issue, poised between the two poles of worship and cross, the highest and lowest points on the honour–shame continuum.

It is not surprising, then, to find that the first part of the gospel story known to pagans in the second century is the fact (and to differing degrees the manner) of Jesus' death. Possibly the earliest references to the gospel narrative occur in two early chronographers, Thallos (?mid to late first century CE) and Phlegon of Tralles (second century CE), who report a solar eclipse in the reign of Tiberius. Both are cited by later Christian writers, who connect the eclipse with the gospel reports of 'darkness' at the time of the crucifixion (a connection denied by Julius Africanus); though it is unclear whether either Thallos or Phlegon mentioned the crucifixion himself.[17] But Origen tells us that Phlegon also 'granted to Christ fore-knowledge of certain future events' and confused Christ with Peter – which would be consistent with a muddled reference to the events and prophecies surrounding the crucifixion.[18]

We are on surer ground with Tacitus (ca. 55–117 CE), who describes Jesus' death in some detail:

Christus, from whom the name had its origin, suffered the extreme penalty during the reign of Tiberius at the hands of one of our procurators, Pontius Pilatus, and a most mischievous superstition, thus checked for the moment, again broke out not only in Judaea, the first source of the evil, but even in Rome, where all things hideous and shameful from every part of the world find their centre and become popular.[19]

Lucian (ca. 115–200 CE) identifies the manner of Jesus' death more pre-cisely. In *The Passing of Peregrinus*, he describes how Peregrinus exploited the gullibility of Christians in Palestine:

---

[16] Tertullian, *Apol.* 16.6–8; Minucius Felix, *Oct.* 9.4; 11.4.

[17] Texts in *FGH* 256 F1, *FGH* 257 F16: Jacoby 1929:1157, 1165. Harris 1985:343–4, Evans 1994:454–5 and van Voorst 2000:20–3 believe that both writers knew the gospels, but Jacoby 1930:836–7 argues that both simply mentioned the eclipse, and that it was the Christian commentators who made the connection with the crucifixion. Thallos' reference comes in the third book of the *Histories*, a world chronicle which (so Eusebius tells us) began with the fall of Troy (*FGH* 256 T1), and cannot have had space for more than the briefest summary of events in any given Olympiad (Jacoby 1930:837); similarly with Phlegon of Tralles. Sections of Phlegon's *Olympiads* (though not this fragment) are translated in Jacoby 1930:58–62.

[18] 'However, Phlegon in the thirteenth or fourteenth book, I think, of his Chronicle even grants to Christ foreknowledge of certain events, although he was muddled and said that some things which really happened to Peter happened to Jesus; and he testified that it turned out in accordance with what Jesus had said' (*C. Cels.* 2.14 = *FGH* 257 F16(c)). Origen is clearly quoting from memory: see also 2.32, 2.59.

[19] Tacitus, *Ann.* 15.44 (Church and Brodribb 1895:304–5); Benko 1980:1062–8.

They revered him as a god, made use of him as a lawgiver, and set him down as a protector, next after that other, to be sure, whom they still worship, the man who was crucified in Palestine because he introduced this new cult into the world.[20]

Both these second-century writers identify Christianity as a sect originating in Palestine, and both implicitly assume that the crime for which the founder was executed was the foundation of a cult which in their own world is clearly identified as degrading and morally reprehensible, if not outright criminal.

One way to neutralize the shame was to claim the crucifixion as a martyr's death which had the power to inspire others in the face of death. For many pagan observers, the gospel was not simply a story about something that happened to Jesus: it was a story that also had the power to make philosophers of his followers. The paradox of Christian achievement of a 'philosophical' attitude to death is a *topos* that recurs in a number of second-century writers. Epictetus (ca. 50–130 CE) refers to the 'Galileans', whose 'habit of mind' (*ethos*) enables them to achieve an enviable level of fortitude when threatened with death by tyrants, despite their lack of formal philosophical training (*Disc.* 4.7.6).[21] Lucian already shows that pagans as well as Christians were prepared to read Christian martyrdom within a Socratic template.[22] Christian readiness to face death also attracted the admiration of Galen (see below). For Marcus Aurelius, however (emperor 161–80 CE), their attitude is not so much courage as obstinacy: without a philosophical foundation, the claim to practise philosophical virtue cannot be sustained.[23]

Celsus too knows of Christian veneration of the cross: 'Everywhere they speak in their writings of the tree of life and of resurrection of the flesh by the tree – I imagine because their master was nailed to a cross and was a carpenter by trade' (*C. Cels.* 6.34). What would the sectaries have venerated, he wonders, if their founder had been strangled or thrown off a cliff? But Celsus also has access to a much greater density of narrative detail on the passion story than anything we have seen so far: 'Do you think that ... the ending of your tragedy is to be regarded as noble and convincing – his cry

---

[20] Lucian, *Peregr.* §13; Benko 1980:1093–5.   [21] Alexander 2002: 245 and n. 19; Benko 1980:1077–8.

[22] Lucian, *Peregr.* §12. The Syriac letter of Mara bar Serapion (probably dating from the second century) also makes a connection between the death of the 'wise king of the Jews' and Socrates: see Evans 1994: 455–7; van Voorst 2000: 53–8. Though the philosophical assessment of Jesus fits with second-century pagan views, the connection with the divine 'punishment' of the Jews makes it likely that the ultimate source of this is Christian.

[23] Marcus Aurelius, *Med.* 11.3; Benko 1980:1092.

from the cross when he expired, and the earthquake and the darkness?' (2.55).
Jesus was convicted and condemned as a criminal by his own people, the Jews
(2.9, cf. 2.5). After his condemnation by the court, he was 'caught hiding
himself and escaping most disgracefully, and indeed was betrayed by those
whom he called disciples' (2.9). Celsus highlights the un-Socratic features of
Jesus' passion: 'Why then does he utter loud laments and wailings, and pray
that he may avoid the fear of death, saying something like this: "O Father, if
this cup should pass by me"?' (2.24). Equally unheroic is his submission to
'those who mocked him and put a purple robe round him and the crown of
thorns and the reed in his hand' (2.34). On the cross, Jesus failed to produce
any philosophical sayings (2.36), and he 'rushed greedily to drink and did not
bear his thirst patiently as even an ordinary man often bears it' (2.37). Jesus
had ordinary blood in his veins, not ichor like the Greek gods (2.36).

The dominant impression left upon Celsus by the gospel story, however,
is the scandal of the crucifixion. He finds it impossible hold together the
two ideas of the 'pure and holy Logos' and the degradation associated with
the cross (2.31); and his counter-arguments reflect three of the main lines of
argument used by Christians in defence of this central paradox of their
faith. (1) One Christian response is to argue that Jesus' death was not an
admission of powerlessness but a deliberate act of self-sacrifice, foretold
both by the biblical prophets and by Jesus himself (2.13). But this, for
Celsus, entangles the believer in an ever more improbable set of paradoxes
(2.54; 2.13–23); and, in any case, the prophets should not be believed if what
they predict is morally and metaphysically repugnant: 'Even if it is really
true that the prophets foretold such things about God's Son, it would be
impossible to believe in the prediction that he should suffer and do such
things' (7.15). (2) Second, Celsus assumes a moral link between the gospel
story and the behaviour of contemporary Christians, and he acknowledges
that Christians are prepared to 'die with' their Lord (2.45, cf. 2.38). In a
world where power had to be demonstrated in persuasive speech, this is an
important argument for the moral effectiveness of the gospel. All the more
telling, therefore, to point out from the gospels themselves that Jesus'
original disciples found his example anything but compelling:

When those who were living with him at the time, who had heard him speak and
were taught by him, saw that he was being punished and was dying, they did not
die with him, or for his sake, nor were they persuaded to despise punishment. But
they even denied that they were disciples. Yet now you die with him. (2.45)

(3) And third, Celsus argues, the Jesus of the gospels fails to display divine
power in action. If Jesus were truly God, he would be able to free himself

from prison at will like Dionysus in Euripides' *Bacchae*, and he would not
have had to endure mocking and humiliation: 'Why, if not before, does he
not at any rate now show forth something divine, and deliver himself from
this shame, and take his revenge on those who insult both him and his
Father?'[24] For this educated Hellenist, the lack of fit between the cross and
the claim to divinity is an insuperable barrier to acceptance of the Christian
message: 'Believe that the person of whom I am telling you is God's Son,
although he was most dishonourably arrested and punished to his utter
disgrace, and though quite recently he wandered about most shamefully in
the sight of all men' (6.10). How can I possibly believe that? asks Celsus:
'How is it anything but blasphemy to assert that the things done to Jesus
were done to God?' (7.15).

WORDS OF POWER

What kind of man was this 'crucified sophist'? Lucian leaves his readers in
little doubt that he was (like Peregrinus) first and foremost a popular
teacher, a 'sophist' (*sophistēs*), i.e. a popular and persuasive orator or street
preacher, and a 'lawgiver' (*nomothētēs*).

The poor wretches have convinced themselves, first and foremost, that they are
going to be immortal and live for all time, in consequence of which they despise
death and even willingly give themselves into custody, most of them.
Furthermore, their first lawgiver persuaded them that they are all brothers of
one another after they have transgressed once for all by denying the Greek gods
and by worshipping that crucified sophist himself and living under his laws.
Therefore they despise all things indiscriminately and consider them common
property, receiving such doctrines traditionally without any definite evidence. So
if any charlatan and trickster, able to profit by occasions, comes among them, he
quickly acquires sudden wealth by imposing upon simple folk.[25]

What we have here is a (probably fairly accurate) pastiche of contemporary Christian teaching, all or most of which is implicitly ascribed to the
teaching of Jesus – i.e. to the gospels.

The standard accusations of 'atheism' (denying the Greek gods) and
anti-social behaviour (despising everything honoured by civilized Graeco-
Roman society) are routinely levelled against Jews as well as Christians.[26]
'Having everything in common' (*koina*) sounds like an allusion to Acts
2.44; Lucian clearly has some information about the early Christian

---

[24] *C. Cels.* 2.34–5, quoting Euripides, *Bacch.* 498; cf. 2.9, 8.41.   [25] Lucian, *Peregr.* §13 (LCL V. 15).
[26] Cf. Tacitus, *Hist.* 5.5.1: *odium humani generis* (Benko 1980:1064).

community's willingness to share their worldly goods (a habit which leaves them vulnerable to charlatans like Peregrinus). The proclamation of Christian 'brotherhood' may be a distant echo of Matt 23.8, 'You are all brothers' – though it could equally reflect the widespread usage of fictive kinship language found in the Epistles.[27] And the allusion to 'receiving such doctrines traditionally without any definite evidence' picks up a common theme of the pagan critique, the insistence of Christians that their teachings have to be accepted on 'faith'.

Some of the same elements occur in Galen (129–ca. 199 CE), a contemporary of Celsus, and an unusually tolerant and dispassionate (if condescending) pagan observer. For Galen, Christians are classed with Jews as 'followers of Moses and Christ', pupils of a defective philosophical 'school' (*diatribe*) which teaches its followers to rely more on faith than on reason.[28] Christ for Galen is above all a popular moral teacher, and the effects of his teachings on followers unable to cope with the rigours of a full philosophical training are by no means despicable. A passage preserved only by an Arabic translator runs:

'Most people are unable to follow any demonstrative argument consecutively; hence they need parables, and benefit from them' – and he (Galen) understands by parables tales of rewards and punishments in a future life – 'just as now we see the people called Christians drawing their faith from parables [and miracles], and yet sometimes acting in the same way [as those who philosophize]. For their contempt of death [and of its sequel] is patent to us every day, and likewise their restraint in cohabitation. For they include not only men but also women who refrain from cohabiting all through their lives; and they also number individuals who, in self-discipline and self-control in matters of food and drink, and in their pursuit of justice, have attained a pitch not inferior to that of genuine philosophers.' (Walzer 1949:15)

The teachings of Christ enable even uneducated Christians to attain to the three cardinal virtues of courage, temperance and justice (Walzer 1949:68). What is interesting for our purposes is the role ascribed to 'parables' here. The 'parable' Galen has in mind is the myth of Er at the end of Plato's *Republic*,[29] a resort to myth-making which at least some ancient commentators were prepared to recognize as necessary in any programme of mass education. If Walzer is right, it is not so much the

---

[27] Interestingly, Lucian does not make the hostile connection between universal 'brotherhood' and sexual promiscuity found already in Fronto:Benko 1980:1082–3.

[28] Walzer 1949:14–15; Benko 1980:1098–1100; Wilken 1984:68–93; Alexander 1994; Alexander 2002:243–9.

[29] Walzer 1949:91; Plato, *Rep.* 10.614b–621b.

gospel parables as the whole gospel story that Galen sees as the 'myth' that enables Christianity to inculcate philosophical virtues in the uneducated masses.[30]

Celsus offers a much sharper critique of Christ the teacher, describing his followers as 'those who believe without rational thought' and comparing them to some of the more colourful oriental cults of his day (*C. Cels.* 1.9). Christians, he says, 'take advantage of the lack of education of gullible people and lead them wherever they wish', using such expressions as 'Do not ask questions; just believe', and 'Thy faith will save thee' (*C. Cels.* 1.9). Here the general charge of reliance on faith, which we have already seen in Lucian and Galen, is supported by a tag from the gospels, heard from Christian street preachers. Christianity's appeal to the 'vulgar and illiterate' is, for Celsus, simply proof of its 'vulgarity and utter illiteracy' (1.27). The sect's open invitation to sinners, and to the poor and simple, demonstrates its depraved character.[31] Celsus' reading of the gospels is deeply coloured by his negative assessment of Christian proselytization. For him, there is a profound and disturbing inconsistency between Jesus' messianic pretensions and his career as a wandering, Cynic-style preacher: this is not the way a king should behave (1.61). Like his followers, Jesus deliberately chose the most uneducated and depraved men he could find as his disciples, 'the most wicked tax-collectors and sailors' (1.62), and adopted the disreputable mendicant lifestyle associated with the Cynics (1.62–5). The implication is that the teaching of Jesus has no persuasive power over educated people, either in his own world or in Celsus' (1.27). The scattered and enigmatic resurrection stories in the gospels are no way to impress the world and 'establish a strong faith' (2.70): if Jesus really wanted 'to teach us even to despise death by the punishments which he suffered, after his resurrection from the dead he ought to have called all men clearly to the light and taught them why he came down' (2.73).

Celsus is no more impressed with the content of Jesus' teaching. As compared with Greek philosophy, it has no claim to originality over against Plato, whom Jesus has plagiarized and misunderstood (6.16, 7.58). And even within its own cultural framework, Jesus fails the novelty test (1.26) as compared with Moses, whose teaching he has corrupted and contradicted (7.18).[32] But the real sting in Celsus' charge against the Christian portrayal of Jesus as a philosophical teacher is his failure to persuade even his own people (1.29). Origen's counter highlights what is

---

[30] Walzer 1949:70–2.   [31] *C. Cels.* 3.44, 50: cf. also 3.55, 59, with Origen's response *ad loc.*
[32] On the importance of antiquity, cf. Swain 1999; Young 1999.

at stake in these exchanges: the message of the gospel *is* both persuasive and morally edifying, and its beneficial effects can be demonstrated to 'anyone who examines the facts' by looking at the large numbers of people around the world who have benefited from his teaching and 'have been so disposed towards his doctrine that they fight for Christianity to the point of death to avoid abjuring him, which no one is related to have done for any other doctrine' (1.26). You want to see power? Look at the success of the gospel in the face of the massed opposition of human power-structures (1.27). Jesus' power as a persuasive speaker is all the more to his credit given the disadvantages of his humble origins (1.29–30). And the power of the gospel continues to bring about 'conversion and moral reformation in those who believe in God through him' (1.43).

DEEDS OF POWER

We see the same tendency to map the gospel story onto contemporary social phenomena in Celsus' treatment of miracle in the gospel story. For Celsus, Jesus was above all a wonder-worker, comparable with the conjurors and street magicians who could be found entertaining the crowds in market-places across the empire:

Celsus pretends to grant that the scriptures may be true when they speak of *cures or resurrection or a few loaves feeding many people, from which many fragments were left over, or any other monstrous tales,* as he thinks, *related by the disciples.* And he goes on to say: *Come, let us believe that these miracles really were done by you.* Then he at once puts them on a level with *the works of sorcerers who profess to do wonderful miracles, and the accomplishments of those who were taught by the Egyptians, who for a few obols make known their sacred lore in the middle of the market-place and drive daemons out of men and blow away diseases and invoke the souls of heroes, displaying expensive banquets and dining-tables and cakes and dishes which are non-existent, and who make things move as though they were alive although they are not really so, but only appear as such in the imagination. (C. Cels. 1.68)*

Like most educated pagans, Celsus is deeply ambivalent about these phenomena. Part of him wants to dismiss them as trickery (and indeed some of what he describes sounds like simple conjuring). So there is a tendency in his gospel critique to dismiss the miracle stories as 'fictions' (6.77), just as later pagan apologetic seeks to undermine the credibility of the miracle stories in detail. But (as Origen points out, 3.22–4) he has no difficulty in believing the miraculous tales recounted of the Greek gods, both in mythology and in present-day healing cults such as that of Asclepius, and sometimes prefers to belittle Jesus' miracles as simply not up to the standards set by the pagan deities (1.67). In fact for Celsus, as for many pagans, the problem was not the reality of the miracles themselves (such things could easily be paralleled) but the Christian attempt to argue that the miracles proved Jesus' divinity. Much simpler to resort to the standard accusation of sorcery: 'Since these men do these wonders, ought we to think them sons of God? Or ought we to say that they are the practices of wicked men possessed by an evil daemon?' (1.68).

The charge of magic was levelled both at contemporary Christian healers and exorcists and at Jesus: 'Impelled by some unknown power', Origen complains, 'Celsus says: *Christians get the power which they seem to possess by pronouncing the names of certain daemons and incantations* ... and he next attacks the Saviour also, saying that *it was by magic that he was able to do the miracles which he appeared to have done*' (1.6). Celsus may have been the first educated pagan to notice this phenomenon, but the accusation of sorcery is standard in early Jewish polemic.[33] Origen's reply is interesting. He shows no sign of rationalistic unease about the miraculous. Miracle is an essential element of the Christian story, both biblical and contemporary; but the power to heal body and mind is a God-given gift, which has to be distinguished sharply from magic. Celsus' attack on Christian exorcists, according to Origen,

seems blatantly to misrepresent the gospel. For they do not *get the power which they seem to possess* by any *incantations* but by the name of Jesus with the recital of the histories (*historiai*) about him. For when these are pronounced they have often made daemons to be driven out of men, and especially when those who utter them speak with real sincerity and genuine belief ... Even if it seems impossible to prove how Jesus did these things, it is clear that Christians make no use of spells, but only of the name of Jesus with other words which are believed to be effective, taken from the divine scripture. (1.6)

Origen's words give us a rare insight into the popular reception of the gospel in the pagan world. In attacking Christian healers, he complains, Celsus 'misrepresents the gospel': in other words, the presentation of the gospel is inextricably bound up with healing and exorcism. In general terms, this confirms other evidence about the spread of Christianity in the second and third centuries, when, in the words of Ramsay MacMullen, the miraculous display of divine power by Christian thaumaturgists was 'the chief instrument of conversion' (MacMullen 1984:27). But Origen also hints at a more intimate connection with gospel narratives. Healing is accomplished by the

---

[33] Cf. *b. Sanh.*107a–b. Further, Stanton 2004:127–47; Aune 1980; Evans 1994:445–6; and see chapter 11 above.

pronunciation of the name of Jesus 'with the recital of the histories about him'. This phrase takes us into the world of the magical papyri, a world in which the magician 'served as a power and communications expert, crisis manager, miracle healer and inflicter of damages and all-purpose therapist and agent of worried, troubled, and troublesome souls' (Betz 1986:xlvii). Here we find examples of short gospel sayings used in healing incantations: 'Come out of your tomb, Christ is calling you', runs a spell for childbearing in *PGM* CXXIIIa.50.[34] The words evoke the iconography of the catacombs with their potent visual presentation of healing and resurrection narratives from the gospels,[35] and suggest another route by which non-literate pagans could access gospel narratives, experienced as part of a discourse of power which has an immediate and visible effect on the physical world. Origen is careful to distance Christian healing from the practice of magic (6.39–41), but he is quite convinced that 'the name of Jesus still takes away mental distractions from men, and daemons and diseases as well' (1.67).

THE SON OF GOD

Up to the end of the second century, then, pagan knowledge of the gospel story is limited. Christians worship a cult leader and teacher who was crucified in Judaea, a dishonoured figure whose death nevertheless inspires his followers to live life with moral conviction and face death with courage. Christ has a growing reputation as a healer and wonder-worker whose teaching appeals to the masses, and his followers continue to exercise these powers in his name. Celsus is the first pagan writer to show indisputable independent knowledge of the gospels as texts, and the first to show knowledge of any events in the gospel story beyond this bare outline. To Celsus, it is not an impressive story: 'an infamous life and a miserable death' (Cook 2000:53), devoid of the 'divine power' and 'gift of persuasion' which are the true marks of the kingdom of God (1.39). But Celsus' selection of texts makes it clear that the message he seeks to counter is a resolutely supernaturalist reading of the gospel story,[36] a reading which highlights signs of divinity in the gospel narratives as planks in a cumulative argument about power and humiliation. The key moments in this story are

---

[34] Betz 1986:319 and n. 20: 'In Christian magic a *historiola* was used according to which Elizabeth says to John ... "Come out, child, Christ is calling you." In our papyrus this *historiola* appears to have been confused with the account of Lazarus in the tomb, thus attesting the analogy of womb and tomb.' Key texts from gospel healing stories are also found in amulets: Cook 1997. Origen may have heard Christian exorcists and healers use short gospel stories in a similar way.

[35] Examples in Stevenson 1978:91–4; Jensen 2000:120–4.   [36] Cf. Chadwick 1953:19 on Justin.

the miraculous birth and resurrection of the crucified Christ, with the baptism and transfiguration providing windows of divine legitimation for a cult-leader whose story seems otherwise all too mundane. Thus it is no surprise that Matthew's birth narrative is more important than Luke's, with the visit of the magi read as proof of Jesus' kingly status – a reading again reflected in early Christian iconography, where the magi (and the star) are much more widespread than the stable and the shepherds.[37]

Part of Celsus' response is to highlight those aspects of the gospel which seem at odds with the extravagant claims made by Christians for their founder: 'You provide your own refutation', he says (2.74). He knows that Jesus' mother was a carpenter's wife (2.32), and pours scorn on Jesus' lowly occupation and village origins (and not even a Greek village! 1.29f.). The evangelists' explanation of Jesus' birth is rejected out of hand: 'The mother of Jesus [was] turned out by the carpenter who was betrothed to her, as she had been convicted of adultery and had a child by a certain soldier named Panthera.'[38] The problem here is not historical criticism of the gospels, but a total inability to accept the Christian doctrine of incarnation.[39] 'Then was the mother of Jesus beautiful? And because she was beautiful did God have sexual intercourse with her, although by nature He cannot love a corruptible body? It is not likely that God would have fallen in love with her since she was neither wealthy nor of royal birth; for nobody knew her, not even her neighbours ... When she was hated by the carpenter and turned out, neither divine power nor the gift of persuasion saved her. Therefore, these things have nothing to do with the kingdom of God' (1.39). The prophetic signs clustering about the birth of Christ merely point up the contrast between his predicted royal status and the actual conditions of his adult life (1.58–61):

If Herod did this in order that when you were grown up you might not reign instead of him, why then when you had grown up did you not become king, but, though son of God, go about begging so disgracefully, cowering from fear, and wandering up and down in destitution? (1.61)

The flight into Egypt is inappropriate behaviour for a son of God (couldn't God protect his own son? 1.66), and provides a convenient link with the charge of sorcery (1.38, cf. Cook 2000:32–3).

Jesus' adult career is equally lacking in 'persuasiveness' (*pithanotēs*): 'What have you ever done in word or deed that is plausible?' (1.67). The

---

[37] Stevenson 1978:85, 87.
[38] 1.32. A version of this story is recorded in the Talmud, *b. Sanh.* 67a. See chapter 11, p. 214 above.
[39] Cf. 1.69, 6.73: (Cook 2000:28–31, 40); 4.2, 4.14–18, 4.52.

gospel portrait of Jesus' life is distressingly human, devoid of any 'fine action like a god' (2.33): 'The body of a god would not eat such food ... The body of a god does not use a voice of that kind, nor that method of persuasion' (1.70). If Christians cite the voice heard at Jesus' baptism as proof of divine approval, Celsus will counter with the argument that such an event needs credible witnesses if it is to stand as convincing evidence.[40] Jesus' failure to persuade his own people is a major stumbling-block: 'What God that comes among men is completely disbelieved?' (2.74, cf. 2.46, 78). The 'Woes' of Matt 23 are simply an index of Jesus' failure to carry conviction (2.76). Jesus' bodily appearance was 'little and ugly and undistinguished' (6.75). Since there is nothing about Jesus' physical appearance in the gospels, Origen concludes that Celsus must be basing this on Isa 53 – another indication of the way Celsus' reading of the gospels is profoundly shaped by the Christian hermeneutical tradition.

Celsus finds the resurrection equally implausible (Cook 2000: 85). Once again there is a two-pronged attack. On the one hand, the gospels fail to provide the stunning and convincing demonstrations of divine power that Celsus thinks appropriate to such an event. Surely Jesus should have been able to open the tomb himself (5.52)? If he wanted to persuade the world, why was there no large-scale epiphany to confound his accusers and convince the masses of his divine status (2.63–7)? The testimony of a 'hysterical female' and a few solitary disciples carry no evidential force (2.59) – and if Christ preached in Hades, as Christians claim, what reason do we have to suppose that his message proved any more persuasive there than it did among his own people (2.43)? But behind this is a more philosophical problem. Celsus is prepared to admit the theoretical possibility that the soul could leave the body (before or after death) and appear in a disembodied state: similar things were claimed in Greek mythology.[41] But the concept of bodily resurrection (like the concept of incarnation) is fundamentally repugnant to the nature of God: 'For the soul He might be able to provide an everlasting life; but as Heraclitus says, "corpses ought to be thrown away as worse than dung". As for the flesh, which is full of things which it is not even nice to mention, God would neither desire nor be able to make it everlasting contrary to reason. For He Himself is the reason of everything that exists: therefore He is not able to do anything contrary to

---

[40] *C. Cels.* 1.40–1. Celsus picks up the variant testimony in the synoptic accounts as to who exactly saw the dove. Conversely, at 2.72 he cites the voice from heaven as a counter to Christian claims that Jesus wanted to keep his mission hidden.

[41] 3.32. *Skia* (3.22) is the Homeric word for 'shade' or 'disembodied spirit' – the normal Greek word for the dead (Garland 2001:12, 123). Cf. 2.55.

reason or to His own character' (5.14). And the incarnate Son of God is no exception to this divinely ordained reason: 'since the Son is a spirit derived from God who was born in a human body, even the Son of God himself would not be mortal ... God would not have received back the spirit which he gave after it had been defiled by the nature of the body' (6.72).[42] Hence, what the disciples saw was either a hallucination (2.60) or a ghost (*skia* 3.22). And when the gospels claim that Jesus showed his wounds to his disciples (2.61), this was a mental impression which he produced on their minds, not a real bodily resurrection, and certainly not (as Origen claims) 'the greatest of all miracles' (2.62).

CONCLUSION

It is beyond the scope of this chapter to pursue the pagan reception of the gospels beyond Celsus; but it is clear that the issues that dominate the second-century debate continue to determine the underlying dialectical structure of later apologetic on both sides.[43] In pagan polemic of the third and fourth centuries we see a progressively more detailed engagement with the text of the gospels, as pagan critics like Porphyry (ca. 232–305) apply to them the principles of higher criticism current in the Greek schools, picking up contradictions (e.g. in the birth stories) and looking for physical or historical howlers in the narratives.[44] Similar criticisms appear in the *Apocriticus*, a fictional pagan–Christian dialogue from the late third or early fourth century, which raises a series of *aporiai* from the gospels: 'How is it said: cast thyself down?' 'What is the meaning of the swine and the demons?'[45] Unlike Celsus, these authors are prepared to engage with the texts at close range; they deal with a wider range of gospel passages than Celsus, and respond to more sophisticated hermeneutical procedures, like the use of allegory to deal with problematic texts (cf., e.g., Cook 2000:182). Later pagan authors also criticize the evangelists for their defective rhetorical skills (Cook 2000:263). But the fundamental issues are still those raised in the dialectic of the second century: Christians have to convince their pagan interlocutors that the gospel message has persuasive power, both at large and in detail, i.e. that it is historically plausible, rhetorically coherent and logically convincing (Cook 2000:180–5).

---

[42] Further, Cook 2000:59–61.
[43] For later pagan writers, see Meredith 1980; Wilken 1984; Cook 2000.
[44] Cook 2000:101–67; Meredith 1980. Origen points out (*C. Cels.* 2.32) that Christians had already begun to notice some of these discrepancies.
[45] Cook 2000:168–249.

Throughout the third and fourth centuries, the lines of apologetic discourse continue to fall into pre-determined patterns, as pagan writers and Christian apologists address the primary points at issue between Graeco-Roman culture of the pagan world and the new religion in progressively more complex epicycles of argument and counter-argument. But we should not close without mentioning a new kind of response, less easy to document but potentially of equal importance, in which pagans respond to the gospel message not with apologetic but with counter-narrative. Bowersock has argued that the 'empty tomb' stories of the Greek novels offer a light-hearted pagan mimicry of the gospel resurrection narratives.[46] More significantly, a major theme in fourth-century polemic is the appearance of a pagan rival to Jesus in the shape of the Pythagorean philosopher and wonder-worker Apollonius of Tyana.[47] Apollonius probably had a real existence in the first century, but his career really takes off in the third century when his story was written up in eight books of carefully crafted prose by Philostratus.[48] There are obvious parallels between Apollonius and Jesus: 'healings, exorcisms, doubting followers, ascension, mission' (Swain 1999:194). But Philostratus' Apollonius has everything the Jesus of the gospels lacks: noble birth, Attic purity of diction, rhetorical power, status as counsellor to the highest in the land, Socratic insouciance and divine power.[49] It is not unreasonable to read Philostratus' *Life of Apollonius* as a deliberate attempt to out-narrate the gospels.[50] Both narratives function as 'vehicles of belief systems, pagan and Christian', embodying not simply a historical account of an individual's life, but a defence of a way of life (Swain 1999:180). Certainly Philostratus addresses some of the fundamental problems that the gospel story raises for educated pagans like Celsus and thus provides indirectly one of the strongest testimonies to the impact of the gospels on the Graeco-Roman world.

[46] Bowersock 1994:99–119; cf. 139.   [47] Cook 2000:250–76.   [48] Bowie 1978; Swain 1999.
[49] E.g. Philostratus, *Vit. Ap.* 1.4, 7, 17; 4.33–8; 5.36; 7.38, 41; 8.1–8, 28–31.
[50] Swain 1999:182, 194.

CHAPTER 13

Forty other gospels

Christopher Tuckett

The four gospels in the NT have always received special attention, partly by virtue of being canonized as part of Christian scripture. Yet it is clear that these four are part of a much wider corpus of texts, either claiming the name of 'gospel' for themselves or being described by others (past or present) as 'gospels'. It is with these 'other' gospels, i.e. gospels other than the canonical gospels of the NT, that this essay is concerned.[1]

These 'other' gospels vary very considerably in scope, content and (probably) genre. The question 'What is a gospel?' is well known as a problem which is by no means simple when applied to the canonical gospels of the NT (cf. Talbert 1977; Burridge 1992). The same question applied to the mass of other writings which have at various times been called 'gospels' is infinitely more complex to try to answer: these writings vary so much that it is hard, if not impossible, to find common denominators in all of them.[2]

I MANUSCRIPT EVIDENCE

Such variation applies even at the mundane level of our knowledge of their text, their extent etc. In the case of the canonical gospels, the huge range of MSS available to us for all four of these gospels means that the broad contours of both their extent and their content are not generally in doubt. The situation is very different in relation to the non-canonical gospels. The fact that, at a relatively early period, the four NT gospels achieved high

---

[1] For presentation and discussions of many of the relevant texts, see Schneemelcher 1991; Koester 1990; Elliott 1993a; Lührmann and Schlarb 2000; Klauck 2004. For an important survey article see Gero 1988. For a slightly more popular treatment, see Ehrman 2003a, 2003b. Whether there are forty such gospels is uncertain: Schneemelcher has far more than forty, though forty is a round number with Biblical overtones! In order to keep the discussion within manageable limits, texts which are probably later than ca. the fifth century are not considered here.

[2] Cf. also Gero 1988:399f.: 'One must guard against an assumption that "apocryphal gospels" or "post-canonical" traditions represent a distinct literary genre'; similarly, Schneemelcher 1991:77–8.

authoritative status[3] had various effects in relation to other 'gospels'. On the one hand, the fact that the latter were not generally considered canonical may have led to greater freedom on the part of scribes in copying them. Thus in relation to the few texts where we have a relatively large number of MSS, the textual evidence is often characterized by very great diversity.[4] On the other hand (and probably more commonly), the 'canonical' (or at least authoritative) status of the NT gospels meant that these were often copied extensively whilst others were not. For many non-canonical gospels, the MS evidence is thus often extremely small in extent.

For some, we have at most one or two MSS containing the whole text. Thus, the Nag Hammadi codices provide complete texts of, e.g., the *Gospel of Thomas* (NHC II.2), the *Gospel of Philip* (NHC II.3) and the *Gospel of Truth* (NHC I.2, XII.2), but even these are only translations of the text into Coptic (probably from Greek).[5] In other cases, we have extant MS attestation for only part of what was evidently a longer text originally. The *Gospel of Mary* is extant in two small Greek fragments (P. Oxy. 3525, P. Ryl. 463); a fuller version of the text is available in Coptic translation in the Berlin codex BG 8502, but the extant part of the codex is lacking the opening few pages of text. The so-called *Gospel of Peter* is available to us in MS form primarily through the Akhmim fragment (P. Cair. 10759), which represents only part of the whole text of the gospel: it starts in the middle of a sentence and breaks off abruptly at the end. How much has been lost we simply do not know.[6] Hence to try to categorize it on the basis of the contents of the Akhmim fragment alone would probably be dangerous.[7] In the case of other MSS we possess, the extant text is so fragmentary and limited in extent that we do not even know if they are 'gospels' or possibly homilies using (or quoting) other gospel material.[8]

---

[3] For the NT gospels as authoritative from a very early date, see Stanton 1997, 2003. When a strict 'canon' of the NT was formed is perhaps another issue.

[4] For example, the textual witnesses of the *Protevangelium of James*, or the *Infancy Gospel of Thomas*, differ enormously, both at the level of detailed wording and also in terms of the content included.

[5] For the *Gospel of Thomas*, there are three Oxyrhynchus papyri, P. Oxy. 1, 654, 655, which give fragments of the text in Greek, but not the complete text.

[6] For other fragmentary material as perhaps part of the same gospel, see Lührmann 2004:55–104, especially in relation to P. Oxy. 4009.

[7] Contra, e.g., Gero 1988:3985, who lists it under the category of 'Passion Gospels'; Klauck 2004:82–8 treats it in the chapter entitled 'Gospels about Jesus' Death and Resurrection'. The extended extant fragment is indeed part of a passion narrative; but there is no way of knowing what else the text contained, and hence whether the passion narrative was the central part of the text or a rather smaller part of a more extended whole. See also below.

[8] See Elliott 1993a:x: 'some fragmentary apocryphal gospels may be mere homilies'.

With other texts, we have no MS of the text as such. We may know of their existence by references in the church fathers who also occasionally quote from them. This is the case with the so-called 'Jewish Christian gospels', the *Gospel of the Hebrews*, the *Gospel of the Nazaraeans* and the *Gospel of the Ebionites*, quoted by people such as Origen, Jerome and Epiphanius,[9] or the so-called *Gospel of the Egyptians*, referred to on occasions by Clement of Alexandria.[10] Methodological problems associated with reconstructing the texts of these gospels are even greater here since we do not know for certain how accurately the text has been quoted.[11] But equally we do not know the full extent of the texts concerned on the basis of the few extracts we have. Hence we can say little about these texts as wholes. There are further texts of whose existence we know, but whose content has been almost completely lost. Thus some of the lists produced of canonical and 'apocryphal' books, or other patristic writers, refer to various texts as 'apocryphal' or heretical,[12] but we have virtually no evidence about their contents at all (e.g. a 'Gospel of Matthias', or a 'Gospel of Judas').[13] In other instances, a writer may be (apparently) claiming to quote from a 'gospel', and yet the identity of that gospel text is otherwise unknown to us.[14]

At some stage, a number of these texts were called 'gospels'. Thus in a few MSS containing these texts, there is a colophon at the end of the text, 'The gospel according to . . .', e.g. in some of the Nag Hammadi texts (the *Gospel of Thomas*, the *Gospel of Philip*, the *Gospel of the Egyptians*) as well as the *Gospel of Mary* in BG 8502. These may well be later scribal additions to the original text, but they do show that others called these texts 'gospels'.[15] The same is shown by lists produced of canonical and non-canonical texts,

---

[9] The whole issue of the nature of the Jewish Christian gospels, and whether there are really three such gospels, is intensely debated and by no means unanimously agreed. See, e.g., Klijn 1992 for the relevant texts and full discussion.

[10] This gospel clearly has nothing to do with the text with the same name/title found at Nag Hammadi (NHC IV.2).

[11] Nor do we know how accurately the text of the church father in question has been transmitted!

[12] The whole question of whether, and in what sense, the word 'apocryphal' is an appropriate one to use here is much debated. See, e.g., the brief, but very helpful, discussion of Klauck 2004:1–3. For more detailed discussion, see Markschies 1998. I have tried to avoid the word for the most part, and have sought simply to refer to texts as, e.g., 'non-canonical'. I am fully aware that even this description begs some questions, but, I hope, not as many as those engendered by the term 'apocryphal'!

[13] A 'Gospel of Matthias' is mentioned in the list of canonical and 'apocryphal' books in the so-called Gelasian Decree. (Clement of Alexandria refers at a few points to some 'Traditions of Matthias', but it is not at all certain if he is referring to this lost gospel: see Lührmann and Schlarb 2000:140; Klauck 2004:206.) A 'Gospel of Judas' is mentioned by Epiphanius, *Pan.* 37.1.5.

[14] E.g. the author of 2 *Clement* gives a number of quotations of sayings of Jesus from what he simply calls 'the gospel', without further specifying his source of information.

[15] Unless the word 'gospel' here has its older meaning of 'good news' or 'saving message', rather than being a reference to the text itself: cf. Vielhauer 1975:258.

where these documents are referred to as 'gospels', and also the way in which quotations of the texts are sometimes introduced by church fathers quoting them. This then raises the question of how justified such a description might be.

2 WHAT IS A 'GOSPEL'?

How we might answer such a question is by no means obvious or clear. One could adopt a very 'theological' standpoint, and say that a 'gospel' should be a text focusing primarily on the primitive Christian kerygma (or 'gospel', *euangelion* in its earliest sense) of the saving death and resurrection of Jesus.[16] Such a definition would probably then exclude all the non-canonical texts considered here as 'genuine' 'gospels' and might even exclude some of the canonical gospels (e.g. Matthew and Luke) as well![17] Further, it would not help very much in seeking to analyse and discuss the actual texts we have: we could not then call them 'gospels', but we would have to call them something else.

A less prejudicial approach would be simply to accept at least ancient descriptions of texts as 'gospels': if a text claimed to be a 'gospel', or was referred to by others as a 'gospel', then this should be accepted and the text concerned included within the broad category of 'gospel'. But then this would not necessarily include all that one wants, since some texts are not explicitly referred to by others at all. Others today might then work with the slightly different criterion that a 'gospel' should be a text purporting to give some account of the life and/or teaching of the historical Jesus (in contrast, say, to a 'letter', sermon or doctrinal treatise).[18]

However, these two broad definitions of a 'gospel' do not always include or exclude the same texts. Thus the so-called *Gospel of Truth* from Nag Hammadi (NHC I.3) is widely believed to be the text mentioned by Irenaeus (*Haer.* 3.11.9, referring to a 'Gospel of Truth' used by Valentinian Gnostics) and probably taking its name from the opening sentence.[19] The text is, however, an extended meditation or homily about the nature of God and of human beings and (in some small part) about Jesus and his

---

[16] This is a common view amongst some seeking to define the genre of the NT gospels.

[17] See, e.g., Koester 1990:43ff. for the 'prejudice' against non-canonical gospel literature engendered by such a tight definition.

[18] Cf. Vielhauer 1975:614; Schneemelcher 1991:78; Koester 1990:46, and see below. This would probably also coincide with the views of many outside academic circles.

[19] 'The gospel of truth is joy for those who have received from the Father of truth the gift of knowing him.' Whether this opening sentence is making any claim for the text as a whole to be regarded as a 'gospel' is more doubtful.

significance; in no sense is it claiming to re-present the life and/or teaching of the historical Jesus. The *Gospel of Philip* from Nag Hammadi (NHC II.3) is similar. It does contain a few 'sayings' claiming to be teaching of Jesus. But the rest of the text is mostly taken up with teaching from the author him/herself *about* God, Jesus and human beings.[20] Yet the colophon of the gospel in the Nag Hammadi codex clearly 'labels' the text 'The Gospel of Philip'. So too the so-called *Gospel of the Egyptians* from Nag Hammadi (NHC IV.2) makes no claim at all to be re-presenting teaching of, or information about, the historical Jesus.[21] Yet it too is called (or calls itself) a 'gospel' in the colophon.

Similarly problematic in this context might be texts such as the *Sophia of Jesus Christ* (NHC III.4) and the *Apocryphon of John* (NHC II.1, III.1, IV.1, BG 8502.2) from Nag Hammadi.[22] Neither is called a 'gospel' in any of the MSS we have, nor, as far as we know, were they called 'gospels' by other people at the time. However, at one level both purport to be accounts of teaching given by Jesus after his resurrection. As such, they might be appropriately considered as 'resurrection dialogues' (see below). On the other hand, in both instances, such a context for the teaching is probably a secondary element. *SJC* is an expansion of material found in another Nag Hammadi tractate, *Eugnostos the Blessed* (NHC III.3). But whereas in *Eugnostos*, the teaching is given uninterrupted, and by the author of the tract, in *SJC* it is given a more Christian context by presenting the same teaching as given by the risen Jesus in response to a series of questions posed by Jesus' disciples (see Tuckett 1986:31–5). In the case of *ApocJohn*, it is widely agreed that the context presenting the teaching as that of the risen Jesus is a secondary, and very superficial, expansion of the earlier tradition (Tuckett 1986: 25–7). Thus although formally both *SJC* and *ApocJohn* appear now as teachings of Jesus, the bulk of the material they contain was not in this form at an earlier stage of their respective traditions.[23]

If one takes a purely phenomenological ('emic') approach and accepts as a potential 'gospel' *any* text which anyone at any time might have once called a 'gospel', then texts like the *Gospel of Truth* or the *Gospel of the Egyptians* can and should be included in the category of 'gospels'. However, such a

---

[20] Cf. Koester 1990:47: 'a collection of aphoristic theological reflections and comments, perhaps derived from a theological treatise'.

[21] Koester calls it 'a mythological description of the work of salvation which was accomplished by the Great Seth, the son of Adam'.

[22] There is a Greek fragment (P. Oxy. 1081) extant of *SJC*. With *ApocJohn*, the substance of the text is also very closely related to the account given in Irenaeus, *Haer.* 1.29 of the beliefs of the Barbelognostics.

[23] The same might be said about some parts of the canonical gospel tradition as well!

criterion on its own might be too restrictive, since some other texts are fragmentary (so we have no equivalent to the colophon extant) and/or they are not referred to by contemporary writers. Thus alongside the purely descriptive approach, an element of critical judgment may be needed, certainly if we are to include other texts as potential 'gospels'. But then, whatever criterion we adopt which might serve to *in*clude some texts[24] may serve to *ex*clude others, despite their possible description as 'gospels' by others.

In this context, the criterion mentioned earlier – that a 'gospel' is a text purporting to give some account of the life and/or teaching of Jesus – might be valuable. With such a criterion, we might then want to exclude the *Gospel of the Egyptians* and perhaps the *Gospel of Truth* as 'gospels' in this (slightly) narrower sense, or at least we might wish to classify them in a category very different from that of other 'gospels'.[25] The status of texts such as *SJC* and *ApocJohn* might be less clear: in their present form they could just be styled 'gospels', though the 'gospel' form is probably a secondary addition to earlier material. They are then texts which have been secondarily 'gospelized'. But maybe this simply shows that a single genre of all 'gospels' is difficult if not impossible to isolate; and the converse of this is perhaps that it is equally difficult to define just what should appropriately be considered, and also what should not be considered, as a 'gospel'. It also illustrates the range of different kinds of 'gospels' that were in existence.

3 TOWARDS A POSSIBLE TAXONOMY OF 'GOSPELS'

Given the great variety of 'gospels' that were evidently around in the early church, some sub-division, or taxonomy, of this diversity may be possible and desirable. However, as already noted, some texts are only available to

---

[24] E.g. Papyrus Egerton 2, called originally 'Fragments of an Unknown *Gospel*' or the 'Egerton *Gospel*'; cf. too the Akhmim fragment, which is widely known today as the 'Gospel of Peter': yet the name is not mentioned as such in the MS and the identification is in part due to equating this text with the 'Gospel of Peter' mentioned by Eusebius as current in Rhossus at the time of Bishop Serapion (*Hist. Eccl.* 6.12).

[25] The solution adopted by, e.g., Klauck 2004:105–44, who treats them as 'gospels', but as a separate category (though he does not attempt to describe this category beyond simply 'Gospels from Nag Hammadi'). Elliott 1993a:xii excludes them from his collection on the pragmatic grounds that good modern editions of most of the Nag Hammadi texts are available elsewhere. Koester 1990:46f. excludes them by a criterion of only including 'all those writings which are constituted by the transmission, use and interpretation of materials and traditions from and about Jesus of Nazareth', and hence lists them under the rubric of 'Writings which are not to be counted as Gospels'. Gero 1988:3970 is even more restrictive, saying at the outset that he will treat only 'connected narrative accounts of Jesus' (which effectively excludes even, say, the *Gospel of Thomas*).

us in fragmentary form, so that we may not know the extent and character of their full contents; other texts may be capable of being fitted into more than one category (e.g. the *Gospel of Thomas*). Thus any taxonomy can be at best provisional and certainly should not foreclose discussion about the nature of any individual text.

3.1 Narrative gospels

One possible sub-group of texts might be labelled 'narrative gospels', i.e. texts that purport to give an account of incidents in Jesus' life in the form of a narrative.[26] As such, these might then be closest in form to the canonical gospels.

One such text might be Papyrus Egerton 2 (called the 'Egerton Gospel' by some today; see Crossan 1991:428; Daniels 1989). The text we have is highly fragmentary. This means that its wording is at times by no means certain; further, we do not know the full extent of the text from which the present fragment comes. Nevertheless, the extant parts appear to contain accounts of Jesus in debate with opponents (e.g. over his healing a leper, and on the issue of paying taxes) and hence seems to be similar, in at least very general terms, to the pericopes of the canonical gospels.

Similarly, P. Oxy. 840, although fragmentary and so giving no indication of its full extent, contains an account of a dispute between Jesus and some Jews about questions of purity. Again in very general terms, the extant fragment looks to be similar in kind to the narratives of the canonical gospels.

Perhaps one might include here the *Gospel of Peter*. As already noted, the most extensive MS witness to the text of this gospel gives a version of a passion narrative. However, another small fragment, P. Oxy. 4009, may also belong to the same text.[27] This records an exchange between Jesus and (possibly) Peter about aspects of martyrdom etc. If this is indeed part of the *Gospel of Peter*, then the gospel may have contained not only an account of Jesus' passion, but also elements of Jesus' teaching as well: thus the gospel may have contained a narrative more extensive than that of the passion alone.[28]

---

[26] As noted above, this is virtually the only category treated by Gero as 'gospels' in his survey article.

[27] See n. 6 above. The *editio princeps* of this fragment is entitled 'Gospel of Peter?' (and edited by Lührmann and P. Parsons): see Coles et al. 1994:1–5. The reconstructed side of P. Oxy. 4009 may be another version of the dialogue recorded in 2 *Clem.* 5.2–4; in 2 *Clement* Jesus speaks to 'Peter', whereas in P. Oxy. 4009 Jesus speaks to someone called 'me' in the text. The fact that Peter might be identified with the 'author' of the text is the main reason for ascribing the fragment to the *Gospel of Peter*.

[28] Hence the danger of simply listing it as a 'passion gospel': see n. 7 above.

Some of the so-called Jewish Christian gospels may also belong in this category. Thus the *Gospel of the Hebrews* (probably) contained a passing reference to Jesus' baptism,[29] as well as an account of a resurrection appearance to James.[30] There is too a version of the story of the rich young man coming to Jesus in the *Gospel of the Nazaraeans*.[31] Similarly, the *Gospel of the Ebionites* seems to have had an account of Jesus' baptism, as well as sayings firmly located in the context of the Last Supper.[32] All this suggests that these gospels contained reasonably extended narrative accounts of the Jesus story.

3.2 Sayings gospels

A second group of 'gospels' might be called 'sayings gospels', i.e. texts consisting primarily of sayings of Jesus collected together with little or no narrative context. Included here might be the *Gospel of Thomas* and possibly too the sayings source Q, believed to lie behind the present gospels of Matthew and Luke.[33] Certainly in the *Gospel of Thomas*, the narrative element has been eliminated almost completely and one has a collection of (only) sayings of Jesus. Here, then, we seem to have a literary entity that is generically different from, say, the narrative gospels of the NT.

Similarly Q, if it existed, appears to have lacked at least significant parts of the narrative that characterizes the other canonical gospels at least in that it lacks a passion narrative. Also the narrative elements in Q are, as far as we can tell, considerably reduced by comparison with the other NT gospels.[34]

---

[29] As quoted in Jerome, *Comm. Isa.* 11.2. This is attributed by Jerome to the *Gospel of the Nazaraeans*, though it is widely assumed to be taken from the *Gospel of the Hebrews* (if indeed the two are to be distinguished): cf. Elliott 1993a:10; Klijn 1992:98.

[30] Cited in Jerome, *Vir. Ill.* 2.

[31] Origen, *Comm. Mt.* 15.14. In Origen's (Latin) text, it is said to come from the *Gospel of the Hebrews*, but this is often assumed to be a mistake for the *Gospel of the Nazaraeans* (cf. Klauck 2004:44–6; Klijn 1992:56).

[32] See Klauck 2004:51–4; Elliott 1993a:14–16. As with all the Jewish Christian gospels, there is doubt about which text might be in mind, and precisely how many different 'gospels' there really were (as opposed to different descriptions of what may have been the same original text).

[33] There is disagreement about whether such a source existed and, if it did, whether it was ever a written text. Even among those who agree about its existence as a text, there is debate about the appropriateness of calling it a 'gospel'. On the minimalist definition adopted above (of a text that purports to give information about the life and/or teaching of Jesus), Q might well qualify as a potential 'gospel' (provided that it was a 'text'!).

[34] Q may have started with some narrative elements, e.g. including an account of the preaching of John the Baptist, the temptation narrative, the Great Sermon, the healing of the centurion's servant and John's question to Jesus. But then a clear narrative line in the Q material seems to dissipate.

Thus Q may be closer in form to a 'sayings collection' than to anything else and hence possibly could be regarded as a 'sayings gospel'.[35]

Other texts might fit into this broad category *if* we had more information about them. For example, most of the quotations ascribed to the *Gospel of the Egyptians* cited by Clement of Alexandria are sayings of Jesus. On the other hand, much of the material cited in Clement appears in the form of Jesus apparently responding to (questions by) Salome. Hence the 'gospel' may be more akin generically to a dialogue form (Klauck 2004:56; cf. 3.4 below).

Perhaps no hard and fast lines can be drawn and it may be a question of tendencies rather than strict definitions; but some (or at least one!) 'gospel' text(s) focused on the sayings of Jesus almost exclusively.

3.3 Infancy gospels

A third group of 'gospels' can be identified as texts which seem consciously to expand one part of the canonical tradition. Thus one group of gospels build on the accounts of Jesus' birth and childhood. For example, the *Infancy Gospel of Thomas* attempts to fill out 'gaps' in the other gospels by giving details of alleged incidents, mostly a series of miracles performed by the child Jesus.[36]

Similarly the so-called *Protevangelium of James* is clearly an attempt to fill out the other (canonical) gospels. Extant in a large number of MSS (thus testifying to its great popularity), this text is perhaps more about Mary than about Jesus (and hence arguably not to be included in the category of 'gospel' at all). Indeed, its title in many MSS is 'The Birth of Mary, Revelation of James', and in fact it gives more space to telling the story of Mary's own birth and virginity. An account of the birth of Jesus does appear in some MSS of the text, but there has been considerable debate about whether this section is a genuine part of the text or not.

3.4 Resurrection discourses/dialogues

If the infancy gospels develop the traditions surrounding Jesus' birth, another group of texts develop the other 'end' of the Jesus story, namely the post-Easter period when Jesus is still present on earth teaching his

---

[35] For the generic similarity between Q and other ancient saying collections in antiquity, see Kloppenborg 1987.

[36] This gospel is not to be confused with the *Gospel of Thomas* known to us from Nag Hammadi.

disciples. In the canonical gospels, not much information is given about the actual contents of Jesus' teaching. Mark notoriously never has the risen Jesus appear at all (Mark 16.8). Matthew has a very brief account of the meeting of Jesus with the disciples on a mountain in Galilee (Matt 28.16–20). Luke and John have slightly longer accounts (Luke 24; Acts 1.1–8; John 20, 21), but the amount of space devoted to the teaching given by Jesus is relatively small.

This potential 'gap' was exploited in particular by Gnostic Christians who developed considerable claims about extensive secret teaching of Jesus given to his chosen disciples, and the time that this teaching was given was often claimed to be the period after Jesus' resurrection. A number of Gnostic (or gnostic)[37] gospel texts thus present the risen Jesus appearing to his disciples and giving them more esoteric teaching. Further, this teaching is often given in the form of a dialogue, with the risen Jesus responding to questions posed by the disciples. For example, the *Gospel of Mary* presents the risen Jesus giving responses to questions posed by a group of twelve men and seven women (including Mary) who are alone with him in a post-resurrection scene. The *Apocryphon of James* (NHC I.2) has a similar setting, presenting Jesus teaching a chosen group of disciples (with here James taking a leading role) in a post-resurrection scene.

Very similar in terms of genre are at least the present forms of the *Sophia of Jesus Christ* and the *Apocryphon of John* from Nag Hammadi, mentioned earlier (though, as noted, in both cases the setting provided is almost certainly a secondary addition to the relevant tradition). Other Nag Hammadi texts may fall into this broad category as well: the *Dialogue of the Saviour* (NHC III.5) and the *Book of Thomas the Contender* (NHC II.7) both present Jesus' teaching in the form of dialogues with the disciples. A post-resurrection setting here is not explicit but may be implied.[38]

The genre is also not confined to Gnostic texts: for example, the so-called *Epistula Apostolorum* should probably be included here. In one way, as its name implies, it is generically a letter (and hence perhaps not a 'gospel'), purporting to be a letter sent to all the churches in the world from the apostolic college. However, this fiction is not maintained consistently, and the text very soon adopts the form of a dialogue between the risen Jesus and the disciples. Moreover, its contents are not necessarily 'Gnostic' (and

---

[37] There is no space here to enter into the vexed question of the legitimacy or appropriateness of labelling texts or ideas 'Gnostic', or 'gnostic'. Suffice it to say that, if anything can be labelled in this way appropriately, then it will include at least some of the material considered here!

[38] The extant text of the *Dialogue of the Saviour* is very fragmentary; hence the precise setting may well be in a part of the text which is missing.

in some sense even anti-gnostic, with its strong stress on the reality of Jesus' bodily resurrection, its insistence on the resurrection of the flesh and its explicit opposition to 'Simon' (presumably Magus) and 'Cerinthus'). Perhaps the work represents a conscious attempt to play the Gnostic 'game' on its own terms in order to oppose it!

It might also be worth considering whether the *Gospel of Thomas* could be appropriately be placed in this category as well. The question of who the speaker is in *Thomas* has always been a conundrum: is it thought of as the earthly, pre-Easter Jesus, or is it the risen, post-Easter Jesus? One of the striking things about the text of *Thomas* is the very brief introduction to each saying, usually translated as 'Jesus said'. The tense of the Coptic *pedje* is ambiguous. However, it is notable that in the extant Greek fragments of *Thomas* the present tense *legei* is consistently used.[39] Thus it may be that the speaker is thought of not as a figure of the historical past, i.e. Jesus speaking to his disciples in the past, but as a figure speaking in the present, i.e. the risen Jesus. Further, dialogue elements are also present: on occasions followers of Jesus, individually or collectively, pose questions to which Jesus responds (sayings 6, 12, 13, 20, 21 etc.). It may be, then, that the *Gospel of Thomas* is rather more like a 'resurrection dialogue' than might appear at first sight, and that in generic terms, not too large a wedge should be driven between *Thomas* (as an alleged 'sayings gospel') and other resurrection dialogues.

3.5 Others

The above survey and suggested taxonomy make no pretence of covering all possible texts which might be considered as 'gospels'. There are, for example, gospel harmonies, texts which appear to have been produced in order to harmonize, and run together, different gospel texts (primarily the canonical gospels). The most famous of these is probably the work of Tatian, who produced his *Diatessaron* towards the end of the second century. However, Tatian may not have been unique: it is widely believed, for example, that Justin Martyr had access to Jesus traditions via a version of the synoptic tradition that had already harmonized the gospels of Matthew and Luke at least. Similarly, the 'gospel' quoted in *2 Clement* may reflect a similar harmonizing version of the tradition already in existence by the time this was written and used by the author.[40]

---

[39] The only exception is in the introduction, where the aorist *eipen* is used.
[40] On these, see Koester 1990:360–402 and 349–60 respectively, with references to further literature.

There is too the phenomenon of isolated sayings and traditions that appear at various places in, e.g., the MS tradition of canonical texts and/or smaller expansions of the texts,[41] as well as a range of other texts from later periods.

4 RELATION TO THE CANONICAL GOSPELS

Interest in the non-canonical gospels has grown considerably in recent years. In part this has been due to a belief or hope that some of the information about Jesus given in these texts might be authentic. Hence our knowledge of, and information about, the historical Jesus might be significantly extended – and perhaps modified – by these texts beyond what we have in the NT gospels. In part this is tied up with questions about the date of these gospels since, according to many, they may well be in part early texts: some may be as early as the canonical gospels; alternatively they might contain traditions which take us back to an early stage of the Jesus tradition. Thus in the context of contemporary Jesus study, some of the non-canonical gospels have been seen as increasingly significant. In particular, texts such as the *Gospel of Thomas*, Papyrus Egerton 2 and the *Gospel of Peter* (or perhaps sources behind the present *Gospel of Peter*) have been regarded by many as providing possible extra information about Jesus which might significantly affect our knowledge about, and assessment of, Jesus' life and/or teaching.[42] What, then, are the dates of these 'forty other gospels', and how do they relate to the canonical gospels?

Such questions are of course too wide-ranging and too complex to be answered in a single essay such as this. In one way clearly, the question about the dates of forty other gospels is really forty quite different questions needing forty different answers. No single blanket answer can cover all the texts concerned.

Some texts are certainly late and probably presuppose the canonical gospels. For example, the infancy gospels were probably written to supplement what were felt to be gaps or deficiencies in the canonical accounts. Thus the relatively small-scale accounts of Jesus' birth and/or childhood were expanded to give much longer, more detailed stories. So too, production of gospel harmonies is only possible on the presupposition that there

---

[41] Included here might be the 'Secret Gospel of Mark', a possible expanded version of Mark quoted in a letter claiming to be by Clement of Alexandria. Space constraints forbid discussion here: see H. Merkel in Schneemelcher 1991:106–10; Koester 1990:293–303.

[42] See, for example, in historical Jesus studies today, the work of Crossan 1991; also the collection of essays in Hedrick 1988, and the work of the 'Jesus Seminar', including Funk and Hoover 1993.

were texts in existence which needed harmonizing: and this in turn implies that the texts concerned were thought to be important enough for the issue of their apparent lack of consistency to be a matter of concern. Thus texts such as Tatian's *Diatessaron* only make sense in the context of the presence of other authoritative, but divergent, gospel texts.

The situation of other gospels is by no means so clear cut. It is not obvious – at least at first sight – whether these gospels presuppose the canonical gospels and, if they do, what their intended relationship to the canonical gospels was: were they intended to supplement other gospels? Or were they written in competition with them, to displace them? Did in fact the canonical gospels have any special status at the time these other gospels were written? Or is the description 'canonical'/'non-canonical' anachronistic, reading back later ecclesiastical decisions into an earlier period so that one can only talk of 'gospels *which became* canonical' and 'gospels *which became* non-canonical'?[43]

In terms of MS attestation, some of the MSS containing the texts of non-canonical gospels are extremely early, often just as early as the earliest MSS of the canonical gospels. MSS of the canonicals gospels dating to the second or early third centuries CE are not that common. Yet this same period produces some of our MSS of non-canonical gospels as well. Thus the three Oxyrhynchus fragments of the *Gospel of Thomas* are probably from ca. 200–50 CE; the Greek fragments of the *Gospel of Mary* are probably early third century; Papyrus Egerton 2 has been dated to the second century;[44] P. Oxy. 4009, which may contain a fragment of the *Gospel of Peter*, has been dated to the second century.[45]

Quite apart from the MSS attestation, the fact that non-canonical gospels were known, written and cited in texts such as *2 Clement*, and the fact that *2 Clement* is probably to be dated to around the mid second century, indicates that non-canonical gospels were current at this time. Similarly, Eusebius' account of the *Gospel of Peter*, its currency in Rhossus and subsequent banning by Serapion (*Hist. Eccl.* 6.12), indicates that the gospel was known and used in the second century. So too we know from Irenaeus and other church fathers of 'gospels' used by second-century

---

[43] So Lührmann and the titles of his books referring to 'apokryph *gewordene* Evangelien'.

[44] Originally dated to ca. 140 CE, it is now generally dated towards the end of the second century, primarily on the basis of some of the details in the handwriting of the fragment P. Köln 255, now accepted as originally belonging to the same MS P. Eg. 2.

[45] Even if not from the *Gospel of Peter*, it is probably from some non-canonical gospel text (with a possible close parallel in *2 Clem.* 5), and so the papyrus provides very early MS attestation for the existence of *a* gospel text which is not one of the canonical gospels.

Gnostics, some of which may now be available to us through the Nag Hammadi library.

All this, however, simply shows what is very widely accepted today, namely that 'gospel' writing was flowering among Christians in the second century; and that, by a mixture of luck and good fortune, we have some of the actual copies of this gospel-writing activity extant in some MSS and texts. But how much of this gospel writing we can trace back into the first century apart from the canonical gospels is another matter.

Again no blanket answers can be given. One group of possible texts should probably be treated separately in this context, namely possible sources used by the canonical evangelists. Thus if Q existed, and it is appropriate to call Q a 'gospel', the fact that Q was used by Matthew and Luke and hence must pre-date Matthew and Luke shows that some other 'gospel'-writing activity apart from the writing of the canonical gospels themselves was taking place in the first century. Similarly, *if* other written sources of Jesus' life and/or teaching were available to, and used by, the canonical evangelists,[46] then this would further enhance the general picture of a wider spread of possible literary activity involving Jesus tradition among first-century Christians.

On the other hand, it is not certain if this would significantly extend our knowledge about Jesus himself. The very fact that such sources are used by the NT evangelists means that the information they contain is already part of the canonical gospel tradition. Awareness of the existence of such activity may sensitize us to the variety of early Christian 'gospel'-making activity, and alert us to different ways in which various Christians presented different parts of the Jesus tradition with different emphases.[47] But on its own, such awareness will not necessarily significantly affect our knowledge of Jesus: it will simply alert us (if we need alerting!) to the complexity of the process of moving back from the NT gospels to recovering information about Jesus himself.[48]

However, apart from possible 'gospel'-type sources of the canonical gospels, it is very uncertain whether other non-canonical gospels are to

---

[46] Possible written sources have been variously postulated: e.g. a parables collection used in Mark 4, a 'Signs source' lying behind the present Johannine miracle stories, one or more accounts of the passion narrative used by the evangelists, etc.

[47] Note the apparent absence of a passion narrative in Q, which has led some to argue that those who preserved the Q tradition may have had less of a cross-centred idea of the Christian message than, say, Paul or John.

[48] Although one should not underestimate the hermeneutical significance of prioritizing different parts of the tradition in one's interpretation of Jesus: the Jesus of Q (or of some parts of Q) might be rather different from the Jesus of Mark.

be regarded as significant in this respect. As already noted, much has been made of texts such as the *Gospel of Thomas*, the *Gospel of Peter*, Papyrus Egerton 2, the *Dialogue of the Saviour* and others as potentially preserving authentic (or at least very early) traditions about Jesus independently of the canonical gospels.[49] Yet in each case, others have argued in some detail that the present form of many of these texts presupposes the texts of the canonical gospels themselves and hence they must post-date the NT gospels and represent a development of the tradition subsequent to those gospels.[50]

Perhaps the text that has given rise to the most debate in this context is the *Gospel of Thomas*. Many have argued that versions of many of the sayings in *Thomas* are independent of parallel versions found in the synoptics, and hence may give us a valuable extra source for recovering information about Jesus.[51] On the other hand, others have pointed out that in some cases, the versions of sayings in *Thomas* seem to presuppose the redactional activity of one of the synoptic evangelists, thus indicating that the text must represent a stage in the developing tradition after that of the canonical gospel concerned.[52]

Others have pointed out that, on its own, such evidence may simply show that some *parts* of *Thomas* presuppose the synoptic gospels; but other parts of the text may still be independent and valuable as a potential witness to Jesus. Further, the full text of *Thomas* is only available to us in a relatively late (fourth-century) Coptic MS. The growing influence of the NT gospels as canonical texts may then have influenced the text of *Thomas* so that those who transmitted and/or translated the text may have at times assimilated its text to that of the canonical gospels. Agreements between *Thomas* and the NT gospels may thus reflect scribal influences in the (later) transmission of the text of *Thomas* rather than the original text of the gospel itself.[53]

Against this it may be argued in part that the case for the dependency of *Thomas* on the synoptics depends not just on the Coptic version of *Thomas* from Nag Hammadi. In one instance the Greek fragments of *Thomas* from Oxyrhynchus show agreement with a redactional element in the

[49] See generally Crossan 1991; Koester 1990; for the *Gospel of Thomas*, see Patterson 1993.
[50] For the *Gospel of Peter*, see Brown 1994:1317–49; for Papyrus Egerton 2, see Neirynck 1991; for the *Dialogue of the Saviour*, see Tuckett 1986:128–35; for the *Gospel of Thomas*, see Tuckett 1988 and others.
[51] See the work of the Jesus Seminar entitled *The Five Gospels* (Funk and Hoover 1993): the 'five' gospels are the canonical four together with the *Gospel of Thomas*.
[52] See Tuckett 1988, with further references to others who have pointed to the same evidence.
[53] This is essentially the argument of Patterson 1993:92–3 (with others).

synoptics.[54] Hence the possible dependence of *Thomas* on the synoptics can be traced back to the earliest – Greek – stage of the Thomas tradition available to us. Further, the fact that at least some redactional elements from the synoptics reappear in *Thomas* in some sayings makes it at least possible to assume that, in instances where *Thomas* parallels material which is not necessarily redactional in the synoptics, the agreements are to be explained in the same way. Issues about the *Gospel of Thomas* are still being debated.[55] The secondary literature generated by this text is now enormous, and there is certainly no unanimity about its value in relation to discussions about Jesus and the earliest stages of the Jesus tradition.

It may be that the greatest contribution of the 'other', non-canonical gospels is to throw light on the period *after* the time of the writing of the canonical gospels and to enable us to see something of the ways in which early Christians used and developed their traditions and beliefs about Jesus in this period. Even if they tell us little about the figure of Jesus himself, they may be far more interesting and fascinating for the light they throw on later periods of Christian history, in some cases (e.g. in the second century) when other sources are sadly lacking.

[54] P. Oxy. 654 lines 29–30 agrees verbatim with Luke 8.17, which represents Luke's redaction of Mark 4.22. At the very least, we cannot 'blame' everything (for making the *Gospel of Thomas* look as if it might be dependent on the synoptic gospels) on the Coptic translator!

[55] For an important essay, highlighting all the major issues and also sensitive to the significance of continuing oral tradition in this context, see Uro 1998.

CHAPTER 14

The One, the Four and the many

Ronald A. Piper

The existence and use of multiple sources of tradition about Jesus in the first and second centuries CE has been clearly demonstrated in the earlier chapters of this volume. Few scholars would be so bold as to claim that an accurate inventory of such sources can actually be compiled today, but this is because many such sources failed to be preserved. Furthermore, a continuing oral tradition is likely to have existed alongside written 'gospels' and other documents incorporating Jesus tradition. Even if some such sources circulated widely amongst Christians in the ancient Mediterranean, it is probable that particular groups or networks of Christians adopted favourite sources of tradition. Insofar as this was the case, the sources of Jesus tradition may not have been merely complementary to one another, but may actually have been in competition with one another.

Yet by the latter half of the second century, Irenaeus argued forcefully for a fourfold gospel, consisting of the four gospels widely recognized as 'canonical' today. How did the choice of these four (the Gospels according to Matthew, Mark, Luke and John) achieve clear support at such an early stage? We shall see that there were many reasons for leaders in the early church to be concerned about the Jesus tradition being used for purposes that they considered theologically suspect. These concerns resulted in efforts to exercise some control over groups or networks choosing their own 'favourites' and over the multiplication of new authoritative sources of Jesus tradition. Yet there were also attempts, as in the case of Marcion, to create a radical reduction of the Jesus tradition to a portrayal considered by early church fathers to be too narrow and too distorted. The conflicting tendencies for the early church to be attracted to an ever-expanding pool of information about Jesus, on the one hand, and to become attached to particular 'favourites' or harmonies, on the other, makes all the more interesting the decisive step reflected in Irenaeus' writings to opt for precisely four gospels as authoritative. It is this step that will be explored in the present chapter.

'THE MANY'

The term 'gospel' is attached to numerous texts surviving from the first five centuries of the Christian era. These works are varied in nature, however, and in many cases differ quite substantially from the four gospels subsequently recognized as canonical. I can only briefly indicate a selection of these works here. The *Infancy Gospel of Thomas*, for example, provides legends about the early activities of Jesus as a child. The *Gospel of Truth*, however, is described by Koester (Koester 1990:22–3) as a 'homily' or 'meditation', deriving probably from the Gnostic Valentinus, and owing the term 'gospel' in its incipit to its purported message of salvation rather than to similarity in genre with the New Testament canonical Gospel literature. The *Gospel of Thomas*, which does purport to record a collection of sayings of Jesus, refers to itself in its incipit as '*the secret sayings* which the living Jesus spoke and which Didymus Judas Thomas wrote down' (*Gos. Thom.* 1; NHC II 32, 10–11, from Koester 1990:21). Thus it did not appear originally to call itself a 'gospel'; rather the title *Gospel of Thomas* seems to derive from the colophon of a later scribe or translator at the end of the document. Other works that preserve purported teaching of Jesus, such as the *Dialogue of the Saviour* (again from the Nag Hammadi Library), do not employ the term 'gospel' at all as a self-designation. Thus the mere designation of a work as 'gospel' tells one little about whether the work is similar in scope or even contains material comparable to the New Testament canonical Gospel literature.[1] The use of the term 'gospel' for the 'good news of salvation' undoubtedly has contributed to the difficulty of associating it with the designation of a specific genre.[2]

Some scholars, such as J. D. Crossan, have sought to identify a number of ostensibly lost or embedded sources that circulated prior to and perhaps alongside the New Testament gospels. For example, Crossan (Crossan 1985:132–3) finds embedded in the *Gospel of Peter* – a narrative preserving part of the passion and resurrection stories – three units of material that are independent of and sources for our 'intracanonical' gospels. He calls this early source of tradition about Jesus' passion the *Cross Gospel*, used by all

---

[1] Koester 1990: xxxi distinguishes between the earliest stages of the history and development of the gospel literature (which includes Q, the *Gospel of Thomas*, the *Dialogue of the Saviour*, the *Unknown Gospel of Papyrus Egerton 2*, the *Apocryphon of James* and the *Gospel of Peter*) and the later stages (the Jewish-Christian Gospels, the *Epistula Apostolorum*, the *Gospel of Nicodemus* and other non-canonical gospels and gospel fragments).

[2] See Gundry 1996:321–5 for the use of 'gospel' for a book, particularly analysing usage prior to Marcion, partly in response to Koester 1989a. Hengel 2000: 61, though, notes that 'in the first half of the second century references to the "Gospel" as a writing are relatively rare'.

four canonical gospels as well as the *Gospel of Peter*.[3] Equally controversial is
Crossan's use of traditions from the *Secret Gospel of Mark*, mentioned by
Clement of Alexandria in a copy of a letter said to have been recently
discovered (and lost) by Morton Smith (Crossan 1985: 90–121).

Apart from such elusive sources, individual sayings attributed to Jesus,
but without parallel in the New Testament gospels, are found scattered in
several early Christian documents.[4] An example is the saying in Acts 20.35
that it is more blessed to give than to receive (see also *1 Clem.* 2.8; 13.1; *Did.*
8.2). Such scattered sayings strongly suggest the continuing presence of an
oral tradition of Jesus sayings, which may have circulated through early
prophets or teachers.[5] The importance of 'sayings' of Jesus is noted in many
early written works. The early-to-mid-second-century bishop Papias of
Hierapolis[6] referred frequently to what Peter, Mark or the presbyters
'remembered' (see Koester 1990: 32–4). Matthew too is said to have written
down 'the sayings' (*ta logia*), which implicitly refer to the continuing
authority of the oral transmission of traditions about Jesus and Jesus'
words. Koester (Koester 1990:38–43), however, detects a shift in emphasis
with Justin Martyr. By designating the gospels as the 'memoirs of the
apostles' and by indicating that it is these that are to be 'read' in worship
(*1 Apol.* 67.3–4), Justin begins to support the use of the written gospels over
against oral traditions.[7] While this provides an important landmark in the
relative value attached to oral and written gospel traditions, it is very
difficult to determine how long oral traditions in practice continued to
have currency alongside written traditions.[8]

The richness and variety of the traditions about Jesus that were likely to
have existed and circulated in the first two centuries CE provide an important context for our considerations in this chapter. Yet by the time of
Irenaeus there emerged a clear bid for recognition of just a four-fold gospel.
What accounts for such a development? To reach a clearer understanding
of this, one must consider one of the fundamental problems of multiple
sources of tradition about Jesus. While ostensibly adding richness to the

---

[3] Crossan 1985:132 also cites in support Cameron 1982:78 and Koester 1980:128–9. See the critique,
  however, in Koester 1990: 218–20.
[4] For a discussion of *Papyrus Egerton 2* ('The Unknown Gospel'), see Stanton 2002:132–3; and Koester
  1980:119–26.
[5] See, for example, Delobel's review of extra-canonical sayings of Jesus in Petersen 1989 (Delobel 1989).
[6] Known from fragments in Eusebius, *Hist. Eccl.* 3.39.3–4.
[7] Koester cites *1 Apol.* 66.3; *Dial.* 10.2 and 100.1. Justin also appears to refer to a record of the *Acts of
  Pilate* in *1 Apol.* 35.9; cf. 48.3. Koester argues that Justin never calls the kerygma itself 'gospel', even
  though Justin does promulgate a kerygmatic statement in *1 Apol.* 31.7.
[8] See Hagner 1985, esp. 250–2.

fabric of early Christianity, in fact a multiplicity of Jesus traditions supported the rise of serious rivalries, not simply about what Jesus did and said but about the nature of the kerygma and Christian faith. Such divergent representations of Christian belief and practice sometimes resulted, as will be discussed, in a process of 'selection' of favoured Jesus traditions by both proponents and opponents. One response to a seemingly uncontrolled diversity of texts and traditions was a move towards establishing an authoritative selection.

AWAY FROM 'THE MANY' AND TOWARDS 'THE ONE'

The suggested tendency of various individuals or groups to have favourite texts is hardly surprising. Even within later canonical discussion, it has not been uncommon to speak of a 'canon within the canon'. Luther, for example, certainly valued Romans more than he valued James. If a selection of preferences has operated within the relatively stable confines of the later New Testament canon, how much more might it have operated within a more fluid situation where the number of texts and traditions was even greater and before a 'canon' was established?

We obtain glimpses of the selective championing of Jesus traditions in some of the writings of the church fathers. Martin Hengel (Hengel 2000:16–18) draws attention to Clement of Alexandria's argument at the close of the second century with Julius Cassian (a Valentinian Gnostic), in which Julius Cassian supports a call for sexual abstinence by citing a conversation between Jesus and Salome about abolishing the distinction between the sexes. Clement notes that this tradition does not occur 'in the four gospels that have been handed down to us, but in that according to the Egyptians' (*Strom.* 3.92 and 3.93.1 (GCS 2.238.27f.)). Nevertheless, Hengel (Hengel 2000:17–19) argues that Clement strikes a distinctive Alexandrian balance between recognizing the fourfold gospel that has been 'handed down' and taking other apocryphal gospels seriously in his discussion with opponents. Clement also quotes elsewhere from the *Gospel of the Hebrews* and other apocryphal traditions. Even more strikingly, Clement seems to acknowledge the Gnostic claim of an esoteric tradition ('gnosis') being handed down by the resurrected Lord to James, John and Peter, but he goes on to claim that they in turn handed it on to the other apostles and the Seventy. Clement thus effectively subverts the Gnostics' claim to their own *secret* teaching of the risen Jesus by suggesting that it was available to all. These examples from the work of Clement of Alexandria provide evidence for some groups of Christians around the end of the second century appealing to special Jesus traditions in support of their distinctive claims. Thus, on the one hand, we find a multiplicity of the traditions still in use. On the other hand, we see some instances of the *selective* preference for particular traditions that lead to the promulgation of distinctive practices or beliefs amongst these opponents of Clement. Clement's own response is perhaps rather distinctive of the intellectual life of Alexandria. His reference to the fourfold gospel that is 'handed down' reflects the fact that by the end of the second century it was possible to attempt to counter one's opponents' selection of Jesus traditions with an 'authorized' selection of Jesus traditions, the four gospels. Yet unlike Irenaeus, whom we shall consider below, Clement appears to be willing to interact with a wider variety of gospel traditions. It would still be some time before a 'canon' was firmly established.

A much more radical step was taken in the first half of the second century by Marcion. Marcion was a wealthy shipowner who settled in Rome ca. 140 CE and who was persuaded that the original message of Jesus had been severely distorted and corrupted in almost all forms in which it was preserved. He held the conviction that Jesus' original message had completely broken free from the Torah and the prophets, just as Paul himself had declared Christ to be the 'end of the law'. Even though this was true of the 'original' message of Jesus, in Marcion's view the church had subsequently introduced Jewish ideas into Jesus' proclamation and had misguidedly tried to understand Jesus' message as fulfilling Old Testament prophecies and motifs. Marcion therefore sought to construct an authoritative collection of writings, in effect a 'Bible', with two parts: a single Gospel, and the 'Apostle' (ten Pauline letters). H. von Campenhausen (Campenhausen 1972:153–5) notes that there was no antecedent for such a collection or existing rationale to reinforce it.[9] Interestingly, Marcion clearly felt that such an authoritative collection did require a gospel and could not simply rely upon Pauline writings. Despite his appreciation of Paul as the preserver of the true 'gospel', he could not do without a 'Gospel' account of Jesus' words. Thus he set about selecting one.

Marcion's choice of Luke's gospel as the basis for the allegedly 'original' gospel is interesting. While Luke was considered a companion of Paul, and thus Luke's gospel was a good candidate on those grounds,

---

[9] Thus Campenhausen 1972: 163 (along with Harnack and Knox) tends to view Marcion as the catalyst, at least in conception, for the creation of the Christian canon of scripture. Hengel 2000: 32, however, speculates that Luke–Acts might already be a 'Gospel' and 'Apostolikon'. The same might apply to the Gospel of John and the three letters of John, Hengel suggests, published together at the beginning of the second century.

H. von Campenhausen rightly observes (Campenhausen 1972:158) that Marcion was actually critical of Luke himself for distorting the gospel.[10] Hence Luke's gospel had to be subjected to critical editing by Marcion, mutilation in the eyes of his opponents, in order to remove lingering Judaizing tendencies. It is perhaps not surprising that even Paul's letters required critical editing for Marcion. Matthew, which was probably the gospel in widest use and circulation, was too wedded to Jewish ways of thinking to be an appropriate candidate for the 'original' gospel, and Mark was probably too lacking in sayings material. Mark was also linked by Papias to Peter, who like Matthew might have been considered a Judaizing apostle. Campenhausen (Campenhausen 1972:159–60) speculates that John might have been more to Marcion's liking, particularly with its strong attacks upon 'the Jews', but he suggests that it might have been rejected by Marcion because of other 'offensive' associations with Jewish symbols and doubts about its age and authenticity. The latter disadvantages would also have been considered to apply to the *Gospel of Peter*, and of course the Jewish Christian apocryphal gospels would have had little chance of being judged suitable by Marcion.

The fact that Marcion not only selected a *single* gospel for his authority but also undertook radical editing of it in order to eliminate legalistic and Judaizing tendencies – including references to Hebrew scriptures – might seem exceptionally bold. Yet Campenhausen (Campenhausen 1972:160) observes that this may have been no bolder that what Matthew or Luke did to their likely source, Mark. The difference is that Marcion's editing is confined to excision rather than addition of new material. His work of restoration was not to add or create material congenial to his viewpoint; it was to recover the portrayal of Jesus that he considered had been obscured by the additions of others.

The attractiveness of what Marcion achieved should not be overlooked. Amidst the confusing proliferation of traditions and texts about Jesus, Marcion provided a simple and clear point of focus for understanding Jesus. Furthermore, that focus was closely aligned with the 'gospel' (*kerygma*) found by Marcion in Paul. Rather than dealing with the confusions and contradictions of varied texts and *kerygmata*, a unified understanding was promulgated by a purged and unified set of authoritative writings.[11] A single 'restored'

---

[10] Campenhausen 1972:159 also notes that 'Marcion supplied no attribution for his corrected text of Luke, but described it simply as "Gospel"'.

[11] This notwithstanding, note Campenhausen's discussion of the efforts of Marcion's disciples to supplement his 'canon' (Campenhausen 1972:163).

gospel reinforced the powerful message found in Paul. An antipathy to Judaizing features, including the Old Testament, was not exclusive to Marcion. It is also found among the Valentinians. Quite apart from the obvious usefulness in clarifying the identity of 'Christians' *vis-à-vis* 'Jews' in the second century, the intellectual and moral issues raised by the Old Testament and its God were widely viewed as problematic well after the time of Marcion. Lest this be considered simply a problem of ancient times, Hengel (Hengel 2000:33) draws attention to the persisting seductiveness of Marcion's solution for German liberal Protestantism of the late nineteenth and early twentieth centuries.

It is arguable that the most powerful early responses to Marcion were also fundamentally reductionist in character. But before discussing these, it is perhaps useful to consider another attempt to limit an uncontrolled diversity of Jesus traditions by reduction to a 'single' gospel, this time by synthesis rather than by extreme selection and excision. This was the *Diatessaron* attributed to Tatian. Tatian was a student of Justin Martyr in Rome. Justin himself published his two *Apologies* in Rome about a decade after Marcion's excommunication in 144 CE and appears to have published a book directly against Marcion that has not survived. Nevertheless, Koester (Koester 1990:36–7) suggests that it is hardly coincidental that Justin avoids quoting Paul in his surviving works (in contrast to his predecessors), firmly links the 'memoirs of the apostles' to the law and the prophets, and quotes from Matthew as well as Luke. In these features we may see a reaction to Marcion and his followers.

It is more difficult to develop a clear view of how Tatian might have related to these controversies (see Petersen 1990:404–5). Tatian was a convert to Christianity, originally from 'the East', but he eventually became a student in Rome under Justin. According to Irenaeus, who mentions Tatian but intriguingly not the *Diatessaron*, Tatian was expelled by the Christian community in Rome after Justin's death[12] for being an Encratite and follower of Valentinus. Encratites are credited with rejecting marriage, abstaining from meat and denying the salvation of Adam. Interestingly, C. D. Allert (Allert 1999:5–6) has recently advocated that any evidence for ascetic Encratite or Valentinian ideologies in the *Diatessaron* is limited at best.[13]

---

[12] Approximately 172 CE, according to Eusebius. See Petersen 1994:427, who dates the *Diatessaron*'s composition to between 165 and 180 CE, but most probably between 172 and 175 CE.

[13] The same is noted for Tatian's *Oratio ad Graecos*. But see Petersen 1990: 428, 430, and below.

With regard to the *Diatessaron* itself, it is from Eusebius that we first learn of the connection between Tatian and the composition of the *Diatessaron*. Eusebius, in the early fourth century, noted the name *Diatessaron* and indicated that it was 'still extant in some places' (*Hist. Eccl.* 4.29.6; see Allert 1999:7). In fact, it appears to have been widely used in Syria well into the fifth and sixth centuries. Unfortunately, despite its apparent popularity, no text of it survives. Thus our knowledge of it is largely through other witnesses. More strikingly, Petersen (Petersen 1990: 403–4) notes that it is the most ancient of the versions (texts translated from the original Greek) of the gospels and

is quite probably the form in which the gospels first appeared in Syriac, Latin, Armenian and Georgian. As such, it occupies a unique position in the history of the dissemination of the gospels.

As the name *Diatessaron* suggests, the work is essentially a gospel harmony. Perhaps using the Gospel according to Matthew as its skeletal structure (Petersen 1990:430),[14] it certainly brings together the texts of Matthew, Mark, Luke and John into a *single* 'synthesized' gospel account. These four gospels constitute the primary sources for Tatian's work. What is less clear is the extent to which the *Diatessaron* also reflects some use of other sources, particularly from the Jewish Christian gospel tradition. For example, the reference in the *Diatessaron* to a great light after Jesus' baptism by John is not found in any of the four gospels, but Epiphanius indicates that it existed in the (lost) *Gospel of the Ebionites*. As Petersen (Petersen 1990:422–3) carefully notes, this suggests either that Tatian used (directly or indirectly) the *Gospel of the Ebionites* here, or else that both the extra-canonical gospel and the *Diatessaron* were dependent upon some other source.[15]

That other source may have been an earlier harmony produced or used by Justin Martyr, Tatian's teacher. Justin knows this particular reading about the great light, as revealed in *Dial.* 88.3. Furthermore, the fact that Justin's quotations of the Jesus tradition at times reveal a harmonization of accounts from Matthew and Luke suggests that Tatian may have had a

---

[14] But Hengel 2000:137 states that Tatian 'bases the *Diatessaron* on the Johannine framework'.

[15] The title *Diatessaron* first appears in Eusebius' *Historia Ecclesiastica*. While Rufinus' Latin translation of Eusebius explains the title as *unum ex quattuor*, the fourth-century Syriac translation explains that it was also known as 'the Gospel of the mixed' (see Allert 1999:7). Because there was no earlier or consistent reference to the title *Diatessaron*, it cannot with certainty be claimed that Tatian was originally restricted to the use of only four sources (the four canonical gospels) on the basis of the title of the work.

predecessor in Justin for his efforts at harmonization.[16] If so, however, a harmony from Justin may well have been compiled with rather specific motives, for Justin was determined to use gospel traditions (including some traditions extraneous to the four gospels) to demonstrate the fulfilment of scriptural prophecies. Even so, as Koester (Koester 1990:402) argues:

> many gospels would not do, either for Marcion or for Justin. While Marcion reduces the record to one single purified gospel, Justin includes as much tradition as is possible. A gospel harmony is the answer, and Justin reveals the process of its composition ... Had Justin prevailed, and not Irenaeus, a harmony of the available gospel literature would have been the answer.

Koester's statement highlights one of the particular advantages of gospel harmonies. Harmonies are a means of being inclusive of several sources of tradition. Yet they achieve this by interweaving the sources into a single 'coherent' account. The reader therefore receives the best of both worlds. The gospel story draws upon favourite traditions drawn from a wide pool of sources. Yet the gospel reader also has a helpfully prepared account of how it all fits together. Moreover, one only needs to possess one document and not many.

In addition, as suggested above, the reader has a reasonably convincing account to offer to critics of how a consistent story of Jesus can be derived from the sometimes confusing and contrasting perspectives that are found in differing gospels. Harmonies can indicate solutions to apparent contradictions in the various gospels. Duplications of stories can be reduced, with the various details being woven together into a single account. The sequence of episodes is also clarified. It is small wonder that the *Diatessaron* had considerable popularity in the early centuries of the church,[17] even when recognition of the authority of the four gospels became largely accepted. On the surface, use of the *Diatessaron* involved no disloyalty to these other gospels. It simply provided a convenient and quite useful compendium.

Yet harmonies should probably not be understood simply as an exercise in sticking pieces together, a kind of jigsaw puzzle. Justin's harmonizations were, as suggested above, linked to an apparent desire to counter the work of Marcion and to highlight correspondences between the gospel texts and the Old Testament scripture. Tatian's harmony may betray occasional

---

[16] For the view that there were written gospel harmonies before Justin, see Bellinzoni 1967:139–42.

[17] The surviving witnesses to the *Diatessaron* range over many centuries, and they show how it was translated into several different languages.

influences of an Encratite agenda.[18] The opportunity to retell the gospel story through harmonization, including editorial additions and deletions, is an opportunity to provide an interpretation of that story. At the very least, it is an opportunity to introduce 'spin'. This, of course, was not the sole prerogative of full-scale harmonies of gospel sources. Even in scribal efforts of copying texts one finds evidence of harmonization and clarification.[19] But full-scale harmonies allowed and encouraged a reworking of the text on a much greater scale. For a significant element of the early church, the *Diatessaron* was a more acceptable reworking and reduction of the gospel sources than the efforts of Marcion, but it was a reduction and a re-shaping of the gospel tradition none the less.

IRENAEUS AND THE ARTICULATION OF THE FOURFOLD GOSPEL

The second-century church father Irenaeus, the bishop of Lyons, articulated an alternative to either the unrestrained competition of multiple sources of Jesus tradition or the reduction of such sources to a single source as in the case of Marcion. Unfortunately, Irenaeus does not provide us with a clear comment on the harmonization of the *Diatessaron*. This is an intriguing puzzle, because while Irenaeus was fully aware of Tatian, he made no reference to the *Diatessaron*. Did he not know of it, or did he have early hesitations about it? If the latter, was it the genre with which he was concerned, or did he detect a potentially dangerous agenda in its editing? Although any answer to such questions is speculative, it is clear that Irenaeus offers a different solution to the church's use of the gospel traditions.

Campenhausen (Campenhausen 1972:170–1) persuasively argued that the problem to be tackled by the early church with respect to its use of gospel traditions was one of 'standardization'. Certainly a good case can be made for this in relation to Irenaeus. He opposed the uncontrolled use of many gospels, not least because this played all too easily into the hands of groups like the Valentinians, who claimed to have their own authoritative sources of tradition. A fluidity of gospel sources offered nothing normative

---

[18] Petersen 1990: 430 discusses the motif of Encratism in Tatian's work and suggestions that an attempt to 'distance Jesus from Judaism' might also be perceived (in contrast to Justin). It appears that the genealogies which linked Jesus to the Davidic lineage were removed in Tatian's work. Nevertheless, Petersen observes that 'the *Diatessaron* was not anti-nomian or pro-Pauline'. See also Petersen 1994: 440–1, 443–4.

[19] Arguing that the same liberty associated with editorial activity for apocryphal texts should be expected to reflect what happened to the synoptic gospels, see Bovon 1988.

at all, particularly if new gospels could appear at any time, and this presented an increasing problem in a situation of competition between various parties with quite different stances in relation to theology, organization and ethos.

Another interesting illustration of this kind of concern is found at the very end of the second century when the *Gospel of Peter* appears to have been used by the church at Rhossos in Syria. Its use was explicitly approved by Serapion, the bishop of Antioch. However, it is recorded by Eusebius that Serapion later withdrew authority for its use, apparently not previously having read it, when he became aware of docetic heretical views associated with the document.[20] Even so, Campenhausen (Campenhausen 1972:170) notes a continuing influence of the *Gospel of Peter* in Syria in the third century, citing the Syrian *Didascalia* and statements attributed to the pagan Celsus. The Serapion incident testifies to the strength of interest or 'curiosity' in new and different gospel writings in the early church, to the tendency to establish favourite gospels, and to the kinds of concerns that arise for church authorities in a rather fluid situation in which many gospels are recognized and in use.[21]

On the other hand, Irenaeus also opposed the reduction of the gospel tradition to a single gospel, heavily edited in ways that might allow it to bend to individual persuasions. This option was of course employed effectively by Marcion to promulgate his views, but it might also be said to apply to the general approach of Tatian. Indeed, even if Irenaeus had no objection to the *Diatessaron* as such, he may well have perceived how the dangers associated with Marcion's creation of a single gospel might also have applied in principle to the creation of a single gospel harmony.

Irenaeus' preferred alternative was defence of a collection of *precisely four* authorized gospels. Here was another way to gain control over the gospel tradition in its varied and competing manifestations. Irenaeus is a particularly valuable source in this respect, because he not only testifies to use of four gospels as authoritative, but also argues the case in his work *Adversus Haereses* (ca. 185 CE).

---

[20] *Hist. Eccl.* 6.12.4–6.
[21] Hengel 2000:112–14 reflects upon the strong desire that existed at the end of the first century and in the early decades of the second century for a plurality of gospel traditions and the theological multiplicity that often accompanied this. He observes that by the second half of the second century such a situation was considered almost 'too lively', because of concerns about splits and heresies. Thus the mainstream church became 'more and more consolidated by the *regula fidei* and the *monarchical episcopate*' (p. 114) and introduced a restriction upon the multiplicity of gospel-like writings.

Irenaeus' solution to the question of authoritative gospels had both strengths and weaknesses. The primary weakness was that the four gospels that he identified as authoritative do not always tell the same story. This left the church open to claims (by the 'false teachers'!) that the gospels contradict one another. One only needs to ask whether Jesus' action to 'cleanse' the Temple was located at the start of his ministry (as in John) or at the end (as in the synoptic gospels). If the gospels are contradictory, then how can they be normative for the church? As Stanton (Stanton 1995:110) notes: 'By opting for four written Gospels instead of one, many Christians in the second half of the second century decided to live with the historical complications which ensued, even though critics were throwing the discrepancies in their faces.' Irenaeus and others of course developed strategies to try to cope with such criticisms, but their willingness to accept the option of four authoritative gospels testifies to the unacceptability of the main alternatives – the one and the many. Indeed, Irenaeus actually defended the use of *four* gospels by highlighting the errors that could result from relying upon just *one* gospel. In effect, he played off different groups of opponents against one another – the Ebionites, who relied on Matthew, the Marcionites, who relied on Luke, some docetists who allegedly relied on Mark and the Valentinians, who relied on John (see Campenhausen 1972:196).[22]

Another, perhaps less obvious, difficulty with accepting four gospels as authoritative is the fact that these gospels were themselves not entirely welcomed with an equal sense of readiness throughout all parts of the early church. Matthew's gospel, with its impressive Sermon on the Mount, its interest in showing Jesus as the fulfilment of scripture, its purported authorship by one of the Twelve and its incorporation of most of Mark's gospel, had wide circulation. As Stanton observes (Stanton 1995:102–3), Matthew may well have been the only gospel which was largely above suspicion and in wide use. Mark was thought to have been only secondarily derived from Peter, and it was largely supplanted by Matthew. Luke contained more teaching material of general interest than Mark, including many distinctive and attractive parables, but Luke was thought to be dependent upon Paul. Doubts about John's gospel arose in no small measure from its popularity not only in Gnostic circles but also amongst the charismatic Montanists.[23] A commitment to these four gospels

[22] For doubts about the connections that Irenaeus makes between particular gospels and particular heresies, see Campenhausen 1972:197 n. 250.

[23] Stanton 1997:324 also notes the necessity for a strong defence of the Fourth Gospel in the Muratorian Fragment and the doubts expressed in the second half of the second century about the Fourth Gospel by the Alogi and the anti Montanist Gaius.

therefore risked a commitment to some potentially weak links. The safer option might have been a commitment to Matthew's gospel alone. Once again, we find that the rejection of this option might well have reflected in part a sensitivity by Irenaeus to falling into the trap of his opponents in relying too greatly on a single gospel.

To proceed further, we need to look at (a) the terms in which Irenaeus justifies the selection of the four gospels, (b) how he complements this selection with the 'canon of truth' and the concept of a single 'gospel', and (c) how far another major factor in opting for use of these four gospels was the extent to which these gospels had begun to overcome their varying degrees of early acceptance and had already begun to be viewed together by the time of Irenaeus.

Irenaeus' justification for the authoritative use of precisely four gospels operated on several levels.[24] Firstly, Irenaeus drew attention to the circumstances in which the Gospels according to Matthew, Mark, Luke and John were created (*Haer.* 3.1.1). Each was said to have an apostolic connection, even if at one remove, and each was claimed to be older than later-appearing works relied upon by Irenaeus' opponents. Provenance and antiquity were therefore significant issues, although one might imagine that Irenaeus' opponents would have claimed apostolic provenance for some of their own distinctive gospels.[25] Secondly, Irenaeus appealed to the consistency and soundness of the truth that these four writings convey (*Haer.* 3.1.2). We shall return to this claim shortly, because Irenaeus' formulation of this truth is carefully crafted to put his opponents on the wrong foot and raises the issue of 'the canon of truth'. He does, however, add to his argument the assertion that the church recognizes these four gospels as the *only* 'true and reliable' ones (*Haer.* 3.11.8–9). Thirdly, Irenaeus employs an oft-quoted argument that operates on a cosmological level:

Since there are four directions of the world, and four principal winds . . . it is only reasonable that she [the church] has four pillars . . . From which it is clear that the Logos . . . gave us the Gospel in four forms but united with one spirit. (*Haer.* 3.11.8)

He goes on to cite the four living creatures of Revelation 4, the four-faced cherubim of Ezekiel 1 and the four principal covenants as further illustrations of the significance of four in the divine economy. Such an appeal to symbolism

---

[24] What follows is helpfully amplified in Campenhausen 1972:195–201.

[25] Also see McDonald 1988:146–8, 152–5. McDonald draws attention to H. Koester's (Koester 1980:105–30) case that on the basis of 'antiquity' several extra-canonical gospels compare well with the dating of the canonical gospels, especially the *Egerton Papyrus* ('The Unknown Gospel'), the *Dialogue of the Saviour*, the *Apocryphon of John*, the *Gospel of Peter* and the *Gospel of Thomas*.

may seem to the modern reader to be highly artificial (see McDonald 1988:96). Yet it attempted to legitimate the fourfold gospel in terms of the very structure of the universe and of salvation history. In doing so, it evoked an image of stability and universality, precisely the concepts that Irenaeus sought to establish for these particular gospels in his effort to make them the norm and standard for the church as a whole. The power for his readers of the symbols to which he appeals for universality should not be underestimated. This point has recently been underscored by Stanton (Stanton 1997:320), who appeals to the gateway called the Tetrapylon in the influential city of Aphrodisias, which was completed slightly before Irenaeus wrote. Its four highly decorative columns testify to the archetypal images that Irenaeus sought to evoke.

Not to be overlooked, however, is Irenaeus' reference (quoted above) to 'the Gospel in four forms but united with one spirit'. The plurality is not uncontrolled. Such a formula is characteristic of Irenaeus' vocabulary. He regularly refers to 'the gospel' in the singular and very rarely to 'four gospels'. We noted earlier how Irenaeus was concerned, against opponents, to affirm the unity of the four gospels, not least because this was one of the potential weaknesses of the option that he adopted. The presentation of a 'fourfold gospel', in effect a *single* 'gospel' in fourfold form, was an attempt to match the reassurance that a 'single' gospel offered. Yet at the same time he retained a limited plurality of gospels that distinguished his stance from that of some of his key opponents, such as Marcion, and that gave some recognition to the general popularity of multiple traditions.

Irenaeus was probably not unique in his day in suggesting that the four gospels were in effect a 'single gospel'. Many scholars have also drawn attention to the titles given to the gospels, namely 'the Gospel according to ... ', in discussions showing how unity was recognized in plurality. Evidence for such usage can be found at the end of the second century in $\mathfrak{P}^{66}$ and $\mathfrak{P}^{75}$, as well as in the Muratorian Fragment. The usage implies some breadth of recognition of a singular 'gospel' in multiple forms. Hengel (Hengel 2000:59) argues that this unusual formulation was already in use in the middle of the second century and that it was imitated also by apocryphal gospels.[26] If so, then it would be further preparation for the conviction of unity found in Irenaeus.

---

[26] Hengel 2000: 77, 97 speculates that the title 'Gospel according to ... ' originated with the circulation of Matthew in Syria, distinguishing this work from its source Mark; in contrast see Koester 1989a:373 n. 2. Stanton 1997: 332–3 states: 'In my judgement all three scholars [Hengel, Zahn and Harnack] have correctly insisted that from early in the second century there was a profound conviction that there was *one* Gospel "according to" individual evangelists.' Stanton further notes that as soon as Christian communities regularly used more than one gospel 'it would have been necessary to distinguish them by some form of title'.

The appeal to 'the Gospel in four forms but united with one spirit' implies a significant claim. It is not just an indication that the tensions or discrepancies in the case of these four works can be accommodated. It is also a positive insistence upon theological unity. Irenaeus argues: 'They have all declared to us that there is one God, Creator of heaven and earth, announced by the law and the prophets; and one Christ, the Son of God' (*Haer.* 3.1.1–2). This theological declaration is of course useful in locating the message of the fourfold gospel within Israel's salvation history and marking points of difference over against opponents such as Marcion and Valentinus. In effect, Irenaeus not only designates the gospels to be accepted as authoritative by the church but also sets the parameters within which they are to be interpreted. An understanding of the Gospel according to Luke or the Gospel according to John that sought to promulgate contrary views ignores the way in which the fourfold gospel is 'united'.[27] Reinforcing this, Irenaeus could engage at times in harmonizing or conflating passages from separate gospels in order to indicate what 'the Lord said' (Stanton 1997: 321).

Thus it is arguable that Irenaeus' defence of four gospels as authoritative could only succeed in providing a real alternative to the simpler solutions of Marcion or Tatian by engaging in a 'reductionist' approach too. There was *one* 'gospel' in fourfold form.[28] A stress upon the theological unity of the gospels, which also defined wherein that theological unity was to be found, provided a powerful base for tackling opponents.[29] Abraham (Abraham 1998:36) observes that even the development of a scriptural canon, on its own, was insufficient to counter the Gnostic challenge, precisely because the Gnostics were clever enough to use any list of authoritative scriptures in order to express their own theological convictions. A plurality of traditions made it even easier for them. Thus the 'rule of truth' of Irenaeus was an essential feature in his conflict with such opponents. An authoritative basis

---

[27] Stanton 1997: 320–1 draws attention to how Irenaeus elected to make his point particularly with reference to the gospel beginnings, where the variation between the gospels is greatest. It is interesting in this regard further to note that Tatian's *Diatessaron* seems to have neglected the beginnings of the gospels in creating a harmony. Is Irenaeus reacting to this? Furthermore, the beginnings of the gospels are rather key passages for legitimating Jesus, whether in terms of an extraordinary birth attended by signs (Matthew, Luke), the announcement and activities of the Baptist (Mark), or a declaration of cosmic origins (John).

[28] See also Koester 1989a: 381.

[29] Hengel 2000: 57–8 notes how Basilides of Alexandria (ca. 120–30), who apparently produced a 'commentary' on 'the gospel', including the Pauline 'gospel', had already affirmed a theological unity between several gospels (which may have included the four gospels and oral tradition) and Paul. Finding unity in multiplicity became an important way of controlling the centrifugal tendencies of the diverse sources of tradition.

for interpretation accompanied the authoritative sources. The truth conveyed by the fourfold gospel was integrated carefully into a view of the saving plan of God, and that saving plan permeated also the 'scripture' of the Old Testament, Acts and the Pauline letters.[30] The comprehensive view from which Irenaeus operated comprised a 'canon of truth' or 'rule of faith',[31] in effect the beliefs on which he understood the church to be founded.

A summary of this 'canon' appears in *Haer.* 1.10.1, which begins 'The Church, though dispersed throughout the whole world, even to the ends of the earth, has received from the apostles and their disciples this faith.' Irenaeus' confidence in the compatibility of his understanding of Christian truth and the gospel and apostolic sources he accepted as authoritative is also found in Book 2:

The preaching of the apostles, the authoritative teaching of the Lord, the announcements of the prophets, the dictated utterances of the apostles, and the ministration of the law – all of which praise one and the same Being, the God and Father of all, and not many diverse beings … are all in harmony with our statements. (*Haer* 2.35.4; cf. McDonald 1988: 93–4)

As McDonald (McDonald 1988:95) notes, these arguments are then further bolstered by appeal to apostolic succession as the guarantor of the truth having been handed down (*Haer.* 3.3.3). As the boundaries of the faith became more precisely drawn, in response to diverse theologies, so also the need to identify authoritative sources and guarantors for this faith arose. A limited plurality of gospel sources became accepted, but only when accompanied by the notion that they conveyed but one gospel, one canon of truth.[32]

THE FOUR BEFORE IRENAEUS

Many scholars have argued that Irenaeus' promulgation of the fourfold gospel is less an innovation than a reflection of the status that the Gospels

---

[30] Following Benoit, Campenhausen 1972: 201 notes, though, that 60 per cent of Irenaeus' 'New Testament' citations come from the 'fourfold gospel'.

[31] As in Tertullian, who also summarized Christian teaching in a way that set the boundaries for authentic belief against those whom he identified as the opponents of the church.

[32] McDonald 1988: 97 observes that the application of the criterion of 'truth' was applied in Serapion's rejection of the *Gospel of Peter*. Eusebius recorded that it was recognized that the *Gospel of Peter* 'was, for the most part, in accordance with the true teaching of the Saviour, but that *some things were added*'.

according to Matthew, Mark, Luke and John had already achieved prior to Irenaeus. Graham Stanton, whom this volume honours, has made a particular contribution to our understanding of how, by the time of Irenaeus, this precise set of four gospels had begun to be accepted as authoritative.

Even though there are no explicit statements about a fourfold gospel before Irenaeus, Stanton (Stanton 1997: 329–31) argues that the roots of this formulation can be found in the first half of the second century. Firstly, he draws attention to Justin. As previously noted, Justin refers to 'memoirs of the apostles' on several occasions, and in both his *1 Apology* and the *Dialogue with Trypho* he identifies them as 'written' gospels. Even though most scholars are only confident about Justin's use of Matthew and Luke (and possibly one reference to Mark), Stanton points to a seldom-noted passage in *Dial.* 103.8 that refers to two groups of authors of 'memoirs', both in the plural – 'the memoirs composed by his apostles and those who followed them'. Logically, this would suggest at least four compositions known to Justin in the category of 'memoirs'. Because Justin shows no knowledge of extra-canonical gospels, the supposition that this refers to Matthew and John (apostles) and Mark and Luke (those who followed apostles) is enticing.[33] Secondly, Stanton (Stanton 1997: 334) cites the use of *euangelion* for a 'writing' (*Did.* 8.2; 11.3; 15.3–4; Ign. *Smyrn.* 5.1; 7.2; *2 Clem.* 8.5) and the extension of this to a title ('the Gospel according to . . .') as also preparing for recognition of one gospel in multiple forms. It prepares for Irenaeus' fourfold gospel, even if it has not yet used Irenaeus' formulation. Thirdly, Stanton (Stanton 1997: 334) notes that the 'very early separation of Luke and Acts is another indication of the deep roots of the fourfold Gospel'. Even though it is not possible to date this separation precisely,[34] it clearly happened by the time of Irenaeus and the Muratorian Fragment. Marcion's use of Luke either reflected or aided such a separation.

A further piece of evidence often cited against Irenaeus being an innovator in his selection of Matthew, Mark, Luke and John as authoritative is the Muratorian Fragment. While this has traditionally been dated around the time of Irenaeus' work *Adversus Haereses*, some scholars have dated it in the fourth century rather than the second. Stanton (Stanton 1997: 322–35)

---

[33] Justin's use or composition of a harmony (noted above) is explained by Stanton 1997: 331–2 as probably being either for catechetical purposes or to counter critics. It is not evidence of a lack of appreciation for the individual written gospels.

[34] Stanton 1997: 334 notes that with the possible exception of $\mathfrak{P}^{53}$, there are no examples of Luke and Acts being juxtaposed in the same codex. See also Farmer and Farkasfalvy 1983: 72–3.

has criticized the arguments used by Sundberg and Hahneman for the later dating. For example, the Fragment's interest in the *Shepherd of Hermas* is more likely in the second century than the fourth, and its genre is less a canonical list than a series of introductory statements about the gospels. Unfortunately, the beginning of the Fragment has been lost, so that comments exist only for 'the Gospel according to Luke' and particularly for the 'fourth' of the gospels, John. The strong defence of the Fourth Gospel is also more easily seen in the context of second-century debates with the Alogi and with Gaius, as are some of the Fragment's statements in relation to the two parousias of Christ. If, as is likely, the Muratorian Fragment belongs to the time of Irenaeus, then it strengthens the likelihood that Irenaeus' comments are less an innovation than the reflection of ideas that had become current by his day.

Interestingly, there has been increasing discussion about how the way in which the gospels circulated may have contributed to this recognition. Stanton (Stanton 1997: 326) observes how the discovery of $\mathfrak{P}^{45}$, the Chester Beatty codex (early third century, containing the four gospels and Acts), led F. G. Kenyon to suggest that Irenaeus might well have had access to codices containing the four gospels. Stanton shows how T. C. Skeat (Skeat 1994: 264) has subsequently argued that $\mathfrak{P}^{75}$, the Bodmer papyrus (late second century to early third century, containing Luke and John), might have been half of a volume that had been brought together with another single-quire codex for Matthew and Mark. Skeat (Skeat 1997:1–34) has followed this more recently by presenting a case for three codex fragments ($\mathfrak{P}^{4}$, $\mathfrak{P}^{64}$ and $\mathfrak{P}^{67}$) belonging to the same codex, stemming from the late second century and possibly being another four-Gospel codex. Stanton (Stanton 1997: 326–9) draws these findings together cautiously to suggest that these works were likely to have had predecessors and thus provide possible confirmation of the circulation of these four gospels together in the second half of the second century.[35]

CONCLUSION

So there is much evidence to suggest that by the end of the second century, even without definition yet of a 'New Testament canon', the fourfold gospel had begun to achieve widening recognition as authoritative. Preparations for this recognition can be detected in the period leading to

---

[35] But contrast Bovon 1988: 20, who argues on the basis of $\mathfrak{P}^{75}$ that before 180 CE the four gospels did not circulate together.

Irenaeus, and it comes to explicit formulation in Irenaeus and the Muratorian Fragment at the end of the second century. Evidence from early papyri codices is suggestive that the fourfold gospel had begun to circulate together near or prior to this time.

Why this occurred is capable of several explanations. The reliance of some figures like Marcion upon a single gospel probably highlighted the danger of commitment to a single gospel, particularly when heavily edited. Yet the greater danger may have been perceived to be the tendency towards multiplicity, particularly in the second half of the second century. There were many sources of Jesus tradition, and it appears that there was considerable interest in these sources. The diversity of sources was sometimes accompanied by a theological diversity. Increasingly this led to painful divisions in the church, the reaction against which was to try to control the diversity by authoritative tradition and authoritative interpretation. A single gospel might have provided the firmest control, while also having the advantage of countering attacks from critics regarding the discrepancies inherent in the use of a plurality of gospels. Perhaps this was in part the motivation behind gospel harmonization. Yet ultimately a limited plurality, the choice of precisely four, best met the competing interests of a desire to control unrestrained multiplicity and a desire to recognize some of the wealth of traditions that existed, circulated and proved popular. The formula of 'the fourfold gospel' seemed to represent the right balance by the end of the second century, a single gospel in fourfold form.

Why precisely *these four* gospels, though? This is a difficult question to answer convincingly. While apostolicity, antiquity and theological unity have been cited by ancient and modern writers in defence of the choice of these particular four gospels, the articulation of the reasons for the recognition of these four over against other contenders is often difficult.[36] The fact that they were so recognized and that they were found useful for the life of the church is clear, however. Interestingly, each of the four gospels gives us a story of the ministry and passion of Jesus in which traditions of Jesus' teaching are also embedded. Unlike 'gospels' that were mainly sayings material (e.g. the *Gospel of Thomas*) or dialogues and sayings (the *Dialogue of the Saviour*) without narrative, the four gospels offer the reader or hearer Jesus' teaching in the context of Jesus' ministry. The popular appeal of such a medium should not be underestimated. Furthermore, unlike narrative 'gospels' that focus upon distinctive but often curious parts

---

[36] Bovon 1988: 34–5 observes how Epiphanius went to some lengths to show how the four gospels complement one another and were written successively to deal with periods of 'darkness'.

of the life of Jesus (e.g. the *Infancy Gospel of Thomas*), the four gospels offer a focus upon Jesus' ministry and passion, bringing the two together. The number of early 'gospels' that can compete on these two grounds – teaching in the context of narrative, and narrative that brings the ministry and passion of Jesus together – is much more limited.[37] It may well be therefore that these four gospels not only met expectations regarding their authors having close apostolic associations, and regarding their content being largely free from the language and concepts of second-century controversies. They also made accessible to popular audiences the heart of the message and ministry of the Jesus whom the church worshipped.

[37] If the *Gospel of Peter*, which had some second-century popularity, were more than a passion narrative, then perhaps it might have been of comparable form.

CHAPTER 15

The making of gospel commentaries

Markus Bockmuehl

Ours is an era saturated in commentaries. By one rough measure of counting, the world's libraries now hold over 120,000 different volumes associated with that genre.[1] The classics of Scriptural and other ancient literature have long since been strip-mined to a point where it goes without saying that, as a famous critic wryly noted three centuries ago, 'learned commentators view / in Homer more than Homer knew'.[2] This is true of the gospels, as of other New Testament writings; today's commentaries, indeed, seem at times to encourage a kind of tertiary scholarship that subsists in texts about meta-texts.

But how and where did it all begin? Drowning as we are in modern biblical commentary, it may be easy to forget that there was a time before commentaries. It was the discovery of the Dead Sea Scrolls in the mid twentieth century that established an exciting and fertile new starting point of the genre in the form of several running expositions of prophetic books in eschatological terms. The history of biblical commentary thus finds a particular focus in the late second century BC, when these running expositions of the prophets first emerged, fully formed and seemingly without precedent, from the pen of monastic scribes in the Judaean wilderness.

This chapter will begin by reviewing the origins of biblical commentary against the background of ancient Graeco-Roman antecedents, before turning to the earliest commentaries on the gospels. 'Commentary' is here used in the narrower sense of a work consisting primarily of sequential, expository annotation of identified texts that are themselves distinguished from the comments and reproduced intact, whether partially

---

[1] This figure is based on a global search of WorldCat, a database of world libraries which in mid 2004 held 54 million records. On a more modest measure purely within a Christian theological context, Princeton Theological Seminary's catalogue offers just over 6,000 entries associated with the word 'commentary'.

[2] Jonathan Swift, *On Poetry*, line 103.

or continuously. This definition differentiates 'commentary' from a range of related intertextual genres such as paraphrase, 'rewritten Bible', and others.

Commentary only becomes possible at the point where the primary text is for the commentator's purposes 'closed' and therefore, at least in some rudimentary sense, 'canonical'. Its perceived authority consists no longer merely in its general content, in which case one could still rewrite it, as in our context Matthew rewrote Mark. Instead, commentary can begin once the received text has achieved the status of a 'classic' whose textual identity is, at least in principle, substantially inviolate. Paradoxically, therefore, it is only the closure of a text or canon which can open up its hermeneutical treasures – and thus invite the possibility of commentary.[3]

This much, of course, is true for all relationships between ancient commentaries and their primary texts, including pagan examples in Greek and Latin. Where Christian and Jewish biblical commentary differs is in the additional assumption that the text is not merely, indeed not even primarily, a literary 'classic' of formative philosophical and religious interest, but has instead become definitive as Holy Scripture. In this sense the *literary* move towards textual fixity is matched by a corresponding *theological* transposition of the text, which shifts from being a sympathetic (but malleable) reflection of possibly authoritative views to a point at which its form and content are themselves a unique and normative disclosure of divine truth. This is particularly significant in the case of the New Testament gospels, which have their primary life and setting in the liturgical context of public reading and exposition.

GREEK AND ROMAN COMMENTARIES

The term *commentarius* (Greek *hypomnēma*) could identify a wide variety of written records, ranging from notebooks, archives, records of spoken communications or legal, religious, or other official decisions, to literary works including both scholarly texts and biographical or autobiographical material ('memoirs', a usage of particular interest for early Christianity – e.g. Justin, *Dial.* 106.2–3). This more loosely identified literary category came to engender a thriving genre of 'commentary' in the more technical sense, i.e. serial explanations of an identified text.

---

[3] Cf. similarly Halbertal 1997:32–40 as cited in Finkelberg 2003: 92.

The Greek tradition

Allegorical exegesis of Homer can be shown to have its oral origins in the performative tradition well before the fifth century BC. It continued despite the studied resistance of Plato and the earlier Platonists,[4] thriving especially under Crates (fl. 159 BC) and his pupils at Pergamum.[5]

Commentaries in the formal sense, by contrast, did not emerge until the third century BC in Greek and the late second or early first century in Latin, although in some recent scholarship the important fifth-century Derveni Papyrus from Macedonia has been described as a 'commentary' on an Orphic poem of theogony.

Commentaries (*hypomnēmata*) and definitive editions of texts (*ekdoseis*) were among the hallmarks especially of the Alexandrian grammarians from about the second century BC, although they arose out of a long-standing tradition of erudite textual explication of demanding texts. In developing this tradition of scholarship, Alexandria derived incalculable benefit from the great royal Library with its affiliated academic institution known as the Museum, both of which were founded in the early third century and generously maintained by the Ptolemaic kings.[6] From the beginning, the Chief Librarians of Alexandria were often among the leading literary scholars of their day; they included men like Lycophron (b. ca. 320 BC), Callimachus (ca. 305–ca. 240), Eratosthenes (ca. 275–195), and Aristophanes of Byzantium (ca. 257–180).[7]

Alexandrian commentaries in the technical sense began to be produced around this same time. A leading pioneer was Callistratus (second century BC), who treated Homer and at least six comedies of Aristophanes. Aristarchus of Samothrace (ca. 216–144), another head of the Library and a laureate scholar (*grammatikotatos*[8]), produced both critical editions and commentaries on Homer, Hesiod, Pindar, Aeschylus, Sophocles, Aristophanes, Herodotus, and others.[9]

The twentieth century's fortunate papyrus discoveries at Oxyrhynchus have brought to light a substantial library of Alexandrian commentaries from the third century BC onwards, although the best examples date from the first three centuries AD.[10] The favoured source text was inevitably

---

[4] See the discussion in Siegert 1996:131–3 and *passim*.
[5] See Forbes et al. 1996; cf. Pfeiffer 1968:140, 235, 237–46.
[6] See, e.g., Reynolds and Wilson 1991:6–17.   [7] See Trojahn 2002:123–7.
[8] Athenaeus, *Deipnosophistae* 15.12 (ed. Kaibel).   [9] See Lazenby et al. 1996.
[10] A pioneering treatment of this material was the survey of 112 such papyri by del Fabbro 1979; see her catalogue, pp. 128–30; and see pp. 92 n. 74, 131–2 for the dominant time frame. More recent literature is discussed in Dorandi 2000, Luppe 2002, and Trojahn 2002. See also above for discussion of the Derveni papyrus.

Homer, the Greek 'Bible' regarded as the fount of all knowledge;[11] but the great tragedians and comedians were soon added, as were Aristotle and Plato, Herodotus, Demosthenes and Thucydides.[12] Scientific commentaries covered great texts in geometry, astronomy, and medicine (e.g. Euclid, Ptolemy, Hippocrates), while in later antiquity scholars in Beirut and Gaza generated an important body of papyrus commentaries on legal texts.[13] In each case the best examples tended to be produced on good mid-sized scrolls, with the text written in wide columns using a clear and functional semi-cursive script and a system of abbreviations and diacritical symbols. The title, with the names of the author and the commentator, was placed at the end.[14]

Perhaps of greater interest for our purposes is the formal execution and setting of these Greek commentaries. Most papyrus commentaries served relatively popular pedagogical rather than strictly scholarly purposes,[15] offering sapiential, moral, and aesthetic interpretation, sometimes derived by means of allegory. The commentators consistently distinguish between *lemma* and exposition, and may include a wide variety of comment covering matters of philological, exegetical, rhetorical, antiquarian, historical and biographical, scientific, religious, and philosophical interest. Under these headings, questions raised might range from breathings and accents to vocabulary, orthography, and the precise meaning of terms. Grammatical and mythological features were equally of interest, and commentators might express critical views as to the text's aesthetic strengths or weaknesses. In the later, more refined examples of Graeco-Roman commentary there could also be interest in the personality of the authors and the historical circumstances in which they worked.

The Latin tradition

Most of the early Latin commentaries were on classic plays or poems like the comedies of Aristophanes, the difficult *Carmen Saliare*, and above all the works of Virgil, although some commentators cover unknown or seemingly more obscure works. On the whole, what distinguishes the

[11] On this subject see usefully Finkelberg 2003:91–6 (esp. pp. 94–5 on *De Homero*); also Ford 1999; Honigman 2003; and previously Lévêque 1959.
[12] See, e.g., del Fabbro 1979:123.
[13] See Wilson 1967, 1968 on Gaza and McNamee 1998 (cf. McNamee 1995) on Beirut.
[14] See del Fabbro 1979:92.
[15] So, e.g., Hadot 2002:184–5, 199, and *passim* on the primary function of philosophical commentaries.

earliest Roman commentaries from their Greek counterparts is that they tended to appear much sooner after the works being commented on.

Among the more mature examples, modern readers of commentaries would find the format of Servius' fourth-century commentary on Virgil in some respects remarkably familiar, not to say contemporary.[16] His critical stance is to highlight questions of particular importance, which are discussed with reference to a range of opinion – and sometimes readers are encouraged to make their own judgment between a variety of options. Servius' introduction deals with standard issues of *Einleitung*: the life of the poet, the title, the character (*qualitas*) of the poem, its 'intention', and the number and order of the books. This is followed by line-by-line or word-by-word explications of the text, aiming to communicate Virgil's intention. The majority of comments are linguistic, concerned with semantic meaning and assessing Virgil's use of language by the criteria of the grammatical rules of his time – departures are explained as 'archaisms' or 'figures'. Finally, Servius turns to a range of matters of textual[17] and rhetorical criticism, intertextual links with Homer and other Greek and Latin poets, philosophical and religious issues in the text, and notes of antiquarian or historical interest.

QUMRAN AND THE EARLIEST BIBLICAL COMMENTARIES

It is in the Dead Sea Scrolls that we have before us the earliest explicit Jewish commentaries on Scripture, dating by common consent from the period ca. 100 BC–AD 70.

Many critical controversies continue to surround these sectarian Hebrew commentaries on the Prophets, known as *pesharim* from their regular identification of their eschatological interpretation as *pesher*.[18] For present purposes we will adopt a standard enumeration of fifteen continuous *pesharim*, five on Isaiah, seven on the minor prophets, and three on the Psalms (Pss 37, 68, 129).

Scrolls reflecting an earlier period of interpretation show an approach marked by relatively free intertextual engagement, conventionally identified as 'Rewritten Bible'.[19] The beginning of commentary, by contrast,

---

[16] Cf. Guthmüller 2000; Marshall 2000:1059–60; Kaster 1999:681–2.
[17] For the Latin commentators' textual criticism see esp. Zetzel 1981:81–147 on Servius and pp. 148–70 on Donatus.
[18] For an overview of recent debate see e.g. Brooke 2000; Charlesworth 2002; Horgan 2002 and Lim 2002.
[19] A somewhat misleading term that was introduced by Harrington 1972 and has come to be widely adopted.

marks the point at which the biblical text becomes a more stable point of reference: it now stands more clearly over against the interpreter, as the object of interpretation and understanding rather than primarily as an available resource or instrument for a writer's literary ends. This point of transition has sometimes been seen in documents like 4Q252 ('Commentary on Genesis'),[20] although arguably this text of mixed genre is still some way from what we might identify as commentary.

Like their classical counterparts, the Qumran commentators quote the relevant portion of text (the *lemma*) before expounding it. Their quotations may at times manifest a degree of continuing textual fluidity, but their often drastic rereading of Scripture tends to be achieved by techniques *other* than textual adaptation.[21]

None of the *pesharim* reproduces the biblical text in its entirety; this is a point to which we will return below. Some quote only brief phrases, while others (like several of the Isaiah commentaries) may cite whole verses or paragraphs of text. Similarly, some expository comments are extensive, while others are little more than parenthetical glosses. In each case, however, the pattern of citation followed by an exposition remains consistent; as does the deliberate separation of the former from the latter by a stereotypical tag usually involving a form of the term *pesher*,[22] and in some cases by a clear space or blank line. Although not straightforwardly continuous, the order of exposition nevertheless follows the canonical sequence. This sequential but somewhat *ad hoc* character of the commentaries could be in keeping with the sort of serial exposition in an oral, homiletical context that Philo of Alexandria envisaged for the Sabbath meetings of Essenes and Therapeutae.[23]

The Dead Sea commentators rarely make reference to the biblical author or circumstances pertaining at the time of the biblical text's composition. Generally speaking, linguistic, philological, and diachronic historical issues remain outside the Qumran commentary's purview.

At the same time, these writers take for granted that the text intends definitive and often surprisingly specific pronouncements or prophecies concerning their own present, near future, or relatively recent past. These contemporary points of reference are in turn understood as part of the

---

[20] See Bernstein 1994a; Brooke 1996; and cf. Bockmuehl 2006 (forthcoming).
[21] So rightly Wagner 2001:176–7.
[22] Trafton 2002 offers a useful index of citation formulae; see also Bernstein 1994b, esp. pp. 67–8 on the significance of the different formulae within the continuous *pesharim*.
[23] *Contempl.* 28–9, 75–8; *Prob.* 80–2. Note already the setting of Neh 8.8, which may similarly imply serial exposition in a liturgical context (as the LXX also appears to take it).

eschatological (and sometimes messianic) conflicts. Such applications of
the text to their contemporary context are themselves implicitly (and
sometimes explicitly[24]) derived from divine revelation, which is said to
have been granted first and foremost to the sect's founding master interpreter, the Teacher of Righteousness, and through him to his followers.
As the Habakkuk commentary famously affirms, even the prophet himself
may not have understood the deeper meaning of his words,[25] and by taking
the prophetic text as *unfulfilled* prophecy the commentator deliberately
interprets *more* than the literal sense of the words.

A feature more familiar from other ancient commentaries is that the
commentator's typological reading is not always univocal. An instructive
example of such hermeneutical multivalency is 4QpNah 3–4.1.1–11. Within
the space of a few lines the commentator on Nahum 2 first identifies the
'lion' (*aryeh*) of verse 12 (ET verse 11) as 'Demetrius, king of Yavan'
(probably Demetrius III Eucareus, 95–88 BC) and then happily identifies
an altogether *different* 'lion' (*aryeh*) in verse 13 (ET verse 12), namely
Alexander Jannaeus, who 'hanged living men from a tree', i.e. who crucified eight hundred Pharisaic dissidents.[26]

COMMON FEATURES OF PRE-CHRISTIAN COMMENTARIES

A number of features shared by the commentaries of Qumran and
Alexandria invite the suggestion of contacts between them. First, exposition in this mode was carried out on *sequential texts*. Qumran and the
Alexandrian commentaries vary considerably in the style and length of
comment provided; but the text was at least in principle treated in its
entirety, from beginning to end, and all of its particularities were in
principle of interest. However, an obvious difference in the developed
classical commentary is its more explicitly philological and scientific
aspect.

Whether fully sequential or not, both Graeco-Roman and Jewish commentaries cited the text by means of consecutive *lemmata*. The most
complete classical commentaries in fact provided a continuous sequence
of *lemmata*, since this obviated the need for a separate edition of the text.
In her study of commentaries on papyrus, Marina del Fabbro noted that
the use of non-continuous *lemmata* presupposed the availability to the

---

[24] E.g. 1QpHab 6.15–7.6; cf. 1QpHab 2.8–10; 4QpIsa[d] (4Q164).
[25] 1QpHab 7.1–14; cf. similarly *4 Ezra* 12.12; note already Isa 16.13–14.
[26] Cf. Josephus, *Ant.* 13.372–83; *J.W.* 1.90–8. See also Lim 2002:32–3.

readers of a separate edition of the complete text[27] – a point of evident relevance for the Qumran commentators, who could take for granted the availability of a written Scriptural text, or at least close familiarity with it. Partly because abbreviated or incomplete *lemmata* tended to preclude the independent circulation of the commentary in the absence of a separate text, later Graeco-Roman commentators increasingly opted to include the entire text.

Commentators, then, deliberately distinguished between the authoritative text and its interpretation, often by means of stereotypical phrases: whereas at Qumran one finds terms like *pishro, pesher ha-dabar,* or the like, classical commentaries employ analogous terminology (e.g. *hoti* or *to semeion hoti* for explanatory comments; *en taute te hode legei hoti* for a paraphrase).[28] In all cases *lemma* citations may sometimes be less than exact; but while variants may represent a deliberate textual adjustment to suit a preferred reading, it is also worth noting in the case of classical texts that the original may not always have been continuously at the commentator's disposal. Both Qumran and Graeco-Roman commentators periodically resort to quotations from elsewhere in the same or another authoritative writer's work (especially Moses or Homer); this often served either to confirm the interpretative position taken by the commentator or else to underline the authority of the work under investigation. In all cases the resulting interpretation was proffered as a valid and implicitly trustworthy exposition of the text's significance.

By the first century, Alexandrian exposition of Homer (and, in the Jewish philosopher Philo's case, of Moses) had come to accept the need to read texts allegorically, to discover under the rough surface of the literal text the polished gems of an interpretation for the life of the readers, both for their knowledge of God and for their present life in the world. In Alexandrian commentary these gems were of course philosophical rather than eschatological. Philo for one, however, found in the liturgically framed biblical interpretation of the Essenes in the Judaean wilderness and the Therapeutae at Lake Mareotis a kindred love for the deeper sense of the sacred text (*Contempl.* 28–9, 75–8). He thought that he saw there hermeneutical concerns and techniques comparable to those of his own systematic exposition of the Pentateuch, which at least in the *Questions and Answers on Genesis* and *on Exodus* shows a distinct debt to the genre of Alexandrian commentary. From this perspective, at least, the sudden appearance at Qumran of a surprisingly mature technique of prophetic

---

[27] So del Fabbro 1979:81.   [28] See del Fabbro 1979:97.

commentary is in some ways suggestive of wider Graeco-Roman cultural influences that may well have facilitated its rapid development.[29]

THE GOSPELS

The interpretation of the Christian gospels began as soon as they were written; indeed, we might say their very genesis represents in each case interpretation of the preceding gospel tradition. At a minimum we may affirm that Matthew and Luke (and possibly, but to a much lesser extent, John) represent a kind of 'rewritten Bible' treatment of Mark, using 90 per cent of that gospel while expounding as well as expanding upon it. Similar views might be taken of the use of gospel tradition in New Testament epistles like 1 Peter or James, or for that matter in the Apostolic Fathers, Justin, and other second-century writers.[30] Another interesting but controversial theory holds that the gospels, Matthew above all, can *themselves* be read as a kind of 'midrashic' commentary on the synagogal lectionary cycle of the Old Testament and on earlier gospel texts.[31]

For all the undoubted dependence on prior text and tradition, however, no New Testament text represents 'commentary' in the sense here in view: neither the gospels nor the Acts or epistles quote explicitly and sequentially from an authoritative Old Testament or gospel text in order then to expound it. Much the same could be said of the great majority of second-century Christian texts. Within and beyond the New Testament there is solid and increasing evidence that the gospels were known, read, and interpreted.[32] But the handling of Mark in Matthew or of the fourfold gospel in Tatian (let alone in the apocryphal 'gospels' of *Thomas* or *Peter*) much more clearly resembles 'rewritten Bible' than any identifiable genre of commentary.

THE EARLIEST GOSPEL COMMENTARIES

By the time the first gospel commentaries made their appearance in the mid second century, the notion of a fourfold gospel was becoming widely

---

[29] This argument, along with a longer discussion of both Qumran and Graeco-Roman commentaries, is more fully developed in Bockmuehl 2006 (forthcoming).

[30] On this subject see, e.g., the perspectives of Hagner 1985 or Stanton 2003 versus those of Koester 1989b, 1990.

[31] See especially Goulder 1974, 1988; cf. Goodacre 1996.

[32] Sunday by Sunday, indeed, as Justin affirms: *1 Apol.* 67.3. Among recent treatments of this issue, see most comprehensively Köhler 1987, Massaux 1990, and Simonetti 2001–2 on Matthew; Kealy 1982, Black 1994, and Oden and Hall 1998 on Mark; Gregory 2003, Just 2003, and Bovon 2004 on Luke; Poffet 1985, Nagel 2000, and Hill 2004 on John.

established in the churches, as is evidenced in the manuscript tradition and gospel superscripts as well as in citations in Justin (ca. 100–65), Irenaeus (ca. 130–200), and even Papias (ca. 60–130).[33]

As might be expected by this stage of the argument, Alexandria turns out to loom large in the early history of Christian gospel commentary. The formal presentation of these commentaries takes its cue from the tried and tested genres of pagan commentary. By accepting multiple levels of meaning, as was the case for Homer, commentary-writing also conveniently deflected the force of such pagan charges as that the gospels were the works of artless and ignorant men whose sheer vulgarity rendered them intellectually worthless (*C. Cels.* 1.27, 62).[34]

Origen (ca. 185–254) and his Valentinian *bête noire* Heracleon (fl. ca. 145–80) are among the pioneering Christian commentators in Alexandria, although Clement's (ca. 150–215) fragmentary eight books of *Hypotyposes* represent another extensive antecedent to Origen, if not perhaps a sequential gospel commentary.[35] Like their pagan predecessors, such commentators quote exegetical *lemmata* of the original text before elucidating their significance. Their exposition proceeds with considerable freedom and with attention to co-texts in the Old Testament and gospel parallels, with more or less attention to the details of the text.

This general form could sometimes be adapted to a pedagogical setting, as in its Graeco-Roman counterpart; and here one also finds a gradually growing body of scholarly apparatus attending to philological (i.e. historical-grammatical) and philosophical matters. Origen is again notable in this connection, as for his attention to matters of synoptic historical and textual criticism.[36] Frances Young notes, 'Origen's exegesis, whether text-critical, explanatory, investigative or symbolic, is grounded in the same traditions of philological scholarship as our own, somewhat differently applied. The underlying assumption was that the scriptures replaced the classics as the literature on which *paideia* was based.'[37] Around this same time, the advent

---

[33] This is a point well demonstrated by Stanton 2004:63–91; see also Schmid 2002 in relation to Marcion. As early as his celebrated prize essay of 1870, Harnack came to the conclusion that Marcion's preference for Luke implied that he had a choice, but had found the others wanting because of their association with apostles of the circumcision (see Harnack 2003:136–7).

[34] See also Gamble 1995:1–2, 6, and *passim* on the implications of this charge for Christian literacy.

[35] According to Eusebius, the *Hypotyposes* contained comment on Luke, *Hist. Eccl.* 6.14; contrast Photius' claim (ninth century) that the *Hypotyposes* covered only Genesis, Exodus, Psalms, and Ecclesiastes as well as Paul and the Catholic epistles (*Bibl.*, Cod. 109, ed. Bekker 89a35).

[36] Note, e.g., his considerations of Matt 16.20 (*Comm. Mt.* 12.15) and 19.19 (*Comm. Mt.* 15.14). see, e.g., Young 1997:82–4. A definitive treatment of Origen's philological scholarship is Neuschäfer 1987.

[37] Young 1997:95.

of classical scholarship applied to Scriptural commentary can be observed in the West in Hippolytus (ca. 170–236) on Daniel and the Song of Songs.[38] Old Testament commentary was prominent among patristic interpreters especially in the East (but also including Hippolytus, Hilary of Poitiers (ca. 315–67), Ambrose (ca. 339–97), Augustine (354–430), and Jerome (ca. 345–420) among Western writers).[39]

More commonly, however, gospel commentary, like Christian commentary on the Old Testament Scriptures which emerges alongside it, finds its original *Sitz im Leben* in a liturgical context, where series of sequentially expository sermons are woven together to constitute a running commentary. Especially in the case of such homiletic commentary, the didactic nature of the more scholastic exposition is moderated or superseded by elements of moral and spiritual edification (paraenesis). Their ecclesial origin makes these expositions in some ways analogous to Philo's depiction of biblical interpretation among Essenes and Therapeutae, as we noted earlier, and perhaps also to some rabbinic homiletical midrashim.[40]

Within patristic literature it is important to distinguish commentary from *ad hoc* or incidental exegetical notes, including the so-called scholia.[41] The latter are almost always later developments, which from about the sixth century may in turn have given rise to the enormously successful 'pick and mix' catena commentaries. These consisted of compilations of influential existing expositions on a given book, a genre that became extremely popular in the Middle Ages. (It may be said to have found its closest modern analogy in the Ancient Christian Commentary on Scripture series.[42]) Despite their generally late date, the catenae nevertheless remain our most important source for many earlier commentaries that do not survive in their original form.

Following the Graeco-Roman pattern of distinguishing between literal ('historical') and allegorical reading, the patristic commentators took it for granted that the normative text should be interpreted in the first place with reference to itself. Just as Homer elucidated Homer, so Scripture interprets Scripture – a principle that became fundamental to Jewish and Christian biblical interpretation alike. This presupposition, rather than merely apologetic concerns, accounts for the fact that gospel commentaries tended

---

[38] Young 1997:76–96 *passim*, esp. 82. Note further the important surveys of Christian OT interpretation in Carleton Paget 1996 and Horbury 1988.
[39] The appendix in Horbury 1988:782–6 provides an invaluable overview.
[40] See Stemberger 1996:239–40.   [41] So Fuhrer 1999:382.
[42] Cf. esp. Oden and Hall 1998; Simonetti 2001–2, and Just 2003 on the Synoptic Gospels.

to draw heavily on cognate or parallel passages in the other gospels – thus producing expositions that were rather less preoccupied with synoptic differences than has been the norm in modern critical scholarship.[43] In this way significant detail in a parallel gospel would be permitted to elucidate the spiritual and even the literal meaning of otherwise unclear matters in the text at hand. So, for example, John's passion narrative might be used to shed light on unclear details in that of Matthew, or Johannine Christology on that of the Synoptics Gospels.[44]

Although typological (i.e. prefigurative) reading was suitably applied only to the Old Testament,[45] the gospels too could be interpreted allegorically on the assumption that the Scriptural text contained a multiplicity of meanings. Examples for the gospels include spiritualizing interpretations of miracles, especially the healings and exorcisms as examples of deliverance from sin, and detailed allegorical paraphrasing of certain favourite parables. Similarly, allegorical interpretation was elicited by juxtaposition with other Scriptural passages, by the widespread acceptance of numerical or etymological symbolisms, or indeed by any situation where the strictly literal sense gives rise to implausible readings or other difficulties (*defectus litterae*, a device used copiously, e.g. by Hilary of Poitiers on Matthew).[46] Even seemingly trivial individual actions or gestures of Jesus may draw attention to their spiritual significance by unexpected features that for the Fathers assume a greater significance – among the examples is Luke's brief description (22.61) of 'the Lord' (*ho kurios*) turning and looking at Peter after his denial.[47]

In what remains of this chapter I will briefly highlight a few of the major gospel commentaries of the first five centuries. Space does not permit more than a rather general description of these writings; specific illustrations are now readily accessible in a number of recent commentary series.[48]

---

[43] In its careful 'synoptic' exposition, Augustine's *De Consensu Evangelistarum* is a notable exception.
[44] See Simonetti 2001–2:I. xl.
[45] For brief treatments see, e.g., Horbury 1988:766–8; also Carleton Paget 1996:495–8 (on Clement), 526–9 (on Origen). Young 1997:152 notes, however, that ancient exegetes did not distinguish carefully between typology and allegory (although she offers methodological criteria for such a distinction on pp. 186–201).
[46] See, e.g., Simonetti 1994:46–7; Simonetti 2001–2:I. xlii.
[47] Augustine, for example, comments on the significance of *ho kurios* here (*De Cons.* 3.6.26). I am grateful to my student Jane F. M. Heath for drawing my attention to the patristic reading of this passage in her Cambridge Diploma dissertation (2004).
[48] At the time of writing, see especially Simonetti 2001–2 on Matthew, Just 2003 on Luke, Oden and Hall 1998 on Mark, and Edwards 2004a on John.

MATTHEW

Matthew and John were the most widely read gospels in antiquity, and also the first to attract the attention of commentators. Although it is true that the earliest known commentary on any gospel is the mid-second-century Gnostic Heracleon's exposition of John (see below), Manlio Simonetti rightly points out that the influence of Matthew both precedes and exceeds that of John in the earliest period; evidence includes the *Didache*, *Barnabas*, and Justin Martyr, but Matthew's importance is also reflected in its assumed chronological priority over (some or all) other gospels ever since Papias of Hierapolis.[49] Papias's five books on the Jesus tradition are usually discussed in relation to the use Eusebius (ca. 260–340) and Irenaeus make of them in discussing gospel origins; but since they explicitly contain *exēgēseis*, it seems reasonable to suspect that these concern expositions of or expository introductions to the gospels – not just for Matthew and Mark, on which Eusebius' quotations are explicit, but for Luke and John as well.[50] But as this is largely a circumstantial argument, we must concentrate here on explicit commentary.

The first and longest-known commentary on Matthew in Greek is the exposition in twenty-five volumes composed by Origen not long before his death (ca. 185–254),[51] while the earliest extant Latin one is Hilary of Poitiers's.[52] Although aware of the Alexandrian exegetical tradition, Hilary in many ways ploughs his own furrow in this pioneering first commentary in Latin.

Once established, Matthean commentary flourished in a variety of expressions, with numerous homiletical (Origen,[53] Chrysostom (ca. 347–407), Chromatius of Aquileia (d. 407)) and scholarly (Hilary, Jerome (ca. 345–420)) specimens surviving at least in fragmentary form.

---

[49] In Eusebius, *Hist. Eccl.* 3.39.16. See Simonetti 2001–2:1. xxxvii, on whose treatment this section depends exensively.

[50] Cf. Hill 1998, Hill 2004:383–96. For Papias see Eusebius, *Hist. Eccl.* 3.39.1.

[51] Only Books 10–17 (on Matt 13.36–22.33) survive.

[52] Five excerpts from another Latin commentary (*Anonymi Chiliastae in Matthaeum Fragmenta*) have sometimes been attributed to the fourth-century Ambrosiaster or to Victorinus of Pettau (ca. 230–304), whose lost commentary on Matthew is cited in Jerome and Cassiodorus. See Geerlings 1999; Schwarte 1999.

[53] Note, however, that Perrone 2000 seeks in this respect to differentiate between the more scholarly commentary on John and the much later one on Matthew, where the more frequent use of question-and-answer diatribe and appeals for the reader's attention suggest more clearly the influence of Origen's years of pedagogical experience. Origen's activity as a preacher after his move to Caesarea in 231 will also be pertinent to this point.

Jerome's four-volume exposition (ca. 398) is the most substantial of the ancient Latin commentaries on Matthew. Despite its somewhat hurried completion the genre here shows itself to have matured to the point where it is able to draw explicitly on a wide range of earlier patristic sources in Greek and Latin. Jerome generally condenses this source material in a remarkably concise discussion that balances historical and spiritual interpretation.

Jerome's friend and correspondent Chromatius of Aquileia produced a commentary partially extant in sixty-one brief exegetical homilies, many of which were unknown until the later twentieth century. His work follows the text up to Matt 9.31 and then covers selected passages up to 18.35. It shows extensive biblical and patristic learning, and his largely didactic and catechetically motivated exegesis makes extensive use of both allegory and Old Testament typology.[54]

Among the homiletical commentaries on Matthew, Chrysostom's (347–407) characteristic serial expositions in ninety substantial sermons still show the attractive marks of their original *Sitz im Leben*, as sequential sermons originally preached in Antioch over a relatively short period of time (ca. AD 390). This setting requires them to retain their original integrity as discrete addresses, and thus to provide less recapitulation and cross-referencing than one finds in the larger scholarly works. At the same time, and despite the preacher's moral and emotional appeal, what distinguishes Chrysostom from individual exegetical preachers on Matthew[55] is precisely the character of these homilies as serial expositions of (mainly) the literal sense, clearly linked through their textual progression – thus providing a clear exegetical discipline for preacher and congregation alike![56] The details of the text here matter not as a licence for allegory but as the stuff of practical moral exhortation; its inconsistencies elicit not speculation about 'deeper meaning' but discussion of pedagogical sensitivity to the audiences in view.[57]

Another major ancient commentary on Matt 1–8, 10–13, and 19–25 is an anonymous fifth-century Arian work, perhaps originally composed in Latin. Known as *Opus Imperfectum in Matthaeum*, it was subsequently divided into fifty-four homilies and rose to extraordinary popularity in

---

[54] Dümler 1999:124; cf. Etaix and Lemarié 1974.
[55] Simonetti 2001–2:1. xxxix lists Augustine, Severus of Antioch, Eusebius of Emesa, and Gregory the Great.
[56] Simonetti 2001–2:1. xxxix wryly comments, 'This prevented readings during liturgical meetings from becoming a pretext for merely generic explanations aimed only at the emotions.'
[57] Simonetti 2001–2:1. xlviii.

the Middle Ages, in part because of its erroneous attribution to Chrysostom.[58] The writer sounds at times polemically anti-Catholic, and includes the 'heretics' (i.e. Catholics) as the heirs of the Jews he finds condemned in the gospel. His moral comments, by contrast, tend to be orthodox in nature, even where they are critical of church hierarchy. The writer's concern for a balance of literal and allegorical interpretation is perceptive and erudite, and shows connections with the commentaries of both Origen and Jerome.[59] Simonetti calls it 'the most important commentary on Matthew written in Latin'.[60]

In the case of Matthew, the *Catenae* are our major source for the fourth- and fifth-century commentaries by Apollinaris of Laodicea (ca. 315–92), Theodore of Heraclea (d. ca. 355), Theodore of Mopsuestia (ca. 350–428), and Cyril of Alexandria (d. 444).[61] Theodore of Mopsuestia represents a classic Antiochene commentator's reaction to the Alexandrian penchant for allegory, placing his emphasis instead on an explanatory paraphrase of the literal sense. The *Catenae*, however, were catholic in their tastes, and extensively excerpted Origen's commentary as well: over 570 fragments have been documented, some of which supply portions of the lost exposition of Matt 1.1–13.35 and Matt 28.[62]

Numerous other homilists are of interest here, but space precludes a fuller discussion; similarly, there are important exegetical texts like the verbatim expositions of the Lord's Prayer in the three well-known treatises on prayer by Tertullian, Cyprian, and Origen.[63]

MARK

It is interesting to note that while several apocryphal gospels circulated widely, none to our knowledge attracted the interest of commentators.

Neither, indeed, did Mark, which appears to have been so rarely read that only a single copy of it ($\mathfrak{P}^{45}$) survives among the thirty or so gospel manuscripts extant from before the year 300 – fewer, that is, than of

---

[58] Two hundred manuscripts are extant; see Simonetti 2001–2:I. xlv.
[59] A christologically sanitized version became the norm in later centuries, and forms the basis of the text in Migne, PL 56:611–946. A 'cleaned-up' critical edition is being produced by Joop van Banning; see Banning 1988 and cf. Christiane Schmidt 1999. See Mali 1991 on the relationship with the commentaries of Origen and Jerome.
[60] Simonetti 2001–2:I. xlvi.   [61] See Reuss 1957 and cf. Simonetti 2001–2:I. xxxviii, xlvi.
[62] See Klostermann and Benz 1935; Simonetti 2001–2: I. xlii.
[63] See the further remarks in Simonetti 2001–2:I. xlix–l.

some apocryphal gospels.[64] Since most of these manuscripts are papyri, this is admittedly most revealing for Egypt,[65] but it does seem to corroborate the situation at least in the East more generally. It took over half a millennium for the first commentaries on Mark to appear: Ps.-Victor of Antioch, writing ca. AD 500, composed a catena compiled from other patristic sources, but 'there is nothing extensive on Mark as such'.[66] We must look to Bede (673–735) and, even later, Theophylact (ca. 1050–ca. 1125) as individuals who can be identified with some confidence as commentators on Mark. Michael Cahill (1998: 6–7) has argued that an anonymous seventh-century Irish composition entitled *Expositio Evangelii Secundum Marcum* (CCSL 82) must be identified as 'the first commentary on Mark'; its monastic author sounds almost apologetic in the acknowledgement that he is something of a pioneer (Cahill 1998: 20).

To modern readers brought up on theories of Marcan priority and studies of this evangelist's literary artistry, this silence of the ancient church may seem perplexing or mildly alarming. The fact is, however, that the contemporary prominence of Mark was wholly without parallel between the composition of Matthew's gospel in the first century and the 'discovery' of Marcan priority in the nineteenth. The explanation for this is not hard to find. Mark was always included within the fourfold gospel because of its perceived (and never questioned) link with the Apostle Peter; Justin, Clement of Alexandria, and others knew and revered it for that reason.[67] But it has no infancy or (in the earliest manuscript tradition) resurrection narratives, and lacks a good deal of Jesus' most familiar teaching discourses. As a result, it was not widely copied or circulated, and entered popular Christian awareness mostly by way of its re-use in Tatian's widely influential harmony known as the *Diatessaron*. Matthew's gospel was arguably written to 'complete' Mark's, and largely replaced it in the early church's use. Commentators, unsurprisingly, concentrated their efforts on John and Matthew, the two most popular gospels.

---

[64] See also the table in Lührmann and Schlarb 2000:22, which shows that out of the thirty canonical gospel manuscripts that predate the year 300, only a single one ($\mathfrak{P}^{45}$) contains the Gospel of Mark (compared to twelve for Matthew, seven for Luke, and sixteen for John).

[65] See Lührmann and Schlarb 2000:182–3 on the implications for the so-called 'Secret Gospel of Mark'.

[66] Oden and Hall 1998:xxxi.

[67] Papias (in Irenaeus, *Haer.* 3.1.1, 10.5; Eusebius, *Hist. Eccl.* 3.39); Justin, *Dial.* 106.2–3; cf. *1 Apol.* 15.2; Clement of Alexandria in Eusebius, *Hist. Eccl.* 6.14.

LUKE

Leaving aside Papias' fragments (mentioned in passing above) and Heracleon on Luke 12.8–9 (see Löhr 2003), the third evangelist appears first to have received sustained philological attention from Marcion of Sinope (fl. ca. 140–60), who famously produced an edited version of Luke as his single normative gospel text. Marcion's *Antitheses* were sometimes thought to have included extensive exegetical comment on his reduced Luke, but this is not now widely believed; indeed, it has been argued that Marcion resisted explicit exegesis, in part because of his opposition to allegory.[68] Conversely, the first commentary has been sought in Book 4 of Tertullian's rebuttal of Marcion;[69] but this certainly does not constitute Lucan commentary in any formal sense.

Indeed, although Luke was less neglected than Mark, it is the case that patristic commentators turned their attention far more commonly to Matthew and John. No early philological commentaries survive, and so for our period we are limited to sequential collections of homilies by Origen, Ambrose, and Cyril of Alexandria, as well as some catena fragments of another fourth-century homiletical commentary by Titus of Bostra.

Origen's homilies on Luke composed in Caesarea, then, may be justly regarded as the earliest 'commentary' on this gospel, even if the extant thirty-nine sermons cover only the first four chapters sequentially before skipping to six brief and unconnected passages in chapters 10, 12, 17, 19, and 20. Originally there appear to have been 150 homilies for morning and evening prayer that treated the entire gospel sequentially;[70] quite possibly this is the first such sermon series transformed into a commentary. As is arguably the case for his interpretation of the gospels more generally, Origen's concern for the literal sense is more clearly in evidence in these homilies than he is often given credit for either in present-day scholarship or indeed among his ancient Antiochene critics who insisted on the primacy of the historical setting.

Cyril of Alexandria likewise produced a series of 150 homiletical expositions of Luke, which in his case strongly underlines his characteristic doctrinal concerns and also offers a strongly christological reading of the Sermon on the Plain.[71]

---

[68] Thus Bovon 2004:15–16.   [69] See, e.g., Just 2003: xvii, citing C. H. Talbert.
[70] Just 2003: xxii, citing Old 1998:1.321–2.   [71] Just 2003: xxiv.

JOHN

Although the earliest named citation of the Fourth Gospel appears in Irenaeus in the late second century (*Haer.* 3.1.1), it is in fact clear that Justin (*1 Apol.* 61.4–5)[72] and Tatian knew and used this gospel in the 160s. Papias of Hierapolis probably did so too, at least a quarter-century earlier;[73] and there are periodic (and in part persuasive) attempts to document familiarity with Johannine ideas in Ignatius' letter to the Ephesian church. It is in Egypt, however, that we encounter the earliest evidence for the copying, reading, and interpretation of this gospel: the earliest of all extant gospel manuscripts is a scrap of papyrus in Manchester's John Rylands Library ($\mathfrak{P}^{52}$), thought to date from around AD 125, while a few years before that the famous Alexandrian theologian Basilides was said by Hippolytus to have derived his 'Gnostic' cosmology partly from his reading of John 1.5.[74]

It was Alexandria, too, which produced the earliest and some of the greatest ancient commentators on the Fourth Gospel. The earliest of them was the infamous and to some extent unjustly maligned 'Gnostic' Heracleon (fl. ca. 145–80), a disciple of Valentinus. He produced *hypomnēmata* on John, which are now known to us only through quotations in Origen, his most vociferous critic. Irenaeus, Clement, and Tertullian, all of whom knew Heracleon as a Valentinian leader, appear to have been unaware of this commentary on John.[75] Origen's extensive interaction with it, however, establishes its importance among the orthodox, at least as a position to be resisted.

Much has often been made of the fact that most of the explicit pre-Irenaean citations of the Fourth Gospel are found in this commentary; but against the conventional supposition of a predominantly Gnostic second-century reception of this gospel must now be held the impressive demolition of the theory of 'orthodox Johannophobia' in Hill 2004. His reading of the evidence confirms Martin Hengel's conclusion that the Valentinian predilection for John seen in Heracleon or Ptolemy was in fact remarkably *un*characteristic of Gnostic groups; and conversely, no

---

[72] See, e.g., Stanton 2004:100–2.
[73] So Hill 1998:586–7 on Eusebius, *Hist. Eccl.* 3.24, cited approvingly in Edwards 2004a:2.
[74] See Hippolytus, *Refut.* 7.10.22, cited in Edwards 2004a:2; see more generally Löhr 1996.
[75] A point rightly noted by Hill 2004:208. Irenaeus, to be sure, does explicitly claim to have 'read the commentaries [*hypomnēmasi*], as they call them' of Valentinus' disciples: *Haer.* 1 Praef.; but as in the case of Basilides' twenty-four books of *Exēgētika* on the gospel (Clement, *Strom.* 4.12.81.1; cf. Agrippa Castor in Eusebius, *Hist. Eccl.* 4.7.7), these need not have been formal 'commentaries' of the kind here in view.

reservations about the Fourth Gospel can be documented in orthodox circles, whose positive reception predates Valentinus.[76]

Heracleon's Johannine text form is difficult to identify; while some have postulated dependence on a Western text form, a more cautious assessment concedes that his extant textual *lemmata* are too brief and few in number to permit confident conclusions. What seems rather clearer, by contrast, is his apparent desire to represent the text faithfully.[77]

Of greater interest is Heracleon's actual commentary, on which for reasons of space I can report here only in passing. Although we cannot be certain, it is now thought that his *hypomnēmata* were perhaps selective exegetical comments used for teaching purposes, rather than a complete running commentary.[78] Origen's claim that Heracleon provided 'very few and unsubstantiated comments in his exposition' (*Comm. Joh.* 6.15.92) is matched by his own somewhat staccato reporting of it, but need not be indicative of the length of either Heracleon's *lemmata* or his comments. Ansgar Wucherpfennig's important new study finds in the papyrus commentaries discussed above the most important analogies to Heracleon's work.[79]

Key passages discussed in recent literature on Heracleon include his commentary on John 1–2, 4, and 8.[80] In substance, Heracleon employs the techniques of classic Alexandrian literary criticism that we encountered above, and which are encountered more fully in Origen and later commentators. Thus, he manifests an intensely *philological* and critical interest in issues of language and historicity: he is concerned with the meanings of unfamiliar expressions and intertextual links and prepared to entertain, for example, that Jesus healed the royal official's son (John 4.46–54) not from a distance but in person.[81] The fact that he draws on the Septuagint as well as Paul's letters (probably including Hebrews) and the Synoptic Gospels as authoritative sources of explanation – but not, interestingly, the *Gospel of Thomas* or other Christian apocrypha – suggests that for all his 'gnosticizing' interpretation he represents a relatively 'orthodox' biblical canon.[82]

---

[76] Similar critiques of twentieth-century scholarship's prevailing consensus emerge in Hengel 1993 and Nagel 2000; see also Wucherpfennig 2002:405–6.

[77] So Wucherpfennig 2002:31 with reference to Ehrman 1994 on the 'Western' text.

[78] Edwards 2004a:3; Wucherpfennig 2002:34.   [79] Wucherpfennig 2002:36.

[80] See, e.g., Poffet 1985; Wucherpfennig 2002:48–331; Blanc 1975; see further Pagels 1973.

[81] See Wucherpfennig 2002:306–7, 373–4 on Heracleon's frag. 40 (in Origen, *Comm. Joh.* 13.60.421: 'he went down to the patient and healed the illness (*katabas pros ton kamnonta kai iasamenos auton tēs nosou*), and having raised that one to life through forgiveness, said, "Your child will live"').

[82] For documentation see Wucherpfennig 2002:375–8; cf. Metzger 1987:82.

Wucherpfennig identifies him, not without some justification, as the earliest-known Christian philologist.[83]

Despite Origen's clear affirmations to this effect, the extent to which Heracleon's commentary is 'gnostic' or more specifically 'Valentinian' remains a controversial question. Some would altogether prescind from any distinction between 'Gnosticism' and 'orthodox' thought (e.g. King 2003, Pagels 2002, and Williams 1996), while others (including Wucherpfennig) prefer to speak more specifically of Heracleon's *Platonizing* Christian exposition of the gospel. This undoubtedly has some value, and in one sense Heracleon's concern to expound Christianity in philosophically respectable terms places him, perhaps like Basilides, alongside Clement or Origen. On the other hand, he does in fact (and again not unlike Basilides) employ certain dualizing moves classically associated with fully fleged 'Gnosticism', including the device of the Demiurge (whom he sees, e.g., in the *basilikos* of John 4.49) or the de-historicizing reference to Jesus as 'Saviour' (rather than by name). Views such as these arguably render Origen's determined resistance more intelligible than on Wucherpfennig's attempted rehabilitation of Heracleon's Platonizing as merely 'in the service of a coherent biblical theology'.[84] One can in fact detect between some of Heracleon's lines the telltale signs of that characteristic Valentinian erasure of the distinction between text and commentary, effectively the reduction of the salvation-historical drama of Scripture to a creative 'psychodrama' – a move that David Dawson has memorably called 'the Apocalypse of the Mind'.[85]

Origen's answer to any Gnostic hijacking of the Fourth Gospel takes shape in his massive commentary in thirty-two books (but extending only to chapter 13), of which only a few hundred pages survive. Although this work amply manifests familiar patterns of Alexandrian philology including allegorical interpretation, we must note against widespread prejudice that the mystical and speculative dimension of Origen's interpretation is in fact remarkably chastened by a deep respect for the literal sense – including a concrete sensitivity to its material, historical, and geographical specificity. It is this that sets him apart from Valentinian speculation. As Edwards 2004a:3 puts it, 'he domesticated the allegorical method by submitting it to a statement of belief which he believed to be held by all churches, and

---

[83] Wucherpfennig 2002:380–1 (and note his title).
[84] Thus Wucherpfennig 2002:402–3. Note also Edwards 2004b, who similarly questions Wucherpfennig's dismissal of Origen's critique.
[85] Dawson 1992:128 and *passim*, also cited in Young 1997:59.

by taking the undisputed sense of one text as the key to the latent meaning of another'. In this sense Origen is the pioneer of an orthodox commentary tradition that aimed to hold together historical and theological truth, fully human with fully divine Christology. He undoubtedly privileges allegory, often to a fault. But despite this preference for the spiritual and invisible rather than the literal and material, the latter nevertheless remains the object of redemption and is never entirely submerged under the former.

Perhaps somewhat ironically in view of the great Alexandrian philo-logical tradition, it was in Antioch rather than Alexandria that Christian commentators came to stress most resolutely an exegetical interest in the historical setting of the gospels and their authors. Antiochene commenta-tors on John include Chrysostom and Theodore of Mopsuestia (ca. 350–428). Although they were by no means averse to spiritual readings of the Fourth Gospel (affirming, for instance, like Eusebius of Emesa (d. ca. 359) or Cyril of Alexandria (d. 444), that the Logos ultimately cannot suffer[86]), their resistance to the excesses of allegory and their vested and more rigorous interest in the setting of the author and of the gospel's *dramatis personae* do make for illuminating contrasts with the Alexandrian commentators. One Antiochene advantage, as William Horbury points out, is that 'Antiochene commentary could appeal to the earnest believer as well as the rational critic.'[87]

Among Latin commentators on the Fourth Gospel, finally, the out-standing figure of the early centuries is without doubt Augustine of Hippo (354–430), whose 124 Tractates on John (written in 414–16) represent a mature synthesis of the best in Alexandrian and Antiochene interpretation. His commentary manifests the affirmation of the historical and plain sense as laid out in his instruction about exegesis in *On Christian Doctrine*, and yet in no way shies away from pressing on to the full theological implications available to the allegorical interpreter. (Indeed, his own appreciation of the Old Testament, initially dismissed as crude, was enabled by his discovery of Ambrose's allegories and his own liturgical experience of the Psalms.[88]) As Edwards 2004a:4 puts it, 'he sees the text as a narrative, veridical, linear, free of inconcinnity or conflict with other Gospels, and yet pregnant in every line with some divine truth or instruc-tion for the soul'.

---

[86] See Edwards 2004a:4.   [87] Horbury 1988:770.
[88] See Horbury 1988:749 n. 109, 781.

CONCLUSION

Ideally we would now turn to a more detailed illustration and exploration of early Christian gospel commentaries, relating them both to other early Christian interpretations of the gospels and also more fully and specifically to contemporary non-Christian commentary. The constraints of the present setting compel us to leave that exploration for another occasion.

Here we may sum up by way of three brief conclusions. The first is to remind ourselves of the earliest gospel commentators' cultural and methodological indebtedness to both Jewish and Graeco-Roman antecedents, especially in Alexandria, where Christian commentary also first took root. These antecedents already manifest the concern to cite intact *lemmata* and to distinguish them from the philological, grammatical, or theological interpretation that would follow.

Somewhat by the way, perhaps, the second- and third-century beginnings of gospel commentary also confirm the extent to which the four canonical gospels had ceased to be freely 'rewritable': even while their precise text form retained a degree of fluidity,[89] their substance had for mainstream Christianity attained a normative fixity to which no 'rewritten' texts could attain. An interesting exception to prove this rule may be the second and third century's prolific output of apocryphal gospels: while these did after a fashion continue to 'write' or 'rewrite' the gospel tradition, none to our knowledge went on to generate commentaries.

Finally, and perhaps most importantly, what is striking about the early patristic gospel commentaries is their ability to hold together academic and pastoral concerns with equal seriousness. Thus they show the scholar's task of painstaking and self-involving gospel interpretation to be vitally relevant and life-giving to the church's faith. That conviction has also marked the work of Graham Stanton, to whom this chapter and this volume are dedicated with heartfelt affection and gratitude.

---

[89] Note on this subject Parker 1997 and Ehrman 1993.

Appendix: Graham Stanton's publications

BOOKS AUTHORED OR CO-AUTHORED

1974 (repr. 2004). *Jesus of Nazareth in New Testament Preaching*. SNTSMS 27. Cambridge: Cambridge University Press.

1978. *Interpreting the New Testament Today*. An Inaugural Lecture in the Chair of New Testament Studies, delivered on 14 November 1978 and published by King's College, London. Repr. in *Ex Auditu* 1 (1985): 63–73.

1989. *The Gospels and Jesus*. Oxford Bible Series. Oxford: Oxford University Press. (Translated into Japanese and Korean.)

1992. *A Gospel for a New People: Studies in Matthew*. Edinburgh: T. & T. Clark.

1995. *Gospel Truth? New Light on Jesus and the Gospels*. London and Valley Forge: HarperCollins and Trinity Press International. (Translated into French, Dutch, Spanish, and Italian.)

1997. *Gospel Truth? Today's Quest for Jesus of Nazareth*. 2nd edn. London: Fount.

2002. *The Gospels and Jesus*. Oxford Bible Series. 2nd edn. Oxford: Oxford University Press.

2003. (With Patrick Collinson and Richard Rex.) *Lady Margaret Beaufort and her Professors of Divinity at Cambridge: 1502–1649*. Cambridge: Cambridge University Press.

2004. *Jesus and Gospel*. Cambridge and New York: Cambridge University Press.

BOOKS EDITED OR CO-EDITED

1983. *The Interpretation of Matthew*. Issues in Religion and Theology 3. London and Philadelphia: SPCK and Fortress.

1994. (With Stephen C. Barton.) *Resurrection: Essays in Honour of Leslie Houlden*. London: SPCK.

1995. *The Interpretation of Matthew*. SNTI. 2nd revised and expanded edn. Edinburgh: T. & T. Clark.

1998. (With Guy G. Stroumsa.) *Tolerance and Intolerance in Early Judaism and Christianity*. Cambridge: Cambridge University Press.

2003. (With David F. Ford.) *Reading Texts, Seeking Wisdom: Scripture and Theology*. London: SCM.

2004. (With Stephen C. Barton and Bruce W. Longenecker.) *The Holy Spirit and Christian Origins: Essays in Honor of James D. G. Dunn*. Grand Rapids: Eerdmans.

ARTICLES AND BOOK CHAPTERS

1971. (With A. A. Macintosh and D. L. Frost.) 'The "New English Bible" Reviewed'. *Theology* 74: 154–66.

1972. 'The Gospel Traditions and Early Christological Reflection'. In *Christ, Faith and History: Cambridge Studies in Christology*, 191–204. Ed. S. W. Sykes and J. P. Clayton. Cambridge: Cambridge University Press.

1973. 'On the Christology of Q'. In *Christ and Spirit in the New Testament: Studies in Honour of Charles Francis Digby Moule*, 27–42. Ed. B. Lindars and S. S. Smalley. Cambridge: Cambridge University Press.

1975. 'Form Criticism Revisited'. In *What About the New Testament? Essays in Honour of Christopher Evans*, 13–27. Ed. M. Hooker and C. Hickling. London: SCM.

1977a. '5 Ezra and Matthean Christianity in the Second Century'. *JTS* N.S. 28: 67–83.

1977b. 'Presuppositions in New Testament Criticism'. In *New Testament Interpretation: Essays on Principles and Methods*, 60–71. Ed. I. H. Marshall. Exeter and Grand Rapids: Paternoster and Eerdmans.

1979a. 'Incarnational Christology in the New Testament'. In *Incarnation and Myth: The Debate Continued*, 151–65. Ed. M. D. Goulder. London and Grand Rapids: SCM and Eerdmans.

1979b. 'Mr Cupitt on Incarnational Christology in the New Testament'. In *Incarnation and Myth: The Debate Continued*, 170–3. Ed. M. D. Goulder. London and Grand Rapids: SCM and Eerdmans.

1979c. 'Rudolf Bultmann: Jesus and the Word'. *Expository Times* 90: 324–8.

1979d. 'Samaritan Incarnational Christology?' In *Incarnation and Myth: The Debate Continued*, 243–46. Ed. M. D. Goulder. London and Grand Rapids: SCM and Eerdmans.

1980. 'Stephen in Lucan Perspective'. In *Studia Biblica 1978: Sixth International Congress on Biblical Studies, Oxford, 3–7 April, 1978*, Vol. III: *Papers on Paul and other New Testament Authors*, 345–60. Ed. E. A. Livingstone. JSNTSup 3. Sheffield: JSOT Press.

1982. 'Matthew 11.28–30: Comfortable Words?' *Expository Times* 94: 3–9.

1983a. 'Matthew as a Creative Interpreter of the Sayings of Jesus'. In *Das Evangelium und die Evangelien: Vorträge vom Tübinger Symposium 1982*, 273–87. Ed. P. Stuhlmacher. WUNT 28. Tübingen: Mohr (Siebeck).

1983b. 'Introduction: Matthew's Gospel: A New Storm Centre'. In *The Interpretation of Matthew*, 1–18. Ed. G. N. Stanton. Issues in Religion and Theology 3. London and Philadelphia: SPCK and Fortress.

1984. 'The Gospel of Matthew and Judaism'. *Bulletin of the John Rylands University Library of Manchester* 66, no. 2: 264–84 (1983 Manson Memorial Lecture).

1985a. 'Aspects of Early Christian-Jewish Polemic and Apologetic'. *NTS* 31: 377–92.

1985b. 'The Origin and Purpose of Matthew's Gospel: Matthean Scholarship from 1945–1980'. *ANRW* II.25.3:1889–1951. Ed. H. Temporini and W. Haase. Berlin and New York: de Gruyter.

1987a. 'Colossians and Philemon'. In *Guidelines to the Bible*, 67–81. Ed. A. E. Harvey. London: Bible Reading Fellowship.

1987b. 'The Origin and Purpose of Matthew's Sermon on the Mount'. In *Tradition and Interpretation in the New Testament: Essays in Honor of E. Earle Ellis for his 60th Birthday*, 181–92. Ed. G. F. Hawthorne and O. Betz. Grand Rapids and Tübingen: Eerdmans and Mohr (Siebeck).

1988. 'Matthew'. In *It is Written: Scripture Citing Scripture: Essays in Honour of Barnabas Lindars, SSF*, 205–19. Ed. D. A. Carson and H. G. M. Williamson. Cambridge: Cambridge University Press.

1989. '"Pray that Your Flight may not be in Winter or on a Sabbath"'. *JSNT* 37: 17–30.

1990a. 'Historical Jesus'. In *A Dictionary of Biblical Interpretation*, 285–90. Ed. R. J. Coggins and J. L. Houlden. London and Philadelphia: SCM and Trinity Press International.

1990b. 'Matthew, Gospel of'. In *A Dictionary of Biblical Interpretation*, 432–5. Ed. R. J. Coggins and J. L. Houlden. London and Philadelphia: SCM and Trinity Press International.

1990c. 'The Revised English Bible: New Wine in Old Wineskins? New Testament'. *Theology* 93: 41–6.

1990d. 'Sermon on the Mount'. In *A Dictionary of Biblical Interpretation*, 625–8. Ed. R. J. Coggins and J. L. Houlden. London and Philadelphia: SCM and Trinity Press International.

1991. 'Interpreting the Sermon on the Mount'. In *Fundamentalism and Tolerance: An Agency for Theology and Society*, 51–60. Ed. A. Linzey and P. Wexler. Canterbury Papers Series. London: Bellew.

1992a. 'Matthew's Christology and the Parting of the Ways'. In *Jews and Christians: The Parting of the Ways A.D. 70 to 135: The Second Durham–Tübingen Research Symposium on Earliest Christianity and Judaism, Durham, September 1989*, 99–116. Ed. J. D. G. Dunn. WUNT 66. Tübingen: Mohr (Siebeck).

1992b. 'Aspects of Early Christian and Jewish Worship: Pliny and the *Kerygma Petrou*'. In *Worship, Theology and Ministry in the Early Church: Essays in Honor of Ralph P. Martin*, 84–98. Ed. M. J. Wilkins and T. Paige. JSNTSup 87. Sheffield: JSOT Press.

1992c. 'The Communities of Matthew'. *Interpretation* 46: 379–91.

1992d. 'Matthew: βίβλος, εὐαγγέλιον, or βίος?' In *The Four Gospels 1992: Festschrift Frans Neirynck*, 2:1187–1201. Ed. F. Van Segbroeck et al. BETL 100. Leuven: Leuven University Press and Peeters.

1992e. 'Sermon on the Mount/Plain'. In *Dictionary of Jesus and the Gospels: A Compendium of Contemporary Biblical Scholarship*, 735–44. Ed. J. B. Green et al. Downers Grove: InterVarsity Press.

1993. 'The Two Parousias of Christ: Justin Martyr and Matthew'. In *From Jesus to John: Essays on Jesus and New Testament Christology in Honour of Marinus de Jonge*, 183–95. Ed. M. C. De Boer. JSNTSup 84. Sheffield: JSOT Press.

1994a. 'Early Objections to the Resurrection of Jesus'. In *Resurrection: Essays in Honour of Leslie Houlden*, 79–94. Ed. S. C. Barton and G. N. Stanton. London: SPCK.

1994b. 'Jesus of Nazareth: A Magician and a False Prophet who Deceived God's People?' In *Jesus of Nazareth Lord and Christ: Essays on the Historical Jesus and New Testament Christology* (Festschrift for I. H. Marshall), 164–80. Ed. J. B. Green and M. Turner. Grand Rapids and Carlisle: Eerdmans and Paternoster.

1994c. 'Revisiting Matthew's Communities'. In *SBL Seminar Papers, 1994*, 9–23. Ed. E. H. Lovering, Jr. SBLSP 33. Atlanta: Scholars. Repr. in *Hervormde Teologiese Studies* 52 (1996): 376–94.

1995a. 'A Gospel among the Scrolls?' *Bible Review* 11: 36–42.

1995b. 'Introduction: Matthew's Gospel in Recent Scholarship'. In *The Interpretation of Matthew*, 1–26. Ed. G. N. Stanton. SNTS. 2nd revised and expanded edition. Edinburgh: T. & T. Clark.

1995c. 'Matthew's Gospel: A Survey of some Recent Commentaries'. *Bible Translator* 46: 131–40.

1996a. 'The Law of Moses and the Law of Christ: Galatians 3:1–6:2'. In *Paul and the Mosaic Law*, 99–116. Ed. J. D. G. Dunn. WUNT 89. Tübingen: Mohr (Siebeck).

1996b. 'Ministry in Matthean Christianity'. In *The Call to Serve: Biblical and Theological Perspectives on Ministry in Honour of Bishop Penny Jamieson*, 142–60. Ed. D. A. Campbell. Sheffield: Sheffield Academic.

1996c. 'Other Early Christian Writings: "Didache", Ignatius, "Barnabas", Justin Martyr'. In *Early Christian Thought in its Jewish Context* (Festschrift for M. D. Hooker), 174–90. Ed. J. Barclay and J. Sweet. Cambridge: Cambridge University Press.

1997a. 'The Fourfold Gospel'. *NTS* 43: 317–46.

1997b. 'Jesus Traditions'. In *Dictionary of the Later New Testament and its Developments: A Compendium of Contemporary Biblical Scholarship*, 565–79. Ed. R. P. Martin and P. H. Davids. Downers Grove: InterVarsity Press.

1998a. '"God-Fearers": Neglected Evidence in Justin Martyr's Dialogue with Trypho'. In *Ancient History in a Modern University, Vol. 2: Early Christianity, Late Antiquity and Beyond* (Festschrift for E. Judge), 43–52. Ed. T. W. Hillard et al. Sydney and Grand Rapids: Macquarie University Ancient History Documentary Research Centre and Eerdmans.

1998b. 'Introduction'. In *Tolerance and Intolerance in Early Judaism and Early Christianity*, 1–6. Ed. G. N. Stanton and G. G. Stroumsa. Cambridge: Cambridge University Press.

1998c. 'Justin Martyr's *Dialogue with Trypho*: Group Boundaries, "Proselytes", and "God-Fearers"'. In *Tolerance and Intolerance in Early Judaism and Early Christianity*, 263–78. Ed. G. N. Stanton and G. G. Stroumsa. Cambridge: Cambridge University Press.

1999. 'Matthew, Gospel of'. In *Dictionary of Biblical Interpretation*, II:136–41. Ed. J. H. Hayes. Nashville: Abingdon.

2001a. 'The Early Reception of Matthew's Gospel: New Evidence from Papyri?' In *The Gospel of Matthew in Current Study: Studies in Memory of William G. Thompson, S. J.*, 42–61. Ed. D. E. Aune. Grand Rapids: Eerdmans.

2001b. 'Galatians'. In *The Oxford Bible Commentary*, 1152–65. Ed. J. Barton and J. Muddiman. Oxford: Oxford University Press.

2001c. 'Message and Miracles'. In *The Cambridge Companion to Jesus*, 56–71. Ed. M. Bockmuehl. Cambridge Companions to Religion. Cambridge: Cambridge University Press.

2001d. 'What is the Law of Christ?' *Ex Auditu* 17: 47–59.

2002. '"I Think, when I Read that Sweet Story of Old": A Response to Douglas Campbell'. In *Narrative Dynamics in Paul: A Critical Assessment*, 125–32. Ed. B. W. Longenecker. Louisville: Westminster John Knox.

2003a. '1 Peter'. In *Eerdmans Commentary on the Bible*, 1493–1503. Ed. J. D. G. Dunn and J. W. Rogerson. Grand Rapids: Eerdmans.

2003b. 'Jesus Traditions and Gospels in Justin Martyr and Irenaeus'. In *The Biblical Canons*, 353–70. Ed. J.-M. Auwers and H. J. de Jonge. BETL 163. Leuven: Leuven University Press and Peeters.

2003c. 'The Law of Christ: A Neglected Theological Gem?' In *Reading Texts, Seeking Wisdom: Scripture and Theology*, 169–84. Ed. D. F. Ford and G. N. Stanton. London: SCM.

2003d. 'Paul's Gospel'. In *Cambridge Companion to St Paul*, 173–84. Ed. J. D. G. Dunn. Cambridge Companions to Religion. Cambridge: Cambridge University Press.

2004a. 'Early Christian Preference for the Codex'. In *The Earliest Gospels: The Origins and Transmission of the Earliest Christian Gospels – The Contribution of the Chester Beatty Gospel Codex P45*, 40–9. Ed. C. Horton. JSNTSup 258. London: T. & T. Clark International.

2004b. 'The Spirit in the Writings of Justin Martyr'. In *The Holy Spirit and Christian Origins: Essays in Honor of James D. G. Dunn*, 321–34. Ed. G. N. Stanton et al. Grand Rapids: Eerdmans.

2005a. 'Evidence in the Pseudo-Clementine Writings for Jewish Believers in Jesus'. In *A History of Jewish Believers in Jesus: The First Five Centuries*. Ed. R. Hvalvik and O. Skarsaune. Peabody: Hendrickson.

2005b. 'Terrorism and Reconciliation'. *Theology* 108.

Bibliography

Abraham, William J. 1998. *Canon and Criterion in Christian Theology: From the Fathers to Feminism*. Oxford: Clarendon.

Achtemeier, P. J. 1990. '*Omne Verbum Sonat*: The New Testament and the Oral Environment of Late Western Antiquity'. *JBL* 109: 3–27.

Ådna, Jostein. 2000. *Jesu Stellung zum Tempel: Die Tempelaktion und das Tempelwort als Ausdruck seiner messianischen Sendung*. WUNT 2.119. Tübingen: Mohr (Siebeck).

Aland, Kurt, ed. 1997. *Synopsis Quattuor Evangeliorum: Locis Parallelis Evangeliorum Apocryphorum et Patrum Adhibitis*. 15th edn. Stuttgart: Deutsche Bibelgesellschaft.

Aland, Kurt and Barbara Aland. 1989. *The Text of the New Testament: An Introduction to the Critical Editions and to the Theory and Practice of Modern Textual Criticism*. Trans. E. F. Rhodes. 2nd rev. edn. Grand Rapids and Leiden: Ecrdmans and Brill.

Albl, Martin C. 1999. *And Scripture Cannot be Broken: The Form and Function of the Early Christian Testimonia Collections*. NovTSup 96. Leiden: Brill.

Alexander, Loveday C. A. 1986. 'Luke's Preface in the Context of Greek Preface-Writing'. *NovT* 28: 48–74.

    1993. *The Preface to Luke's Gospel: Literary Convention and Social Context in Luke 1.1–4 and Acts 1.1*. SNTSMS 78. Cambridge: Cambridge University Press.

    1994. 'Paul and the Hellenistic Schools: The Evidence of Galen'. In *Paul in his Hellenistic Context*, 60–83. Ed. T. Engberg-Pedersen. Edinburgh: T. & T. Clark.

    1995. '"In Journeyings Often": Voyaging in Acts of the Apostles and in Greek Romance'. In *Luke's Literary Achievement*, 17–49. Ed. C. M. Tuckett. JSNTSup 116. Sheffield: Sheffield Academic.

    1996. 'The Preface to Acts and the Historians'. In *History, Literature, and Society in the Book of Acts*, 73–103. Ed. B. Witherington, III. Cambridge: Cambridge University Press.

    2002. '"Foolishness to the Greeks": Jews and Christians in the Public Life of the Empire'. In *Philosophy and Power in the Graeco-Roman World: Essays in Honour of Miriam Griffin*, 229–49. Ed. G. Clark and T. Rajak. Oxford: Oxford University Press.

Alexander, Philip S. 2005 (forthcoming). 'Jewish Christians in Early Rabbinic Literature (2nd–5th Centuries)'. In *A History of Jewish Believers in Jesus: The First Five Centuries*. Ed. R. Hvalvik and O. Skarsaune. Peabody: Hendrickson.

Allegro, J. M. 1956. 'Further Messianic References in Qumran Literature'. *JBL* 75: 174–87.

Allen, O. W. 1997. *The Death of Herod: The Narrative and Theological Function of Retribution in Luke–Acts*. SBLDS 158. Atlanta: Scholars.

Allen, W. C. 1912. *A Critical and Exegetical Commentary on the Gospel according to St. Matthew*. ICC. 3rd edn. Edinburgh: T. & T. Clark.

Allert, Craig D. 1999. 'The State of the New Testament Canon in the Second Century: Putting Tatian's *Diatessaron* in Perspective'. *BBR* 9: 1–18.

Allison, Dale C. 1988. 'Was There a "Lukan Community"?' *IBS* 10: 62–70.

   1998. *Jesus of Nazareth: Millenarian Prophet*. Minneapolis: Fortress.

Ascough, Richard S. 2001. 'Matthew and Community Formation'. In *The Gospel of Matthew in Current Study: Studies in Memory of William G. Thompson, S. J.*, 96–126. Ed. D. E. Aune. Grand Rapids: Eerdmans.

Ashton, J. 1991. *Understanding the Fourth Gospel*. Oxford: Clarendon.

Asiedu-Peprah, M. 2001. *Johannine Sabbath-Conflicts as Juridicial Controversy*. WUNT 2.132. Tübingen: Mohr (Siebeck).

Augustine. 1995. *The Works of Saint Augustine: A Translation for the 21st Century*, Vol. X: *Sermons on Various Subjects, 341–400*. Trans. E. Hill. Ed. J. E. Rotelle. Brooklyn: New City Press.

Aune, David E. 1980. 'Magic in Early Christianity'. *ANRW* II.23.2: 1507–57.

   1987. *The New Testament in its Literary Environment*. LEC 8. Philadelphia: Westminster.

Aune David E., ed. 2001. *The Gospel of Matthew in Current Study: Studies in Memory of William G. Thompson, S.J.* Grand Rapids: Eerdmans.

Avi-Yonah, Michael. 1976. *The Jews of Palestine: A Political History from the Bar Kokhba War to the Arab Conquest*. Oxford: Blackwell.

Bacher, W. 1899, 1905. *Die exegetische Terminologie der jüdischen Traditionsliteratur*. 2 vols. Leipzig: J. C. Hinrich. Repr. in one vol., Darmstadt: Wissenschaftliche Buchgesellschaft, 1965.

Bacon, Benjamin Wisner. 1930. *Studies in Matthew*. New York: Holt.

Bailey, Kenneth E. 1976. *Poet and Peasant: A Literary-Cultural approach to the Parables in Luke*. Grand Rapids: Eerdmans.

Balch, David L., ed. 1991. *Social History of the Matthean Community: Cross-Disciplinary Approaches*. Minneapolis: Fortress.

Ball, D. M. 1996. *'I am' in John's Gospel: Literary Function, Background and Theological Implications*. JSNTSup 124. Sheffield: Sheffield Academic.

Bammel, Ernst. 1966–7. 'Christian Origins in Jewish Tradition'. *NTS* 13: 317–35. Repr. in *Kleine Schriften I*, 220–38.

   1968. 'Origen *Contra Celsum* i.41 and the Jewish Tradition'. *JTS* N.S. 19: 211–13. Repr. in *Kleine Schriften I*, 194–5.

   1986a. 'Der Jude des Celsus'. In *Judaica: Kleine Schriften I*, 265–83. WUNT 37. Tübingen: Mohr (Siebeck).

1986b. *Judaica: Kleine Schriften I*. WUNT 37. Tübingen: Mohr (Siebeck).

Banning, Joop van. 1988. *Opus Imperfectum in Matthaeum*. CCSL 87. Turnhout: Brepols.

Barrett, C. K. 1971. *The Prologue of St. John's Gospel*. London: Athlone Press. Repr. in *New Testament Essays*, 27–48. London: SPCK, 1972.

1972. *New Testament Essays*. London: SPCK.

1975. *The Gospel of John and Judaism*. Trans. D. M. Smith. London: SPCK.

1994. *A Critical and Exegetical Commentary on the Acts of the Apostles*. ICC. Vol. I. Edinburgh: T. & T. Clark.

1996. 'The First New Testament?' *NovT* 38: 94–104.

Barth, Gerhard. 1963. 'Matthew's Understanding of the Law'. In *Tradition and Interpretation in Matthew*, 58–164. By G. Bornkamm et al. Trans. P. Scott. NTL. Philadelphia: Westminster.

Barthes, Roland. 1968. 'La Mort de l'Auteur'. *Mantéia* 5. ET: 'The Death of the Author'. In *Image–Music–Text*, 142–8. Trans. S. Heath. London: Fontana, 1977.

Barton, Stephen C. 1988. 'Can we Identify the Gospel Audiences?' In *The Gospels for All Christians: Rethinking the Gospel Audiences*, 173–94. Ed. R. Bauckham. Grand Rapids: Eerdmans.

Bauckham, Richard. 1990. *Jude and the Relatives of Jesus in the Early Church*. Edinburgh: T. & T. Clark.

1998a. 'A Response to Philip Esler'. *SJT* 51: 249–53.

Bauckham, Richard, ed. 1998b. *The Gospels for All Christians: Rethinking the Gospel Audiences*. Grand Rapids: Eerdmans.

Bauer, W. 1909. *Das Leben Jesu im Zeitalter der neutestamentlichen Apokryphen*. Tübingen: Mohr (Siebeck).

Bauer, W. et al. 2000. *A Greek–English Lexicon of the New Testament and Other Early Christian Literature*. 3rd edn. Chicago and London: University of Chicago Press.

Baum, A. D. 1998. 'Papias, der Vorzug der Viva Vox und die Evangelienschriften'. *NTS* 44: 144–51.

2003. 'Oral Poetry und synoptische Frage: Analogien zu Umfang, Variation und Art der synoptischen Wortlautidentität'. *TZ* 59: 17–34.

Bauman, Clarence. 1985. *The Sermon on the Mount: The Modern Quest for its Meaning*. Leuven and Macon: Peeters and Mercer University Press.

Beasley-Murray, G. R. 1986. *Jesus and the Kingdom of God*. Grand Rapids and Carlisle: Eerdmans and Paternoster.

1987. *John*. WBC 36. 2nd edn. Dallas: Word.

Beaton, Richard. 2002. *Isaiah's Christ in Matthew's Gospel*. SNTSMS 123. Cambridge: Cambridge University Press.

Beavis, Mary Ann. 1989. *Mark's Audience: The Literary and Social Setting of Mark 4.11–12* JSNTSup 33. Sheffield: Sheffield Academic.

Bekkum, W. J. van. 1998. *Hebrew Poetry from Late Antiquity: Liturgical Poems of Yehudah: Critical Edition with Introduction and Commentary*. AGJU 43. Leiden: Brill.

Bellinzoni, A. J. 1967. *The Sayings of Jesus in the Writings of Justin Martyr.* NovTSup 17. Leiden: Brill.

Benko, Stephen. 1980. 'Pagan Criticism of Christianity during the First Two Centuries AD'. *ANRW* II.23.2: 1054–118.

Bernstein, Moshe J. 1994a. '4Q252: From Re-Written Bible to Biblical Commentary'. *JJS* 45: 1–27.

1994b. 'Introductory Formulas for Citation and Re-citation of Biblical Verses in the Qumran Pesharim'. *DSD* 1: 30–70.

Best, E. 1983. *Mark: The Gospel as Story.* Edinburgh: T. & T. Clark.

Betz, Hans Dieter. 1995. *The Sermon on the Mount: A Commentary on the Sermon on the Mount, Including the Sermon on the Plain (Matthew 5:3–7:27 and Luke 6:20–49).* Hermeneia. Minneapolis: Fortress.

Betz, Hans Dieter, ed. 1986. *The Greek Magical Papyri in Translation,* Vol. I: *Texts.* Chicago: University of Chicago Press.

Bi(c)kerman, Elias. 1938. *Les Institutions des Séleucides.* Paris: Geuthner.

Bieringer, R., D. Pollefeyt, and F. Vandercasteele-Vanneuville, eds. 2001. *Anti-Judaism and the Fourth Gospel: Papers of the Leuven Colloquium 2000.* JCH 1. Assen: Van Gorcum.

Bilezikian, Gilbert G. 1977. *The Liberated Gospel: A Comparison of the Gospel of Mark and Greek Tragedy.* Grand Rapids: Baker.

Biondi, Alessandro. 1983. *Gli accenti nei papiri greci biblici.* PapyCast 9. Rome and Barcelona: distributed by Biblical Institute Press.

Black, C. Clifton. 1994. *Mark: Images of an Apostolic Interpreter.* SPNT. Columbia and Edinburgh: University of South Carolina Press and T. & T. Clark.

Blanc, Cécile. 1975. 'Le Commentaire d'Héracléon sur Jean 4 et 8'. *Aug* 15: 82–124.

Bockmuehl, Markus. 2006 (forthcoming). 'The Dead Sea Scrolls and Ancient Commentary'. In *Text, Thought, and Practice in Qumran and Early Christianity: Proceedings of the Ninth International Symposium of the Orion Center for the Study of the Dead Sea Scrolls and Associated Literature.* Ed. D. R. Schwartz and R. Clements. STDJ. Leiden: Brill.

Borg, Marcus J. 1984. *Conflict, Holiness, and Politics in the Teachings of Jesus.* SBEC 5. New York: Edwin Mellen. Repr. Harrisburg: Trinity Press International, 1998.

1986. 'A Temperate Case for a Non-Eschatological Jesus'. *Forum* 2, no. 3: 81–102.

1987. *Jesus: A New Vision: Spirit, Culture, and the Life of Discipleship.* San Francisco: Harper.

Borgen, Peder. 1965. *Bread from Heaven: An Exegetical Study of the Concept of Manna in the Gospel of John and the Writings of Philo.* NovTSup 10. Leiden: Brill.

1969–70. 'Observations on the Targumic Character of the Prologue of John'. *NTS* 16: 288–95.

Bousset, Wilhelm. 1921. *Kyrios Christos: Geschichte des Christusglaubens von den Anfängen des Christentums bis Irenaeus.* FRLANT 21. 2nd edn. Göttingen: Vandenhoeck & Ruprecht.

Bovon, François. 1988. 'The Synoptic Gospels and the Non-Canonical Acts of the Apostles'. *HTR* 81: 19–34.

2003. 'The Synoptic Gospels and the Noncanonical Acts of the Apostles'. In *Studies in Early Christianity*, 209–25. Ed. F. Bovon. WUNT 161. Tübingen: Mohr (Siebeck).

2004. 'The Reception and Use of the Gospel of Luke in the Second Century' (unpub. MS).

Bowden, J. 1988. *Jesus: The Unanswered Questions*. London: SCM.

Bowersock, G. W. 1994. *Fiction as History: Nero to Julian*. Berkeley: University of California Press.

Bowie, E. L. 1978. 'Apollonius of Tyana: Tradition and Reality'. *ANRW* II. 16.2: 1652–99.

Boyarin, D. 2001. 'The Gospel of the *Memra*: Jewish Binitarianism and the Prologue to John'. *HTR* 94: 243–84.

Brock, Sebastian P. 1967. 'Greek Words in the Syriac Gospels (*VET* and *PE*)'. *Mus* 80: 389–426.

Brooke, A. E., N. McLean, and H. St J. Thackeray, eds. 1927. *The Old Testament in Greek*, Vol. II: *The Later Historical Books*, Pt I: *I and II Samuel*. Cambridge: Cambridge University Press.

Brooke, George J. 1996. '4Q252 as Early Jewish Commentary'. *RevQ* 17.65–8: 385–401.

2000. 'Pesharim'. *DNTB*: 778–82.

Brooks, Stephenson H. 1987. *Matthew's Community: The Evidence of his Special Sayings Material*. JSNTSup 16. Sheffield: JSOT Press.

Brown, R. E. 1966, 1970. *The Gospel according to John*. AB 29, 29A. 2 vols. New York: Doubleday.

1979. *The Community of the Beloved Disciple*. London and New York: Chapman and Paulist.

1994. *The Death of the Messiah: From Gethsemane to the Grave: A Commentary on the Passion Narratives in the Four Gospels*. ABRL. 2 vols. New York: Doubleday.

1997. *An Introduction to the New Testament*. ABRL. New York: Doubleday.

2003. *An Introduction to the Gospel of John*. Ed. F. J. Moloney. ABRL. New York: Doubleday.

Buckwalter, H. D. 1996. *The Character and Purpose of Luke's Christology*. SNTSMS 89. Cambridge: Cambridge University Press.

Bultmann, R. 1921. *Die Geschichte der synoptischen Tradition*. FRLANT N. S. 12 (1st edn). Göttingen: Vandenhoeck & Ruprecht.

1951–5. *Theology of the New Testament*. Trans. K. Grobel. 2 vols. New York: Scribner.

1966. *Die Erforschung der synoptischen Evangelien*. 5th edn. Berlin: A. Töpelmann.

1967. 'Das Verhältnis der urchristlichen Christusbotschaft zum historischen Jesus [1960]'. In *Exegetica: Aufsätze zur Erforschung des Neuen Testaments*, 445–69. Ed. E. Dinkler. Tübingen: Mohr (Siebeck).

1969. 'Liberal Theology and the Latest Theological Movement [1924]'. In *Faith and Understanding I*, 28–52. Ed. R. W. Funk. Trans. L. P. Smith. London: SCM.

1971. *The Gospel of John: A Commentary*. Trans. G. R. Beasley-Murray. et al. Oxford and Philadelphia: Blackwell and Westminster.

1972. *The History of the Synoptic Tradition*. Trans. J. Marsh. 3rd edn. Oxford: Blackwell.

1995. *Geschichte der synoptischen Tradition* (1921/1931/1957). FRLANT N. S. 29. 10th edn. Göttingen: Vandenhoeck & Ruprecht.

Burridge, Richard A. 1992. *What Are the Gospels? A Comparison with Graeco-Roman Biography*. SNTSMS 70. Cambridge: Cambridge University Press.

1994. *Four Gospels, One Jesus? A Symbolic Reading*. Grand Rapids and London: Eerdmans and SPCK. 2nd edn. forthcoming in 2005.

1998. 'About People, by People, for People: Gospel Genre and Audiences'. In *The Gospels for All Christians: Rethinking the Gospel Audiences*, 113–45. Ed. R. Bauckham. Grand Rapids: Eerdmans.

2000. 'Gospel Genre, Christological Controversy and the Absence of Rabbinic Biography: Some Implications of the Biographical Hypothesis'. In *Christology, Controversy and Community: New Testament Essays in Honour of David Catchpole* 137–56. Ed. D. G. Horrell and C. M. Tuckett. NovTSup 99. Leiden: Brill. Repr. in *What Are the Gospels?*, Appendix II: 322–40. 2nd rev. edn. Grand Rapids: Eerdmans, 2004.

2004. *What Are the Gospels? A Comparison with Graeco-Roman Biography*. Foreword from Graham N. Stanton. BRS. 2nd rev. edn. Grand Rapids: Eerdmans.

Byrskog, Samuel. 2000. *Story as History – History as Story: The Gospel Tradition in the Context of Ancient Oral History*. WUNT 123. Tübingen: Mohr (Siebeck). Repr. Boston and Leiden: Brill Academic, 2002.

2004. 'A New Perspective on the Jesus Tradition: Reflections on James D. G. Dunn's *Jesus Remembered*'. *JSNT* 26: 459–71.

Cadbury, H. J. 1922a. 'Commentary on the Preface of Luke'. In *The Beginnings of Christianity*, Part 1, Vol. II, Appendix C: 488–510. Ed. F. J. Foakes-Jackson and K. Lake. London: Macmillan.

1922b. 'The Knowledge Claimed in Luke's Preface'. *Exp* 8: 401–20.

1922c. 'The Purpose Expressed in Luke's Preface'. *Exp* 8: 431–41.

1927. *The Making of Luke–Acts*. New York and London: Macmillan. Repr. London: SPCK, 1958.

1955. *The Book of Acts in History*. New York: Harper.

1956–7. '"We" and "I" Passages in Luke–Acts'. *NTS* 3: 128–32.

Cahill, Michael. 1998. *The First Commentary on Mark: An Annotated Translation*. Oxford and New York: Oxford University Press.

Caird, George B. 1994. *New Testament Theology*. Completed and edited by L. D. Hurst. Oxford: Clarendon.

Cameron, Ron, ed. 1982. *The Other Gospels: Non-Canonical Gospel Texts*. Philadelphia: Westminster.

Campenhausen, Hans von. 1972. *The Formation of the Christian Bible.* Trans. J. A. Baker. London and Philadelphia: A. & C. Black and Fortress.

Cancik, Hubert. 1984a. 'Bios und Logos. Formengeschichtliche Untersuchungen zu Lukians "Leben des Demonax"'. In *Markus-Philologie: Historische, literargeschichtliche und stilistische Untersuchungen zum zweiten Evangelium,* 115–30. Ed. H. Cancik. WUNT 33. Tübingen: Mohr (Siebeck).

　1984b. 'Die Gattung Evangelium: Markus im Rahmen der antiken Historiographie'. In *Markus-Philologie: Historische, literargeschichtliche und stilistische Untersuchungen zum zweiten Evangelium,* 85–113. Ed. H. Cancik. WUNT 33. Tübingen: Mohr (Siebeck).

Carleton Paget, J. N. B. 1996. 'The Christian Exegesis of the Old Testament in the Alexandrian Tradition'. In *Hebrew Bible/Old Testament: The History of its Interpretation,* I.1: 478–542. Ed. M. Sæbø. Göttingen: Vandenhoeck & Ruprecht.

Carter, W. 2000. *Matthew and the Margins: A Sociopolitical and Religious Reading.* Sheffield: Sheffield Academic.

Casey, M. 1996. *Is John's Gospel True?* London: Routledge.

　1998. *Aramaic Sources of Mark's Gospel.* SNTSMS 102. Cambridge: Cambridge University Press.

Catchpole, D. R. 1971. *The Trial of Jesus: A Study in the Gospels and Jewish Historiography from 1770 to the Present Day.* StPB 18. Leiden: Brill.

Chadwick, Henry. 1953. *Origen: Contra Celsum.* Cambridge: Cambridge University Press.

Charlesworth, James H. 2002. *The Pesharim and Qumran History: Chaos or Consensus?* Grand Rapids: Eerdmans.

Chilton, Bruce. 1996. *Pure Kingdom: Jesus' Vision of God.* SHJ. Grand Rapids and London: Eerdmans and SPCK.

Church, Alfred John and William Jackson Brodribb, eds. 1895. *Annals of Tacitus.* London: Macmillan.

Clines, D. J. A. and J. Elwolde, eds. 1995. *The Dictionary of Classical Hebrew.* Vol II. Sheffield: Sheffield Academic.

Coles, R. A., M. W. Haslam, and P. J. Parsons, eds. 1994. *The Oxyrhynchus Papyri LX.* London: Egypt Exploration Society.

Collins, Adela Yarbro. 1999. 'The Worship of Jesus and the Imperial Cult'. In *The Jewish Roots of Christological Monotheism: Papers from the St. Andrews Conference on the Historical Origins of the Worship of Jesus,* 234–57. Ed. C. C. Newman et al. JSJSup 63. Leiden: Brill.

Conzelmann, Hans. 1960. *The Theology of St. Luke.* Trans. G. Buswell. London and New York: Faber and Harper & Row.

　1966. 'Luke's Place in the Development of Early Christianity'. In *Studies in Luke–Acts: Essays Presented in Honor of Paul Schubert,* 298–316. Ed. L. E. Keck and J. L. Martyn. Nashville: Abingdon.

Cook, E. M. 1994. 'A New Perspective on the Language of Onkelos and Jonathan'. In *The Aramaic Bible: Targums in their Historical Context,* 142–56.

Ed. D. R. G. Beattie and M. J. McNamara. JSOTSup 166. Sheffield: JSOT Press, published in Association with the Royal Irish Academy.

Cook, John G. 1997. 'In Defence of Ambiguity: Is There a Hidden Demon in Mark 1.29–31?' *NTS* 43: 184–208.

2000. *The Interpretation of the New Testament in Greco-Roman Paganism.* STAC 3. Tübingen: Mohr (Siebeck).

Cremer, Hermann. 1893. *Biblisch-theologisches Wörterbuch der neutestamentlichen Gräzität.* 7th edn: Gotha: F. A. Perthes, 1893; 10th edn: ed. J. Kögel, 1911.

Cross, Frank Moore. 1975. 'The History of the Biblical Text in the Light of Discoveries in the Judean Desert'. In *Qumran and the History of the Biblical Text,* 177–95. Ed. F. M. Cross and S. Talmon. Cambridge, Mass. and London: Harvard University Press. Repr. from *HTR* 57 (1964): 281–99.

Crossan, John Dominic. 1985. *Four Other Gospels: Shadows on the Contour of Canon.* Minneapolis: Winston.

1991. *The Historical Jesus: The Life of a Mediterranean Jewish Peasant.* San Francisco and Edinburgh: Harper and T. & T. Clark.

Dalman, Gustaf. 1898. *Die Worte Jesu.* Leipzig: Hinrichs (2nd edn. 1930). ET: *The Words of Jesus Considered in the Light of Post-Biblical Jewish Writings and the Aramaic Language.* Trans. D. M. Kay. Edinburgh: T. & T. Clark, 1902.

Daniels, Jon B. 1989. 'The Egerton Gospel: Its Place in Early Christianity'. Unpublished dissertation, Claremont Graduate School.

Davies, W. D. 1963. *The Setting of the Sermon on the Mount.* Cambridge: Cambridge University Press.

Davies, W. D. and D. C. Allison. 1988–97. *A Critical and Exegetical Commentary on the Gospel according to Saint Matthew.* ICC. 3 vols. Edinburgh: T. & T. Clark.

Dawson, David. 1992. *Allegorical Readers and Cultural Revision in Ancient Alexandria.* Berkeley: University of California Press.

de Lange, N. R. M. 1976. *Origen and the Jews: Studies in Jewish–Christian Relations in Third-century Palestine.* UCOP 25. Cambridge: Cambridge University Press.

Degenhardt, H.-J. 1965. *Lukas Evangelist der Armen: Besitz und Besitzverzicht in den lukanischen Schriften: Eine traditions- und redaktionsgeschichtliche Untersuchung.* Stuttgart: Katholisches Bibelwerk.

Deines, Roland. 2004. *Die Gerechtigkeit der Tora im Reich des Messias: Mt 5, 13–20 als Schlüsseltext der matthäischen Theologie.* WUNT 177. Tübingen: Mohr Siebeck.

Deissmann, Adolf. 1923. *Licht vom Osten: Das Neue Testament und die neuent-deckten Texte der hellenistisch-römischen Welt.* 4th rev. edn. Tübingen: Mohr (Siebeck). ET: *Light from the Ancient East: The New Testament Illustrated by Recently Discovered Texts of the Graeco-Roman World.* Trans. L. R. M. Strachan. London: Hodder & Stoughton, 1910.

del Fabbro, Marina. 1979. 'Il commentario nella tradizione papiracea'. *SPap* 18: 69–132.

Delcor, M. 1962. *Les Hymnes de Qumrân (Hodayot): Texte Hébreu, Introduction, Traduction, Commentaire.* Autour de la Bible. Paris: Letouzey et Ané.

Delobel, Joël. 1989. 'Extra-Canonical Sayings of Jesus: Marcion and Some "Non-received" Logia'. In *Gospel Traditions in the Second Century: Origins, Recensions, Text, and Transmission*, 105–16. Ed. W. L. Petersen. CJA 3. Notre Dame: University of Notre Dame Press.

Denaux, A. 1997. 'Old Testament Models for the Lukan Travel Narrative: A Critical Survey'. In *The Scriptures in the Gospels*, 271–305. Ed. C. M. Tuckett. Leuven: Leuven University Press and Peeters.

Di Segni, R. 1985. *Il Vangelo del Ghetto*. Rome: Newton Compton.

Dibelius, Martin. 1919. *Die Formgeschichte des Evangeliums* (1st edn). Tübingen: Mohr (Siebeck).

1922. Review of R. Bultmann, *Geschichte der synoptischen Tradition*, Göttingen: Vandenhoeck & Ruprecht, 1921. *DL 43*, no. 7/8: 128–34.

1932. Review of R. Bultmann, *Geschichte der synoptischen Tradition*, Göttingen: Vandenhoeck & Ruprecht, 1931. *DL 53*, no. 24: 1105–11.

1933. *Die Formgeschichte des Evangeliums*. 2nd edn. Tübingen: Mohr (Siebeck).

1971. *From Tradition to Gospel*. Trans. B. L. Woolf. London: James Clarke.

Dihle, A. 1987. *Die Entstehung der historischen Biographie*. Heidelberg: Universitätsverlag.

Dillon, R. J. 1978. *From Eyewitnesses to Ministers of the Word*. AnBib 82. Rome: Biblical Institute.

Doble, P. 1996. *The Paradox of Salvation: Luke's Theology of the Cross*. SNTSMS 87. Cambridge: Cambridge University Press.

Dodd, C. H. 1952. *According to the Scriptures: The Sub-Structure of New Testament Theology*. London: Nisbet.

1963. *Historical Tradition in the Fourth Gospel*. Cambridge: Cambridge University Press.

Donahue, J. R. 1973. *Are You the Christ? The Trial Narrative in the Gospel of Mark*. SBLDS 10. Missoula: Scholars.

Dorandi, Tiziano. 2000. 'Le Commentaire dans la Tradition Papyrologique: Quelques Cas Controversés'. In *Le Commentaire entre Tradition et Innovation: Actes du Colloque International de l'Institut des Traditions Textuelles, Paris et Villejuif, 22–25 septembre 1999*, 15–27. Ed. M.-O. Goulet-Cazé and T. Dorandi. BHP. N.S. Paris: Vrin.

Downing, F. G. 2000. 'Markan Intercalation in Cultural Context'. In *Narrativity in Biblical and Related Texts / La Narrativité dans la Bible et les Textes Apparentés*, 105–18. Ed. G. J. Brooke and J.-D. Kaestli. BETL 149. Leuven: Leuven University Press and Peeters.

Droysen, J. G. 1977. *Historik: Vorlesungen über Enzyklopädie und Methodologie der Geschichte* (1932). Ed. R. Hübner. 7th edn. Darmstadt: Wissenschaftliche Buchgesellschaft.

Drury, John. 1976. *Tradition and Design in Luke's Gospel: A Study in Early Christian Historiography*. London: Darton, Longman and Todd. Repr. Atlanta: John Knox, 1977.

Dubrow, Heather. 1982. *Genre*. CrIS 42. London: Methuen.

Dümler, Bärbel. 1999. 'Chromatius von Aquileia'. *LACL*: 123–4.

Dunn, James D. G. 1991. 'John and the Oral Gospel Tradition'. In *Jesus and the Oral Gospel Tradition*, 351–79. Ed. H. Wansbrough. JSNTSup 64. Sheffield: JSOT Press.

   2003a. 'Altering the Default Setting: Re-envisaging the Early Transmission of the Jesus Tradition'. *NTS* 49: 139–75.

   2003b. *Christianity in the Making*, Vol. I: *Jesus Remembered*. Grand Rapids: Eerdmans.

   2004. 'On History, Memory and Eyewitnesses: In Response to Bengt Holmberg and Samuel Byrskog'. *JSNT* 26: 473–87.

Earl, D. 1972. 'Prologue-form in Ancient Historiography'. *ANRW* I.2: 842–56.

Edwards, J. R. 1999. 'Markan Sandwiches: The Significance of Interpolations in Markan Narratives'. In *The Composition of Mark's Gospel: Selected Studies from Novum Testamentum*, 192–215. Ed. D. E. Orton. BRBS 3. Leiden: Brill. Repr. from *NovT* 31 (1989): 193–216.

   2002. *The Gospel according to Mark*. PillNTC. Grand Rapids and Leicester: Eerdmans and Apollos.

Edwards, Mark. 2004a. *John*. BBCom. Oxford: Blackwell.

   2004b. Review of Ansgar Wucherpfennig, *Heracleon Philologus*, Tübingen: Mohr (Siebeck), 2002. *JEH* 55: 129–30.

Ehrman, Bart D. 1993. *The Orthodox Corruption of Scripture: The Effect of Early Christological Controversies on the Text of the New Testament*. Oxford and New York: Oxford University Press.

   1994. 'Heracleon and the "Western" Textual Tradition'. *NTS* 40: 161–79.

   2003a. *Lost Christianities: The Battles for Scripture and the Faiths We Never Knew*. Oxford and New York: Oxford University Press.

   2003b. *Lost Scriptures: Books that Did Not Make It into the New Testament*. Oxford and New York: Oxford University Press.

Elliott, J. K. 1993a. *The Apocryphal New Testament: A Collection of Apocryphal Christian Literature in an English Translation*. Oxford and New York: Clarendon and Oxford University Press.

   1993b. *The Language and Style of the Gospel of Mark: An Edition of C. H. Turner's 'Notes on Markan Usage' Together with Other Comparable Studies*. NovTSup 71. Leiden: Brill.

Elmslie, W. A. L. 1911. *The Mishna on Idolatry: Aboda Zara*. TS 8.2. Cambridge: Cambridge University Press.

Enslin, Morton. 1983. 'Luke and Matthew'. *ANRW* II.25.3: 2363.

Esler, Philip Francis. 1987. *Community and Gospel in Luke–Acts: The Social and Political Motivations of Lucan Theology*. SNTSMS 57. Cambridge: Cambridge University Press.

   1998. 'Community and Gospel in Early Christianity: A Response to Richard Bauckham's *Gospels for All Christians*'. *SJT* 51: 235–48.

Etaix, R. and Joseph Lemarié. 1974. *Chromatii Aquileiensis Opera*. CCSL 9A. Turnhout: Brepols.

Evans, C. F. 1990. *Saint Luke*. TPINTC. London and Philadelphia: SCM and Trinity Press International.

Evans, Craig A. 1982. '"Peter Warming Himself": The Problem of an Editorial "Seam"'. *JBL* 101: 245–9.

1994. 'Jesus in Non-Christian Sources'. In *Studying the Historical Jesus: Evaluations of the State of Current Research*, 443–78. Ed. B. Chilton and C. A. Evans. NTTS 19. Leiden: Brill.

2000. 'Mark's Incipit and the Priene Calendar Inscription: From Jewish Gospel to Greco-Roman Gospel'. *JGRCJ* 1: 67–81.

2001. *Mark 8:27–16:20*. WBC 34B. Nashville: Nelson.

Farmer, William R. and Denis M. Farkasfalvy. 1983. *The Formation of the New Testament Canon: An Ecumenical Approach*. ThI. New York: Paulist.

Fascher, E. 1924. *Die formgeschichtliche Methode: eine Darstellung und Kritik, zugleich ein Beitrag zur Geschichte des synoptischen Problems*. BZNW 2. Giessen: A. Töpelmann.

Feldmeier, R. 1985. 'The Portrayal of Peter in the Synoptic Gospels'. In *Studies in the Gospel of Mark*, 59–63. By M. Hengel. London and Philadelphia: SCM and Fortress.

Fernández Marcos, Natalio. 1998. *Introducción a las versiones griegas de la Biblia*. 2nd edn. Madrid: Instituto de Filología del Consejo Superior de Investigaciones Científicas. ET: *The Septuagint in Context: Introduction to the Greek Versions of the Bible*. Trans. W. G. E. Watson. Leiden: Brill, 2000.

Fernández Marcos, Natalio and José Ramón Busto Saiz. 1989. *El texto antioqueño de la Biblia griega*, Vol. I: *1–2 Samuel*. Madrid: Instituto de Filología del Consejo Superior de Investigaciones Científicas.

Finkelberg, Margalit. 2003. 'Homer as a Foundation Text'. In *Homer, the Bible, and Beyond: Literary and Religious Canons in the Ancient World*, 75–96. Ed. M. Finkelberg and G. A. G. Stroumsa. JSRC 2. Leiden and Boston, Mass.: Brill.

Fish, Stanley. 1980. *Is There a Text in This Class? The Authority of Interpretive Communities*. Cambridge, Mass: Harvard University Press.

Fitzmyer, J. A. 1981. *The Gospel According to Luke I–IX: A New Translation with Introduction and Commentary*. AB 28. New York: Doubleday.

1985. *The Gospel According to Luke X–XXIV: A New Translation with Introduction and Commentary*. AB 28A. New York: Doubleday.

1989. *Luke the Theologian: Aspects of His Teaching*. New York: Paulist.

Forbes, Peter Barr Reid, Robert Browning, and Nigel Guy Wilson. 1996. 'Crates of Mallus'. *OCD*: 406.

Ford, Andrew. 1999. 'Performing Interpretation: Early Allegorical Exegesis of Homer'. In *Epic Traditions in the Contemporary World: The Poetics of Community*, 33–53. Ed. M. H. Beissinger et al. Berkeley: University of California Press.

Ford, J. M. 1983. 'Reconciliation and Forgiveness in Luke's Gospel'. In *Political Issues in Luke–Acts*, 80–98. Ed. R. J. Cassidy and P. J. Scharper. Maryknoll: Orbis.

Fortna, R. 1970. *The Gospel of Signs: A Reconstruction of the Narrative Source Underlying the Fourth Gospel*. SNTSMS 11. Cambridge: Cambridge University Press.

1988. *The Fourth Gospel and its Predecessor: From Narrative Source to Present Gospel.* Edinburgh and Philadelphia: T. & T. Clark and Fortress.

Foster, Paul. 2004. *Community, Law and Mission in Matthew's Gospel.* WUNT 2.117. Tübingen: Mohr (Siebeck).

Fowler, Alastair. 1982. *Kinds of Literature: An Introduction to the Theory of Genres and Mode.* Oxford: Oxford University Press.

Frankenberg, W. 1896. *Die Datierung der Psalmen Salomos.* BZAW 1. Giessen: J. Ricker'sche Buchhandlung.

Frede, Michael. 1999. 'Origen's Treatise against Celsus'. In *Apologetics in the Roman Empire: Pagans, Jews, and Christians,* 131–55. Ed. M. Edwards et al. Oxford: Oxford University Press.

Frey, Jörg. 1997–2000. *Die johanneische Eschatologie I–III.* WUNT 96/110/117. 3 vols. Tübingen: Mohr (Siebeck).

Frickenschmidt, Dirk. 1997. *Evangelium als Biographie: die vier Evangelien im Rahmen antiker Erzählkunst.* TANZ 22. Tübingen: Francke.

Friedrich, G. 1935. '*Euangelizomai*'. In *TWNT* II:705–35. ET: *TDNT* II: 707–37.

Fuhrer, Therese. 1999. 'Kommentar'. *LACL*: 381–3.

Funk, F. and K. Bihlmeyer. 1924. *Die Apostolischen Väter: Neubearbeitung der Funkschen Ausgabe.* SAQ. Tübingen: Mohr (Siebeck).

Funk, Robert W. 1996. *Honest to Jesus: Jesus for a New Millennium.* San Francisco: Polebridge/Harper.

Funk, Robert W. and Roy W. Hoover, eds. 1993. *The Five Gospels: The Search for the Authentic Words of Jesus.* New York: Macmillan.

Gadamer, Hans-Georg. 1975. *Truth and Method.* London: Sheed and Ward.

Gamble, Harry Y. 1995. *Books and Readers in the Early Church: A History of Early Christian Texts.* New Haven: Yale University Press.

García Martínez, Florentino and Eibert J. C. Tigchelaar , eds. 1997–8. *The Dead Sea Scrolls Study Edition.* 2 vols. Leiden and Grand Rapids: Brill and Eerdmans.

García Martínez, Florentino, Eibert J. C. Tigchelaar, and Adam S. van der Woude, eds. 1998. *Qumran Cave 11.ii: 11Q2–18, 11Q20–31.* DJD 23. Oxford: Clarendon.

Garland, Robert. 2001. *The Greek Way of Death.* 2nd edn. Bristol: Bristol Classical Press.

Gasque, W. Ward. 1975. *A History of the Criticism of the Acts of the Apostles.* BGBE 17. Tübingen and Grand Rapids: Mohr (Siebeck) and Eerdmans. Repr. Peabody: Hendrickson, 1989.

Geerlings, Wilhelm. 1999. 'Anonymi Chiliastae in Mt Fragmenta'. *LACL*: 31.

Gerhardsson, Birger. 1961. *Memory and Manuscript: Oral Tradition and Written Transmission in Rabbinic Judaism and Early Christianity.* Uppsala: C. W. K. Gleerup.

1998. *Memory and Manuscript: Oral Tradition and Written Transmission in Rabbinic Judaism and Early Christianity, with Tradition and Transmission in Early Christianity* (1961/1964). Trans. E. J. Sharpe. BRS. Grand Rapids and Livonia: Eerdmans and Dove.

Gero, S. 1988. 'Apocryphal Gospels: A Survey of Textual and Literary Problems'. *ANRW* II.25.5: 3969–96.

Gianotto, C. 1984. *Melchisedek e la sua tipologia*. RivBSup 12. Brescia: Paideia.

Gill, D. 1970. 'Observations on the Lukan Travel Narrative and Some Related Passages'. *HTR* 63: 200–5.

Ginzberg, Louis. 1922. 'Some Observations on the Attitude of the Synagogue towards the Apocalyptic-Eschatological Writings'. *Journal of Biblical Literature* 41: 115–36.

Glare, P. G. W. et al., eds. 1996. H. G. Liddell, R.Scott, H. Stuart Jones, and R. McKenzie, eds. *Greek–English Lexicon: Revised Supplement*. Oxford: Clarendon.

Glover, R. 1964–5. 'Luke the Antiochene and Acts'. *NTS* 11: 97–106.

Goldschmidt, [E.] D. 1970. *Mahzor la-yamim ha-nora'im*. 2 vols. Jerusalem: Koren.

Goodacre, Mark S. 1996. *Goulder and the Gospels: An Examination of a New Paradigm*. JSNTSup 133. Sheffield: Sheffield Academic.

　　2002. *The Case Against Q*. Harrisburg: Trinity Press International.

Goody, Jack. 1986. *The Logic of Writing and the Organization of Society*. Cambridge: Cambridge University Press.

Goranson, Stephen. 1999. 'Joseph of Tiberias Revisited: Orthodoxies and Heresies in Fourth-Century Galilee'. In *Galilee through the Centuries: Confluence of Cultures*, 335–43. Ed. E. M. Meyers. DJSS 1. Winona Lake: Eisenbrauns.

Goulder, Michael D. 1974. *Midrash and Lection in Matthew: The Speaker's Lectures in Biblical Studies, 1969–71*. London: SPCK.

　　1988. *Luke: A New Paradigm*. JSNTSup 20. Sheffield: JSOT Press.

Grant, Patrick. 1989. *Reading the New Testament*. London and Grand Rapids: Macmillan and Eerdmans.

Green, Joel B. 1995. *The Theology of the Gospel of Luke*. NTTh. Cambridge: Cambridge University Press.

　　1996. 'Internal Repetition in Luke–Acts: Contemporary Narratology and Lucan Historiography'. In *History, Literature, and Society in the Book of Acts*, 283–99. Ed. B. Witherington, III. Cambridge: Cambridge University Press.

Gregory, Andrew. 2003. *The Reception of Luke and Acts in the Period before Irenaeus*. WUNT 2.169. Tübingen: Mohr (Siebeck).

Grotius, H. 1641. *Annotationes in Libros Evangeliorum*. Amsterdam: J. & C. Blaeuw.

Guelich, Robert A. 1989. *Mark 1–8:26*. WBC 34A. Dallas: Word.

　　1991. 'The Gospel Genre'. In *The Gospel and the Gospels*, 173–208. Ed. P. Stuhlmacher. Grand Rapids: Eerdmans.

Gundry, Robert H. 1993. *Mark: A Commentary on His Apology for the Cross*. Grand Rapids: Eerdmans.

　　1996. 'EUANGELION: How Soon a Book?' *JBL* 115: 321–5.

Guthmüller, Bodo. 2000. 'Kommentar'. *DNP* 14: 1055–7.

Hadot, Ilsetraut. 2002. 'Der fortlaufende philosophische Kommentar'. In *Der Kommentar in Antike und Mittelalter: Beiträge zu seiner Erforschung*, 183–99.

Ed. W. Geerlings and C. Schulze. CCAMA 2. Leiden and Boston, Mass.: Brill.

Haenchen, E. 1968. Review of C. H. Dodd, *Historical Tradition in the Fourth Gospel*, Cambridge: Cambridge University Press, 1963. *TLZ* 93: 346–8.

1971. *The Acts of the Apostles: A Commentary.* Trans. R. M. Wilson et al. Oxford and Philadelphia: Blackwell and Westminster.

Hagner, Donald A. 1985. 'The Sayings of Jesus in the Apostolic Fathers and Justin Martyr'. In *Gospel Perspectives*, Vol. V: *The Jesus Tradition Outside the Gospels*, 233–68. Ed. D. Wenham. Sheffield: JSOT Press.

1993. *Matthew 1–13.* WBC 33A. Dallas: Word.

1995. *Matthew 14–28.* WBC 33B. Dallas: Word.

1996. 'The *Sitz im Leben* of the Gospel of Matthew'. In *Treasures New and Old: Recent Contributions to Matthean Studies*, 27–68. Ed. D. R. Bauer and M. A. Powell. SBLSymS 1. Atlanta: Scholars.

Halbertal, Moshe. 1997. *People of the Book: Canon, Meaning, and Authority.* Cambridge, Mass.: Harvard University Press.

Hall, David R. 1998. *The Gospel Framework – Fiction or Fact? A Critical Examination of* Der Rahmen der Geschichte Jesu. Carlisle: Paternoster.

Hanson, A. T. 1991. *The Prophetic Gospel: A Study of John and the Old Testament.* Edinburgh: T. & T. Clark.

Harmless, William. 1995. *Augustine and the Catechumenate.* Collegeville: Liturgical Press.

Harnack, A. 1910. 'Evangelium: Geschichte des Begriffs in der ältesten Kirche'. In *Entstehung und Entwickelung der Kirchenverfassung und des Kirchenrechts in den zwei ersten Jahrhunderten*, 199–239. Leipzig: Hinrichs. ET: 'Gospel: History of the Conception in the Earliest Church'. In *The Constitution and Law of the Church in the First Two Centuries*, 275–331. London: Williams & Norgate, 1910.

1925. *The Origin of the New Testament and the Most Important Consequences of the New Creation.* Trans. J. R. Wilkinson. New York: Macmillan.

2003. *Marcion, der moderne Gläubige des 2. Jahrhunderts, der erste Reformator: Die Dorpater Preisschrift (1870). Kritische Edition des handschriftlichen Exemplars mit einem Anhang.* Ed. F. Steck. TUGAL 149. Berlin: de Gruyter.

Harrington, Daniel J. 1972. 'Abraham Traditions in the Testament of Abraham and in the "Rewritten Bible" of the Intertestamental Period'. In *International Organization for Septuagint and Cognate Studies and the SBL Pseudepigrapha Seminar, 1972 Proceedings*, 155–64. N.p.: Society of Biblical Literature.

Harris, Murray J. 1985. 'References to Jesus in Early Classical Authors'. In *Gospel Perspectives*, Vol. V: *The Jesus Tradition Outside the Gospels*, 343–68. Ed. D. Wenham. Sheffield: JSOT Press.

Hartin, P. J. 1991. *James and the Q Sayings of Jesus.* JSNTSup 47. Sheffield: JSOT Press.

Hawkins, J. C. 1909. *Horae Synopticae: Contributions to the Study of the Synoptic Problem.* Oxford: Clarendon.

Hays, Richard B. 1998. Foreword to paperback edition of *Lord of the Banquet: The Literary and Theological Significance of the Lukan Travel Narrative* by D. P. Moessner. Harrisburg: Trinity Press International.

Hedrick, C., ed. 1988. *The Historical Jesus and the Rejected Gospels. Semeia* 44.

Held, Heinz Joachim. 1963. 'Matthew as Interpreter of the Miracle Stories'. In *Tradition and Interpretation in Matthew*, 165–300. By G. Bornkamm et al. Trans. P. Scott. NTL. Philadelphia: Westminster.

Hengel, Martin. 1963. 'Maria Magdalena und die Frauen als Zeugen'. In *Abraham unser Vater: Juden und Christen im Gespräch über die Bibel. Festschrift für Otto Michel zum 60. Geburtstag*, 243–56. Ed. O. Betz et al. AGSU 5. Leiden: Brill.

1971. 'Kerygma oder Geschichte?' *TQ* 151: 323–36.

1977. *Crucifixion in the Ancient World and the Folly of the Message of the Cross.* Trans. J. Bowden. London and Philadelphia: SCM and Fortress.

1984a. *Die Evangelienüberschriften.* SHAW.PH 3. Heidelberg: Carl Winter, Universitätsverlag.

1984b. *Zur urchristlichen Geschichtsschreibung.* 2nd edn. Stuttgart: Calwer Verlag.

1985a. *Studies in the Gospel of Mark.* Trans. J. Bowden. London and Philadelphia: SCM and Fortress.

1985b. 'The Titles of the Gospels'. In *Studies in the Gospel of Mark*, 64–84. London and Philadelphia: SCM and Fortress.

1988. *Judentum und Hellenismus: Studien zu ihrer Begegnung unter besonderer Berücksichtigung Palästinas bis zur Mitte des 2. Jahrhunderts v. Chr.* (1969). WUNT 10. 3rd edn. Tübingen: Mohr (Siebeck).

1993. *Die Johanneische Frage: Ein Lösungsversuch.* WUNT 67. Tübingen: Mohr (Siebeck).

1999. 'Das Johannesevangelium als Quelle für die Geschichte des antiken Judentums'. In *Judaica, Hellenistica et Christiana: Kleine Schriften II*, 292–334. WUNT 109. Tübingen: Mohr (Siebeck).

2000. *The Four Gospels and the One Gospel of Jesus Christ: An Investigation of the Collection and Origin of the Canonical Gospels.* Trans. J. Bowden. London and Harrisburg: SCM and Trinity Press International.

2002a. 'Paulus und die frühchristliche Apokalyptik'. In *Paulus und Jakobus: Kleine Schriften III*, 302–42. WUNT 141. Tübingen: Mohr (Siebeck).

2002b. *Paulus und Jakobus: Kleine Schriften III.* WUNT 141. Tübingen: Mohr (Siebeck).

2002c. 'Zwischen Jesus und Paulus. Die "Hellenisten", die "Sieben" und Stephanus (Apg 6: 1–15; 7: 54–8:3)'. In *Paulus und Jakobus: Kleine Schriften III*, 1–67. WUNT 141. Tübingen: Mohr (Siebeck).

2003a. 'Die ersten heidnischen Leser der Evangelien'. *Hyp* 9: 89–111.

2003b. 'Eine junge theologische Disziplin in der Krise'. In *Neutestamentliche Wissenschaft: autobiographische Essays aus der Evangelischen Theologie*, 18–29. Ed. E. -M. Becker. UTB 2479. Tübingen: Francke.

2003c. '"Salvation History": The Truth of Scripture and Modern Theology'. In *Reading Texts, Seeking Wisdom*, 229–44. Ed. G. N. Stanton and D. F. Ford. Trans. J. Bowden. London: SCM.

2004a. 'Abba, Maranatha, Hosanna und die Anfänge der Christologie'. In *Denkwürdiges Geheimnis: Festschrift für E. Jüngel zum 70. Geburtstag*, 143–81. Ed. U. Dalferth. WUNT. Tübingen: Mohr (Siebeck).

2004b. 'Das Mahl in der Nacht, "in der Jesus ausgeliefert wurde" (1 Kor 11,23)'. In *Le Repas de Dieu / Das Mahl Gottes*, 115–59. Ed. C. Grappe. WUNT 169. Tübingen: Mohr (Siebeck).

Hengel, Martin and C. Markschies. 1996. 'Das Problem der "Hellenisierung" Judäas im 1. Jahrhundert nach Christus'. In *Judaica et Hellenistica: Kleine Schriften I*, 1–90. By M. Hengel. WUNT 90. Tübingen: Mohr (Siebeck).

Hengel, Martin and Anna Maria Schwemer. 1998. *Paulus zwischen Damascus und Antiochien: die unbekannten Jahre des Apostels*. WUNT 108. Tübingen: Mohr (Siebeck).

2001. *Der messianische Anspruch Jesu und die Anfänge der Christologie: vier Studien*. WUNT 138. Tübingen: Mohr (Siebeck).

Henige, David P. 1982. *Oral Historiography*. London: Longman.

Herford, R. Travers. 1903. *Christianity in Talmud and Midrash*. London. Repr. Clifton: Reference Book Publishers, 1966.

Higgins, A. J. B. 1970. 'The Preface to Luke and the Kerygma in Acts'. In *Apostolic History and the Gospel: Biblical and Historical Essays Presented to F. F. Bruce on his 60th Birthday*, 78–91. Ed. W. W. Gasque and R. P. Martin. Exeter and Grand Rapids: Paternoster and Eerdmans.

Hill, Charles E. 1998. 'What Papias said about John (and Luke)'. *JTS* 49: 582–629.

2004. *The Johannine Corpus in the Early Church*. Oxford: Oxford University Press.

Hirsch, E. D., Jr. 1967. *Validity in Interpretation*. New Haven: Yale University Press.

1976. *The Aims of Interpretation*. Chicago: University of Chicago Press.

Hoegen-Rohls, C. 1996. *Der nachösterliche Johannes*. WUNT 2.84. Tübingen: Mohr (Siebeck).

Hofrichter, P. L., ed. 2002. *Für und wider die Priorität des Johannesevangeliums*. Hildesheim: Olms.

Holmberg, Bengt. 2004. 'Questions of Method in James Dunn's *Jesus Remembered*'. *JSNT* 26: 445–57.

Holm-Nielsen, Svend. 1960. *Hodayot: Psalms from Qumran*. ATDan 2. Aarhus: Universitetsforlaget.

Honigman, Sylvie. 2003. *The Septuagint and Homeric Scholarship in Alexandria: A Study in the Narrative of the Letter of Aristeas*. London and New York: Routledge.

Hooker, Morna D. 1969–70. 'John the Baptist and the Johannine Prologue'. *NTS* 16: 354–8.

1974–5. 'The Johannine Prologue and the Messianic Secret'. *NTS* 21: 40–58.

1993. 'The Beginning of the Gospel'. In *The Future of Christology: Essays in Honor of Leander E. Keck*, 18–28. Ed. A. J. Malherbe and W. A. Meeks. Minneapolis: Fortress.

1997. *Beginnings: Keys that Open the Gospels.* London and Harrisburg: SCM and Trinity Press International.

2003. *Endings: Invitations to Discipleship.* London and Peabody: SCM and Hendrickson.

Horbury, William. 1970. 'A Critical Examination of the Toledoth Yeshu'. Unpublished dissertation, University of Cambridge.

1988. 'Old Testament Interpretation in the Writings of the Church Fathers'. In *Mikra: Text, Translation, Reading, and Interpretation of the Hebrew Bible in Ancient Judaism and Early Christianity*, 727–87. Ed. M. J. Mulder and H. Sysling. CRINT 2:1. Assen and Philadelphia: Van Gorcum and Fortress.

1997. 'Appendix: The Hebrew Text of Matthew in Shem Tob Ibn Shaprut's *Eben Bohan*'. In *A Critical and Exegetical Commentary on the Gospel according to Saint Matthew*, 3: 729–38. By W. D. Davies and D. C. Allison. ICC. 3 vols. Edinburgh: T. & T. Clark.

1998a. 'The Benediction of the Minim'. In *Jews and Christians in Contact and Controversy*, 67–110. Edinburgh: T. & T. Clark. Repr. from *JTS* N.S. 33 (1982): 19–61.

1998b. 'Christ as Brigand in Ancient Anti-Christian Polemic'. In *Jews and Christians in Contact and Controversy*, 162–73. Edinburgh: T. & T. Clark. Repr. from *Jesus and the Politics of His Day*, 183–95. Ed. E. Bammel and C. F. D. Moule. Cambridge: Cambridge University Press, 1984.

1998c. *Jewish Messianism and the Cult of Christ.* London: SCM.

1998d. *Jews and Christians in Contact and Controversy.* Edinburgh: T. & T. Clark.

1999. 'The Hebrew Matthew and Hebrew Study'. In *Hebrew Study from Ezra to Ben-Yehuda*, 122–31. Ed. W. Horbury. Edinburgh: T. & T. Clark.

2003. *Messianism among Jews and Christians: Twelve Biblical and Historical Studies.* London and New York: T. & T. Clark International.

Horgan, Maurya. 2002. 'Pesharim'. In *The Dead Sea Scrolls: Hebrew, Aramaic, and Greek Texts with English Translations*, 1–193. Ed. J. H. Charlesworth. PTSDSSP 6B. Tübingen and Louisville: Mohr (Siebeck) and Westminster/ John Knox.

Horsley, G. H. R. 1983. *New Documents Illustrating Early Christianity: A Review of the Greek Inscriptions and Papyri Published in 1978.* Macquarie University: Ancient Documentary Research Centre.

Horsley, Richard A. and Neil Asher Silberman. 1997. *The Message and the Kingdom: How Jesus and Paul Ignited a Revolution and Transformed the Ancient World.* New York: Grossett/Putnam. Repr. Minneapolis: Fortress, 2002.

Horst, P. W. van der. 1972. 'Can a Book End with γάρ? A Note on Mark xvi.8'. *JTS* N.S. 23: 121–4.

Howard, George. 1987. *The Gospel of Matthew according to a Primitive Hebrew Text.* Macon: Mercer University Press.

1995. *Hebrew Gospel of Matthew.* Macon: Mercer University Press.

Iser, Wolfgang. 1974. *The Implied Reader: Patterns of Communication in Prose Fiction from Bunyan to Beckett*. Baltimore: Johns Hopkins University Press.

1978. *The Art of Reading*. Baltimore: Johns Hopkins University Press.

Jacoby, Felix. 1929. *Die Fragmente der griechischen Historiker*, Vol. IIB3: *Historiker des Hellenismus u. der Kaiserzeit. Chronographen*. Berlin: Weidmann.

1930. *Die Fragmente der griechischen Historiker*, Vol. IIBD: *Kommentar*. Berlin: Weidmann.

Jensen, Robin Margaret. 2000. *Understanding Early Christian Art*. London and New York: Routledge.

Jeremias, Joachim. 1930. *Jesus als Weltvollender*. BFCT 33.4. Gütersloh: Evangelischer Verlag.

1963. *The Parables of Jesus*. Trans. S. H. Hooke. London: SCM.

1971a. *Neutestamentliche Theologie I*, Vol. I: *Die Verkündigung Jesu*. Gütersloh: Gütersloher Verlagshaus G. Mohn.

1971b. *New Testament Theology*, Vol. I: *The Proclamation of Jesus*. London and New York: SCM and Scribner.

Johnson, L. T. 1979. 'On Finding the Lukan Community: A Cautionary Essay'. In *SBL Seminar Papers, 1979*, I: 87–100. SBLSP 18. Missoula: Scholars.

1991. *The Gospel of Luke*. SP 3. Collegeville: Liturgical Press.

1992. 'Luke–Acts, Book of '. In *ABD*, IV: 403–20.

Just, Arthur A., Jr, ed. 2003. *Luke*. ACCSNT 3. Downers Grove: InterVarsity Press.

Kähler, M. 1964. *The So-Called Historical Jesus and the Historic, Biblical Christ* (1892). Trans. C. E. Braaten. Philadelphia: Fortress.

Karris, R. J. 1986. 'Luke 23:47 and the Lucan View of Jesus' Death'. *JBL* 105: 65–74.

Käsemann, Ernst. 1964. *Essays on New Testament Themes*. Trans. W. J. Montague. SBT 41. London: SCM. Repr. Philadelphia: Fortress, 1982.

1968. *The Testament of Jesus: A Study of the Gospel of John in the Light of Chapter 17*. Trans. G. Krodel. London and Philadelphia: SCM and Fortress.

1969. 'The Structure and Purpose of the Prologue to John's Gospel'. In *New Testament Questions of Today*, 138–67. Trans. W. J. Montague and W. F. Bunge. London and Philadelphia: SCM and Fortress.

Kaster, Robert A. 1999. 'Kommentar'. *DNP* 6: 680–2.

Kealy, Sean P. 1982. *Mark's Gospel: A History of its Interpretation*. New York: Paulist.

Keck, Leander E. 1965–6. 'The Introduction to Mark's Gospel'. *NTS* 12: 352–70.

Kee, Howard Clark. 1977. *Community of the New Age: Studies in Mark's Gospel*. Philadelphia: Westminster.

Kelber, Werner H. 1982. *The Oral and the Written Gospel: The Hermeneutics of Speaking and Writing in the Synoptic Tradition, Mark, Paul, and Q*. Philadelphia: Fortress. Repr. with a new introduction by the author and a foreword by Walter J. Ong. Bloomington and Indianapolis: Indiana University Press, 1997.

Kermode, Frank. 1967. *The Sense of an Ending: Studies in the Theory of Fiction*. New York: Oxford University Press.

Kilpatrick, G. D. 1946. *The Origins of the Gospel according to St. Matthew.* Oxford: Clarendon.

Kimelman, R. 1981. 'Birkat Ha-Minim and the Lack of Evidence for an Anti-Christian Jewish Prayer in Late Antiquity'. In *Jewish and Christian Self-Definition*, Vol. II: *Aspects of Judaism in the Graeco-Roman Period*, 226–44. Ed. E. P. Sanders et al. London and Philadelphia: SCM and Fortress.

King, Karen L. 2003. *What is Gnosticism?* Cambridge, Mass. and London: Belknap/Harvard University Press.

Kingsbury, Jack Dean. 1988. *Matthew as Story.* 2nd edn., rev. and enl. Philadelphia: Fortress.

Klauck, Hans-Josef. 2004. *Apocryphal Gospels: An Introduction.* Trans. B. McNeil. London and New York: T. & T. Clark/Continuum.

Klijn, A. F. J. 1992. *Jewish-Christian Gospel Tradition.* VCSup 17. Leiden: Brill.

Kloppenborg, J. S. 1987. *The Formation of Q: Trajectories in Ancient Wisdom Collections.* Philadelphia: Fortress.

1988. *Q Parallels: Synopsis, Critical Notes, and Concordance.* FF. Sonoma: Polebridge.

1995. 'Jesus and the Parables of Jesus in Q'. In *The Gospel Behind the Gospels: Current Studies on Q*, 275–319. Ed. R. A. Piper. NovTSup 75. Leiden: Brill.

2001. 'Discursive Practices in the Sayings Gospel Q and the Quest of the Historical Jesus'. In *The Sayings Source Q and the Historical Jesus*, 149–90. Ed. A. Lindemann. Leuven: Leuven University Press.

Kloppenborg Verbin, J. S. 2000. *Excavating Q: The History and Setting of the Sayings Gospel.* Minneapolis: Fortress.

Klostermann, Erich and Ernst Benz. 1935. *Origenes Matthäuserklärung.* GCS. 3 vols. Leipzig: Hinrichs.

Knowles, Michael. 1993. *Jeremiah in Matthew's Gospel: The Rejected-Prophet Motif in Matthean Redaction.* JSNTSup 68. Sheffield: JSOT Press.

Knox, J. 1987. 'Marcion's Gospel and the Synoptic Problem'. In *Jesus, the Gospels, and the Church: Essays in Honor of William R. Farmer*, 25–31. Ed. E. P. Sanders. Macon: Mercer University Press.

Koester, Helmut. 1980. 'Apocryphal and Canonical Gospels'. *HTR* 73: 105–30.

1989a. 'From the Kerygma-Gospel to Written Gospels'. *NTS* 35: 361–81.

1989b. 'The Text of the Synoptic Gospels in the Second Century'. In *Gospel Traditions in the Second Century: Origins, Recensions, Text, and Transmission*, 19–37. Ed. W. L. Petersen. CJA 3. Notre Dame: University of Notre Dame Press.

1990. *Ancient Christian Gospels: Their History and Development.* London and Philadelphia: SCM and Trinity Press International.

Köhler, Wolf-Dietrich. 1987. *Die Rezeption des Matthäusevangeliums in der Zeit vor Irenäus.* WUNT 2.24. Tübingen: Mohr (Siebeck).

Kokkinos, Nikos. 1998. *The Herodian Dynasty: Origins, Role in Society, and Eclipse.* JSPSup 30. Sheffield: Sheffield Academic.

Krauss, S. 1902. *Das Leben Jesu nach jüdischen Quellen.* Berlin: S. Calvary.

Kuhn, Karl Georg. 1960. 'Giljonim und sifrei minim'. In *Judentum-Urchristentum-Kirche: Festschrift für Joachim Jeremias*, 24–61. Ed. W. Eltester. BZNW 26. Berlin: Töpelmann.

Kümmel, W. G. 1975. 'Current Theological Accusations Against Luke'. *ANQ* 16: 134, 138.

Kurz, William S. 1984. 'Luke 3: 23–38 and Greco-Roman and Biblical Genealogies'. In *Luke–Acts: New Perspectives from the Society of Biblical Literature Seminar*, 169–87. Ed. C. H. Talbert. New York: Crossroad.

———. 1999. 'Promise and Fulfillment in Hellenistic Jewish Narratives and in Luke and Acts'. In *Luke the Interpreter of Israel*, Vol. I: *Jesus and the Heritage of Israel: Luke's Narrative Claim upon Israel's Legacy*, 147–70. Ed. D. P. Moessner. Harrisburg: Trinity Press International.

Kürzinger, J. 1977. 'Die Aussage des Papias von Hierapolis zur literarischen Form des Markusevangeliums'. *BZ* 21: 245–64.

Kvalbein, Hans. 2000. 'Has Matthew Abandoned the Jews?' In *The Mission of the Early Church to Jews and Gentiles*, 45–62. Ed. J. Ådna and H. Kvalbein. WUNT 127. Tübingen: Mohr (Siebeck).

Lagrange, Marie-Joseph. 1929. *Evangile selon Saint Marc*. EBib. 4th edn. Paris: Gabalda.

Lake, Kirsopp, trans. 1926. *Eusebius: Ecclesiastical History*. LCL 153. Vol. I. London and Cambridge, Mass: Heinemann and Harvard University Press.

Lampe, G. W. H. 1961. *A Patristic Greek Lexicon*. Oxford: Clarendon.

Landmesser, Christof. 2001. *Jüngerberufung und Zuwendung zu Gott: Ein exegetischer Beitrag zum Konzept der Matthäischen Soteriologie im Anschluss an Mt 9, 9–13*. WUNT 133. Tübingen: Mohr (Siebeck).

Lane Fox, Robin. 1986. *Pagans and Christians*. London: Viking.

Lazenby, J. F., Robert Browning, and N. G. Wilson. 1996. 'Aristarchus of Samothrace'. *OCD*: 159.

Lee, D. A. 1994. *The Symbolic Narratives of the Fourth Gospel: The Interplay of Form and Meaning*. JSNTSup 95. Sheffield: Sheffield Academic.

Leith, M. J. W. 1997. *Wadi Daliyeh, I, The Wadi Daliyeh Seal Impressions*. DJD 24. Oxford: Clarendon.

Lévêque, Pierre. 1959. *Aurea Catena Homeri: Une Etude sur l'Allegorie Grecque*. ALUB. Paris: Belles Lettres.

Liddell, H. G. et al. 1940. *A Greek–English Lexicon*. 9th edn. Oxford: Clarendon. Repr. with a Revised Supplement edited by P. G. W. Glare. Oxford: Clarendon, 1996.

Lieu, Judith M. 1996. *Image and Reality: The Jews in the World of the Christians in the Second Century*. Edinburgh: T. & T. Clark.

———. 2000. 'Narrative Analysis and Scripture in John'. In *The Old Testament in the New Testament: Essays in Honour of J. L. North*, 144–63. Ed. S. Moyise. JSNTSup 189. Sheffield: Sheffield Academic.

Lightfoot, J. B. 1891. *The Apostolic Fathers*. Ed. J. R. Harmer. London and New York: Macmillan.

Lightfoot, J. B. and J. R. Harmer, eds. 1989. *The Apostolic Fathers: Second Edition.* Edited and revised by Michael W. Holmes. Grand Rapids: Baker.

Lightfoot, R. H. 1938. *Locality and Doctrine in the Gospels.* London: Hodder and Stoughton.

1950. *The Gospel Message of St. Mark.* Oxford: Oxford University Press.

Lim, Timothy H. 2002. *Pesharim.* CQS 3. London and New York: Sheffield Academic.

Lincoln, A. 2000. *Truth on Trial: The Lawsuit Motif in the Fourth Gospel.* Peabody: Hendrickson.

2002. 'The Beloved Disciple as Eyewitness and the Fourth Gospel as Witness'. *JSNT* 85: 3–26.

Lindars, B. 1992. *Essays on John.* Ed. C. M. Tuckett. SNTA 17. Leuven: Leuven University Press.

Lods, M. 1941. 'Étude sur les Sources Juives de la Polémique de Celse contre les Chrétiens'. *RHPR* 21: 1–33.

Lohmeyer, Ernst. 1919. *Christuskult und Kaiserkult.* Tübingen: Mohr (Siebeck).

Löhr, Winrich A. 1996. *Basilides und seine Schule: Eine Studie zur Theologie und Kirchengeschichte des zweiten Jahrhunderts.* WUNT 83. Tübingen: Mohr (Siebeck).

2003. 'Valentinian Variations on Lk 12, 8–9/Mt 10, 32'. *VC* 57: 437–55.

Lord, A. B. 1978. 'The Gospels as Oral Traditional Literature'. In *The Relationships Among the Gospels: An Interdisciplinary Dialogue,* 33–91. Ed. W. O. Walker. TUMSR 5. San Antonio: Trinity University Press.

Lührmann, Dieter. 2004. *Die apokryph gewordenen Evangelien: Studien zu neuen Texten und zu neuen Fragen.* NovTSup 112. Leiden: Brill.

Lührmann, Dieter and Egbert Schlarb. 2000. *Fragmente apokryph gewordener Evangelien in griechischer und lateinischer Sprache.* MThS 59. Marburg: Elwert.

Luppe, Wolfgang. 2002. 'Scholia, Hypomnemata und Hypotheseis zu griechischen Dramen auf Papyri'. In *Der Kommentar in Antike und Mittelalter: Beiträge zu seiner Erforschung,* 55–77. Ed. W. Geerlings and C. Schulze. CCAMA 2. Leiden and Boston: Brill.

Luz, Ulrich. 1992. *Matthew 1–7.* Trans. W. C. Linss. CC. Minneapolis: Fortress.

1995a. 'The Disciples in the Gospel according to Matthew'. In *The Interpretation of Matthew,* 115–48. Ed. G. N. Stanton. SNTI. 2nd edn. Edinburgh: T. & T. Clark. Trans. by Robert Morgan from *ZNW* 62 (1971): 142–71.

1995b. *The Theology of the Gospel of Matthew.* Trans. J. B. Robinson. NTTh. Cambridge: Cambridge University Press.

MacDonald, D. R. 2000. *The Homeric Epics and the Gospel of Mark.* New Haven: Yale University Press.

McDonald, Lee Martin. 1988. *The Formation of the Christian Biblical Canon.* Nashville: Abingdon.

Mack, Burton L. 1988. *A Myth of Innocence: Mark and Christian Origins.* Philadelphia: Fortress.

1993. *The Lost Gospel: The Book of Q and Christian Origins.* San Francisco: Harper.

McKnight, Scot. 1999. *A New Vision for Israel: The Teachings of Jesus in National Context.* SHJ. Grand Rapids: Eerdmans.

MacMullen, Ramsay. 1984. *Christianizing the Roman Empire AD 100–400.* New Haven: Yale University Press.

McNamee, Kathleen. 1995. 'Missing Links in the History of Scholia'. *GRBS* 36: 399–414.

1998. 'Another Chapter in the History of Scholia'. *CQ* 48: 269–88.

Maddox, Robert. 1982. *The Purpose of Luke–Acts.* FRLANT 126. Göttingen: Vandenhoeck & Ruprecht.

Magness, J. Lee. 1986. *Sense and Absence: Structure and Suspension in the Ending of Mark's Gospel.* SBL SemeiaSt. Atlanta: Scholars.

Maier, Johann. 1978. *Jesus von Nazareth in der talmudischen Überlieferung.* EdF 82. Darmstadt: Wissenschaftliche Buchgesellschaft.

1982. *Jüdische Auseinandersetzung mit dem Christentum in der Antike.* Darmstadt: Wissenschaftliche Buchgesellschaft.

Mali, Franz. 1991. *Das 'Opus Imperfectum in Matthaeum' und sein Verhältnis zu den Matthäuskommentaren von Origenes und Hieronymus.* IThS 34. Innsbruck: Tyrolia-Verlag.

Maloney, E. C. 1981. *Semitic Interference in Marcan Syntax.* SBLDS 51. Chico: Scholars.

Marcus, Joel. 1992. *The Way of the Lord: Christological Exegesis of the Old Testament in the Gospel of Mark.* Louisville: Westminster/John Knox. Repr. SNTW. Edinburgh: T. & T. Clark, 1993.

Marguerat, D. 1998. 'Voyages et Voyageurs dans le Livre des Actes et dans la Culture Gréco-romaine'. *RHPR* 78: 33–59.

2002. *The First Christian Historian: Writing the 'Acts of the Apostles'.* Trans. K. McKinney et al. SNTSMS 121. Cambridge: Cambridge University Press.

Markschies, C. 1991. 'Platons König oder Vater Jesu Christi? Drei Beispiele für die Rezeption eines griechischen Gottesepithetons bei den Christen in den ersten Jahrhunderten und deren Vorgeschichte'. In *Königsherrschaft Gottes und himmlischer Kult im Judentum, Urchristentum und in der hellenistischen Welt*, 385–439. Ed. M. Hengel and A. M. Schwemer. WUNT 55. Tübingen: Mohr (Siebeck).

1998. '"Neutestamentliche Apokryphen": Bemerkungen zu Geschichte und Zukunft einer von Edgar Hennecke im Jahr 1904 begründeten Quellensammlung'. *Apoc* 9: 97–132.

Marshall, Christopher D. 1989. *Faith as a Theme in Mark's Gospel.* SNTSMS 64. Cambridge: Cambridge University Press.

Marshall, I. Howard. 1971. *Luke: Historian and Theologian.* Grand Rapids: Zondervan.

Marshall, Peter K. 2000. 'Kommentar: II. Lateinische Literatur'. *DNP* xiv: 1057–62.

Martin, R. P. 1973. *Mark: Evangelist and Theologian.* Grand Rapids: Zondervan.

Martyn, J. L. 1978. *The Gospel of John in Christian History.* New York: Paulist Press.

2003. *History and Theology in the Fourth Gospel.* NTL. 3rd edn. Louisville: Westminster John Knox.

Marxsen, Willi. 1959. *Der Evangelist Markus: Studien zur Redaktionsgeschichte des Evangeliums.* FRLANT 67. 2nd edn (1st edn 1956). Göttingen: Vandenhoeck & Ruprecht.

1969. *Mark the Evangelist: Studies on the Redaction History of the Gospel.* Trans. J. Boyce et al. New York: Abingdon.

Mason, Steve. 1992. *Josephus and the New Testament.* Peabody: Hendrickson.

Massaux, Edouard. 1990. *The Influence of the Gospel of Saint Matthew on Christian Literature before Saint Irenaeus,* Vol. I: *The First Ecclesiastical Writers.* Trans. N. J. Belval and S. Hecht. Ed. A. J. Bellinzoni. NGS. Leuven and Macon: Peeters and Mercer University Press.

Mattill, A. J., Jr. 1970. 'The Purpose of Acts: Schneckenburger Reconsidered'. In *Apostolic History and the Gospel: Biblical and Historical Essays presented to F. F. Bruce on his 60th Birthday,* 108–22. Ed. W. W. Gasque and R. P. Martin. Exeter and Grand Rapids: Paternoster and Eerdmans.

1975. 'The Jesus–Paul Parallels and the Purpose of Luke–Acts'. *NovT* 17: 15–46.

Mauser, Ulrich. 1963. *Christ in the Wilderness: The Wilderness Theme in the Second Gospel and its Basis in the Biblical Tradition.* SBT 39. London and Naperville: SCM and Allenson.

1992. *The Gospel of Peace: A Scriptural Message for Today's World.* SPS. Louisville: Westminster/John Knox.

Meeks, Wayne A. 1972. 'The Man from Heaven in Johannine Sectarianism'. *JBL* 91: 44–72. Repr. in *The Interpretation of John,* 169–205. Ed. J. Ashton. SNTI. 2nd edn. Edinburgh: T. & T. Clark, 1997.

1983. *The First Urban Christians: The Social World of the Apostle Paul.* New Haven: Yale University Press.

Meier, John P. 1976. *Law and History in Matthew's Gospel: A Redactional Study of Mt.5: 17–48.* AnBib 71. Rome: Biblical Institute Press.

1992. 'John the Baptist in Josephus: Philology and Exegesis'. *JBL* 111: 225–37.

1994. *A Marginal Jew: Rethinking the Historical Jesus,* Vol. II: *Mentor, Message, and Miracles.* ABRL. New York: Doubleday.

Meijering, R. 1987. *Literary and Rhetorical Theories in Greek Scholia.* Groningen: E. Forsten.

Meredith, Anthony. 1980. 'Porphyry and Julian against the Christians'. *ANRW* II.23.2: 1119–49.

Metzger, Bruce M. 1987. *The Canon of the New Testament: Its Origin, Development, and Significance.* Oxford and New York: Clarendon and Oxford University Press.

Meyer, Ben F. 1979. *The Aims of Jesus.* London: SCM. Repr. PTMS 48. Eugene: Pickwick/Wipf & Stock, 2002.

Millar, Fergus. 1993. *The Roman Near East, 31 BC–AD 337.* Cambridge, Mass.: Harvard University Press.

Mirsky, S., ed. 1977. *Yosse ben Yosse: Poems.* Jerusalem: Bialik Institute.

Mitchell, Stephen. 1993. *Anatolia: Land, Men, and Gods in Asia Minor.* 2 vols. Oxford and New York: Clarendon and Oxford University Press.

Moessner, D. P. 1988. 'The Ironic Fulfillment of Israel's Glory'. In *Luke–Acts and the Jewish People: Eight Critical Perspectives,* 35–50. Ed. J. B. Tyson. Minneapolis: Augsburg.

1989. *Lord of the Banquet: The Literary and Theological Significance of the Lukan Travel Narrative.* Minneapolis: Augsburg Fortress. Repr. Harrisburg: Trinity Press International, 1998.

1990. '"The Christ Must Suffer", the Church Must Suffer: Rethinking the Theology of the Cross in Luke–Acts'. In *SBL Seminar Papers, 1990,* 165–83. Ed. D. J. Lull. SBLSP 29. Atlanta: Scholars.

1991. 'Re-reading Talbert's Luke: The *Bios* of "Balance" or the "Bias" of History?' In *Cadbury, Knox, and Talbert: American Contributions to the Study of Acts,* 203–28. Ed. J. B. Tyson and M. C. Parsons. Atlanta: Scholars.

1993. 'Suffering, Intercession, and Eschatological Atonement: An Uncommon Common View in the Testament of Moses and in Luke–Acts'. In *The Pseudepigrapha and Early Biblical Interpretation,* 202–27. Ed. J. H. Charlesworth and C. A. Evans. JSPSup 14. SSEJC 2. Sheffield: JSOT Press.

1996a. '"Eyewitnesses", "Informed Contemporaries", and "Unknowing Inquirers": Josephus' Criteria for Authentic Historiography and the Meaning of *Parakoloutheō*'. *NovT* 38: 105–22.

1996b. 'The "Script" of the Scriptures in Acts: Suffering as God's "Plan" (*Boulē*) for the World for the "Release of Sins"'. In *History, Literature, and Society in the Book of Acts,* 218–50. Ed. B. Witherington, III. Cambridge: Cambridge University Press.

1998. Preface to paperback edition of *Lord of the Banquet: The Literary and Theological Significance of the Lukan Travel Narrative.* Harrisburg: Trinity Press International.

1999a. 'The Appeal and Power of Poetics (Luke 1: 1–4): Luke's Superior Credentials (*Parēkolouthēkoti*), Narrative Sequence (*Kathexēs*), and Firmness of Understanding (*hē Asphaleia*) for the Reader'. In *Luke the Interpreter of Israel,* Vol. 1: *Jesus and the Heritage of Israel: Luke's Narrative Claim upon Israel's Legacy,* 84–123. Ed. D. P. Moessner. Harrisburg: Trinity Press International.

1999b. 'The Lukan Prologues in the Light of Ancient Narrative Hermeneutics: *Parēkolouthēkoti* and the Credentialed Author'. In *The Unity of Luke–Acts,* 399–417. Ed. J. Verheyden. BETL 142. Leuven: Leuven University Press and Peeters.

2002. 'Dionysius' Narrative "Arrangement" (*Oikonomia*) as the Hermeneutical Key to Luke's Re-Vision of the "Many"'. In *Paul, Luke and the Graeco-Roman World: Essays in Honour of Alexander J. M. Wedderburn,* 149–64. Ed. A. Christophersen et al. JSNTSup 217. Sheffield: Sheffield Academic.

2004a. '"Completed End(s)ings" of Historiographical Narrative: Diodorus Siculus and the End(ing) of Acts'. In *Die Apostelgeschichte und hellenistische Geschichtsschreibung. Festschrift für Dr. Plümacher*, 193–221. Ed. C. Breytenbach and J. Schröter. Leiden: Brill.

2004b. 'Ministers of Divine Providence: Diodorus Siculus and Luke the Evangelist on the Rhetorical Significance of the Audience in Narrative "Arrangement"'. In *Literary Encounters with the Reign of God [Studies in Honor of R. C. Tannehill]*, 304–23. Ed. S. H. Ringe and H. C. P. Kim. London and New York: T. & T. Clark.

2005 (forthcoming). '"Managing" the Audience: Diodorus Siculus and Luke the Evangelist on Designing Authorial Intent'. In *Festschrift A. Denaux*. Ed. J. Verheyden. BETL. Leuven: Leuven University Press and Peeters.

Moessner, D. P. and D. L. Tiede. 1999. '*Two* Books but *One* Story?' In *Luke the Interpreter of Israel*, Vol. I: *Jesus and the Heritage of Israel: Luke's Narrative Claim upon Israel's Legacy*, 1–4. Ed. D. P. Moessner. Harrisburg: Trinity Press International.

Mohrmann, Christine. 1965. *Etudes sur le Latin des Chrétiens*. Vol. III: *Latin Chrétien et liturgique*. Rome: Edizioni di Storia e Letteratura.

Moloney, F. 1998. *The Gospel of John*. SP 4. Collegeville: Liturgical Press.

Momigliano, A. 1993. *The Development of Greek Biography*. Expanded edn. Cambridge, Mass.: Harvard University Press.

Moore, Stephen D. 1989. *Literary Criticism and the Gospels: The Theoretical Challenge*. New Haven and London: Yale University Press.

Morgenthaler, R. 1971. *Statistische Synopse*. Zurich and Stuttgart: Gotthelf.

Moule, C. F. D. 1982. *Essays in New Testament Interpretation*. Cambridge: Cambridge University Press.

Moxnes, Halvor. 1991. 'Patron–Client Relations and the New Community in Luke–Acts'. In *The Social World of Luke–Acts: Models for Interpretation*, 241–68. Ed. J. H. Neyrey. Peabody: Hendrickson.

1994. 'The Social Context of Luke's Community'. *Int* 48: 379–89.

Nagel, Titus. 2000. *Die Rezeption des Johannesevangeliums im 2. Jahrhundert: Studien zur vorirenäischen Aneignung und Auslegung des vierten Evangeliums in christlicher und christlich-gnostischer Literatur*. ABG 2. Leipzig: Evangelische Verlagsanstalt.

Neirynck, F. 1988. *Duality in Mark: Contributions to the Study of the Markan Redaction*. BETL 31. Leuven: Leuven University Press and Peeters.

1991. 'Papyrus Egerton 2 and the Healing of the Leper'. In *Evangelica II: 1982–1991: Collected Essays*, 773–84. BETL 99. Leuven: Leuven University Press and Peeters.

Neuschäfer, Bernhard. 1987. *Origenes als Philologe*. SBAltW 18: 1–2. 2 vols. Basle: Friedrich Reinhardt.

Neusner, Jacob. 1988. *Why No Gospels in Talmudic Judaism?* Atlanta: Scholars.

1993. *Are There Really Tannaitic Parallels to the Gospels? A Refutation of Morton Smith*. SFSHJ 80. Chico: Scholars.

Newman, Hillel I. 1999. 'The Death of Jesus in the *Toledot Yeshu* Literature'. *JTS* 50: 59–79.

Neyrey, Jerome H. 1985. *The Passion according to Luke: A Redaction Study of Luke's Soteriology.* New York: Paulist.

1991. 'The Symbolic Universe of Luke–Acts: "They Turn the World Upside Down"'. In *The Social World of Luke–Acts: Models for Interpretation,* 271–304. Ed. J. H. Neyrey. Peabody: Hendrickson.

Niederwimmer, K. 1993. *Die Didache.* KAV 1. 2nd edn. Göttingen: Vandenhoeck & Ruprecht.

Nisbet, R. G. M. and Margaret Hubbard. 1970. *A Commentary on Horace, Odes, Book I.* Oxford: Clarendon.

Nock, Arthur Darby. 1933. *Conversion: The Old and the New in Religion from Alexander the Great to Augustine of Hippo.* Oxford: Clarendon.

Oberman, A. 1996. *Die christologische Erfüllung der Schrift im Johannesevangelium: Eine Untersuchung zur johanneischen Hermeneutik anhand der Schriftzitate.* WUNT 2.83. Tübingen: Mohr (Siebeck).

O'Day, G. 1986. *Revelation in the Fourth Gospel: Narrative Mode and Theological Claim.* Philadelphia: Fortress.

Oden, Thomas C. and Christopher A. Hall, eds. 1998. *Mark.* ACCSNT 2. Downers Grove: InterVarsity Press.

Old, Hughes Oliphant. 1998. *The Reading and Preaching of the Scriptures in the Worship of the Christian Church.* 4 vols. Grand Rapids: Eerdmans.

Olmstead, Wesley G. 2003. *Matthew's Trilogy of Parables: The Nation, the Nations and the Reader in Matthew 21.28–22.14.* SNTSMS 127. Cambridge: Cambridge University Press.

Ong, Walter J. 1982. *Orality and Literacy: The Technologizing of the Word.* London and New York: Routledge.

Orchard, Bernard and Harold Riley. 1987. *The Order of the Synoptics: Why Three Synoptic Gospels?* Macon: Mercer University Press.

Origen. 1996. *Homilies on Luke, Fragments on Luke.* Trans. J. T. Lienhard. FC 94. Washington D.C.: Catholic University of America Press.

Orton, David E. 1989. *The Understanding Scribe: Matthew and the Apocalyptic Ideal.* JSNTSup 25. Sheffield: Sheffield Academic.

Overbeck, F. 1882. 'Über die Anfänge der patristischen Literatur'. *HZ* N.S. 12 (48): 417–72.

Overman, J. Andrew. 1990. *Matthew's Gospel and Formative Judaism: The Social World of the Matthean Community.* Minneapolis: Fortress.

1996. *Church and Community in Crisis: The Gospel according to Matthew.* NTC. Valley Forge: Trinity Press International.

Oyen, G. Van. 1992. 'Intercalation and Irony in the Gospel of Mark'. In *The Four Gospels 1992: Festschrift Frans Neirynck,* 2: 949–74. Ed. F. Van Segbroeck et al. BETL 100. Leuven: Leuven University Press and Peeters.

Pagels, Elaine H. 1973. *The Johannine Gospel in Gnostic Exegesis: Heracleon's Commentary on John.* Nashville: Abingdon.

2002. 'Irenaeus, the "Canon of Truth", and the Gospel of John: "Making a Difference" through Hermeneutics and Ritual'. *VC* 56: 337–71.

Parker, David C. 1997. *The Living Text of the Gospels.* Cambridge and New York: Cambridge University Press.

Parker, P. 1987. 'Herod Antipas and the Death of Jesus'. In *Jesus, the Gospels, and the Church: Essays in Honor of William R. Farmer,* 197–208. Ed. E. P. Sanders. Macon: Mercer University Press.

Parsons, Mikeal C. and Richard I. Pervo. 1993. *Rethinking the Unity of Luke and Acts.* Minneapolis: Fortress.

Patterson, Stephen J. 1993. *The Gospel of Thomas and Jesus: Thomas Christianity, Social Radicalism, and the Quest of the Historical Jesus.* FF. Sonoma: Polebridge.

Paul, Shalom M. et al., eds. 2003. *Emanuel: Studies in Hebrew Bible, Septuagint, and Dead Sea Scrolls in Honor of Emanuel Tov.* VTSup 94. 2 vols. Leiden: Brill.

Peabody, David B. 1987. *Mark as Composer.* NGS 1. Leuven and Macon: Peeters and Mercer University Press.

Perrin, Norman. 1969. *What is Redaction Criticism?* GBS. Philadelphia: Fortress.

Perrone, Lorenzo. 2000. 'Continuité et Innovation dans les Commentaires d'Origène: Un Essai de Comparaison entre le *Commentaire sur Jean* et le *Commentaire sur Matthieu*'. In *Le Commentaire entre Tradition et Innovation: Actes du Colloque International de l'Institut des Traditions Textuelles, Paris et Villejuif, 22–25 septembre 1999,* 183–97. Ed. M.-O. Goulet-Cazé and T. Dorandi. BHP. N.S. Paris: Vrin.

Pervo, Richard I. 1999. 'Israel's Heritage and Claims upon the Genre(s) of Luke and Acts: The Problems of a History'. In *Luke the Interpreter of Israel,* Vol. 1: *Jesus and the Heritage of Israel: Luke's Narrative Claim upon Israel's Legacy,* 127–43. Ed. D. P. Moessner. Harrisburg: Trinity Press International.

Pesch, R. 1977, 1991. *Das Markusevangelium.* HTKNT 2.1–2.2 vols. Freiburg: Herder.

Petersen, Norman R. 1980. 'When is the End not the End? Literary Reflections on the Ending of Mark's Narrative'. *Int* 34: 151–66.

Petersen, William L. 1990. 'Tatian's Diatessaron'. In *Ancient Christian Gospels: Their History and Development,* 403–30. By H. Koester. London and Philadelphia: SCM and Trinity Press International.

  1994. *Tatian's Diatessaron: Its Creation, Dissemination, Significance, and History in Scholarship.* VCSup 25. Leiden: Brill.

Petersen, William L., ed. 1989. *Gospel Traditions in the Second Century: Origins, Recensions, Text, and Transmission.* CJA 3. Notre Dame: University of Notre Dame Press.

Pfeiffer, Rudolf. 1968. *History of Classical Scholarship from the Beginnings to the End of the Hellenistic Age.* Oxford: Clarendon.

Piper, R. A. 1989. *Wisdom in the Q-Tradition: The Aphoristic Teaching of Jesus.* SNTSMS 61. Cambridge: Cambridge University Press.

Plümacher, E. 1972. *Lukas als hellenistischer Schriftsteller: Studien zur Apostelgeschichte.* SUNT 9. Göttingen: Vandenhoeck & Ruprecht.

1979. 'Die Apostelgeschichte als historische Monographie'. In *Les Actes des Apôtres. Traditions, Rédaction, Théologie,* 457–66. Ed. J. Kremer. Leuven and Gembloux: Leuven University Press and Duculot.

Poffet, Jean-Michel. 1985. *La Méthode Exégétique d'Héracléon et d'Origène: Commentateurs de Jn 4 – Jésus, la Samaritaine et les Samaritains.* Paradosis 28. Fribourg: Editions Universitaires.

Pokorný, Petr. 1983. 'Das Markusevangelium: Literarische und theologische Einleitung mit Forschungsbericht'. *ANRW II.*25.3: 1969–2035.

Poole (Pole), Matthew (Matthæus). 1684–6. *Synopsis Criticorum Aliorumque Sacræ Scripturæ Interpretum et Commentatorum: Summo Studio et Fide Adornata.* Ed. J. Leusden. 5 vols. Utrecht: Ribb, van de Water & Halma.

Puech, Emile. 1998. *Qumrân Grotte 4, xviii: Textes Hébreux (4Q521–4Q528, 4Q576–4Q579).* DJD 25. Oxford: Clarendon.

Rajak, T. 1987. 'Josephus and Justus of Tiberias'. In *Josephus, Judaism, and Christianity,* 81–94. Ed. L. H. Feldman and G. Hata. Detroit: Wayne State University Press.

Reicke, Bo. 1986. *The Roots of the Synoptic Gospels.* Philadelphia: Fortress.

Reid, B. E. 1996. *Choosing the Better Part? Women in the Gospel of Luke.* Collegeville: Liturgical Press.

Reid, R. S. 1996. 'Dionysius of Halicarnassus' Theory of Compositional Style and the Theory of Literate Consciousness'. *RhetR* 15: 46–64.

1997. '"Neither Oratory nor Dialogue": Dionysius of Harlicarnassus and the Genre of Plato's Apology'. *RhetSQ* 27: 63–90.

Reinhartz, A. 2001. *Befriending the Beloved Disciple: A Jewish Reading of the Gospel of John.* New York: Continuum.

Reiser, Marius. 1997. *Jesus and Judgment: The Eschatological Proclamation in its Jewish Context.* Trans. L. M. Maloney. Minneapolis: Fortress.

Renan, Ernst. 1877. *Les Evangiles et la Seconde Génération Chrétienne.* HOC 5. Paris: Calmann Lévy.

Resseguie, James L. 1984. 'Reader-Response Criticism and the Synoptic Gospels'. *JAAR* 52: 307–24.

Reuss, Joseph. 1957. *Matthäus-Kommentare aus der griechischen Kirche.* TUGAL 61. Berlin: Akademie-Verlag.

Reynolds, L. D. and N. G. Wilson. 1991. *Scribes and Scholars: A Guide to the Transmission of Greek and Latin Literature.* 3rd edn. Oxford and New York: Clarendon and Oxford University Press.

Richter, G. 1977. *Studien zum Johannesevangelium.* Ed. J. Hainz. Regensburg: Pustet.

Riesenfeld, Harald. 1970. *The Gospel Tradition: Essays.* Trans. E. M. Rowley and R. A. Kraft. Foreword by W. D. Davies. Philadelphia: Fortress.

Riesner, Rainer. 1981. *Jesus als Lehrer: Eine Untersuchung zum Ursprung der Evangelien-Überlieferung.* WUNT 2.7 (1st edn). Tübingen: Mohr (Siebeck).

1988. *Jesus als Lehrer: Eine Untersuchung zum Ursprung der Evangelien-Überlieferung.* WUNT 2.7. 3rd edn. Tübingen: Mohr (Siebeck).

Roberts, C. H. 1936. *Two Biblical Papyri in the John Rylands Library, Manchester.* Manchester: Manchester University Press.

Robinson, J. M., P. Hoffmann, and J. S. Kloppenborg, eds. 2000. *The Critical Edition of Q*. The International Q Project/Hermeneia. Leuven and Minneapolis: Peeters and Fortress.

Robinson, John A. T. 1962–3. 'The Relation of the Prologue to the Gospel of St John'. *NTS* 9: 120–9. Repr. in *Twelve More New Testament Studies*, 65–76. London: SCM, 1984.

1985. *The Priority of John*. London: SCM.

Rohrbaugh, R. L. 1993. 'The Social Location of the Markan Audience'. *Int* 47: 380–95.

Roloff, Jürgen. 1970. *Das Kerygma und der irdische Jesus: historische Motive in den Jesus-Erzählungen der Evangelien*. 2nd edn. Göttingen: Vandenhoeck & Ruprecht.

Rowland, C. 1992. 'The Parting of the Ways: The Evidence of Jewish and Christian Apocalyptic and Mystical Material'. In *Jews and Christians: The Parting of the Ways, AD 70 to 135: The Second Durham-Tübingen Research Symposium on Earliest Christianity and Judaism, Durham, September 1989*, 213–37. Ed. J. D. G. Dunn. WUNT 66. Tübingen: Mohr (Siebeck).

Saldarini, Anthony J. 1994. *Matthew's Christian-Jewish Community*. CSHJ. Chicago: University of Chicago Press.

Sanders, E. P. 1969. *The Tendencies of the Synoptic Tradition*. SNTSMS 9. Cambridge: Cambridge University Press.

1985. *Jesus and Judaism*. Philadelphia: Fortress.

Sanders, James A. 1975. 'From Isaiah 61 to Luke 4'. In *Christianity, Judaism and Other Greco-Roman Cults: Studies for Morton Smith at Sixty*, Part 1:75–106. Ed. J. Neusner. SJLA 12. 4 vols. Leiden: Brill.

1993. 'From Isaiah 61 to Luke 4'. In *Luke and Scripture: The Function of Sacred Tradition in Luke–Acts*, 46–69. By Craig A. Evans and James A. Sanders. Minneapolis: Fortress (revision of Sanders 1975).

Sato, Migaku. 1988. *Q und Prophetie: Studien zur Gattungs- und Traditionsgeschichte der Quelle Q*. WUNT 2.29. Tübingen: Mohr (Siebeck).

Scafuro, A. C. 1984. 'Universal History and the Genres of Greek Historiography'. Unpublished dissertation, Yale University.

Schlatter, Adolf. 1947. *Das Evangelium nach Matthäus*. Stuttgart: Calwer Verlag.

2002. 'Die heilige Geschichte und der Glaube'. In *Die Bibel verstehen. Aufsätze zur biblischen Hermeneutik*. Ed. W. Neuer. Giessen: Brunnen Verlag.

Schmid, Ulrich. 2002. 'Marcions Evangelium und die neutestamentlichen Evangelien: Rückfragen zur Geschichte und Kanonisierung der Evangelienüberlieferung'. In *Marcion und seine kirchengeschichtliche Wirkung = Marcion and his Impact on Church History: Vorträge der Internationalen Fachkonferenz zu Marcion, gehalten vom 15.–18. August 2001 in Mainz*, 67–77. Ed. G. May and K. Greschat. TUGAL 150. Berlin and New York: de Gruyter.

Schmidt, Christiane. 1999. 'Opus Imperfectum in Matthaeum'. *LACL*: 459.

Schmidt, Daryl D. 1999. 'Rhetorical Influences and Genre: Luke's Preface and the Rhetoric of Hellenistic Historiography'. In *Luke the Interpreter of Israel*, Vol. 1:

Jesus and the Heritage of Israel: Luke's Narrative Claim upon Israel's Legacy, 27–60. Ed. D. P. Moessner. Harrisburg: Trinity Press International.

Schmidt, Karl Ludwig. 1919. *Der Rahmen der Geschichte Jesu: literarkritische Untersuchungen zur ältesten Jesusüberlieferung*. Berlin: Trowitzsch. Repr. Darmstadt: Wissenschaftliche Buchgesellschaft, 1964.

1923. 'Die Stellung der Evangelien in der allgemeinen Literaturgeschichte'. In *Eucharistērion: Studien zur Religion und Literatur des Alten und Neuen Testaments. Hermann Gunkel zum 60. Geburtstage, dem 23. Mai 1922 dargebracht von seinen Schülern und Freunden*, II: 50–134. Ed. H. Schmidt. FRLANT N.S. 19 [36]. 2 vols. Göttingen: Vandenhoeck & Ruprecht.

1981. 'Die Stellung der Evangelien in der allgemeinen Literaturgeschichte [1923]'. In *Neues Testament – Judentum – Kirche: Kleine Schriften*, 37–130. Ed. G. Sauter. TB 69. Munich: Kaiser Verlag.

Schnackenburg, R. 2002. *The Gospel of Matthew*. Trans. R. R. Barr. Grand Rapids: Eerdmans.

Schneemelcher, Wilhelm, ed. 1991. *New Testament Apocrypha*, Vol. I: *Gospels and Related Writings*. Ed. R. M. Wilson. Rev. edn. Cambridge and Louisville: James Clarke and Westminster/John Knox.

Schoedel, W. R. 1967. *Polycarp, Martyrdom of Polycarp, Fragments of Papias*. AF 5. London: Thomas Nelson & Sons.

Scholtissek, K. 2000. *In ihm sein und bleiben: Die Sprache der Immanenz in den johanneischen Schriften*. Freiburg: Herder.

Schotroff, Luise. 1970. *Der Glaubende und die feindliche Welt: Beobachtungen zum gnostischen Dualismus und seiner Bedeutung für Paulus und das Johannesevangelium*. WMANT 37. Neukirchen: Neukirchener Verlag.

Schröter, J. 1997. *Erinnerung an Jesu Worte: Studien zur Rezeption der Logienüberlieferung in Markus, Q und Thomas*. WMANT 76. Neukirchen-Vluyn: Neukirchener.

Schürmann, Heinz. 1968. 'Die vorösterlichen Anfänge der Logientradition'. In *Traditionsgeschichtliche Untersuchungen zu den synoptischen Evangelien: Beiträge*, 39–65. KBANT. Düsseldorf: Patmos-Verlag.

Schwarte, Karl-Heinz. 1999. 'Victorinus von Pettau'. *LACL*: 627–8.

Schwartz, Seth. 2001. *Imperialism and Jewish Society, 200 B.C.E. to 640 C.E.* Princeton: Princeton University Press.

Scott, M. 1992. *Sophia and the Johannine Jesus*. JSNTSup 71. Sheffield: JSOT Press.

Segovia, F. 1991. *The Farewell of the Word: The Johannine Call to Abide*. Minneapolis: Fortress.

Segovia, F., ed. 1996. *What is John? Readers and Readings of the Fourth Gospel*. 2 vols. Atlanta: Scholars.

Shellard, B. 2002. *New Light on Luke: Its Purpose, Sources and Literary Context*. JSNTSup 215. Sheffield: Sheffield Academic.

Shepherd, T. 1993. *Markan Sandwich Stories: Narration, Definition, and function*. AUSDDS 18. Berrien Springs: Andrews University Press.

1995. 'The Narrative Function of Markan Intercalation'. *NTS* 41: 522–40.

Siegert, Folker. 1996. 'Early Jewish Interpretation in a Hellenistic Style'. In *Hebrew Bible/Old Testament: The History of its Interpretation*, I.I: 130–98. Ed. M. Sæbø. Göttingen: Vandenhoeck & Ruprecht.

Sim, David C. 2001. 'The Gospels for All Christians? A Response to Richard Bauckham'. *JSNT* 84: 3–27.

Simonetti, Manlio. 1994. *Biblical Interpretation in the Early Church: An Historical Introduction to Patristic Exegesis*. Trans. J. A. Hughes. Ed. A. Bergquist and M. Bockmuehl. Edinburgh: T. & T. Clark.

Simonetti, Manlio, ed. 2001–2. *Matthew*. ACCSNT I.A–B. 2 vols. Downers Grove: InterVarsity Press.

Skeat, T. C. 1994. 'The Origin of the Christian Codex'. *ZPE* 102: 263–8.

  1997. 'The Oldest Manuscript of the Four Gospels?' *NTS* 43: 1–34.

Smith, D. M. 2001. *John among the Gospels: The Relationship in Twentieth Century Research*. 2nd edn. Columbia: University of South Carolina Press.

Smith, Dennis E., ed. 1991. *How Gospels Begin. Semeia* 52.

Snodgrass, Klyne R. 1999. 'Reading and Overreading the Parables in *Jesus and the Victory of God*'. In *Jesus and the Restoration of Israel: A Critical Assessment of N. T. Wright's Jesus and the Victory of God*, 61–76. Ed. C. C. Newman. Downers Grove and Carlisle: InterVarsity Press and Paternoster.

Sokoloff, Michael and Joseph Yahalom. 1999. *Jewish Palestinian Aramaic Poetry from Late Antiquity: Critical Edition with Introduction and Commentary*. Jerusalem: Israel Academy of Sciences and Humanities.

Sproston North, Wendy. 2001. *The Lazarus Story within the Johannine Tradition*. JSNTSup 212. Sheffield: Sheffield Academic.

  2003. Review of Richard Bauckham, ed., *The Gospels for All Christians: Rethinking the Gospel Audiences*, Grand Rapids: Eerdmans, 1998. *JSNT* 25.4: 449–68.

Squires, J. T. 1993. *The Plan of God in Luke–Acts.* SNTSMS 76. Cambridge: Cambridge University Press.

Stanton, Graham N. 1974. *Jesus of Nazareth in New Testament Preaching*. SNTSMS 27. Cambridge: Cambridge University Press.

  1983. 'The Origin and Purpose of Matthew's Gospel: Matthean Scholarship from 1945–1980'. *ANRW* II.25.3: 1889–1951.

  1989. '"Pray that your Flight may not be in Winter or on a Sabbath"'. *JSNT* 37: 17–30.

  1992a. *A Gospel for a New People: Studies in Matthew*. Edinburgh: T. & T. Clark. Repr. Louisville: Westminster/John Knox, 1993.

  1992b. 'The Communities of Matthew'. *Int* 46: 379–91.

  1994a. 'Jesus of Nazareth: A Magician and a False Prophet who Deceived God's People?' In *Jesus of Nazareth Lord and Christ: Essays on the Historical Jesus and New Testament Christology*, 164–80. Ed. J. B. Green and M. Turner. Grand Rapids and Carlisle: Eerdmans and Paternoster. Repr. in *Jesus and Gospel*, 127–47.

  1994b. 'Revisiting Matthew's Communities'. In *SBL Seminar Papers, 1994*, 9–23. SBLSP 33. Atlanta: Scholars.

1995. *Gospel Truth? New Light on Jesus and the Gospels.* London and Valley Forge: HarperCollins and Trinity Press International.

1997. 'The Fourfold Gospel'. *NTS* 43: 317–46.

2002. *The Gospels and Jesus.* Oxford Bible Series. 2nd edn (1st edn 1989). Oxford: Oxford University Press.

2003. 'Jesus Traditions and Gospels in Justin Martyr and Irenaeus'. In *The Biblical Canons*, 353–70. Ed. J.-M. Auwers and H. J. De Jonge. BETL 163. Leuven: Leuven University Press and Peeters.

2004. *Jesus and Gospel.* Cambridge and New York: Cambridge University Press.

Stemberger, Günter. 1996. *Introduction to the Talmud and Midrash.* Ed. and trans. M. Bockmuehl. 2nd edn. Edinburgh: T. & T. Clark.

2000. *Jews and Christians in the Holy Land: Palestine in the Fourth Century.* Trans. R. Tuschling. Edinburgh: T. & T. Clark.

Stendahl, Krister. 1968. *The School of St. Matthew and its Use of the Old Testament.* 1st American edn. With a New Introduction by the Author. Philadelphia: Fortress. First published ASNU 20, Lund and Copenhagen: Gleerup and Munksgaard, 1954; 2nd edn Lund: Gleerup, 1967.

Stevenson, James. 1978. *The Catacombs: Rediscovered Monuments of Early Christianity.* London: Thames & Hudson.

Stibbe, M. 1992. *John as Storyteller: Narrative Criticism and the Fourth Gospel.* SNTSMS 73. Cambridge: Cambridge University Press.

Strack, Hermann L. 1910. *Jesus, die Häretiker und die Christen nach den ältesten jüdischen Angaben.* SIJB 37. Leipzig: Hinrichs.

Strack, Hermann L. and Paul Billerbeck. 1922–61. *Kommentar zum Neuen Testament aus Talmud und Midrasch.* Vol. V indexes compiled by K. Adolph, Vol. VI indexes compiled by J. Jeremias. 6 vols. Munich: Beck.

Strecker, Georg. 1962. *Der Weg der Gerechtigkeit: Untersuchung zur Theologie des Matthäus.* FRLANT 82. Göttingen: Vandenhoeck & Ruprecht.

Stuhlmacher, Peter. 1968. *Das paulinische Evangelium*, Vol I: *Vorgeschichte.* FRLANT 95. Göttingen: Vandenhoeck & Ruprecht.

1991. 'The Pauline Gospel'. In *The Gospel and the Gospels*, 149–72. Ed. P. Stuhlmacher. Grand Rapids: Eerdmans.

1992. *Biblische Theologie des Neuen Testaments*, Vol. I: *Grundlegung von Jesus zu Paulus.* Göttingen: Vandenhoeck & Ruprecht.

Suhl, A. 1965. *Die Funktion der alttestamentlichen Zitate und Anspielungen im Markusevangelium.* Gütersloh: Mohn.

Swain, Simon. 1999. 'Defending Hellenism: Philostratus, In Honour of Apollonius'. In *Apologetics in the Roman Empire: Pagans, Jews, and Christians*, 157–96. Ed. M. Edwards et al. Oxford: Oxford University Press.

Talbert, C. H. 1977. *What is a Gospel? The Genre of the Canonical Gospels.* London and Philadelphia: SPCK and Fortress.

2003. 'Succession in Luke–Acts and in the Lukan Milieu'. In *Reading Luke–Acts in its Mediterranean Milieu*, 19–55. NovTSup 107. Leiden: Brill.

Tannehill, Robert C. 1975. *The Sword of his Mouth: Forceful and Imaginative Language in Synoptic Sayings*. SBLSemeiaSup 1. Philadelphia and Missoula: Fortress and Scholars.

—— 1988. 'Rejection by Jews and Turning to Gentiles: The Pattern of Paul's Mission in Acts'. In *Luke–Acts and the Jewish People: Eight Critical Perspectives*, 83–101. Ed. J. B. Tyson. Minneapolis: Augsburg.

Taylor, Miriam S. 1995. *Anti-Judaism and Early Christian Identity: A Critique of the Scholarly Consensus*. StPB 46. Leiden: Brill.

Theissen, Gerd. 1999. *A Theory of Primitive Christian Religion*. London: SCM.

Theissen, Gerd and Annette Merz. 1998. *The Historical Jesus: A Comprehensive Guide*. Trans. J. Bowden. Minneapolis: Fortress.

Theissen, Gerd and Dagmar Winter. 1997. *Die Kriterienfrage in der Jesusforschung: vom Differenzkriterium zum Plausibilitätskriterium*. NTOA 34. Göttingen and Freiburg: Vandenhoeck & Ruprecht and Universitätsverlag Freiburg Schweiz.

Thompson, Marianne Meye. 1988. *The Humanity of Jesus in the Fourth Gospel*. Philadelphia: Fortress. Repr. as *The Incarnate Word: Perspectives on Jesus in the Fourth Gospel*. Peabody: Hendrickson, n.d. (ca. 1993).

Thompson, Michael. 1991. *Clothed with Christ: The Example and Teaching of Jesus in Romans 12.1–15.13*. JSNTSup 59. Sheffield: JSOT Press.

Thornton, Timothy C. G. 1990. 'The Stories of Joseph of Tiberias'. *VC* 44: 54–63.

Thrall, Margaret E. 1962. *Greek Particles in the New Testament*. NTTS 4. Leiden: Brill.

Thyen, H. 1977. 'Entwicklungen innerhalb der johanneischen Theologie und Kirche im Spiegel von Joh 21 und der Lieblingsjüngertexte des Evangeliums'. In *L'Evangile de Jean: Sources, Rédaction, Théologie*, 259–99. Ed. M. de Jonge. BETL 44. Leuven and Gembloux: Leuven University Press and Duculot.

Tiede, David L. 1980. *Prophecy and History in Luke–Acts*. Philadelphia: Fortress.

—— 1988. '"Glory to Thy People Israel": Luke–Acts and the Jews'. In *Luke–Acts and the Jewish People: Eight Critical Perspectives*, 21–34. Ed. J. B. Tyson. Minneapolis: Augsburg.

Torrey, C. C. 1912. 'The Translations Made from the Original Aramaic Gospel'. In *Studies in the History of Religions Presented to Crawford Howell Toy by Pupils, Colleagues, and Friends*, 269–317. Ed. D. G. Lyon and G. F. Moore. New York: Macmillan.

—— 1933. *The Four Gospels: A New Translation*. New York: Harper & Brothers.

—— 1937. *Our Translated Gospels: Some of the Evidence*. London: Hodder & Stoughton.

—— 1941. *Documents of the Primitive Church*. New York and London: Harper & Brothers.

Tov, Emanuel. 1999. *The Greek and Hebrew Bible: Collected Essays on the Septuagint*. VTSup 72. Leiden: Brill.

Trafton, Joseph L. 2002. 'Commentary on Genesis A'. In *The Dead Sea Scrolls: Hebrew, Aramaic, and Greek Texts with English Translations*, Vol. 6B: 203–19.

Ed. J. H. Charlesworth. PTSDSSP. Tübingen and Louisville: Mohr (Siebeck) and Westminster John Knox.

Trilling, Wolfgang. 1961. *Das Evangelium nach Matthäus.* Düsseldorf: Patmos Verlag.

Trocmé, Etienne. 1957. *Le 'Livre des Actes' et L'Histoire.* Paris: Presses Universitaires de France.

1975. *The Formation of the Gospel according to Mark.* London: SPCK.

Trojahn, Silke. 2002. *Die auf Papyri erhaltenen Kommentare zur alten Komödie: Ein Beitrag zur Geschichte der antiken Philologie.* BAlt 175. Munich: K. G. Saur.

Trompf, G. W. 1979. *The Idea of Historical Recurrence in Western Thought: From Antiquity to the Reformation.* Berkeley: University of California Press.

Tuckett, C. M. 1986. *Nag Hammadi and the Gospel Tradition: Synoptic Tradition in the Nag Hammadi Library.* SNTW. Edinburgh: T. & T. Clark.

1988. 'Thomas and the Synoptics'. *NovT* 30: 132–57.

1996. *Q and the History of Early Christianity: Studies on Q.* Edinburgh: T. & T. Clark.

Turner, N. and J. H. Moulton. 1976. *A Grammar of New Testament Greek,* Vol. IV: *Style.* Edinburgh: T. & T. Clark.

Tyson, Joseph B. 1988a. 'The Problem of Jewish Rejection in Acts'. In *Luke–Acts and the Jewish People: Eight Critical Perspectives,* 124–37. Ed. J. B. Tyson. Minneapolis: Augsburg.

Tyson, Joseph B., ed. 1988b. *Luke–Acts and the Jewish People: Eight Critical Perspectives.* Minneapolis: Augsburg.

Ulrich, E. 1996. 'Multiple Literary Editions: Reflections toward a Theory of the History of the Biblical Text'. In *Current Research and Technological Developments on the Dead Sea Scrolls: Conference on the Texts from the Judean Desert, Jerusalem, 30 April 1995,* 78–105. Ed. D. W. Parrey and S. D. Ricks. STDJ 20. Leiden: Brill.

Ungern-Sternberg, Jürgen von and Hansjörg Reinau, eds. 1988. *Vergangenheit in mündlicher Überlieferung.* CR I. Stuttgart: B. G. Teubner.

Unnik, W. C. van. 1979. 'Luke's Second Book and the Rules of Hellenistic Historiography'. In *Les Actes des Apôtres: Traditions, Rédaction, Théologie,* 37–60. Ed. J. Kremer. BETL 48. Leuven and Gembloux: Leuven University Press and Duculot.

Uro, Risto. 1998. '*Thomas* and Oral Gospel Tradition'. In *Thomas at the Crossroads: Essays on the* Gospel of Thomas, 8–32. Ed. R. Uro. SNTW. Edinburgh: T. & T. Clark.

Uytfanghe, M. Van. 2001. 'Biographie II (Sprituelle)'. In *RAC Supplement I,* 1088–1363. Ed. T. Klauser and E. Dassmann. Stuttgart: Anton Hiersemann.

Vaage, L. E. 1995. 'Composite Texts and Oral Mythology: The Case of the "Sermon" in Q (6: 20–49)'. In *Conflict and Invention: Literary, Rhetorical, and Social Studies on the Sayings Gospel Q,* 75–97. Ed. J. S. Kloppenborg. Valley Forge: Trinity Press International.

Vanhoozer, Kevin J. 1998. *Is There a Meaning in This Text? The Bible, The Reader and the Morality of Literary Knowledge.* Grand Rapids: Zondervan.

Vansina, Jan. 1985. *Oral Tradition as History.* Madison and London: University of Wisconsin Press and Currey.

Verheyden, J., ed. 1999. *The Unity of Luke–Acts.* BETL 142. Leuven: Leuven University Press and Peeters.

Vielhauer, Philipp. 1975. *Geschichte der urchristlichen Literatur: Einleitung in das Neue Testament, die Apokryphen und die Apostolischen Väter.* Berlin and New York: de Gruyter.

Voorst, Robert E. van. 2000. *Jesus Outside the New Testament: An Introduction to the Ancient Evidence.* SHJ. Grand Rapids: Eerdmans.

Votaw, C. W. 1970. *The Gospels and Contemporary Biographies in the Greco-Roman World.* FBBS 27. Philadelphia: Fortress.

Wagner, J. Ross. 2001. Review of Timothy H. Lim, *Holy Scripture in the Qumran Commentaries and Pauline Letters.* Oxford: Clarendon, 1997. *JBL*, 120: 175–8.

Walsh, M. 1986. *Roots of Christianity.* London: Grafton (Collins).

Walzer, Richard. 1949. *Galen on Jews and Christians.* Oxford: Oxford University Press.

Watson, F. 1998. 'Towards a Literal Reading of the Gospels'. In *The Gospels for All Christians: Rethinking the Gospel Audiences,* 195–217. Ed. R. Bauckham. Grand Rapids: Eerdmans.

Watts, R. E. 1997. *Isaiah's New Exodus in Mark.* WUNT 2.88. Tübingen: Mohr (Siebeck). Repr. BSL. Grand Rapids: Baker Academic, 2000.

Weeden, Theodore J. 1971. *Mark: Traditions in Conflict.* Philadelphia: Fortress.

Wellhausen, J. 1911. *Einleitung in die drei ersten Evangelien.* Berlin: G. Reimer.

Wenham, David. 1995. *Paul: Follower of Jesus or Founder of Christianity?* Grand Rapids: Eerdmans.

Westcott, B. F. 1881. *Introduction to the Study of the Gospels.* 6th edn. London: Macmillan.

Wilckens, U. 1974. *Die Missionsreden der Apostelgeschichte.* WMANT 5. Neukirchen-Vluyn: Neukirchener Verlag.

Wilken, Robert L. 1984. *The Christians as the Romans Saw them.* New Haven: Yale University Press.

Williams, Michael A. 1996. *Rethinking 'Gnosticism': An Argument for Dismantling a Dubious Category.* Princeton: Princeton University Press.

Wilson, N. G. 1967. 'A Chapter in the History of Scholia'. *CQ* N.S. 17: 244–56. 1968. 'A Chapter in the History of Scholia: A Postscript'. *CQ* N.S. 18: 413.

Witherington, Ben, III. 1995. *John's Wisdom: A Commentary on the Fourth Gospel.* Cambridge and Westminster: Lutterworth and John Knox.

Wright, G. A., Jr. 1985. 'Markan Intercalations: A Study in the Plot of the Gospel'. Unpublished dissertation, Southern Baptist Theological Seminary, Louisville.

Wright, N. T. 1996. *Christian Origins and the Question of God,* Vol. II: *Jesus and the Victory of God.* Minneapolis: Fortress.

Wucherpfennig, Ansgar. 2002. *Heracleon Philologus: Gnostische Johannesexegese im zweiten Jahrhundert.* WUNT 142. Tübingen: Mohr (Siebeck).

Yahalom, J. 1996. *Priestly Palestinian Poetry: A Narrative Liturgy for the Day of Atonement* (Hebrew title begins *Az be-eyn kol*). Jerusalem: Magnes.

Young, Frances M. 1997. *Biblical Exegesis and the Formation of Christian Culture.* Cambridge and New York: Cambridge University Press.

1999. 'Greek Apologists of the Second Century'. In *Apologetics in the Roman Empire: Pagans, Jews, and Christians*, 81–104. Ed. M. Edwards et al. Oxford: Oxford University Press.

Zeller, D. 1977. *Die weisheitlichen Mahnsprüche bei den Synoptikern.* Würzburg: Echter.

1992. 'Eine weisheitliche Grundschrift in der Logienquelle?' In *The Four Gospels 1992: Festschrift Frans Neirynck*, I: 389–401. Ed. F. Van Segbroeck et al. BETL 100. Leuven: Leuven University Press and Peeters.

Zetzel, James E. G. 1981. *Latin Textual Criticism in Antiquity.* MCS. New York: Arno Press.

Zimmermann, F. 1979. *The Aramaic Origin of the Four Gospels.* New York: Ktav.

Zumstein, J. 1996. 'Der Prozess der Relecture in der johanneischen Literatur'. *NTS* 42: 394–411.

Zuntz, G. 1984. 'Ein Heide las das Markusevangelium'. In *Markus-Philologie: Historische, literarische und stilistische Untersuchungen zum zweiten Evangelium*, 205–22. Ed. H. Cancik. WUNT 33. Tübingen: Mohr (Siebeck).

Index of ancient sources

BOOKS OF THE BIBLE

337

LXX/DEUTERO-CANONICAL BOOKS

NEW TESTAMENT

OLD TESTAMENT PSEUDEPIGRAPHA

ANCIENT CHRISTIAN WRITINGS

NT APOCRYPHA

CLASSICAL AND HELLENISTIC WRITINGS